SYRIAN INTERVENTION IN LEBANON

SYRIAN INTERVENTION IN LEBANON

The 1975–76 Civil War

NAOMI JOY WEINBERGER

New York   Oxford
OXFORD UNIVERSITY PRESS
1986

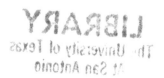

Oxford University Press

Oxford   New York   Toronto
Delhi   Bombay   Calcutta   Madras   Karachi
Petaling Jaya   Singapore   Hong Kong   Tokyo
Nairobi   Dar es Salaam   Cape Town
Melbourne   Auckland

and associated companies in
Beirut   Berlin   Ibadan   Nicosia

Published by Oxford University Press, Inc.
200 Madison Avenue, New York, New York 10016

Oxford is a registered trademark of Oxford University Press

Library of Congress Cataloging-in-Publication Data

Weinberger, Naomi Joy.
Syrian Intervention in Lebanon.

Bibliography: p.
Includes index.
1. Lebanon—History—Civil War, 1975–1976.
2. Syria—Foreign relations—Lebanon. 3. Lebanon—
Foreign relations—Syria. I. Title.
DS87.5.W45 1986   956.92′044   86-8353
ISBN 0-19-504010-4

2 4 6 8 9 7 5 3 1

Prinited in the United States of America
on acid-free paper

To my mother and
in memory of my father

whose inspiring examples of professional
dedication and personal commitment will
always guide my endeavors

Preface

A decade after its initial intervention in Lebanon's civil strife, Syria remains deeply embroiled in its neighbor's dilemmas. This costly engagement stemmed from long-standing ties between the two countries, nourished by Syria's regional leadership ambitions. Yet the goal of restoring stability to Lebanon remains elusive, while the frustration of ongoing occupation bedevils both Lebanese and Syrians.

Despite its distinctive characteristics, this case is highly revealing about the dynamics of intervention in general. Many factors favored Syria over other great and small power interveners elsewhere in the globe. Syria was intimately acquainted with its neighbor's political system and society. A multiplicity and diversity of contacts spanning the Lebanese political spectrum yielded manifold channels of influence. By the eve of its intervention in the Lebanese Civil War of 1975–76, the paramountcy of Syrian influence over that of any other external actor was widely acknowledged by Lebanese. Moreover, Syria's bilateral ties with domestic Lebanese parties were augmented by its predominant influence over Palestinian guerrillas in Lebanon.

Yet despite the advantages of intimacy and influence in the Lebanese arena, Syria fell into the same trap as most interveners in miscalculating the potential costs of its commitment. President Hafiz al-Asad and his advisers were unable to assess correctly the balance of forces between the parties into Lebanon's civil strife. They also erred in overestimating Syria's leverage over its traditional allies in Lebanon. As a consequence of both miscalculations, Syria's expectation that Lebanese stability could be restored through a finite, measured commitment proved invalid. Despite impressive tactical flexibility, Syria was caught in a dynamic of escalation that carried its Lebanese commitment far beyond desired limits.

A distinguishing feature of Syria's intervention in Lebanon was the fragmented nature of each of the key actors—Lebanon, the Palestine Liberation Organization, and Syria itself. The splintering of Lebanon along sectarian, socioeconomic, and ideological lines—defying clear-cut categories of analysis—gave rise to unstable coalitions during the Civil War and invited external manipulation. Palestinian guerrilla organizations maintained a symbiotic partnership with anti-establishment groups in Lebanon, but divisions within Palestinian ranks led to ambivalent relations with Lebanese authorities as well as with Syria. The apparent decisiveness of Syria's authoritarian regime projected a contrasting image of coherence. In reality, however, the underlying fragmentation of Syrian society was a perennial source of apprehension for Syria's leaders. Syrian objectives in Lebanon therefore reflected a gnawing defensiveness, lest Lebanese unrest spark comparable threats to Syria's narrowly based military elite.

Baffling associations and divisions, within and across key players, account for the inherent complexity of analyzing Syria's intervention in Lebanon. Significantly, realization of Syrian objectives was stymied by these internal divisions rather than by external constraints. Although both regional and great powers sought to influence Syria's Lebanese strategy, neither Arab states, Israel, nor the superpowers fundamentally altered the course of the Syrian intervention. Syria gained pervasive acknowledgment of the paramountcy of its influence, yet the draining commitment in Lebanon ultimately complicated Syria's bid for recognition as a leader in the Arab world.

The full saga of Syria's adventure in Lebanon would fill many volumes, and the final outcome is yet to be determined. Striving for depth of analysis, this volume focuses on the opening chapter of Lebanese civil strife—and of the Syrian commitment—in 1975–76. The developments of subsequent years are alluded to in the concluding chapter and will also provide the motif for my second book, *Peacekeeping Strategies: Lessons from Lebanon*.

The preparation of this book benefited from the inspiration of many colleagues. Those whose constructive criticism helped shape the manuscript include J. C. Hurewitz, Donald J. Puchala, Marius

K. Deeb, Itamar Rabinovich, William J. Foltz, Richard W. Bulliet, Yaacov Bar-siman-Tov, Robert O. Keohane, Fred Donner, Maan Z. Madina, Lisa Anderson, Raymond Baker, and Mike M. Mochizuki. The excellent editorial guidance of Susan Rabiner and Joan Bossert at Oxford University Press was also much appreciated, as was Roberta Dulong's dedicated processing of many drafts of the manuscript.

I am grateful for access to the research facilities of the Shiloah Institute of Tel Aviv University, whose primary source materials in Arabic were indispensable for this study. Ghassan Nakad paid meticulous attention to the accuracy of my Arabic translations. Generous grants from the Institute for the Study of World Politics and the Josephine de Karman Foundation were enormously helpful. Beyond a doubt, the warm encouragement and supportiveness of my husband, Dr. Sylvain Weinberger, was the critical ingredient in seeing this project through to completion.

May 1986   N.J.W.
New Haven, Connecticut

Contents

List of Maps

I

INTERVENTION IN CIVIL WARS

1

Miscalculations by Interveners

The outbreak of civil strife in Lebanon in 1975 presented both opportunities and risks for the Syrian leadership. Successful resolution of the crisis by Syria would enhance its Arab nationalist credentials, increasing its influence over Lebanon and the Palestine Liberation Organization. An unfavorable outcome to Lebanon's civil conflict, however, would benefit regional rivals at Syria's expense. Negative repercussions of Lebanese strife could also spill over and disrupt the stability of the Syrian regime.

Several distinctive features of the Syrian intervention in Lebanon make this a particularly fascinating case. Most of the literature on intervention in civil wars focuses on great power interveners, rather than small states. As a state of modest size and resources, Syria aspired to become a regional power, and had gained recognition for that status in its immediate Arab environment by the eve of the Lebanese Civil War. Syria's behavior therefore sheds light on the significance of the regional environment for small state interveners.

Second, the dynamics of the Syrian intervention display several highly unusual characteristics. Most interveners act in support of either incumbents or insurgents in a state undergoing civil conflict. Syria, having received appeals for support from both pro-establishment and anti-establishment groups in Lebanon, shifted its alignments in the midst of the Lebanese Civil War from its traditional allies (the insurgents) to the incumbents. Syria's behavior raises important questions about fluctuations in commitment during the intervention process.

Another noteworthy feature of the Syrian intervention is the

critical role played by a transnational actor, the Palestine Liberation Organization. Most theories of intervention are exclusively
concerned with two parties, the intervener and the target state.
The ambiguous status of the Palestinian Resistance derived from
the backing it enjoyed from many Arab states, while it was also
a key actor in the domestic Lebanese arena. Syria's relationship
with the Resistance was a critical factor in its commitment in Lebanon and in its redefinition of objectives once the intervention was
under way.

Finally, although the escalation of Syria's commitment in Lebanon paralleled the experience of other great and small power
interveners, the outcome of the conflict was unusual. In most cases
of intervention, decommitment eventually occurs. A clear-cut end
to the intervention may be defined and an assessment of its success
or failure may be made. Instead, the demarcation point ending
this study is the transformation of Syria's intervention into an
enduring military occupation, albeit under the guise of a peacekeeping mission sponsored by the Arab League. The reasons for
this outcome, and its consequences for both Lebanon and Syria,
warrant careful analysis.

Motivations for Intervention

Penetrational, defensive, and invitational motives were all at play
in Syria's decision to intervene in the Lebanese Civil War of 1975–
76. Guided by penetrational motives, an intervener may pursue
an activist policy when a state undergoing civil strife lies within its
presumed sphere of influence. In conformity to a realist view of
international politics, the intervener seeks an outcome to the conflict that maximizes its influence in the target state. In so doing,
the intervener seeks to ward off challenges to, and even enhance,
its status in the local balance of power.[1]

Syrian foreign policy, increasingly activist since the consolidation
of power by President Hafiz al-Asad in the early 1970s, was bound
to regard Lebanon as central to its sphere of influence. As a result

---

[1]Richard Little, *Intervention: External Involvement in Civil Wars* (Totowa, N.J.:
Rowman and Littlefield, 1975), pp. 16–17.

of close historic ties as well as geographic proximity, there was no other state more critical to Syria's regional ambitions. Lebanon's role as the major base for PLO operations raised the stakes still higher for Syria, whose title as champion of the Palestinian cause was integral to its claim to Arab leadership.

Exclusive emphasis on penetrational objectives, however, would overlook the defensive motives of the Syrian intervention. Elites in one state may intervene in an unstable neighbor because of apprehension over potential imitative unrest at home, known as the "fear of contagion." This phenomenon may be especially pronounced if the intervener's society has cleavages parallel to those in the target state.[2] Defensive motives compel an intervener to respond to perceived threats, instead of shaping its environment to conform to its ambitions in a penetrational style. Moreover, whereas penetrational theories are based on a state's status in the international system, defensive theories are associated with "linkage politics," which studies the interplay of a state's domestic and foreign policy.[3]

Beyond a doubt, Syria's leaders were apprehensive about repercussions of turmoil in Lebanon for stability in Syria. Both Lebanese and Syrian societies are fragmented along religious and—to a lesser extent—ethnic, regional, and socioeconomic lines. In each country, predominant political influence has been exercised by members of one sectarian minority group. Syria's oft-cited determination to prevent partition of Lebanon along sectarian lines reflected anxiety over Syria's vulnerability to a similar fate.

Whereas either defensive or penetrational motives may prompt an initiative by an intervener in another state's domestic troubles, invitational motives attribute the initiative to an appealer within the target state. Although Syria's ties in Lebanon were closest with anti-establishment groups prior to the Civil War, both insurgents and members of the Lebanese establishment appealed for Syrian

[2]Frederic Pearson, "Foreign Military Intervention and Domestic Disputes," *International Studies Quarterly* 18 (September 1974): 266–267.

[3]See James N. Rosenau, "Toward the Study of National-International Linkages," in *Linkage Politics*, ed. James N. Rosenau (New York: Free Press, 1969) pp. 44–63; and also Yaacov Bar-Simon-Tov, *Linkage Politics in the Middle East: Syria Between Domestic and External Conflict, 1961–1970* (Boulder, Col.: Westview Press, 1983), pp. 9–57.

support by January 1976. This rare instance of appeals by both incumbents and insurgents to the same external actor reflects the depth and breadth of Syrian ties to parties traversing the Lebanese political spectrum. The primacy of Syrian influence in Lebanon persuaded both pro- and anti-establishment forces that they had better seek Syrian assistance in order to prevail.

In most instances of invitational intervention, an appeal for outside support is issued by one of the parties to civil strife. Whether or not the recipient of the appeal responds positively depends on the nature and intensity of prior links between elites and societal groups in the two states. If these linkages are strong, a decision to intervene is seen merely as an extension of a prior commitment. From the appealer's perspective, however, a request for assistance is generally issued reluctantly. Recognizing the risks of involving an external actor in their quarrel, the parties to civil strife delay as long as possible before reaching their "threshold of appeal."[4]

Syria cited Lebanese pleas for support as indications that its intervention was purely invitational and, by implication, both welcome to the overwhelming majority of Lebanese and morally justifiable. The normative overtones of appeals may profoundly affect perceptions of the legitimacy of the intervention both within the target state and by the rest of the international community. However, it is inaccurate to counterpose invitational motives with other incentives for intervention as if they were mutually exclusive. For the analyst, it is not sufficient to ask who made the first move in initiating intervention. An intervener may harbor penetrational ambitions, even if its intervention was initially solicited by an appealer. Having responded to an invitation does not bind an intervener to subsequent conformity to the policy preferences of an appealer. By June 1976, when Syrian leaders dramatically escalated the level of their commitment in Lebanon, they did so in response to Syrian policy imperatives, not because of appeals by parties to the Lebanese conflict.

At what level, therefore, are invitational explanations helpful in understanding an intervener's motives? Surely, receiving an invitation for assistance affects a state's calculation of the costs of

---

[4]C.R. Mitchell, "Civil Strife and the Involvement of External Parties," *International Studies Quarterly* 14 (June 1970): 175–189.

intervening in civil strife. In this instance, the multiplicity and diversity of Lebanese appeals led Syrian leaders to expect that a favorable solution to the Lebanese crisis would not entail inordinate burdens.

Calculation of Costs

The overriding goal of any intervener is to realize its objectives in the target state at an acceptable cost. Yet even if the intervener is a rational actor pursuing clear-cut objectives, calculation of costs involves considerable uncertainty.[5] Observing the evolution of civil strife in another state raises doubts over who is likely to "win" the confrontation and what the consequences of "winning" will be for each side. The intervener may assist the side it favors as a means of decreasing uncertainty. However, inability to assess correctly the balance of forces between contending parties in the target state may undermine the intervener's intent. Instead of decreasing uncertainty, intervention may actually increase unpredictability by reinforcing chronic elite and institutional instability.[6] In fact, empirical studies suggest that the level of conflict in a target state generally peaks after an outside party intervenes, falsifying the intervener's common expectation that its actions will restore stability.[7]

Psychological factors also affect an intervener's calculations, introducing irrational elements into the decisionmaking process. When ambiguous information is received about circumstances in the target state, observers formulate divergent images, each representing a simplification of reality. A decision to intervene corresponds to only one of these images, and post-decision dissonance sets in as contradictory evidence is received. The intervener's re-

[5]The limitations of the "rationality assumption" in realist theories are evaluated in Robert O. Keohane, "Theory of World Politics: Structural Realism and Beyond," in *Political Science: The State of the Discipline*, ed. Ada W. Finifter (Washington, D.C.: American Political Science Association, 1983), pp. 508, 529, 531.

[6]Ted Gurr, "The Relevance of Theories of Internal Violence for the Control of Intervention," in *Law and Civil War in the Modern World*, ed. John N. Moore (Baltimore: Johns Hopkins University Press, 1974), pp. 73–75.

[7]Pearson, "Foreign Military Intervention," pp. 279–281.

sponse is often self-justification or rationalization, selecting only information that substantiates its accepted image.[8]

Obstacles to prescient analysis bedeviled Syrian decisionmakers when civil strife erupted in Lebanon. As a result, the Syrians made fundamental miscalculations, underestimating the commitment required to pursue their objectives. The pitfalls in analysis were revealing, for Syria was far more intimately acquainted with its neighbor's political circumstances than are many interveners. Nevertheless, Syria misjudged the balance of forces between the Lebanese regime and its opponents, underestimating the fragility of the Lebanese state under challenge. Syria was therefore taken by surprise when the Lebanese Army collapsed in March 1976. Syria then felt obliged to raise the level of its commitment, since no indigenous Lebanese force was capable of restoring order.

Still another vital set of calculations confronted Syrian decisionmakers. They had to evaluate how much leverage Syria could potentially wield over the Lebanese contestants, to assure that Syria's political preferences would prevail. In this respect as well, Syria from the outset had substantial sensitivity to the diversity of power centers in the Lebanese state and maintained numerous channels of communication and mechanisms for influence. Nevertheless, Syrian leaders overestimated their leverage over parties to the Lebanese conflict—and particularly over members of the anti-establishment coalition in the Civil War.

The Syrian elite was distressed when the leader of Lebanon's domestic insurgents, Kamal Junbalat, refused to accept a February 1976 plan advanced by Syria for reforming the Lebanese political system. Syria realized that its proposals fell short of demands for radical redistribution of power advanced by Junbalat's Lebanese National Movement (LNM). Nevertheless, as the principal supplier of military assistance to LNM, Syria expected to exact political compliance.

Even more devastating from the Syrian perspective were unexpected problems in exercising influence over the Palestine Liberation Organization. The ultimate source of frustration was the stubborn refusal by PLO Chairman Yasir 'Arafat to break ranks with Junbalat after Syrian-LNM relations went sour. The long-

---

[8]Little, *Intervention*, pp. 30–32, 37–38, 53–54, 115–120.

standing dependence of the PLO on Syria as its major backer in the Arab world politically and militarily had convinced the Syrians that they could manipulate 'Arafat's behavior. When he refused to submit to their will in Lebanon, Syria launched an out-and-out struggle to suppress the PLO's capacity for independent action. Unhappiness over their inability to influence Lebanese clients prompted Syrian leaders to reevaluate their initial calculations. Instead of irrationally dismissing information that contradicted their preconceived views, the Syrians displayed substantial flexibility in tactical maneuver. A shift in the direction of Syrian alignments away from its traditional allies was then accompanied by an increase in the intensity of Syrian determination to shape the outcome of the Lebanese Civil War.

Process of Commitment

Syria's dramatic shift of alignments in the midst of the Lebanese Civil War is the most astonishing feature of its intervention. This behavior does not conform to the pattern of most interventions and calls into question the consistency of Syrian actions. However, closer examination reveals that Syria's leaders maintained consistent objectives in Lebanon, despite opportunism in means employed to reach those objectives.

Definitions of intervention advanced by theorists do not adequately explain Syrian behavior. For example, James N. Rosenau asserts that "an intervention begins when one national society explicitly, purposefully, and abruptly undertakes to alter or preserve one or more essential structures of another society through military means, and it ends when the effort is either successful, abandoned, or routinized." Rosenau further explains that the concept of intervention "refers to an action and not a process—to a single sequence of behavior, the initiation and termination of which is easily discernible and the characteristics of which are dependent on the use or threat of force."[9]

This definition does not conform to the Syrian case for three

[9]James N. Rosenau, "Theorizing Across Systems: Linkage Politics Revisited," in *Conflict Behavior and Linkage Politics,* ed. Jonathan Wilkenfeld (New York: David McKay, 1973), p. 38.

reasons. First, Rosenau assumes consistency in alignments on the part of the intervener, acting either to alter or to preserve authority structures in the target state. Second, he focuses exclusively on the use of military means. Third, his emphasis on purposeful and abrupt intervention overlooks possible fluctuations in the intervener's level of commitment. A more satisfactory definition should distinguish between two key dimensions of intervention—the *direction* and *intensity* of an intervener's commitment.

Because most interveners maintain consistency in alignments with either incumbents or insurgents in a target state, theorists tend to assume that the purpose of intervention is to preserve or alter existing authority structures. A closer look calls into question whether interveners ever fully embrace the political goals of the actors they support in a target state. Certainly Syria's key objective was not to advance the cause of any particular party in Lebanon's civil strife, but rather to assure that Lebanon's authority structures were compatible with its own preferences.

Syrian diplomacy revealed the utmost consistency throughout the Lebanese Civil War in articulating Syria's preferred political outcome. Syria endorsed moderate reform of the Lebanese political system along with preservation of the status of the Palestinian Resistance in Lebanon. Syria's diplomacy revealed penetrational and defensive motives, insofar as the objectives of the Lebanese parties presented polar dangers of either partition or radicalization of Lebanon. Extreme elements in the Maronite-dominated pro-establishment camp called for a mini-state of Mount Lebanon under their control, leaving the rest of the country to the insurgents. Syria could not identify with this proposal because of its potential contagion effects. Extreme elements in the anti-establishment coalition wanted a secularized and leftist-oriented Lebanese regime, whose Arabism would be asserted in staunch support for the Palestinian Resistance. This outcome would challenge Syria's position of regional leadership, taking the foreign policy initiative out of Syrian hands and possibly leading to war with Israel at an inauspicious moment.

Syria's considered diplomatic stance enabled tactical support for either Lebanese coalition, using military assistance to prod the respective parties to endorse its own preferred political outcome. This accounts for the disjuncture between consistent diplomacy and inconsistent military alignments. When the traditional recipients of Syrian largesse (the Lebanese National Movement and the PLO) refused Syrian diplomatic proposals, they were punished. Acceptance of the Syrian reform plan by the pro-establishment coalition was then rewarded by generous support.

The means employed by an intervener to reach its objectives reflect the *intensity* of its commitment. Instead of confining the concept of intervention to military means, some theorists believe that intervention passes through both noncoercive and coercive phases. These phases correspond to the evolution of political violence in the target state. When civil strife erupts, discontent is first generated, then politicized, and finally actualized in political violence. Meanwhile, the intervener uses its influence either to help maintain or to alter the regime. Noncoercive intervention is more common when discontent in the target state is being generated and politicized, whereas coercive intervention accompanies the stage of actualized political violence.[10] There are, however, conceptual difficulties in applying the term *intervention* to preliminary, non-coercive phases, because there is no way of knowing whether an external actor had escalatory intentions from the outset. Perhaps the actor was merely an interested party, with no intent of resorting to coercive means until later. In such a case, noncoercive phases may be deemed part of an intervention process only in retrospect.

On balance, therefore, it is preferable to refer to a process of commitment that may culminate in intervention. When a state is undergoing civil strife, *commitment* by an external actor seeks to determine the target state's authority structures by noncoercive or coercive means. The most intense form of commitment is *intervention,* involving direct military engagement for the purpose of determining the authority structures of the target state. This conceptual distinction emphasizes that the period prior to intervention is part of a continuous process of commitment, shaping the expectations of all concerned parties. Moreover, noncoercive means remain vital instruments for exerting influence even once intervention begins.

In determining the intensity of its commitment in a target state,

---

[10]Gurr, "Relevance of Theories," pp. 71–77, 84–90; idem, *Why Men Rebel* (Princeton: Princeton University Press, 1970), pp. 3–15.

an external actor has an entire spectrum of means at its disposal. These instrumentalities vary from low-cost, low-risk means such as mediation or economic assistance to high-cost, high-risk means such as direct military engagement. The choice of instrumentality depends on calculations of the costs and risks involved. Syria initially hoped and preferred to achieve its objectives in Lebanon without recourse to intervention. In a cautious, incremental decisionmaking process, Syrian leaders sought to restrict their country's level of commitment to strategies involving the lowest possible costs and risks. Only when they discovered that they lacked sufficient leverage over their traditional allies to achieve compliance did the Syrian elite embark on direct military engagement in June 1976.

The phases of Syria's commitment in Lebanon's civil strife may be demarcated according to gradual increases in the level of intensity. From the outbreak of the Lebanese Civil War in April 1975 until the end of that year, Syria assumed the role of mediator, while simultaneously supplying military assistance to the Lebanese insurgents. In January 1976, a new phase of indirect Syrian intervention began, as Palestinian guerrilla forces crossed the Syrian border and participated in the Lebanese combat. Indirect intervention (discussed below) entails military engagement by a client, proxy, or agent of an external actor in a situation of civil strife. In this circumstance, the external actor serves as a patron, supplying the military wherewithal for the intervention and coordinating or directing the intervention strategy. During this transitional phase, a shift of alignments prompted Syria to command Palestinian guerrillas sent from Syria to Lebanon to throw their support to the incumbents. Finally, in June, the most intense stage of Syrian commitment was reached, culminating in the direct engagement of 30,000 regular Syrian forces.

The pattern of Syria's commitment in Lebanon reveals that, despite distinctions between three definable stages, there was an ongoing blending of modalities for exercising influence. Even during the initial, mediatory phase, provision of military assistance entailed a coercive dimension. An interested party striving for a given diplomatic outcome may exploit dependence by parties in the target state on economic or military assistance as an instrument of leverage in negotiations. Conversely, even once intervention occurs, efforts at mediation rely on intangible and symbolic instrumentalities as well as the use or threat of force. For this reason, labeling phases of commitment as purely noncoercive or purely coercive is inaccurate.

In its overall thrust, the Syrian commitment in Lebanon reveals a clear escalatory dynamic. Nevertheless, the process cannot be characterized as a "single sequence of behavior." Instead of being "explicit, purposeful and abrupt" (to cite Rosenau's phrase), Syria's commitment both before and during the stage of intervention revealed fluctuations and even reversals in levels of intensity. This is because ongoing calculations and reassessments were occurring at each stage.

Escalation reflects a progressive redefinition of stakes by an intervener. A balancing of costs and benefits occurs not only when the initial decision to intervene is made, but at each stage of the intervention process. Because the cost of intervention increases as time passes, the intervener, hoping to recover its initial costs, is willing to raise its level of commitment. As the utility attached to the outcome continues to increase, the result is an ongoing expansion of the initial commitment.

Obviously, an element of determinism is implied in the image of a ladder of escalation, proceeding relentlessly toward the top. However, escalation is not a mindless, undifferentiated process. A series of thresholds define the ladder of escalation, and decisionmakers are conscious of the symbolic significance of each threshold. Fluctuations in commitment are reflected in differential levels of resources expended over time. Moreover, decommitment eventually occurs, although decisionmakers hesitate to specify conditions for reversal or termination of intervention commitments. Instead, they issue ambiguous declarations of intent, hoping to keep their options open. The decisive factor in triggering decommitment is often an erosion of elite consensus within the intervener.

The difficulty of maintaining elite consensus depends on how much dissent initially surfaces within the elite about the decision to intervene. Predecision conflict may occur over which regime (incumbents or insurgents) to support in the bifurcated target state, as well as over the intensity of the intervention commitment. As the costs of intervention increase, a growing divergence may occur within an elite over the acceptability of the level of commitment.

Ultimately, the intervener's willingness to decommit depends on opportunity costs foregone and on the current costs which decommitment entails. Once the process begins, it is usually portrayed as the termination of a commitment that has been fulfilled, rather than a reversal of policy.[11] As a result of the closed, authoritarian nature of the Syrian political system, the analyst is left in the dark about the process whereby consensus for intervention may have been built and may have subsequently eroded within the Syrian elite. Information about which key actors were involved in the decisionmaking process does not suffice to identify their specific points of view in policy debates. For this reason, an outside observer is obliged to adhere to a "rational actor" model, seeking clues about fluctuations in Syrian commitment based on Syrian behavior. By October 1976, when a cease-fire accord marked a formal end to the Syrian intervention process, there were no discernible indications of an erosion of elite consensus. In effect, however, the cease-fire did not signify a true process of decommitment, but rather a redefinition of the Syrian presence in Lebanon.

Indirect Intervention

The complex relationship between Syria and the Palestinian Resistance is in large measure responsible for the distinctive features of Syria's experience in Lebanon in 1975–76. The transnational dimension of Syria's intervention was decisive in three respects. First, Syria's prior links to the Palestinian Resistance were its strongest ties within the target state, generating expectations by domestic Lebanese parties that Syria would intervene once the Resistance became a party to Lebanon's civil strife. Second, the internal fragmentation of the Resistance permitted individual Arab states to gain predominant influence over some of its component guerrilla organizations. Consequently, when Syrian leaders chose to intervene indirectly in Lebanon, they could count on certain guerrilla groups to serve as instruments of Syria's policy objectives. However, the limits of Syrian leverage over the Resistance as a

[11]Little, *Intervention*, pp. 9–11, 91–95, 134–141, 156–160.

whole were revealed when Syrian policies threatened vital interests of the Palestinian leadership. At this point, a third feature of Syrian-Palestinian relations came to the surface. The core group within the Resistance, Fath, was unwilling to serve as a Syrian proxy in the Lebanese arena.

The ambiguous status of the Palestinian Resistance in Lebanon derived from its transnational character. Because the Palestine Liberation Organization operated in and derived support from various Arab states, it could not be classified as a domestic actor in Lebanon. Nevertheless, the PLO formed close political ties to anti-establishment groups in Lebanon, and therefore was a participant in domestic Lebanese politics.

The single most highly charged issue in Lebanese politics for years before the outbreak of the Civil War was whether or not Lebanese authorities should condone raids by Palestinian guerrillas against Israel. Some Lebanese viewed the guerrillas as intruders; others welcomed their presence as a symbol of Lebanon's identification with pan-Arab goals. Support for the PLO was a cause célèbre for anti-establishment forces in Lebanon, and the issue became a catalyst polarizing the Lebanese political environment.

Since the late 1960s, Syria had actively sponsored Palestinian guerrilla operations in Southern Lebanon. When clashes erupted between the Resistance and Lebanese authorities in 1969 and 1973, Syria assisted the guerrillas. Although Lebanese authorities viewed Syrian backing of the Resistance as an unfriendly gesture, they recognized Syrian leverage over the PLO and sought to encourage Syrian restraint. When Lebanese civil strife in April 1975 was triggered by clashes between the Maronite-dominated Kata'ib (Phalangist) militia and the PLO, Lebanese authorities wondered whether Syria would support direct Palestinian involvement.

The different postures adopted by Palestinian guerrilla groups in the early months of the Lebanese Civil War stemmed from deep political and ideological differences. Yasir 'Arafat's principal group, Fath, was officially committed to noninterference in domestic Lebanese politics, and attempted to maintain that posture throughout 1975. The Popular Front for the Liberation of Palestine (PFLP) was the leading exponent of an alternative approach, based on an ideology advocating social revolution throughout the Arab world. The PFLP identified explicitly with Kamal Junbalat's Lebanese National Movement long before the Civil War, and fought alongside the LNM from the outset of the war.

The fragmentation of the Resistance created opportunities as well as frustrations for Syria's efforts to present itself as a champion of the Palestinian cause. Despite Syria's early support for Fath, Yasir 'Arafat's efforts at autonomy from Syrian control led to strains in the relationship, and Syria's ties to the PFLP were also tense. Units of the Palestine Liberation Army (the military arm of the PLO) deployed in Syria were kept under the command of the regular Syrian Army. Moreover, in 1968, Syria sponsored the creation of al-Sa'iqah, a Palestinian guerrilla group subordinate to Syrian control that was active in conducting operations against Israel from Southern Lebanon.

As Lebanon's Civil War evolved, Syria initially acted in its mediatory capacity to encourage 'Arafat's posture of non-involvement in Lebanese domestic strife. Then, after Kata'ib attacks on Palestinian refugee camps precipitated direct PLO participation in the war, Syria deepened its commitment in Lebanon in the name of saving the Palestinian Resistance. At this point, however, Syria's leaders were unwilling to risk direct military engagement. Indirect intervention appeared to offer a perfect mechanism for incrementally escalating Syria's level of commitment. Forces of Sa'iqah as well as PLO units stationed in Syria intervened in support of the Lebanese insurgents in January 1976.

Subsequent developments illustrate the utility as well as the fuzziness of the concept of indirect intervention. This concept has usually been applied to intervention by a client state on behalf of a great power, a problematic usage that will be analyzed below. Indirect intervention is a more useful explanatory tool for the behavior of subnational or transnational actors. In effect, a spectrum of possible relationships between a patron and a subordinate actor may lead the latter to indirect intervention. Varying with the subordinate actor's degree of dependence, it may either be referred to as an agent, a proxy, or a client. In each case, one must ask what costs the actor would incur for refusing to advance its patron's goals through the act of intervention.

AUTONOMY◄ ● ● ●► DEPENDENCE

CLIENT	PROXY	AGENT
(strategic	(tactical	(no
flexibility)	flexibility)	flexibility)

Vulnerability of a subordinate actor to manipulation by a patron varies directly with the actor's dependence on the patron for military, economic, or political backing. Vulnerability varies inversely with the availability to the actor of alternative sources of support. For a subnational actor, the existence of a strong domestic base of support may enhance its autonomy. For a transnational actor, the availability of alternate patrons would decisively increase its flexibility and decrease the patron's leverage.

Syria's effort at indirect intervention in Lebanon illustrates the applicability of these categories. Sa'iqah served as an agent for Syrian interests, lacking any identifiable constituency outside its organizational ranks. A totally artificial creation, Sa'iqah lacked sufficient autonomy even to articulate preferences of its own. If its leaders refused to follow Syrian guidelines and consequently lost the patron's support, Sa'iqah would cease to exist as an organization. In fact, Sa'iqah was a mere extension of Syria's will in Lebanon, explaining the ease with which Syria could employ the organization for indirect intervention. In reaction to the involvement of Sa'iqah in clashes with other Palestinian guerrillas after Syria shifted alignments in the Lebanese Civil War, the PFLP called for the expulsion of the Syrian-sponsored group from the ranks of the PLO.

By contrast, groups within the PLO loyal to the leadership of Yasir 'Arafat retained substantial autonomy, despite their status as Syrian clients. 'Arafat coordinated Palestinian activities with Syria as long as a convergence of interests existed. In January 1976, when PLO units nominally subordinate to 'Arafat's command were infiltrated by Syria across the Lebanese border to support the anti-establishment coalition of LNM and PLO forces, 'Arafat applauded the move. However, by the spring of 1976, when Syria instructed PLO forces to support Lebanese incumbents, spokesmen for the PLO contested Syria's right to deploy PLO units without their approval. Despite heavy Syrian pressure, 'Arafat refused to break with the LNM. This led to the spectacle of Palestinians loyal to Syria fighting those loyal to Yasir 'Arafat.

The deeper significance of this episode is that the PLO had the wherewithal, despite long-standing dependence on Syria, to say no to the Syrian leadership and still maintain its integrity. The strategic flexibility of the PLO meant that on an issue of vital importance to PLO leaders, they were able to absorb the costs of the patron's disapproval. The PLO leadership could do so because, first of all, they could turn to other Arab states as alternate patrons and second, they derived strength from a symbiotic relationship with the LNM. Although Syrian officials accused the PLO of "fighting for the goals of others" in Lebanon, the alliance with the LNM was useful to the PLO in enhancing its autonomy. The LNM, as a subnational actor, had a solid base of domestic support, but needed Palestinian fighting strength to make a credible military showing in the Lebanese Civil War.

The availability of alternate sources of support to the PLO enabled its leaders to reject Syrian demands, although at a very heavy price. While a client may have strategic flexibility, the cost of following its own preferences on an issue of vital significance varies based on whether the issue is of strategic significance to its patron as well. In this case, Syria considered the outcome of the Lebanese Civil War a matter of vital interest, and therefore Palestinian insubordination led to a suspension of the patron-client relationship. The upshot was that, beginning in June 1976, Syria and the PLO became the prime combatants in the Lebanese Civil War.

Syria's most critical miscalculation in the Civil War was its expectation that the PLO could be manipulated to serve as a proxy, rather than a client. A proxy at most enjoys tactical flexibility in implementing objectives spelled out by its patron. This is because a proxy is exclusively dependent on its patron for support (lacking potential alternate patrons) and also has a narrow indigenous constituency. If a proxy were to say no to a patron's request to intervene in a situation of civil strife, it would not cease to exist as an actor (as would an agent), but neither would it have the wherewithal to intervene on its own. The willingness of a proxy to intervene on a patron's behalf may be reinforced if there is a convergence of interests between the two—that is, if the proxy has motivations of its own for intervening, but lacks the wherewithal to do so without the patron's support.

A good example of patron-proxy interaction was the relationship between Israel and the militia led by Major Sa'ad Haddad in Southern Lebanon from 1976 to 1984. Haddad and his Israeli backers shared the objective of curtailing PLO presence and operations in Southern Lebanon. Nevertheless, Haddad often strained at the bit of Israeli control and tested the outer limits of his autonomy. Because of his ultimate vulnerability to Israeli leverage, he could only diverge from Israeli preferences on minor tactical matters.[12]

Although it was a patron to transnational and subnational actors in Lebanon, Syria itself was a client vis-à-vis a superpower patron. The possibility of "dual layers of patronage," whereby "weak states can try to behave as patrons of even weaker states,"[13] applies also to small states' relations with nonstate actors. In a global perspective, Syria is a relatively small and weak state, heavily dependent on military and economic support from its Soviet patron. The conceptual question raised is how intervention may be affected by the dependence of a small state intervener on a great power.

Some observers of the Syrian intervention in Lebanon have characterized Syria as a proxy for the Soviet Union, or even for the United States. According to one interpretation, the U.S.S.R. viewed Syrian hegemony in Lebanon as a means of enlarging its own sphere of influence in the Middle East. The opposing theory is that the United States was "using" President Asad as a tool for "taming" the PLO, whose opposition posed a major obstacle to American diplomatic designs in the region.

Those who speak of indirect intervention by great powers advance a rigidly hierarchical image of the international system. A great power presumably uses a regional actor as its proxy in situations of civil strife when it is either unwilling or unable to intervene directly on its own. One common explanation for an increased trend toward indirect intervention by the United States

---

[12]Naomi Joy Weinberger, "Peacekeeping Options in Lebanon," *The Middle East Journal* 37,3 (Summer 1983): 344–347.

[13]Michael Handel, *Weak States in the International System* (London: Frank Cass, 1981), p. 13.

in the 1970s is that when the fiasco of the Vietnam War discredited direct military engagement as an instrument of American policy, alternate strategies were sought. The cultivation of "special relationships" with regional "subimperial" powers made it possible to delegate intervention to junior partners.[14] These regional actors are characterized as "strong middle powers" which "exercise hegemony over neighboring countries, yet are still subordinate to major powers."[15]

Analysts who argue that a state may serve as a proxy suggest that the initiative in indirect intervention is taken by a great power "activator." The patron is reluctant to intervene on its own because either it lacks viable military options, perceives the risks of intervention as too high, or lacks vital interests in the target state to justify the cost of intervening. For the proxy, the decision to intervene on the activator's behalf may be taken either voluntarily or against its will. If a proxy lacks interests of its own in the target state, the costs of saying no may be too high in terms of its dependent relationship with its patron. If a proxy does have interests in the target, the request to intervene may be perceived as an opportunity to advance its own objectives. Nevertheless, without the patron's request, the proxy would not pursue military action. Even for the voluntary proxy, there is an element of explicit or implicit coercion in the decision to intervene.[16]

On closer scrutiny, the attempt to prove that one state is a proxy for another is highly problematic. Empirically, it is often impossible to document a specific request on the activator's part. Moreover, if a convergence of interests exists between the patron and a "voluntary proxy," it is difficult to substantiate the element of coercion—that is, to demonstrate that the proxy would not intervene without the activator's request. The fact that the small state lacks the material capabilities to intervene, or to intervene on as large a scale, is not sufficient to prove a proxy relationship. If a small state, while receiving material support from its patron, coordinates

[14]Richard Falk, "The Prospects of Intervention: Exporting Counterrevolution," *The Nation* 228 (9 June 1979): 659–662.

[15]James Mittleman, "Intervention in Southern Africa: America's Investment in Apartheid," *The Nation* 228 (9 June 1979): 684–689.

[16]Yaacov Bar-Siman-Tov, "The Strategy of War by Proxy," *Cooperation and Conflict* 19 (1984):263–273.

an intervention strategy without pressure to intervene, it may be considered a partner rather than a proxy.[17]

On an even more fundamental level, the reason that it is accurate to apply the proxy label to subnational or transnational actors but not to a state is that the latter possesses the attribute of sovereignty. A nonstate actor may lack strategic flexibility because it cannot absorb the costs of saying no to a patron's request. If the patron cuts off support, the subordinate actor may have nowhere to turn because it lacks potential alternate patrons or a viable indigenous constituency. Even a weak state, by contrast, enjoys some options in its international alignments and some measure of domestic legitimacy. For a state to serve as a proxy, intervening in a conflict in which it would not autonomously decide to become committed, involves a suspension of its own sovereign will. Intervening under pressure implies that the state ceases to make its own calculations of interest, deferring to the primacy of the activator's objectives.

The type of state least likely to engage in proxy intervention is a regional power. Although as a small state its interests and influence are limited to its local environment,[18] its ambitions in that regional arena involve vital interests and deep historic roots. In framing a decision to intervene, a regional power will be reluctant to subordinate its priorities to those of a great power patron. By contrast, the great power's interests are global in scope, and its priorities in any region are evaluated in the context of broader goals. Vital interests may or may not be considered at stake in the outcome of a given situation of civil strife.[19]

In various conflict situations, including intervention in civil wars, the commitment of a small state to the outcome may be stronger than that of a great power patron. As a result, the small state may be willing to devote more resources to influence the outcome and may also be willing to incur the costs of its patron's wrath if a divergence of interests arises. The phenomenon of "asymmetry in motivation" favoring a small state[20] challenges the realist theorists'

---

[17]Bertil Duner, "Proxy Intervention in Civil Wars," *Journal of Peace Research* 18, 4 (1981): 353–361.

[18]Handel, *Weak States*, pp. 21, 42.

[19]For a discussion of the different incentives for intervention by great powers and regional powers, see Pearson, "Foreign Military Intervention," pp. 262–263.

[20]Alexander George, "Comparisons and Lessons," in *The Limits of Coercive*

assumption about the "fungibility" of power. If power is fungible, this means that an overall preponderance of power resources would allow a patron to assert its will on virtually any issue. A more convincing interpretation, however, is that "power resources are differentially effective across issue areas."[21]

In Lebanon's civil strife, Syria displayed stronger motivation than either of the superpowers. Neither the Soviet Union nor the United States had vital interests at stake in the outcome of the Lebanese Civil War. Syria could therefore exercise strategic flexibility without incurring heavy cost. Insofar as the Syrian client diverged from preferences of its Soviet patron, this did not entail refusal of an activator's request to intervene. On the contrary, Soviet pressures were ultimately aimed at restraining Syria's initiatives. Because of the asymmetry in motivation, Syria sustained Soviet disapproval without unduly damaging its relationship with its patron.

External Constraints

To what extent was Syria's freedom of action in Lebanon constrained by its global or regional environment? What actors had the capacity to curb Syria's freedom of maneuver? *Potential* constraints might derive from an actor's leverage over Syria, through military or economic support. Alternatively, potential constraints could stem from an actor's capacity for counterintervention. What motivation did other actors have to constrain Syria's behavior based on their own interests in the target state? Only by answering the latter question can one evaluate the *actual* constraints presented by Syria's external environment.

Reactions by external actors were responsive to the complex pattern of Syria's commitment in Lebanon. In calculating whether their interests were challenged by Syrian behavior, other states implicitly distinguished between the two dimensions of Syria's commitment. Some were most concerned with the *intensity* of the com-

---

Diplomacy, by Alexander George et al. (Boston: Little Brown, 1971), pp. 218–220.
    [21]Keohane, "Theory of World Politics," pp. 508, 522–525, 529.

mitment and its implications for the local balance of power. Others were more worried about the shift in *direction* of Syria's alignments in the midst of the Lebanese war, because of power-political or normative repercussions.

As argued above, although the Soviet Union had the potential to impose constraints on Syrian behavior (or at least to raise the costs of Syrian divergence from its preferences), it lacked serious motivation to do so. Soviet leaders had no intrinsic objection to the intensity of Syria's commitment in Lebanon, since an increase in its client's regional stature would benefit Soviet interests. Soviet discomfiture arose only after the shift in Syrian alignments. Although the Soviets cared little about domestic contestants in the Lebanese war, they were embarrassed to witness Syrians and Palestinian guerrillas locked in combat, each equipped with Soviet arms. The Soviets were also troubled by President Asad's assertions of autonomy, manifested both in lack of consultation with the Soviet patron and in a worrisome increase in contacts with the United States.

Asad's flirtation with the United States during the Lebanese Civil War increased his bargaining leverage with the Soviet Union by suggesting that an alternate patron might be available. In reality, Syria's new fluidity in global alignments did not significantly decrease its dependence on the Soviet patron. Asad considered the American connection useful for the specific purpose of precluding Israeli counterintervention in Lebanon. He was therefore concerned with potential constraints that the United States could pose to Israel's actions, rather than his own.

From the American perspective, increased interaction with an Arab state previously considered securely in the Soviet orbit was welcome. The United States, like the Soviet Union, had little intrinsic interest in domestic Lebanese developments, despite an American preference for victory by the incumbents. The prime American concern was the risk that Syrian intervention might spark a widening of the Lebanese conflict if Israeli counterintervention occurred. Washington served as a channel of communications between Israel and Syria in an effort to avoid confrontation. Although the United States was primarily concerned with the intensity of Syria's commitment, the shift in direction of Syria's alignments was ultimately appreciated by Washington, and the United States applauded Syria's "constructive" intervention on the Lebanese incumbents' behalf. Actual constraints were more decisively posed by Syria's regional, rather than its global, environment. Israel, as the only state other than Syria with vital security interests at stake in the outcome of Lebanon's civil strife, was also the only state with credible prospects for counterintervention. Israel was concerned that victory by the Lebanese insurgents would lead to increased Palestinian guerrilla operations against its population. For this reason, Israel was preoccupied, during the initial stage of Syria's commitment in Lebanon, with the direction of Syrian alignments in support of the LNM and PLO. Once Syria shifted its support to the pro-establishment coalition in Lebanon, Israel toned down its threats of counterintervention.

Nevertheless, the intensity of Syria's eventual commitment in Lebanon troubled the Israelis independent of its direction. As a major partner in the Arab confrontation with Israel, Syria's military posture could benefit from access to an additional front in Lebanon. Insofar as Lebanon's former status as a noncombatant had created a buffer between Israel and Syria, direct Syrian intervention in Lebanon threatened to reverse that condition. At minimum, Israeli leaders wished to deter the presence of Syrian forces in Southern Lebanon, immediately adjacent to their border.

Counterintervention often sparks a process of escalation by the original intervener. A "self-feeding process" impels competing interveners to progressively higher levels of violence, associated with rising stakes.[22] In this case, potential counterintervention had a restraining, rather than an escalatory, effect on Syrian behavior. The threat of Israeli counterintervention profoundly affected Syria's calculation of the risks involved in its Lebanese commitment. Reluctance by Syrian leaders to intervene directly in Lebanon was largely attributable to the danger of confrontation with Israel. The incremental and cautious escalation of Syria's commitment, initially restricted to military assistance to the Lebanese combatants and then to indirect intervention, reflects this perception of risk. By the time Syria contemplated direct intervention, its shift of

[22]Richard Smoke, "Analytic Dimensions of Intervention Decisions," in *The Limits of Military Intervention*, ed. Ellen P. Stern (Beverly Hills: Sage, 1977), pp. 29–30.

alignments had considerably lowered the probability of Israeli counterintervention. However, the geographic scope of Syria's intervention was restricted to exclude Southern Lebanon, through successful Israeli deterrence.

As distinct from the power-political constraints posed by Israel, Syria's actions were limited by other Arab states primarily through normative sanctions. Moreover, as opposed to Israel's continuous restraining influence on Syrian behavior, Arab opposition did not present actual constraints until direct intervention began in June 1976.

Arab nationalist ideology is a significant element in the legitimacy formulae of Arab regimes,[23] as well as a vital criterion for credibility of Arab leadership claims. Syria was obliged to pay heed to Arab consensual norms to fulfill the subjective requirements for regional leadership. Whereas the status of regional power may be determined by objective power resources, leadership requires recognition by members of the group one wishes to lead.

Arab nationalist ideology creates a permissive normative climate for intervention among Arab states. The symbol of a single Arab nation, historically preceding the emergence of territorially demarcated states, renders state frontiers highly permeable. Ostensibly sovereign Arab states become merely a facade masking the overarching Arab nation, and their leaders emerge as "interim caretakers" until Arab unity is concretely realized. The "super-legitimacy" of the Arab nation, superseding the legitimacy claims of individual leaders, may justify intervention in favor of either incumbents or insurgents—depending on whose ideological credentials are deemed superior.[24]

There would be no Arab opposition in principle, therefore, to Syrian intervention in Lebanon so long as the direction of its alignments was ideologically sound. Syria consistently justified its intervention as an effort to protect the Palestinian Resistance and restore the stability and territorial integrity of the Lebanese state. Support for the Palestinian cause was a recognized criterion of

[23]Michael Hudson, *Arab Politics: The Search for Legitimacy* (New Haven: Yale University Press, 1977), pp. 1–30.

[24]Walid Khalidi, "Thinking the Unthinkable: A Sovereign Palestinian State," *Foreign Affairs* 56 (July 1978): 695–696.

pan-Arab commitment. Even after shifting alignments in Lebanon, Syrian leaders continued to pose as guardians of the true interests of the Palestinians, accusing the Palestinian leadership of inappropriate entanglement in parochial Lebanese pursuits. Contesting these charges, Yasir 'Arafat sought "Arabization" of the crisis. 'Arafat won backing in the Arab League for his complaint that Syria had gone too far in directly attacking PLO forces, thereby exceeding the normative limits permitted by the Arab consensus.

The fact that Arab condemnation of Syrian behavior was cast solely in normative terms does not mean that power-political considerations were absent. Other Arab states contesting Syria's leadership claims harbored unarticulated anxieties about the increased capabilities Syria might accrue through successful domination of Lebanon and the PLO. On this level, Arab rivals were concerned about the intensity of Syria's commitment in Lebanon as well as its direction. The dynamics of inter-Arab politics may be explained in terms of fluctuations in power relations among Arab states. A persistent tension exists between internally weak states, seeking stability through coalition with stronger partners, and more stable states seeking regional dominance. When one actor emerges as the leader of a powerful coalition, other states seek to create counterweights, as classic balance of power theory would predict. The outcome is polarization in the Arab state system.[25]

During the early 1970s, Syria's attempts at coalition building were confined to the immediate geographic area of the Fertile Crescent, emphasizing close ties with Jordan, Lebanon, and the PLO. During the early stages of the Syrian commitment in Lebanon, both "moderate" and "rejectionist" Arab coalitions recognized Syria's increased stature, each offering incentives to Syria to join their ranks. Then, after Syria's military engagement in Lebanon aroused Arab anxieties, no single state possessed the capacity or will for full-scale counterintervention. Unilateral measures were taken only by Iraq, a Fertile Crescent state whose own regional leadership ambitions were challenged by Syrian actions. Only when a consensus within the Arab League developed for restraining Syrian behavior did collective action become possible.

[25]Yair Evron and Yaacov Bar Simantov, "Coalitions in the Arab World," *Jerusalem Journal of International Relations* 1 (1975): 71–88.

Syria was then persuaded to attend an Arab League meeting in October 1976 through pressure by Saudi Arabia, upon whom Syria had become heavily dependent financially during the Civil War. Saudi Arabia's leverage, derived from tangible assets, was exercised in in the name of implementing the normative consensus of the Arab League.

In negotiating the terms of the October cease-fire accord, Arab League members were satisfied with symbolic concessions on Syria's part. Once Syria pledged to safeguard the status of the PLO in Lebanon and to redesignate its forces as members of the Arab Deterrent Force, its military presence in Lebanon was not only permitted but also funded by the Arab League. Thus, despite the limits set by the Arab states collectively on the scope of Syria's intervention, they retrospectively conferred a measure of legitimation on unilateral actions of the Syrian regime.

Determining Relative Weights

On balance, Syria's external environment was remarkably permissive, allowing unusual autonomy to Syria as a small state intervener. Insofar as Syria's choices were limited by regional or global constraints, the effect was to set outer limits for Syrian policymakers, rather than inhibiting pursuit of major objectives.

The foremost obstacles to achieving Syrian goals in Lebanon derived not from its external environment, but rather from circumstances in the target state. Syria lacked sufficient leverage over parties to the Lebanese conflict to achieve its objectives at an acceptable cost. Its initial miscalculations were superseded by subsequent reappraisal, displaying impressive tactical flexibility. Nonetheless, the net result was an undesirable escalatory dynamic, bringing Lebanon no closer to a resolution of its conflicts compatible with Syrian interests.

One of the most important—and difficult—tasks confronting an analyst of the Syrian intervention is to assess the relative weights of different variables in the Syrian decisionmaking process. What were the most compelling motives for Syria's decision to intervene in Lebanon? Were penetrational, defensive, or invitational goals predominant? Or, perhaps, did the relative salience of these motives vary during the process of commitment? How did Syria's prior links to the Lebanese combatants color its expectations of exercising leverage once civil strife erupted? How well did Syrian leaders anticipate whether the potential of other states to limit Syrian freedom of maneuver would be transformed into actual constraints? Before addressing these questions in depth with respect to the 1975–76 Lebanese Civil War, Syria's stake in Lebanon must first be appreciated in its historical context.

II

THE SYRIAN STAKE
IN LEBANON

2

Historical Bonds

The Syrian stake in Lebanon long predates the independence of both countries. During four centuries of Ottoman rule, Mount Lebanon was considered part of the larger geographic entity of Syria. Ambiguous administrative divisions prompted persistent questions over Lebanon's autonomy as well as its boundaries. Competing claims were not resolved when France gained a mandate over Syria and Lebanon in 1920. French designation of new boundaries for each state favored Lebanon at Syria's expense. The subsequent refusal by Syria to establish diplomatic relations with Lebanon reflected an enduring perception that Lebanon was rightfully part of Syria.

The pre-independence period was also critical to the social development of Syria and Lebanon. Lebanese society evolved from a feudal order to a system in which religious sects (or confessions) were the principal social cleavages. Diverse mechanisms for containing conflict between sects, ranging from partition to proportional representation, furnished important precedents. Parallels with the social cleavages emerging in Syria encouraged transnational links, despite differing political settings.

History also provides important precedents for external intervention. The most conspicuous and consistent extra-regional intervener in Lebanese and Syrian affairs during the Ottoman period was France, although other European states played an active role. The impact of European rivalries in accentuating Lebanese confessional cleavages, influencing administrative arrangements, and highlighting Lebanon's distinctive status came to a head under the French mandate. Undoubtedly, foreign interference complicated the Syrian-Lebanese relationship from the very outset.

Administrative Anomalies

The ambiguity of Lebanon's status during the Ottoman period stemmed from fluid administrative divisions throughout Syria. Since medieval times the geographic designation of *al-Sham* (or *bilad al-Sham)* covered the subsequent states of Syria, Lebanon, Jordan, and Israel. Syria gradually acquired a predominantly Arab-Muslim character after the seventh-century Arab conquest, and Damascus served as the capital of the Islamic Umayyad Empire until A.D. 750. Syria then preserved its distinctive cultural tone through two centuries of occupation by European crusaders and four centuries of rule by the Ottoman Turks.[1]

After its conquest by Ottoman Sultan Selim I in 1516, Syria was divided into provinces whose contours repeatedly fluctuated. Even the name of the basic provincial unit was changed from *pashaliks,* to *eyalets,* and finally to *vilayets.* Ambitious provincial governors, known as *pashas* or *valis* (in Arabic, *walis),* strove incessantly to enlarge their domains at each other's expense. Thereby, the initial three provinces of Damascus, Aleppo, and Tripoli were modified and a fourth province of Sidon (later redesignated as the province of Beirut) emerged. The province of Tripoli was then intermittently absorbed by either the Sidon or Damascus provinces.[2]

Fluctuations in provincial size reflected not only rivalries among competing *valis,* but also attempts at control by the Sublime Porte, the seat of Ottoman authority in Istanbul. In Syria, as in other peripheral areas of the Ottoman Empire, decentralization of authority encouraged the rise of strong local rulers who enjoyed substantial autonomy. As long as they acknowledged the overlordship of the Sultan and collected a stipulated amount of revenue for the state treasury, the *valis* experienced few constraints from Istanbul. At best, the Porte could hope to balance the local forces against each other to prevent any one from becoming too powerful.[3]

[1] Abdul Latif Tibawi, *A Modern History of Syria, Including Lebanon and Palestine* (London: Macmillan; New York: St. Martin's, 1969), pp. 19–20.

[2] Moshe Ma'oz, *Ottoman Reform in Syria and Palestine, 1840–1861* (Oxford, England: Clarendon Press, 1968), pp. 31–32.

[3] Tibawi, *Modern History of Syria,* pp. 23, 30; Ma'oz, *Ottoman Reform,* pp. 4–5.

Since the beginning of Ottoman rule, a distinctive status was accorded to the Mountain, as Lebanon was known because of the mountain ranges traversing its length. Although nominally subordinate to the *valis* of the adjacent Syrian provinces, two successive dynasties of local Lebanese rulers (known as *hakims,* or princes) pressed their independent prerogatives to the outer limits. The Ma'ni dynasty was established by Fakhr al-Din I, whose southern Shuf region of the Mountain was recognized by Sultan Selim I in 1516. His son, Fakhr al-Din II, was the first to promote a vision of "greater Lebanon," expanding the area under his control (from the northern city of Aleppo to the borders of Egypt) and winning the title of governor of Syria. Eventually, however, the Sultan felt threatened by his power and ordered him beheaded.[4]

Rulers of the subsequent Shihabi dynasty (1697–1841) also strove to enlarge the domain and autonomy of the Mountain. Bashir II, who ruled from 1788 to 1840, achieved the most success in realizing a "greater Lebanon." Not only did he gain jurisdiction over all of Mount Lebanon, but he also incorporated the coastal towns along the Mediterranean and controlled the eastern Biqa' valley, despite the strenuous objections of the *vali* of Damascus.[5]

The final years of Bashir II's rule coincided with an eight-year interlude of Egyptian control over all of Syria (1832–40). In an unusual episode in Ottoman history, the powerful *vali* of Egypt, Mehmed Ali (1805–49) mounted a far-reaching challenge to the authority of the Sublime Porte. After unsuccessful petitions to Sultan Mahmud II to gain control of the Syrian provinces, Mehmed Ali sent out forces commanded by his son, Ibrahim Pasha. Ibrahim was supported by Bashir II in gaining control of the Mountain as well as other parts of Syria.[6]

The Egyptian occupation of Syria was a jarring affront to the Sultan. Mahmud II had recently launched a series of comprehensive reforms, the *tanzimat,* aimed at restoring centralized control in the outlying provinces. The Sultan embarked in 1826 on a major program to modernize his army along Western lines, but had not progressed far enough to withstand the Egyptian challenge. His

[4]Philip Hitti, *History of Syria, Including Lebanon and Palestine* (London: Macmillan, 1951), pp. 679–684.
[5]Ibid., pp. 692–694.
[6]Ibid.; Tibawi, *Modern History of Syria,* pp. 64–71; Ma'oz, *Ottoman Reform,* p. 12.

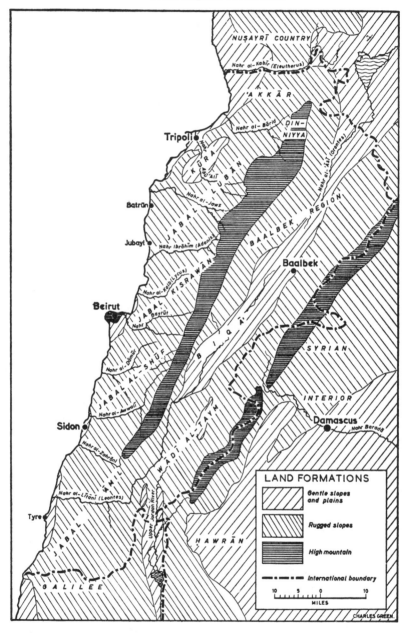

NUṢAYRĪ COUNTRY

Nahr al-Kabīr (Eleutherus)

'AKKĀR

Nahr al-Bārid   DIN-
                 NIYYA

Tripoli

Nahr al-'Āṣī (Orontes)

K Ū R A

'AIT

Batrūn

Nahr al-Jaws

J A B A L

L U B N Ā N

B A A L B E K   R E G I O N

Jubayl

Nahr Ibrāhim (Adonis)

Baalbek

K I S R A W Ā N

Nahr al-Kalb (Lycus)

Beirut

J A B A L

Nahr   Bayrūt

Nahr al-Dāmūr

B I Q Ā '

S Y R I A N

J A B A L   A L - S H Ū F

I N T E R I O R

Nahr al-Awwali

Damascus

Nahr Baradā

Sidon

Nahr al-Zahrāni

W Ā D Ī   A L - T A Y M

J A B A L

Nahr al-Līṭāni (Leontes)

Tyre

J A B A L

Upper Jordan River

H A W R Ā N

G A L I L E E

LAND FORMATIONS

	Gentle slopes and plains
	Rugged slopes
	High mountain
–·–·–	International boundary

10   5   0   10
MILES

CHARLES GREEN.

Source: Kamal Salibi, *A Modern History of Lebanon*, p. 218. Reprinted by permission of the author.

successor, Sultan Abdelmecid, was eager to proceed with administrative centralization, and when Ottoman control was finally restored to Syria in 1840, he decreed new administrative guidelines. The basic provincial system was maintained, with provinces now designated as *eyalets,* each headed by a *vali.* Provinces were further divided into *sancaks* (in Arabic, *sanjaqs*), each governed by a *kaymakam* (in Arabic, *qa'im maqam).*

A distinctive application of the new guidelines to the Mountain occurred in 1841, the year in which the Shihabi dynasty ceased to rule. At this point, the Mountain was divided into two districts and designated as a dual *kaymakamate.* One district was governed by a Maronite Catholic *kaymakam* and the other, by a Druze *kaymakam.*[7] The unique status of Mount Lebanon, which was in effect partitioned along sectarian lines, reflected two major processes that had long been under way. One, to be discussed below, was the intervention of European powers, who played a key role in devising the dual *kaymakamate.* Another was the evolution of Lebanon's social structure from a feudal to a confessional system, providing an indigenous rationale for the partition scheme. This process was accelerated by changes in the status of religious minorities in the Ottoman Empire as a whole.

Social Transformation

The Ottoman Empire was traditionally conceived as a religious state. In a community of believers, the Sultan was to administer the sacred law of Islam. Because religion was the fundamental criterion of affiliation, non-Muslims were not considered members of the political community, although they lived under the Sultan's protection. Christians and Jews were associated with distinct structures of local authority, known as communities or *millets.* Each *millet* administered its own religious laws, covering personal and property matters. The *millets* were also entitled to full control of their properties and schools and had the right to be heard by the Sultan through the appointed heads of their communities. However, they were obliged to pay special taxes and experienced social

[7]Ma'oz, *Ottoman Reform,* pp. 3–11, 30–37.

discrimination. By contrast, no separate status was conferred on members of Muslim sects who dissented from orthodox, Sunni Islam. Heterodox sects such as the Shi'is, as well as the Druze (whose identity as Muslims is subject to debate), were under the jurisdiction of the Sunni *qadi* (or judge), and their separate religious hierarchies were not officially recognized by Ottoman authorities.

The dominant Sunni Muslim majority was spread fairly evenly throughout Syria, interspersed with a variety of sectarian minorities. The largest non-Muslim group was the Christians, residing primarily in towns and villages. Mount Lebanon was distinguished by its high concentration of sectarian minorities. This was in part attributable to the active role of the Maronite Church, which traces its origins to the seventh century. It was the first Eastern church to enter into full communion with Rome in 1180, during the Crusader period. Thereafter, the Maronite patriarch received investiture from the Pope, while the Church retained its own priesthood and distinctive Syriac liturgy. The other predominant community, the Druze, was concentrated in the southern part of the Mountain, as well as in the Hawran region and the Jabal al-Duruz of the adjacent province of Damascus. Still other significant Shi'i Muslim, Greek Orthodox, and Greek Catholic communities resided in the Mountain and its immediate environs. The appeal of the Mountain to these sectarian groups stemmed from the policy of both Ma'ni and Shihabi *hakims* of welcoming religious minorities and political refugees from other parts of Syria.[8]

The social structure of the Mountain evolved over time from a "feudal" order to a "confessional" order. In the earlier phase, horizontal (socioeconomic) cleavages prevailed, reflecting distinctions between the dominant feudal lords and their tenants. Vertical (sectarian or confessional) cleavages only gradually became politicized, emerging as the most salient social divisions in Mount Lebanon by the mid-nineteenth century. The interplay between

[8]Albert Hourani, "Race, Religion, and Nation-State in the Near East," in *Readings in Arab Middle Eastern Societies and Cultures,* ed. Abdullah Lutfiyya and Charles Churchill (The Hague: Mouton, 1970), pp. 1–4; Stephen Hemsley Longrigg, *Syria and Lebanon Under the French Mandate* (New York: Octagon Books, 1972), , pp. 6–14; Tibawi, *Modern History of Syria,* pp. 19–21; Hitti, *History of Syria,* pp. 679, 684, 694.

the two dimensions of social cleavage ultimately exploded in civil strife. Social unrest was first sparked by horizontal cleavages within the Maronite community, challenging the bases of the feudal order. In later decades, socioeconomic grievances were overshadowed by intersectarian strife.

The first Ma'ni *hakim,* Fakhr al-Din I, was himself a feudal lord, and he and his descendants extended their authority through the Mountain by winning the allegiance of other feudal lords. The locally predominant feudatories were hereditary chiefs, each of whom owned the larger portion of a *muqata'ah* (i.e., a fief held in the name of a clan). Ruling clans were each composed of one kinship group of the same sect. In contrast to the social cohesion of the ruling clans, the subjects in a given *muqata'ah* were often heterogeneous in family and religion. The peasants were either tenants or small landowners, who cultivated the land of the feudatories and shared the produce with them in designated proportions.

The gradual erosion of the feudal system was in part attributable to rivalry among the feudatories. Another contributing factor was the growing social and political role of the Maronite Church. Although relations between the Church and the feudatories were initially cordial, Church reform weakened the influence of the feudatories in selection of the clerical elite. As the Church gained increased following, wealth, and organizational strength, it sought a more influential role in social and political affairs, accentuating the sectarian identification of Maronite adherents.

Consciousness of sectarian differences was intensified by increased contact between members of different confessional communities, as a result of large-scale migration of Maronite peasants in the eighteenth century. The migrants, seeking employment as agricultural workers, moved from the north to the districts of Kisrawan and the Shuf, predominantly populated by Druze feudatories and peasants. Although Druze feudal lords initially welcomed the additional manpower, they felt threatened by the growing influence of the Maronite Church throughout the Mountain by the late eighteenth century. Druze communal organization developed largely as a means of counteracting Maronite solidarity.[9]

[9]Enver M. Koury, *The Operational Capability of the Lebanese Political System* (Beirut: Catholic Press, 1972), pp. 13–45.

Civil Strife

Four localized uprisings in the early nineteenth century each re-flected grievances against the feudal system. Over time, however, sectarian tensions played an increasingly important contributory role. The first uprising, in 1820, was confined exclusively to peas-ants, angered by the high taxes imposed by the Shihabi *hakim,* Bashir II. The peasants were backed by a Maronite bishop, who joined them in drafting a "covenant" repudiating payment of more than the traditional basic tax. As a result of the rebellion, Bashir II was temporarily forced into exile.[10]

The second uprising was confined to the Druze, who were an-gered by the partisan policies of Bashir II once he was reinstated as *hakim.* Bashir II, himself a Maronite, stripped many Druze feudatories of their privileges and appropriated their property. During the period of Egyptian rule, Bashir II cultivated Maronite support as a power base, while the Druze were forcibly disarmed and conscripted into the Egyptian army. In response, the Druze shifted their allegiance to the Ottoman authorities in opposition to the Egyptian presence. When, in 1838, a Druze rebellion broke out in both the southern part of the Mountain and the adjacent Syrian district of Hawran, Bashir II raised a Maronite army to quell the uprising. Many Druze leaders were forcibly exiled from the Mountain by the *hakim.*[11]

The third uprising was unique in that it involved coordination between Maronites and Druze. In a mass revolt against Bashir II's rule by the *'ammiyyah* (commoners) in June 1840, representatives of both sects met to discuss their grievances. A major complaint was that innovative measures introduced by Ibrahim Pasha in the rest of Syria were not extended to the Mountain. Elsewhere, the Egyptian ruler undermined the authority of local feudal leaders, depriving them of their autonomy and their function as tax farmers. He created a *meclis* (in Arabic, *majlis*) or consultative council, in each locality, allowing the Christians to participate in these councils

---

[10]Ibid., pp. 42–44.
[11]Tibawi, *Modern History of Syria,* pp. 68, 99.

for the first time on an equal footing with Muslims. In the Mountain, however, Bashir II was rewarded for his cooperation with the Egyptians by the nonapplication of these measures challenging the traditional social order. The rebels of the *'ammiyyah* unsuccessfully demanded the establishment of consultative councils with representatives of all sectarian groups, as well as an end to forced labor, excessive taxation, and conscription orders. When Egyptian rule over Syria ended, Bashir II was succeeded in September 1840 by Bashir III. Although the new *hakim* reduced the powers of both Maronite and Druze feudatories, he remained heavily dependent politically on the Maronite Church. The Druze feudatories were angered by Bashir III's attitude toward them and also suspicious of the motives of the Church, rebelling against both in October 1841. This fourth uprising sparked sectarian clashes between Druze and Maronites, until intervention by outside powers precipitated the dismissal of Bashir III, ending the Shihabi dynasty.[12]

It was at this point that the dual *kaymakamate* was introduced, dividing the Mountain along clear-cut sectarian lines. As such, the *kaymakamate* marked a decisive turning point in the evolution of Lebanon's social order from a feudal to a confessional system. Under the new formula, the Beirut-Damascus road designated the partition of Lebanon into two districts, with a Maronite *kaymakam* in the north and a Druze *kaymakam* in the south. Although the rationale was to provide communal autonomy, the proposal anticipated problems in confessionally mixed localities. Such districts were governed by two *wakils* (people's representatives), one Christian and one Druze, granting each individual the right to be judged by his coreligionist. Residents of the Mountain who were neither Maronite nor Druze had no special representatives under this system.

The partition scheme proved difficult to implement, and relations between Maronites and Druze became embittered. During clashes in 1845, Maronites burned fourteen Druze villages, and

---

[12]Koury, *Operational Capability,* pp. 45–50; Tibawi, *Modern History of Syria,* pp. 71–75, 84, 91; Ma'oz, *Ottoman Reform,* pp. 15–18; David Smock and Audrey Smock, *The Politics of Pluralism: A Comparative Study of Lebanon and Ghana* (New York: Elsevier, 1975), pp. 31–35.

the Maronite Patriarch endorsed the attacks as part of a holy war against the Druze.[13] The sectarian conflict of 1845 provided the Sultan, bent on administrative centralization, with a pretext to dilute the distinctive status of the Mountain. Ottoman authorities moved forcibly to quell the civil strife, sending eighteen batallions to restore order and disarm the populace. The Sultan then introduced a new administrative scheme, establishing in each *kaymak-amate* a council representing all communal groups, not only the Maronites and the Druze. This forum resembled the *meclis,* the consultative councils functioning in the rest of Syria, and thereby joining the Mountain in a system of governance similar to those of other provinces.[14]

Despite a temporary respite in social unrest in Mount Lebanon, latent socioeconomic and sectarian grievances erupted on an unprecedented scale in 1859–60. In this instance, not only the Mountain but also Damascus was involved. The background to the widespread turmoil lay in resentment by Syria's Sunni Muslim majority of decrees by the Sultan, under the *tanzimat,* affecting the right of religious minorities in the Ottoman Empire. Particularly objectionable was an 1856 edict proclaiming the equal rights of "the Christian communities and other non-Muslim subjects," and providing representation for all sects in mixed councils and mixed tribunals on the local level.[15]

Civil strife began with an 1859 revolt in Kisrawan (the central sector of the Mountain) by Maronite peasants against Maronite feudal lords. The peasants, reminding the feudatories of the Sultan's 1856 decree, demanded equality before the law and representation on a district council. When these demands were refused, peasants drove lords off their lands and divided their property.[16]

---

[13]Koury, *Operational Capability,* pp. 50–54; Smock and Smock, *Politics of Pluralism,* pp. 32–33.

[14]J. C. Hurewitz, *The Middle East and North Africa in World Politics: A Documentary Record,* Vol. I: *European Expansion, 1535–1914,* 2nd ed. (New Haven: Yale University Press, 1975), pp. 295–297; Hurewitz, "Lebanese Democracy in Its International Setting," in *Politics in Lebanon,* ed. Leonard Binder (New York: John Wiley, 1966), pp. 220–221; Tibawi, *Modern History of Syria,* p. 101.

[15]Ma'oz, *Ottoman Reform,* pp. 21–29.

[16]Kamal Salibi, *The Modern History of Lebanon* (London: Weidenfeld and Nicolson, 1965), pp. 80–87; Tibawi, *Modern History of Syria,* pp. 122–123.

Peasant revolt then spread to the south, where a new, communal dimension emerged. The majority of the peasants working the lands of the Druze feudatories were Christians. After trying unsuccessfully to incite Druze peasants to join them, some Christians took provocative measures. In predominantly Christian villages and towns, armed bands threatened to exterminate the Druze. However, Christian-Druze clashes beginning in May 1860 revealed the relative weakness of the Maronites, who believed that Druze attacks on them had the sympathy of Ottoman authorities. Moreover, Maronite appeals to leaders of the earlier peasant revolt in Kisrawan to come to their assistance with reinforcements went unheeded. One after another, southern districts fell under Druze control, and clashes leading to heavy Christian casualties did not subside until 10 July 1860.[17]

While the conflict in the Mountain was still under way, massacres of Christians occurred in Damascus on 9–10 July 1860. The massacres were sparked by the resentment of the Muslims of Damascus over newly accorded Christian rights that challenged their privileged status, in a city long regarded as a major center of Islam. Muslim indignation grew when Damascene Christians refused to pay a tax known as the *bedel* in lieu of army service, on the grounds that Christians in the Mountain had not been obliged to do so. The local *meclis* accused the Christians of revolting against authority, a view shared by the *vali* of Damascus, Ahmed Pasha.

Significant transnational linkages surfaced in the outbreak of violence in the Mountain and Damascus. With the controversy over the conscription tax still unresolved, rumors reached Damascus in June 1860 that Christians in Lebanon were being massacred by Druze with government backing. Ahmed Pasha made no effort to halt the flow of men and arms from Jabal Duruz and Damascus to assist the Lebanese Druze. Nor did he prevent groups of Druze from both the Mountain and Hawran from entering Damascus and inciting Muslims against Christians. When attacks against Christians were begun by an angry crowd, composed primarily of Damascene Muslims, the *vali* refrained from using his

[17]Tibawi, *Modern History of Syria,* pp. 99–100, 123–124; Kouri, *Operational Capability,* p. 54; Salibi, *Modern History of Lebanon,* pp. 87–104.

troops to protect the Christians. Ahmed Pasha was subsequently executed by order of the Porte for his role in the Damascus massacres.[18]

European Intervention

The civil strife of 1860 set the stage for direct European intervention in the affairs of the Mountain. There were actually many previous instances of either individual or collective involvement by European states in Syria. Collectively, European pressure on Ottoman authorities to redefine administrative arrangements in the Mountain were rationalized as promotion of representative institutions. Individually, European powers contended for influence in Syria, with French ambitions for paramountcy repeatedly challenged by Britain and Russia. European powers supported different sectarian groups in the Mountain, exacerbating communal tensions.

As early as 1649, France formally "adopted" the Maronite community in Lebanon. King Louis XIV proclaimed that

> we do take and place our protection and safeguard the Most Reverend Patriarch and all the prelates, ecclesiastics and Maronite Christian laics, who dwell particularly in Mount Lebanon.[19]

From then on, France assumed the role of guardian of European Catholicism throughout the Ottoman Empire. Russia later espoused the interests of the Orthodox Christian communities, and in the early nineteenth century Britain entered into an alliance with Druze leaders in the Mountain.[20]

When the power of the Ottoman Empire declined in the nineteenth century, members of the Concert of Europe were collectively concerned about the destabilizing implications, but individually eager to reap the spoils. Mehmed Ali's challenge to the Sultan won the support of France, whereas the other members

---

[18]Ma'oz, *Ottoman Reform*, pp. 231–240; Tibawi, *Modern History of Syria*, pp. 126–129.

[19]Hurewitz, *European Expansion*, p. 28.

[20]Tibawi, *Modern History of Syria*, pp. 101–103.

of the Concert of Europe offered their guarantee to the Sultan to help contain Egyptian influence. In 1840, Austria, Great Britain, Prussia, and Russia negotiated a convention with the Ottoman Empire permitting Mehmed Ali to retain control of Syria if he accepted other specified provisions within ten days. When he refused to do so, the Europeans backed the Sultan in insisting on an Egyptian withdrawal from Syria.[21]

However, termination of Egyptian rule failed to restore stability to the Mountain, and the European Concert sought to shape a new governmental arrangement to replace the Shihabi dynasty. The European input in devising the dual *kaymakamate* was presented as an attempt to curb Ottoman authoritarianism and to institute a more representative form of government.[22] This unprecedented arrangement both highlighted the distinctiveness of the Mountain from the rest of Syria and reinforced confessional cleavages in the Mountain through the principle of partition.

Although the consuls of the five European powers at first met frequently to monitor implementation of their proposal, rivalries soon surfaced. When intercommunal conflict erupted in the southern district of the Mountain in 1845, the British backed the Druze while the French supported the Christians. In the north, where Maronite peasants opposed the Maronite feudatories, the French supported the former and the British assisted the latter.[23] The violence of 1845 allowed the Sultan to seize the initiative in diluting the European-sponsored partition scheme. Were it not for the 1860 events, and the opportunity they again afforded for collective European intervention, Lebanon's distinctive status might have been further undermined in the Ottoman drive for centralization.[24]

When the disorders of 1860 spread throughout the Mountain, France prepared an initiative to intervene militarily in the crisis. Other members of the European Concert, suspecting Napoleon III of seeking to annex the territory, negotiated a convention with the Ottoman authorities in August 1860 endorsing a joint European role in pacifying the area. Although the convention provided

---

[21]Hurewitz, *European Expansion,* p. 271.

[22]Hurewitz, "Lebanese Democracy," pp. 219–221.

[23]Koury, *Operational Capability,* pp. 50–54.

[24]Hurewitz, "Lebanese Democracy," pp. 220–221; Idem., *European Expansion,* pp. 295–297.

for sending up to 12,000 European troops to restore tranquillity, Ottoman authorities in fact achieved stability on their own. The only European troops introduced were members of a French military force that arrived in August 1860 and remained until the following June.[25]

Meanwhile, a commission was created by the Concert to investigate the causes of the 1860 massacres and recommend changes in the administration of Lebanon. The regulation which ensued, the Organic Statute of 9 June 1861, provided the Mountain with the most explicit administrative autonomy it had experienced to date. Defined as a distinct district, or *sanjaq*, its ruler was directly responsible to the Porte, rather than reporting through the *vali* of an adjacent Syrian province. Lebanon's domain was confined to the Mountain, thereby excluding the coastal cities and the Biqa' which had been incorporated during the Shihabi period. It was now known as a *mutasarrifiyyah*, whose governor-general, or *mutasarrif*, was a non-Lebanese Ottoman Christian appointed by the Sublime Porte after consultation with the European powers.[26]

Despite limitations posed by the fact that the *mutasarrif* was a non-Lebanese, answerable to both the Porte and the Europeans, the new form of governance was a move toward broader representation. A Central Administrative Council was created, based on the principle of proportional confessional representation. The various sectarian groups in the Mountain took part according to set formulae. Of the twelve members of the council, the Maronite, Druze, Greek Orthodox, Greek Catholic, Mutawila (Shi'i) and Sunni Muslim communities each initially sent two members. In 1864, the allocation of seats in the Central Administrative Council was revised to reflect more accurately the relative size of the sectarian groups.[27]

The experience of the *mutasarrifiyyah* was vital in inculcating the principle of "confessionalism" in Lebanese political culture. Allocation of government positions on the basis of religious sect meant that government served as a trustee for the interests of the

[25]Hurewitz, *European Expansion*, pp. 344–345; Idem., "Lebanese Democracy," p. 223.

[26]Hitti, *History of Syria*, p. 695; Hurewitz, "Lebanese Democracy," pp. 222.

[27]Hurewitz, *European Expansion*, pp. 346–347; Smock and Smock, *Politics of Pluralism*, pp. 33–34.

Ottoman Divisions of Syria after 1860

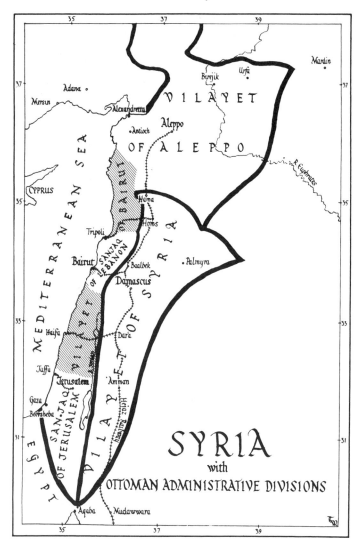

Source: George Antonius, *The Arab Awakening*, map opposite p. 176. Reprinted by permission of the Putnam Publishing Group. Copyright © 1939 by The Institute of Current World Affairs.

various communal groups. The leader of each group strove to ensure that his clients received their due measure of benefits and privileges. This system was representative in a narrow sense, but did not advance a participatory democracy in which "a team of leaders, backed by the majority of public opinion, carry out a coherent program of state action within the limits of a national consensus."[28] Despite its limitations, the *mutasarrifiyyah* marked a period of relative tranquillity, allowing the wounds of previous turbulent decades to heal. However, in October 1915, Ottoman rulers took advantage of the outbreak of war in Europe to abrogate the Organic Statute unilaterally and absorb Lebanon into the regular provincial system.[29]

Creation of Greater Lebanon

The defeat of the Ottoman Empire during World War I permitted realization of European ambitions in the empire's Arab provinces. Under the secret Sykes-Picot agreement of May 1916, France and Britain carved out spheres of influence in anticipation of Allied victory. They did so despite British promises in 1914–15 to the ruler of Mecca, the Sharif Husayn, that the Arabs would be granted independence in exchange for their support in the war against the Turks.[30] Moreover, in November 1918 France and Britain issued a joint declaration to the Arabs, promising "the setting up of national governments and administrations that shall derive their authority from the free exercise of the initiative and choice of the indigenous populations in Syria and Mesopotamia."[31]

A commission sent in 1919 by American President Woodrow Wilson, the King-Crane Commission, was instructed to ascertain the wishes of the population. The commission reported that 80.4 percent of the petitions received demanded a united Syria, while 73.5 percent favored independence. The prospect of a French man-

---

[28]Malcolm Kerr, "Political Decision-Making in a Confessional Democracy," in *Politics in Lebanon,* ed. Leonard Binder (New York: John Wiley, 1966), pp. 187–188.

[29]Hurewitz, "Lebanese Democracy," pp. 219–222.

[30]George Antonius, *The Arab Awakening,* pp. 164–183, 243–253.

[31]Longrigg, *Syria and Lebanon,* pp. 52, 59, 68.

date was overwhelmingly rejected if it would be "obligatory" and advocated by only 14.5 percent of the petitions if it arose by consent. Accordingly, the commission recommended the establishment of a united Syria-Palestine after an interim mandatory period, with the mandate allocated to the United States or Britain, but not to France.[32] Nevertheless, a mandate for Syria and Lebanon was granted by the Principal Allied Powers to France in April 1920, and confirmed by the Council of the League of Nations in July 1922. Britain, in turn, was awarded the mandate for Palestine as well as Iraq.

Arab disillusionment with European failure to honor pre-war promises of independence was deepened as a result of French policies in administering their mandate. In August 1920, France took a critical decision to enlarge the boundaries of the Mountain, creating a State of Greater Lebanon. This act doubled the land area of the *mutasarrifiyyah* and increased Lebanon's population from 400,000 to 600,000. The inhabitants of the annexed areas differed, especially in religion, from the population of the Mountain. In the eastern Biqa' valley, the Sunni, Mutawilah (Shi'i), and Druze population was nearly double that of the Christians. Of the coastal cities that were added, Beirut was about half Muslim and half Christian; Tripoli was predominantly Muslim; and in Sidon and Tyre, Mutawilah formed about three-fifths of the population, most of the rest of whom were Christian. Whereas the Maronites had comprised 59 percent of the population in the *mutasarrifiyyah,* they were only 29 percent in Greater Lebanon. However, the Maronites were still the single largest sect, and the Christian population as a whole comprised a majority of Greater Lebanon.[33]

Critics charged that Greater Lebanon was an artificial creation, differing territorially and demographically from the entity referred to as the Mountain in the Ottoman period. In response, proponents of Greater Lebanon argued that all of the annexed

[32]Walid Khalidi, *Conflict and Violence in Lebanon: Confrontation in the Middle East,* Harvard Studies in International Affairs, no. 38 (Cambridge, Mass.: Center for International Affairs, Harvard University, 1979), p. 33 n.2; Longrigg, pp. 89–92.

[33]Smock and Smock, *Politics of Pluralism,* p. 24; Longrigg, *Syria and Lebanon,* p. 123.

French Mandatory Divisions

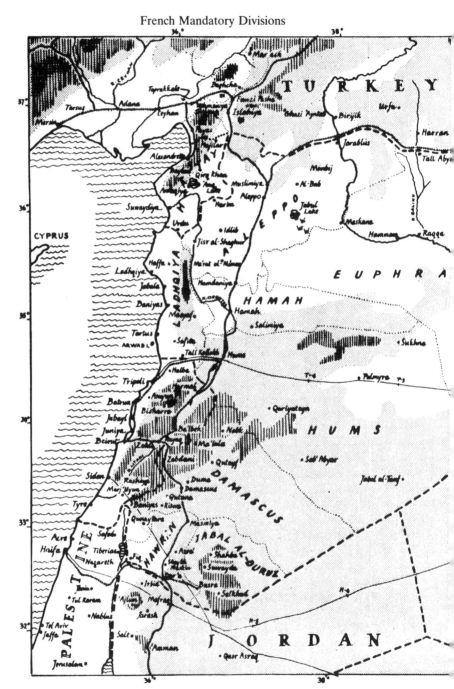

Source: S. Longrigg, *Syria and Lebanon under French Mandate*, map opposite p. 404.

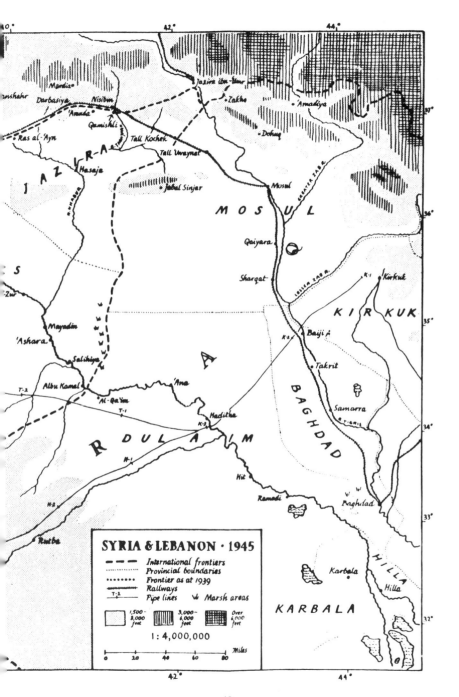

SYRIA & LEBANON · 1945

– – –	*International frontiers*
....	*Provincial boundaries*
••••••••	*Frontier as at 1939*
┼┼┼┼┼	*Railways*
T-2	*Pipe lines*
↯	*Marsh areas*

1,500 – 3,000 feet
3,000 – 6,000 feet
Over 6,000 feet

1 : 4,000,000

Miles
0   20   40   60   80

areas had at some point fallen under the domain of a given Lebanese *hakim,* and that there was nothing immutable about the reduced boundaries of the *mutasarrifiyyah.* Moreover, they considered Greater Lebanon's autonomy from Syria merely an expansion of the semi-autonomous status of the Mountain under Ottoman rule.

The most vigorous advocates of Greater Lebanon were found in the Maronite community, and indeed the French decision was widely perceived as an act of favoritism to the Maronites. As the most Francophile of the indigenous groups, the Maronites traditionally enjoyed French protection and maintained cultural, educational, and social bonds with France. Maronites believed that their status would be more secure in an enlarged, independent Lebanese state. Moreover, the economic viability of Lebanon was enhanced by the addition of the productive coastal cities bordering the Mediterranean, the rich Biqa' valley in the east, and the Jabal 'Amil area in the south.

However, a minority of Maronites expressed reservations about Lebanon's enlargement. They maintained that if Lebanon were to serve its desired function as a Christian sanctuary, it would be preferable to confine its scope to the area of the *mutasarrifiyyah.* In a Greater Lebanon, they worried, the slim Christian majority would disappear if the Muslim population increased at a more rapid rate.

Most vocal in their opposition were the sectarian groups whose status was jeopardized by Lebanon's enlargement. Sunni Muslims, especially, feared being reduced in Lebanon to a minority community, whereas they constituted the majority of the population in Syria and in the Arab world as a whole. They suspected France's ambitions in Lebanon and its obvious preference for the Christians. Sunni spokesmen advocated instead a united and independent Lebanon-Syria. This alternative was widely endorsed by members of smaller sectarian groups, although they recognized that whether Lebanon ultimately emerged under Maronite or Sunni domination, they would retain minority status.[34]

[34]Hurewitz, "Lebanese Democracy," pp. 223–225; Smock and Smock, *Politics of Pluralism,* pp. 24–27, 42–43; Longrigg, *Syria and Lebanon,* pp. 41–44, 70–71; Iliya F. Harik, "The Ethnic Revolution and Political Integration in the Middle East," *International Journal of Middle East Studies* 3 (July 1972): 313–314.

Nationalist Mobilization in Syria

Also outraged by the creation of Greater Lebanon were the increasingly articulate nationalists in Syria. They were perturbed not only by Lebanon's enlargement at Syria's expense, but also by the dissection of Palestine, which they regarded as "Southern Syria." They were appalled by administrative divisions within the rump Syrian states. Moreover, they were indignant at the termination by France of the short-lived rule of King Faysal, who raised hopes of an independent constitutional monarchy in a united Syria.

Syrian grievances against the French were nourished by the growing appeal of Arab nationalist ideology. The most encompassing form of pan-Arabism, or *qawmiyyah 'arabiyyah,* aims at uniting all branches of the Arab people into a single national unit. Syrians were among the foremost early exponents of Arab nationalism, which crystallized into a political movement by the late nineteenth century. When Arab state boundaries were designated after the breakup of the Ottoman empire, *qawmiyyah* came into tension with a narrower form of patriotism, or *wataniyyah.* While embracing the ultimate goal of overall unity for the Arab nation, the first priority of Arab nationalists in Syria was to oppose the fragmentation of Syria itself, adopting the broad definition of "geographic Syria" common in Ottoman usage.

The contradiction between the goals of the Syrian nationalists and of the French mandatory came to a head very quickly. In October 1918, upon the defeat of Ottoman forces in Syria, the Amir (Prince) Faysal was installed as ruler in Damascus with the assistance of French and British liaison officers. Faysal, a son of the Sharif Husayn of Mecca and military leader of the Arab Revolt against the Turks, claimed authority to rule throughout Syria. A Syrian National Council, proclaiming itself the legally representative body for all of Syria, was convened in June 1919. The council demanded sovereignty for a united Syria-Palestine under Faysal's leadership, and its March 1920 plenary session unanimously elected Faysal as King. The council included both Christian and Muslim representatives from Lebanon, which was to be guaranteed special status in an all-Syrian National Government.

France, however, rejected the legitimacy and the demands of

the National Council. Although a provisional agreement was worked out by Faysal on a visit to Paris late in 1919 whereby his rule in inland Syria was assured, he was obliged to agree to recognize a separate, mandated Lebanon and to accept enduring French influence in Syria. Once France gained the mandate for Syria and Lebanon in April 1920, Faysal was presented with an ultimatum further curtailing his powers. His telegram of acquiescence did not arrive by the stated deadline, and the movement of French troops toward Damascus obliged him to flee the country in July, bringing an end to the brief period of Arab rule in Syria.[35]

Bitterness over the ouster of Faysal was compounded by subsequent French policies. French unwillingness to sponsor a unified Syria was reflected not only in the creation of Greater Lebanon, but also in the truncation of two Syrian mini-states in which sectarian minorities predominated. The designation of 'Alawi and Druze "states" was rationalized as protecting the rights of minorities, but Syrian nationalists saw it as further evidence of a strategy of "divide and rule." The 'Alawis, a Shi'i sect also known as Nusayris, were predominantly rural and mountain dwellers concentrated along Syria's western coast. After their initial armed resistance to the imposition of French control was suppressed, France announced in July 1922 the creation of an 'Alawi state. The French cited 'Alawi preferences for separate status—in fact, some 'Alawi spokesmen preferred union with Lebanon to union with Syria. Nevertheless, Sunnis and most Greek Orthodox, who comprised two-thirds of the population in the newly designated "state," advocated merger with Syria to no avail.[36]

The Druze of Syria were concentrated in the Jabal al-Duruz (i.e., the Mountain of the Druze) and nearby Hawran region, in the southern tip of Syria adjacent to southern Lebanon. After a Druze "state" was created in March 1922, French public works and land reform programs aroused consternation among Druze feudal leaders. Sultan al-Atrash, of the leading Druze family, mounted a revolt in July 1925. He endorsed the unity of all Syria (including Greater Lebanon), provided there was home rule for the Druze. The Druze Rebellion of 1925–27 was a significant ep-

[35]Longrigg, *Syria and Lebanon,* pp. 63–106.
[36]Ibid., pp. 80, 120–125, 209–210.

isode in activating transnational Lebanese-Syrian linkages in opposition to France. Sultan al-Atrash mobilized hundreds of recruits in Southern Lebanon as well as in the Druze state. Despite the lack of central organization or visible coordination, the rebellion spread through much of Syria and briefly centered in Southern Lebanon. France provided arms to Christian civilians, contributing to clashes between Christians and Druze, and then launched a vigorous military campaign obliging the rebels to lay down their arms.[37]

Despite French determination to prevent broad Syrian unity, transnational bonds between Syria and Lebanon were selectively promoted by the mandatory. A single High Commissioner was designated, with his headquarters in Beirut. A common currency, commercial code, and customs system were established, with no internal economic barriers separating Lebanon from the Syrian states. The High Commissioner drew up a single budget, whose revenues were known as the Common Interests, and which was used to cover the costs of services and subventions to individual state budgets. In practice, however, there was little Lebanese-Syrian coordination in the realm of economics. In September 1923, a joint Lebanese-Syrian commission appointed by the French was unable to agree on a division of the Common Interests surplus between the two states. When the High Commissioner determined that 47 percent should go to Lebanon and 53 percent to the Syrian states, neither side was satisfied.[38]

The French obviously differentiated between Syria and Lebanon in interpreting their mandatory responsibility to promote constitutional government. The 1920 League of Nations mandate called on the French to frame "an organic law for Syria and Lebanon" within three years. They were instructed to seek the agreement of "native authorities" and to encourage local autonomy "as far as circumstances permit."[39] In Syria, France was unable to reach a constitutional accord with nationalist spokesmen, provoking an increasingly confrontational atmosphere.

France never acknowledged the credibility of the nationalist leadership in Syria. Generally originating from socially privileged

[37]Ibid., pp. 8–9, 127, 152–177, 208–209, 245–247.
[38]Ibid., pp. 133, 272.
[39]Ibid., pp. 111–112.

groups, the nationalist spokesmen did not achieve an integrated movement until the formation of the National Bloc in 1930. Although the nationalists enjoyed a countrywide following, the French dismissed them as "extremists," preferring to deal with "moderates" who were less insistent in their demands.[40] Elections for a Constituent Assembly to participate in drafting a Syrian constitution were finally held in April 1928. Outspoken nationalists took the initiative in calling for Syrian unity and independence, announcing in Article 2 of their draft that

> the Syrian territories detached from the Ottoman Empire constitute an indivisible unity; the divisions which have taken place between the end of the war and the present time leave this unity unaffected.

This article sought to reverse the fragmentation of the 'Alawi and Druze zones, the creation of Greater Lebanon, as well as the detachment of Palestine. In response, the French High Commissioner declared the draft constitution unacceptable and dissolved the Constituent Assembly. In 1930, he promulgated an imposed constitution, omitting the offensive Article 2.[41]

When the imposed constitution came into effect in 1932 and the Syrian Republic was proclaimed, the nationalists turned their efforts to seeking an acceptable treaty with France. Ironically, when a treaty acceptable to the Syrian nationalists was finally negotiated, a change of government in France precluded its ratification. Under a draft concluded with the left-wing French government of Léon Blum in September 1936 and unanimously adopted by the Syrian Chamber of Deputies, significant concessions were made by both parties. France agreed that the Druze and 'Alawi areas would be annexed by Syria, while retaining a special administrative regime. Syria, in turn, did not press its claim to Lebanon, nor did it insist on modification of the boundaries of Greater Lebanon. Under parallel treaties with Syria and Lebanon, both states were to become independent and sovereign members of the League of Na-

---

[40]Ibid., pp. 24–30, 151, 183–187.

[41]Tibawi, *Modern History of Syria,* pp. 348–349; Longrigg, *Syria and Lebanon,* pp. 180–188.

tions. However, the Blum government was voted out of office in June 1937 and its successor did not support the treaty.[42]

Cooperation in Undermining the Mandate

Lebanon's relationship with France was substantially less acerbic, primarily because of the influence of the Francophile Maronite Catholic community. Lebanon achieved a constitution several years earlier than Syria, and the issue of a treaty with France never aroused great political passion. Nevertheless, diverse groups continued to protest the creation of Greater Lebanon, intermittently coordinating their efforts with Syrian nationalists. Eventually, politically conscious Christians committed to full Lebanese independence came to share disenchantment with French tactics.

Lebanon's distinctiveness was reflected in the political institutions established by the French. The principle of confessionalism determined the sectarian distribution of seats in a newly created Representative Council. This council then served as a Constituent Assembly, in which the French High Commissioner heavily influenced the deliberations of the drafting committee despite objections by the Muslim minority. In May 1926, adoption of the constitution inaugurated the Lebanese Republic. The constitution designated the boundaries of Greater Lebanon as immutable, and gave France the right to direct Lebanon's foreign relations and to dissolve the Lebanese parliament (known as the Chamber of Deputies) at will.[43]

During the deliberations over the constitution, Lebanese advocates of union with Syria protested consecration of the boundaries of Greater Lebanon. The Muslims of Beirut refused to participate in the Constituent Assembly and subsequently submitted a memorandum to the High Commissioner calling for the truncation of Greater Lebanon. Similar sentiments surfaced during negotiations in 1936 for parallel French treaties with Lebanon and Syria. Lebanese Muslims held a "Conference of the Coast" in Beirut, unanimously advocating the transfer of the Muslim areas

[42]Tibawi, *Modern History of Syria*, pp. 350–360; Longrigg, *Syria and Lebanon*, pp. 189–197, 218–224, 231–236.

[43]Longrigg, *Syria and Lebanon*, pp. 169–171, 178–179.

annexed to Greater Lebanon in 1920 back to Syrian control. Delegations or demonstrations were also initiated by Muslims of the Biqa', Southern Lebanon, Tyre, Sidon, and Tripoli. These efforts bore no fruit, and Greater Lebanon's integrity was guaranteed by France in the 1936 treaty.[44]

Transnational contacts between Lebanese unionists (i.e., advocates of unity with Syria) and Syrian nationalists occurred frequently in the 1930s. Syrian nationalists kept in close touch with sympathetic Lebanese, as well as with unionist elements in the 'Alawi and Druze states. When the National Bloc called a general strike in support of Syrian unity and independence in January 1936, many shops were shut in sympathy in Beirut and there were demonstrations in Tripoli and Sidon.[45] Significantly, aspirations for union with Syria were not confined to Lebanese Muslims. Whereas Greek Catholics tended to share Maronite Francophile sentiments, Greek Orthodox Christians frequently did not. The latter resented the predominant Maronite political influence and their favored status with the French, often preferring incorporation in a unified Syria to subordination to the Maronites in Lebanon.

The Syrian Social Nationalist Party (SSNP), advocating a unified Greater Syria, was founded by a Greek Orthodox Lebanese, Antun Sa'ada. Committed to a single Syrian state within its "natural boundaries," the party strove to reincorporate Lebanon as well as Palestine. However, the SSNP did not embrace the broader goal of pan-Arabism, believing that a merger with other Arab states might compromise Greater Syria's autonomy. Originally functioning as a secret society, the SSNP attracted a large following in both Lebanon and Syria when it began to operate openly in 1935. Subsequent French efforts at suppressing the party and frequent imprisonment of its leaders did not prevent its rapid growth in membership during the mandate years.[46]

The sporadic coordination between opposition elements in Lebanon and Syria was superseded during World War II by a new level of cooperation. The rise in each country of nationalist leaders, whose highest priority was the termination of French authority,

---

[44]Ibid., pp. 169–170, 176, 219–220.

[45]Ibid., pp. 189, 215–216, 252, 343.

[46]Ibid., pp. 44, 200, 225–226; Hourani, *Syria and Lebanon,* pp. 118–120; Tibawi, *Modern History of Syria,* pp. 363–364.

encouraged consultation between political elites. The backdrop to this new phase was common allegations about French betrayal of promises of independence.

After France came under Nazi occupation and the Vichy government was installed in 1940, a new High Commissioner in Beirut asserted that Germany would be allowed access to Syrian airfields. In response, Britain joined forces with the Free French under Gen. Charles de Gaulle, launching an invasion of Syria and Lebanon in June 1941. Hoping to secure popular goodwill, the French commander of the operation, General Catroux, dispersed thousands of leaflets in which he declared:

> In the name of the Free French, . . . I come to put an end to the Mandate and to proclaim you free and independent. . . . Your independent and sovereign status will be guaranteed in a treaty in which our mutual relations will be defined.

Nevertheless, once securely in control of Syria and Lebanon, de Gaulle asserted that the mandate was still in effect, and that independence would be conferred only after the conclusion of satisfactory treaties safeguarding the "rights and special interests" of France.[47]

Nevertheless, Syrian and Lebanese nationalists were encouraged by the weakening of France's political position. They believed that France lost its title to the mandate when the Vichy government withdrew from the League of Nations in 1941, and resented attempts by the Free French to maintain control after the pledge of imminent independence. Delays in negotiating acceptable treaties encountered progressively less willingness by Syrian and Lebanese officials to surrender autonomy to the French. The nationalists also drew confidence from a divergence of views between France and Britain. The latter repeatedly prodded the Free French to respect the constitution in each state and allow a greater measure of self-government.[48]

Although the French High Commissioner (now known as the

---

[47]Longrigg, *Syria and Lebanon,* pp. 296–311.

[48]Hurewitz, *Middle East Politics: The Military Dimension* (New York: Praeger, 1969), pp. 385–386; Idem., "Lebanese Democracy," pp. 227–228; Longrigg, *Syria and Lebanon,* pp. 293, 300, 317–322.

Délégué-Général) legislated by decree at the inception of Free French control, by the end of 1941 the suspended constitutions of Syria and Lebanon were restored and formal sovereignty was granted to each country. The governments quickly recognized each other, in a move connoting further Syrian acceptance of Lebanese integrity. The nationalists, however, remained dissatisfied with the privileges accorded to France in the existing constitutions, demanding new constitutional arrangements as well as free general elections. After heavy British urging, the Free French permitted general elections in 1943, which brought the National Bloc firmly to power in Syria under the leadership of Shukri al-Quwatli, and respected nationalists to the helm in Lebanon led by President Bishara al-Khuri (a Maronite) and Prime Minister Riyadh al-Sulh (a Sunni).

The newly elected governments entered into unprecedented cooperation in subsequent dealings with the French. They addressed identical notes to the Délégué-Général in October 1943, demanding full legislative powers and freedom from French interference in their national affairs. In particular, they sought autonomy in financial and security affairs. French High Commissioners had exercised exclusive control over the Common Interests, which were defrayed in accordance with their preferences. They were also in charge of the *troupes spéciales,* forces which were recruited locally to form part of the French Army, as well as of the internal security forces. When the Free French rejected these demands, the Lebanese Chamber of Deputies defiantly decided to amend its constitution unilaterally. In response, the French arrested the President and most of his Cabinet, dissolved the Chamber, and suspended the constitution. This move antagonized every sectarian group in the country, promoting solidarity against the French, and precipitating widespread strikes and rioting. Britain demanded the release of the imprisoned officials, implying that it would intervene militarily if the French did not comply.

De Gaulle was obliged to retract these punitive measures, and he subsequently allowed a broad transfer of powers to Syria and Lebanon. Nevertheless, he insisted on retaining French control of the *troupes spéciales,* as the last remaining French card in negotiating treaties that would guarantee continued French influence in Syria and Lebanon after independence. The Syrian and Lebanese governments both announced their unwillingness to conclude such agreements in May 1945, and clashes between demonstrators and French forces in both countries followed. A joint declaration by both governments on 21 June indicated their resolve to press for the withdrawal of French troops and to take over the *troupes spéciales*. When an Anglo-French agreement of December 1945 provided for a phased withdrawal of foreign military forces, Syria and Lebanon insisted on an immediate and unconditional withdrawal. They presented a joint protest to the United Nations, and the United Nations secured a French promise to evacuate at the earliest possible date. The last French forces were withdrawn from Syria in April 1946 and from Lebanon in December 1946.[49]

The cooperation and mutual recognition by Syria and Lebanon during their quest for independence was reinforced when both became founding members of the Arab League. In the Alexandria Protocol of October 1944, the Arab states collectively acknowledged their "respect for the independence and sovereignty of Lebanon within its present frontiers."[50] By this point, substantial evidence had accumulated for Syrian reconciliation to the integrity and sovereignty of its Lebanese neighbor. In agreeing to the wording of the 1936 draft treaty with France, as well as the Alexandria Protocol, Syria implicitly renounced both its minimalist claim to the districts annexed to Lebanon in 1920 and the maximalist claim to the whole of Lebanon. In February 1977, President Hafiz al-Asad of Syria went so far as to say that Syria had willingly given away four provinces in the past, so as to prevent France from establishing a sectarian (i.e., Christian) state in Lebanon.[51]

Dubious Legacy

Nevertheless, Syria's unwillingness to establish diplomatic relations with Lebanon after independence symbolized a lingering ir-

[49]Longrigg, *Syria and Lebanon*, pp. 332–333, 340–349, 353–356; Tibawi, *Modern History of Syria*, pp. 368–378; Hurewitz, *Middle East Politics*, pp. 387–388.

[50]Longrigg, *Syria and Lebanon*, pp. 351–352; Hurewitz, *Middle East Politics*, pp. 387–388.

[51]Itamar Rabinovich, "The Limits of Military Power: Syria's Role," in *Lebanon in Crisis: Participants and Issues*, ed. P. Edward Haley and Lewis W. Snider (Syracuse: Syracuse University Press, 1979), p. 56, n. 2.

redentist claim. Publicly, Syrian governments refrained from articulating claims to all or part of Lebanon. Aspirations for the union of Syria and Lebanon were, however, sustained in the doctrine of the Syrian Social Nationalist Party, which functioned both in Syria and Lebanon. In addition, advocates of pan-Arab unity, or *qawmiyyah,* foresaw the emergence of a larger Arab entity of which Syria and Lebanon would merely constitute two regions.

From both the Syrian and Lebanese perspectives, allusions to Greater Syria or Greater Lebanon epitomized the jumbled historical links between these two neighbors. As spokesmen in both countries explored their broader Arab identifications, they were especially ambivalent in their attitudes toward each other. Although the administrative anomalies of Ottoman rule were superseded by more clearly defined boundaries in the mandatory period, new grievances arose then as well.

Precedents for intervention by external powers may also be traced to the Ottoman period, when European powers became progressively bolder in constraining Ottoman authorities. European solicitude promoted a relatively autonomous status for Mount Lebanon; and European rivalries led to the "adoption" of different indigenous sectarian communities. During the period of exclusive French mandatory control, preference for one religious community over others further exacerbated intercommunal tensions.

Consensus over the goal of independence from France did, however, spark a closing of ranks in Lebanon and a high point in Lebanese-Syrian cooperation. Transnational linkages between Lebanese and Syrian societies often came to the surface during periods of civil strife. Linkages between Druze in the Mountain and in the Syrian south were influential in the uprisings of 1838 and in 1925–27. Sectarian conflict between Christians and Sunni Muslims in Damascus in 1860 were sparked by news of Christian-Druze conflict in the Mountain. Finally, nationalist and unionist elements in both countries forged political bonds during the mandate period.

The interplay of sectarian tensions and socioeconomic grievances, which surfaced in the civil strife of 1860, continued to characterize both Lebanese and Syrian societies in the twentieth century. Parallels and interactions between these societies continued to grow after independence, despite dramatic contrasts in the political systems of the two states.

3

Syria's Military Elite

Syria began its experience as an independent state without a coherent sense of national identity or direction. Unable to avert the truncation of historic Syria by French mandatory authorities, Syrian nationalists were obliged to modify their ambitions within narrower frontiers.

Yet it was not insufficient territorial expanse that impeded nation-building by Syria's post-independence rulers, but rather divisions within the area under their rule. Social cleavages were deep and persistent. Instead of being reduced through political accommodation, Syria's social divisions shaped the evolution of its political system. The dominant institution in Syrian politics—the Army—conspicuously reflected tensions between the country's sectarian and ethnic groups. The evolution of the Ba'th Party—a second pillar of every Syrian regime since 1963—also mirrored the country's plural society.

Nevertheless, despite disproportionate influence by sectarian minorities in Syria's military elite, the country achieved relative domestic stability by the early 1970s. The ability of a determined and relatively homogeneous group to control the instruments of coercion enabled the regime of President Hafiz al-Asad to chart a decisive course in both domestic and foreign policy. One consequence was a deepening of Syria's interest and effective influence in Lebanon.

Roots of Social Cleavage

Consciousness of sectarian and ethnic divisions in society arose under the Ottoman Empire and took on increased political sig-

61

nificance as nationalism grew in the nineteenth century. For minority groups in a plural society, the political consequences were profound.

Historically, distinctions of race, based on physical characteristics or common biological origin, were not prevalent among Arabs. The reason is that the Middle East had experienced a succession of great empires, involving a continual moving and mingling of peoples. In almost all of its national communities, as a result, one finds people of different physical types and varying origins. Islam, the dominant religion, also played down consciousness of racial distinctions.

The culture of Islam did, however, call attention to other social differences. In addition to primary divisions based on religion, secondary divisions into ethnic groups emerged. Ethnic communities shared a common historical experience, language, culture, and some similar physical characteristics (resulting from a common environment and intermarriage). Differences between groups were accentuated during the Ottoman period, and over time it became harder to cross the barriers that separated communities. Religious sects came to be seen as "national groups," and what counted was not an individual's religious belief but the fact that his ancestors held that belief. The Ottoman Empire progressively took on the complexion of a multi-ethnic polity.

Although the communities of the empire were shut off from each other in terms of belief, personal status law, and close personal relations, there was considerable economic interdependence. Most of the empire formed a single trading unit for hundreds of years, with no legal restrictions on the movement of populations. Although some regions had a relatively homogeneous population, there were others in which groups were mixed at every level above that of the village. Social distinctions between communities were often functional rather than geographical, in that different groups tended to predominate in different occupations.[1]

The social system of the Ottoman Empire began to break down in the early nineteenth century. As the supremacy of the Sultan

[1]Albert Hourani, "Race, Religion, and Nation-State in the Near East," in *Readings in Arab Middle Eastern Societies and Cultures,* ed. Abdallah Lutfiyya and Charles Churchill (The Hague: Mouton, 1970), pp. 1–4.

and the Turkish Muslim element which he represented eroded, the collective will of districts and communities reasserted itself. There was also an erosion of strict compartmentalization of relations between groups under the impact of the communications revolution. Increased interaction resulting from freer communications did not, however, dilute differences between groups. Instead, greater contact often intensified ethnic consciousness by highlighting differences among groups, arousing each community's sense of identity.[2]

Stimulation of ethnic consciousness coincided with the rise of nationalist sentiment, influenced by Western beliefs that ethnic identity was the appropriate basis for political consciousness and organization.[3] Under the impact of the Western imperial presence, new social groups were created—including commercial and industrial classes as well as professional groups who embraced the concept of nationalism, both as a product of their Western education and their desire to rise to positions of power in their societies.

Fulfillment of nationalist aspirations at the time of independence did not, however, resolve underlying ethnic dilemmas. Ethnic groups that were small or scattered and lacking in political influence were often incorporated in a larger state, with no clear prescription for political integration. In newly created nation-states, those who "did not belong to the nation in whose name the State was established" were not considered full members of the political community.[4]

Most problematic was the status of minority groups "whose communal identities lack either the Arab or the Islamic character, or both, which define the majority community." The status of these groups often came into question as a result of economic and political developments. Communal tensions were triggered during periods of rapid social change, sparking awareness of social inequalities and of class identity. In addition, external interventions activated sensitivity to communal distinctions. Therefore, in Arab societies, "the possibility for ethnosectarian conflict remains a

[2]Iliya Harik, "The Ethnic Revolution and Political Integration in the Middle East," *International Journal of Middle East Studies* 3 (July 1972): 308.

[3]Hourani, "Race, Religion, and Nation-State," p. 3.

[4]Ibid., pp. 6–11.

constant danger should the conflict-precipitating circumstances arise."[5]

Syrian Agro-Cities

Social cleavages in Syria spanned several different dimensions. Sectarian identifications were complemented by regional differentiation, urban-rural distinctions, and socioeconomic disparities. These dimensions of fragmentation often overlapped and reinforced each other.

Regional loyalties remained a prime focus of political identification for Syrians. The indigenous unit of geopolitical association in Syria is the traditional Arab agro-city. Nine agro-cities in Syria each comprise a city of at least 50,000 people, several large towns, and scores of outlying villages. Each forms an interdependent economic and communications network and a center of political activity. Syrian political consciousness accentuates subnational loyalties at the agro-city level, especially because the many truncations of Syrian state boundaries before independence impeded loyalty to a cohesive state unit. Political identifications in the agro-city are further defined by the ethnic composition of the region in which it is located, and especially by the distribution of ethnic groups.[6]

The concentration of minority communities in Syria is highly significant politically. In sectarian terms, Sunni Muslims, who constitute a majority of the population, are scattered throughout the country, as is the Christian minority. The 'Alawis and Isma'ilis (two Shi'i Muslim sects) and the Druze form compact minorities, by contrast. Members of these communities are concentrated in particular districts, in which they form a local majority.[7]

The geographic concentration of communal groups engendered an overlapping of sectarian and socioeconomic cleavages in Syrian society. Socioeconomic distinctions between groups, and between

---

[5]Michael Hudson, *Arab Politics: The Quest for Legitimacy* (New Haven: Yale University Press, 1977), pp. 56–81.

[6]Michael Van Dusen, "Political Integration and Regionalism in Syria," *The Middle East Journal* 26 (Spring 1972): 123–125.

[7]Nikolaos Van Dam, "Sectarian and Regional Factionalism in the Syrian Political Elite," *The Middle East Journal* 32,2 (Spring 1978): 201.

Contemporary Syria

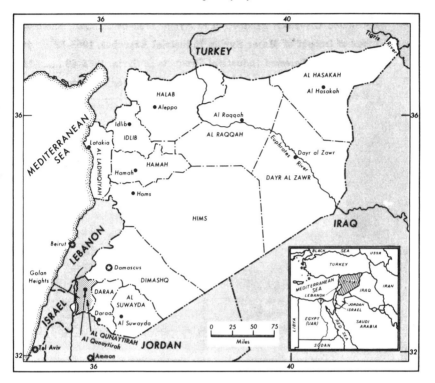

Source: Anne Sinai and Allen Pollack, eds., *The Syrian Arab Republic: A Handbook*, p. 9.
Reprinted by permission of the U.S. Government Printing Office.

rural and urban sectors of the economy, have often been associated
by compact minority groups with their sectarian identity. In the
Syrian sociopolitical mosaic, as in other Fertile Crescent societies,
horizontal (or class) cleavages are "criss-crossed" by vertical cleavages among ethnic, linguistic, tribal, and sectarian groups. Although economic growth gives rise to class changes in each
(vertical) community, intercommunal barriers endure and are
often even reinforced.[8]

The distinctive overlap of vertical and horizontal cleavages in

[8]J. C. Hurewitz, *Middle East Politics: The Military Dimension* (New York: Praeger, 1969), pp. 427–428.

Syria reflected the geographic and numerical balance between its sectarian communities. Urban-rural divisions took on particular significance, insofar as the richer and larger cities were primarily Sunni, while compact minorities concentrated in poor rural areas. For members of compact minorities, the reinforcement of minoritarian communal status by low socioeconomic status generated an overall sense of deprivation in traditional Syrian society.[9]

Military Politics

In the Syrian Army, communal minorities have attained disproportionate representation and power. Although the Army was initially a vehicle of social mobility for members of deprived communal groups, it became an instrument for minority group leaders to dominate other sectors of society.

The principal means whereby communal divisions penetrated the Army was the formation of personal clienteles by Syrian officers. This occurred because "[f]or minority officers, allegiance to the sectarian-communal and/or ethnic identity takes precedence over a wider political loyalty to the Syrian state." Competition between rival clienteles led to persistent coups d'état since independence, representing "minute officer cabals, wresting power from one another."[10]

Interestingly, the communal background of officers contending for power in Syria was transformed in 1963. Before that year, the heads of Syria's military regimes were always Sunni Muslim, although several were Kurds (an ethnic minority). After 1963, members of sectarian minorities, and particularly of the 'Alawi sect, increasingly rose to prominence.

The high representation of minority recruits in the Syrian Army originated during the French mandate period. After carving Syria into several ethnically distinct units, France intentionally sought minority members to serve in the armed forces. The French hoped

[9]Nikolaos Van Dam, *The Struggle for Power in Syria,* 2d ed. (London: Croom Helm, 1981), pp. 25–27.

[10]P. J. Vatikiotis, "The Politics of the Fertile Crescent," in *Political Dynamics in the Middle East,* ed. Paul Hammond and Sidney Alexander (New York: Elsevier, 1972), pp. 227–228.

to temper nationalist aspirations in the Army, presumably strongest among members of the Sunni majority. Skewed sectarian recruitment also resulted from the practice, in effect until 1964, of permitting exemption from Army service for those who paid a *badal* (or financial substitute) of 500 Syrian pounds. While most Sunni city dwellers could afford to do so, rural minorities (especially the impoverished 'Alawis) rarely had the wherewithal. Moreover, minority recruits often viewed the Army as a welcome avenue for social mobility, not available in other professions.[11]

For the first three years of independence, Syria was ruled by a civilian regime dominated by a "club" of fifty families. These were primarily Sunni politicians from the traditional leading families of the agro-cities of Damascus and Aleppo. Discreditation of the civilian regime, which diverted parliamentary institutions to promote oligarchical rule, facilitated the subsequent military seizure of power. Until 1963, periods of military intervention alternated with periods of parliamentary or quasi-parliamentary rule.[12]

Syria's early coups d'état (three of which took place in 1949 alone) revealed that officers from minority communities would play a conspicuous role in Syrian politics. Some analysts emphasize that competition took place primarily between Sunni officers through the 1950s, and were led by urban upper- and middle-class Sunnis.[13] The evidence, however, reveals that both an ethnic minority (Kurds) and a sectarian minority (Druze) were major players in these early coups.

In the first coup, of March 1949, for example, a Sunni Arab

[11]Eliezer Be'eri, *Army Officers in Arab Politics and Society,* trans. Dov Ben-Abba (Jerusalem: Israel Universities Press, 1969), pp. 336–337; Vatikiotis, "Politics of the Fertile Crescent," pp. 226–228; Hanna Batatu, "Some Observations on the Social Roots of Syria's Ruling, Military Group and the Causes for Its Dominance," *The Middle East Journal* 35, 3 (Summer 1981): 341–342.

[12]Van Dusen, "Political Integration," pp. 125–127; Hurewitz, *Middle East Politics,* p. 145; Amos Perlmutter, "From Obscurity to Rule: The Syrian Army and the Ba'th Party," *Western Political Quarterly* 22,4 (1969): 827.

[13]Van Dam, "Sectarian and Regional Factionalism," pp. 203, 205; Moshe Ma'oz, "'Alawi Military Officers in Syrian Politics," in *The Military and State in Modern Asia,* ed. H. Z. Schiffrin (Jerusalem: Academic Press, 1976), pp. 277–278. These analysts both emphasize the Sunni dimension of Kurdish identity, overlooking the fact that minoritarian ethnic status is salient in the political consciousness of Kurds in Syria (who are not ethnic Arabs and speak a different language).

civilian politician enlisted the military assistance of a Kurdish colonel to suppress the power base of a leading Druze family. The Kurdish officer was overthrown five months later by a rival who successfully mobilized the support of resentful Druze armored unit commanders. By December 1949, still another coup was led by a Kurd, Colonel Adib Shishakli, with the support of Druze officers and politicians. Shishakli succeeded in remaining at the helm until February 1954, when his suppression of a Druze uprising provided a pretext for his ouster.[14]

Within several years, therefore, the coup d'état was "institutionalized" as a means of regime change in Syria.[15] In a series of personal dictatorships, officers consistently promised a speedy return to the barracks but failed to make good on this pledge. An unprecedented departure occurred when the officers who seized power from Shishakli actually did hand over the reigns of government to civilian politicians. For four years, a variety of political parties competed for power both in Parliament and in the Army.

The rise of the Ba'th Party to prominence from 1954 to 1958 is attributable in part to its leaders' ability to gain support in the Syrian officer corps. Many officers were persuaded to support the Ba'th Party by Akram al-Hawrani, a politician whose reputation in his native agro-city of Hamah enabled him to recruit officers from Hamah. Ba'th officers were then instrumental in launching the January 1958 initiative for union with Egypt in the United Arab Republic.[16]

Syrian leaders were convinced that Egypt was striving to dominate the United Arab Republic, which lasted from February 1958 to September 1961. Egyptian interference was manifested in the predominant selection of Sunni Muslims for Syrian cabinet positions (95.5 percent), corresponding to the primarily Sunni population of Egypt.[17] Resentment by minority communities was reflected in the officer corps, and a secret Syrian Ba'thi military committee was formed in 1959, led by three 'Alawis and two

---

[14]Be'eri, *Army Officers,* pp. 57–70.

[15]Hurewitz, *Middle East Politics,* p. 150.

[16]Malcolm Kerr, *The Arab Cold War: Gamal 'Abd al-Nasir and His Rivals, 1958–1970,* 3rd ed. (London: Oxford University Press, 1971), p. 8; Be'eri, *Army Officers,* p. 232.

[17]Van Dam, "Sectarian and Regional Factionalism," p. 205.

Isma'ili officers. Its leaders included Salah Jadid and Hafiz al-Asad, two future Syrian heads of state. The secret committee continued to function after Syria's secession from the United Arab Republic, while the country was ruled by a conservative-dominated civilian regime.[18]

The emergence of an explicitly Ba'thi regime in 1963 transformed civil-military relations in Syria. Previously, civilian politicians sought to enhance the influence of the Ba'th Party through coalition with Army officers. At this point, officers identifying with the Ba'th Party succeeded in gaining ascendancy over other factions in the Syrian Army.

The regime led by Gen. Amin al-Hafiz initiated significant changes in the composition of the Syrian military elite. 'Alawi and Druze officers played a crucial role in the 1963 coup, and then designated Hafiz, a Sunni, as the front man for the regime. He, in turn, succeeded in playing officers of minority background off against each other for three years, until they finally prevailed over him in 1966.[19] The minority members of the Hafiz regime lacked affiliation with the historical leadership of the Ba'th Party, exerting influence through their domination of the military committee of the Ba'th.[20]

The sectarian dimension of the power struggle between General Hafiz and the minority officers was complemented by other lines of cleavage in the elite. There was a generational change from Hafiz, associated with the Old Guard of the Ba'th, and the minority officers, identified with the neo-Ba'th. There was also a center-periphery dichotomy, with the Sunni elite originating largely in the agro-cities of Damascus and Aleppo, while minority officers derived from Ladhaqiyyah and Hamah.[21] In short, this was a transitional regime, in which a new type of elite began to emerge with distinctive communal origins and firmer mechanisms for military ascendancy over civilian politicians.

The predominant representation of members of minority com-

[18]R. D. McLaurin, Mohammed Mughisuddin, and Abraham Wagner, *Foreign Policy Making in the Middle East* (New York: Praeger, 1977), pp. 223–224.

[19]Hurewitz, *Middle East Politics,* p. 154.

[20]Malcolm Kerr, "Hafiz Asad and the Changing Patterns of Syrian Politics," *International Journal* 28 (1973): 693–694.

[21]Perlmutter, "From Obscurity to Rule," p. 843.

munities reached a climax under Salah Jadid, an 'Alawi officer who ruled from 1966 to 1970. During this period, the regional center of gravity of the regime shifted to the agro-city of Ladhaqiyyah, where the 'Alawi community is concentrated. Representation of officers from Ladhaqiyyah in the Regional (i.e., Syrian) Command of the Ba'th Party reached an all-time high of 63 percent,[22] prompting the Secretary General of the Ba'th Party, Munif al-Razzaz, to denounce the "sectarian grouping" of 'Alawis in the officers' cadre.[23] The image of a narrowly based regime relying increasingly on the instruments of coercion was reinforced during the June 1967 Arab-Israel war. Some of the best-trained armed units were held back from the front and mobilized around Damascus, presumably to guard the regime from its domestic enemies.[24]

Although Jadid rose to power with the assistance of both Druze and 'Alawi officers, he gradually undermined the influence of the Druze faction and evicted its members from important positions. By 1969, the struggle for power was confined to members of the 'Alawi community. Jadid himself officially headed the civilian wing of the Ba'th Party. His most important rival, Hafiz al-Asad, contended for influence in his capacity as Minister of Defense. The contest came to a head in November 1970, and Asad seized power in a bloodless coup.[25]

Asad continued Jadid's reliance on members of his own minority community, removing 'Alawi officers loyal to his rival in favor of those whom he trusted personally. The most sensitive positions in the regime were largely restricted to 'Alawis, and occasionally even to members of his own family. Rif'at al-Asad, his brother, became commander of the Defense Companies, an elite unit of the Syrian Army with responsibilities for defense of the regime. 'Adnan Asad, his nephew, was placed in charge of the Special Forces, additional security units for the regime.[26] By surrounding himself with a coterie of trusted men, Asad formed a regime possibly more homogeneous, at its core, than that of his predecessor.

However, Asad organized his regime on a dualistic basis. The

[22]Van Dam, "Sectarian and Regional Factionalism," p. 207.
[23]As cited in Ma'oz, "'Alawi Military Officers," p. 293.
[24]Kerr, "Hafiz Asad," p. 697.
[25]Ma'oz, "'Alawi Military Officers," pp. 282–284.
[26]McLaurin *et al., Foreign Policy Making*, pp. 232–233, 251.

central, informal network of authority was masked by a more broadly based formal structure.[27] This distinction was evident in the officer corps. Asad filled many senior—although less sensitive—positions with Sunnis and members of minority groups other than the 'Alawis. He probably hoped that an intercommunal officer corps would broaden the regime's base of support. Then the Army could serve "as a solid foundation for the regime and as a melting pot for the emerging Syrian political community."[28]

However, to achieve genuine support and legitimation for the regime, its appeal obviously had to extend beyond the confines of the Army. No regime can rely exclusively on the coercion represented by military power and hope to maintain its authority. A critical element in the quest for legitimacy by Syrian regimes since 1963 has been their identification with the ideology of the Ba'th Party. The popular appeal of Ba'thi ideology was authentic and well suited to indigenous circumstances in Syria. However, the institutional apparatus of the Ba'th Party was so effectively subordinated to the military elite that Party spokesmen became mere instruments of the regime.

Since the first coup d'état in which Ba'thi officers seized power, both the military and civilian wings of the party were brought under Army control. In one view, "the officers in the coalition that had seized power in 1963 so militarized the regime . . . that the Ba'th Party became in effect the private property of the military junta."[29] As early as 1966, Michel Aflaq, a founder of the Ba'th Party, complained:

> We hope to change the function of the Army by preventing the officers from forming a bloc inside the leadership of the party. . . . There is no real revolutionary party in the world whose leaders are military men continuing to command army units.[30]

[27]Itamar Rabinovich, "The Limits of Military Power: Syria's Role," in *Lebanon in Crisis,* ed. P. Edward Haley and Lewis W. Snider (Syracuse, N.Y.: Syracuse University Press, 1979), p. 67.

[28]Moshe Ma'oz, *Syria Under Hafiz al-Asad: New Domestic and Foreign Policies,* Jerusalem Papers on Peace Problems, no. 15 (Jerusalem: Hebrew University, 1975), p. 7; see also Van Dam, *Struggle for Power,* p. 89.

[29]Hurewitz, *Middle East Politics,* p. 147.

[30]As cited in Adeed Dawisha, "The Transnational Party in Regional Politics: The Arab Ba'th Party," *Asian Affairs* 61,1 (February 1974): 29.

Ideological Orientations

The impact of Ba'thi ideology on Syrian politics derives from its appeal on both the elite and popular levels. Has ideology determined the political affiliations of the military elite or influenced their policies? To what extent did communal origins condition ideological orientations?

Analysts who view Syria as a praetorian state discount the impact of ideology on the military elite. P. J. Vatikiotis, for example, declares that "because the personal factor outweighs all others in the Syrian experience, prescriptive ideology and institutional affiliations have limited relevance in Syrian politics."[31] Dismissing ideology out of hand, however, overlooks several vital functions served by Ba'thi ideology. It provides a synthesis of traditional and modern values well suited to the needs of a society in transition. Ba'thi ideology also suits Syria in its emphasis on pan-Arabism, since "the diffuse idea of pan-Arabism has remained perhaps the most widely and intensely held symbol of political identification in Syria since independence." A popular perception of Syria as the heartland of the Arab nation was reinforced by recent memories of the paring down of the state's boundaries by Western imperial powers. Finally, Ba'thi ideological appeal enhanced the structural solidarity of the Syrian regime. The destruction of traditional Syrian ruling structures after independence created a legitimacy vacuum, and a formula was needed to transform new structures into authoritative institutions. Syria was plagued by intraparty factionalism and by the lack of nationally based associational constituencies as vehicles for political participation. The cohesiveness provided by the Ba'th Party promoted a spread of central authority in the state.[32]

The pan-Arab dimension of party ideology identifies the Ba'th as a transnational party. Ba'thi ideology considers the Arabs members of one nation in which individual Arab states are merely regional segments. Founded in Syria in 1940, the Party's influence spread to other Arab states, especially Iraq. The structural reflec-

---

[31]Vatikiotis, "Politics of the Fertile Crescent," pp. 228, 237.
[32]Hudson, *Arab Politics,* pp. 257–266.

tion of the party's transnational character was that a National (i.e., pan-Arab) Command was formally superior to the Regional Commands of the party in each state. In practice, the distinction between national and regional levels generated substantial friction. For example, under the regime of Amin al-Hafiz (1963–66), 'Alawi and Druze officers used their dominant positions in the Regional Command of the party to gain influence over Hafiz, a member of the National Command.[33]

The Ba'th Party was flexible in adapting its internal structure to local circumstances. Most Syrians identified politically either at the subnational (regional) or supranational (pan-Arab) level, rather than harboring loyalty to the Syrian nation-state. In effect, "the lack of any middle ground loyalty has meant that local political struggles have been projected to the national political arena."[34] To accommodate Syrian realities, the Ba'th Party became decentralized and cell oriented. A cellular structure enabled the party to win adherence to pan-Arab and socialist goals by phrasing them in terms relevant to local circumstances. This method assisted the party in recruiting local support and penetrating the population, but it did have associated costs. By catering to and perpetuating subnational loyalties, the party emerged on the national level as a network of relatively autonomous cells, subject to interregional conflict.[35]

The regional and sectarian appeals of Ba'thi ideology often coincided. In general, Arab nationalist ideology had the strongest appeal to Sunni Muslims, who form the majority community throughout the Arab world. In Syria, the option of a non-Muslim, particularist national identification was offered by the Syrian Social Nationalist Party (SSNP), which was active in the early years of independence. However, the Ba'th Party had the advantage of attracting both Sunnis and members of minority communities through its arguments for pan-Arab nationalism on secular grounds.[36]

If the pan-Arab appeal of the Ba'th cut across social groups, its socialist ideology was especially popular among minority com-

---

[33]Dawisha, "Transnational Party," pp. 23–26.
[34]Van Dusen, "Political Integration," p. 125.
[35]Ibid., p. 135.
[36]Vatikiotis, "Politics of the Fertile Crescent," p. 263.

munities. Ba'thi calls for social justice were compelling to socio-economically deprived groups, particularly in rural areas. The 'Alawis, as the poorest community in the country, were mostly peasants concentrated in the southwestern agro-city of Ladha-qiyyah. Another agro-city, Hamah, played a critical role in the evolution of the Ba'th Party.

Ideology in Practice

In the early post-independence period, Akram al-Hawrani recruited support for the Ba'th Party through his popularity and connections in the agro-city of Hamah. His regional reputation was derived from earlier leadership of a peasant revolt in Hamah, as an enemy of the local landed families. Hawrani's socialism was therefore targeted to local realities. When his Arab Socialist Party merged with Ba'th in 1954, the consolidated party gained grass-roots support among peasants and Army officers from Hamah. The Ba'th then agitated against the military regime of Adib Shi-shakli and effectively contested the popularity of the Syrian Social Nationalist Party.[37]

As it happened, Ladhaqiyyah was the only agro-city in which both the Ba'th and the SSNP had strong appeal in the 1950s. Ideological commitments were nurtured at the high school level, when regional identifications and ties were most intense. The pervasive poverty in Ladhaqiyyah enhanced the appeal of Ba'thi socialist ideals. The Army and teaching were the only two careers in which an individual could hope to achieve social mobility. For 'Alawi officers identified with the Ba'th Party, communal attachments first gained crucial political significance in the 1960s. When factional rivalries between Ba'thi officers intensified, absolute trust between officers of the same sect became a vital bond.[38]

The ideological commitments of Syria's leaders were put into practice in the 1960s, when Ba'th-dominated regimes embarked on programs of social reform. At their first party congress after the 1963 coup, Ba'thi spokesmen announced a move from belief

[37]Kerr, *Arab Cold War*, p. 8; Dawisha, "Transnational Party," p. 24.
[38]Van Dusen, "Political Integration," pp. 132–134.

in socialism to implementation of socialism. Decrees nationalizing industrial concerns were soon enacted.[39] A Ba'thi officer rationalized the nationalizations in explicit communal terms:

> Don't expect us to eliminate socialism in Syria; for the real meaning of such steps would be the transfer of all the political, industrial and commercial advantages to the towns, i.e., the members of the Sunni community. We the 'Alawis and the Druze, will then again be the poor and the servants. . . . What property do we have which we could lose by nationalization? None![40]

Under protest from urban business and agrarian interests, however, the Hafiz regime relaxed its socialist policy in 1965. This reversal also reflected the ongoing power struggle between Hafiz, a Sunni, and the minority officers in the regime. Hafiz's attempt to contain 'Alawi and Druze influence was reflected in his retreat from socialist measures. When Salah Jadid seized power in 1966, he announced his determination to "rectify the deviation," accelerating nationalizations and agrarian reforms.[41]

The subsequent rivalry between Jadid and Asad had clear ideological overtones. However, since both were 'Alawis, a distinction based on communal background is not convincing. Many issues in debate between the two derived from the strict interpretation of ideological imperatives by Jadid, as opposed to Asad's attempt to liberalize somewhat so as to broaden the regime's base of support.

On domestic policy, Asad felt that the Army should receive a larger budget at the expense of economic development projects. He advocated a less interventionist government role in the economy. Promoting an "outwardly directed" Arab nationalist posture, Asad argued for political and military cooperation with Egypt, Jordan, and Iraq, to counter Syria's isolation under the Jadid regime and to improve Syria's preparedness for armed struggle against Israel. He also urged stronger control by the Syrian Army over Palestinian guerrilla activities.

---

[39] George Haddad, *Revolutions and Military Rule in the Middle East: The Arab States,* II (New York: Robert Speller, 1971), p. 325.

[40] Be'eri, *Army Officers,* p. 337.

[41] Haddad, *Revolutions and Military Rule,* p. 357; Be'eri, *Army Officers,* pp. 160–161, 167.

In February 1969, Asad staged a limited coup. For close to two years, he shared power in an uneasy alliance with Jadid. Both participated in the Regional Command of the Ba'th Party. The issue that brought matters to a head was the circumscribed Syrian intervention in the Jordanian Civil War of September 1970. The Regional Command of the Ba'th authorized intervention by Syrian tanks in support of the Palestinian Resistance. Asad, as Minister of Defense, opposed the intervention and deliberately withheld air support. When a special session of the National (pan-Arab) Congress of the Ba'th was convened to pass judgment, Asad contended that Syria must "refrain in the future from all gratuitous acts of provocation which the enemy [i.e., Israel] could use as a pretext to challenge the Syrian Army." The Jadid faction accused Asad of "defeatism," and the Congress upheld their position. In response, Asad staged a coup d'état the next day (13 November 1970), assumed full power, and replaced the membership of the Ba'th Regional Command with a slate of his own supporters.[42]

Once in power, Hafiz al-Asad maintained substantial continuity with the two previous Ba'thi regimes in which he had participated. However, there were significant changes both in substance and style, revealing an effort at broader legitimation. Perhaps "the revolutionary potential which brought the Ba'th to power ... [was] largely spent by the early 1970s".[43] Asad's selective liberalization was in tune with a more pragmatic and conservative mood in the country.

Increased scope for popular political participation was permitted, as Asad introduced a "personal-presidential" regime. National referenda were held on important issues, and the President emerged as a national Syrian and an all-Arab leader.[44] Asad also sought to modify the image of the Army. His predecessor, Jadid, opposed efforts to convert the Syrian Army from an "ideological" to a professional Army. Asad, while still proclaiming commitment to an "ideological" Army, stressed the identification between the Army and the people, rather than between the Army and the Ba'th Party.[45]

[42]Kerr, "Hafiz Asad," pp. 676–700; Van Dam, *Struggle for Power,* pp. 83–88.
[43]Rabinovich, "Limits of Military Power," p. 61.
[44]Ma'oz, *Syria Under Hafiz al-Asad,* pp. 9–12.
[45]Ma'oz, *Alawi Military Officers,* pp. 288–289.

Asad believed that excessive emphasis had been placed in the past on the centrality of the Ba'th Party. In 1972, therefore, he sponsored creation of a National Progressive Front (NPF). This coalition of "progressive" groups included the Ba'th, the Communist Party, the Arab Socialist Union (a Nasirist group), the Socialist Union, and the Arab Socialist Party. The NPF provided a vehicle of expression for some groups excluded from political participation since 1963, when the Ba'th had become the sole political party.

However, there were built-in limits to the influence and autonomy available to constituent members of the NPF. The Ba'th was designated as the "vanguard" party, responsible for direction of the NPF. According to the charter by which the NPF was established, all political activity by groups other than the Ba'th was prohibited in the armed forces and in educational institutions. Participation by the other political groups in the cabinet was confined to peripheral ministries, and Ba'thi officers also retained the most influential positions in the Army's Revolutionary Command Council. Overall, therefore, the formation of the NPF was a symbolic measure, rather than a significant move toward broader political participation.[46]

In the economic sphere, Asad's policies of liberalism were aimed at tempering the urban-rural cleavages accentuated by the Jadid regime's socialist policies. Those measures had hurt the interests not only of the larger industrialists and merchants, but also of urban petty traders, artisans and members of the professions. In the early 1970s, Asad courted the urban traders by permitting increased scope for private enterprise, as well as attracting substantial aid and some investment capital from Arab Gulf states.

It became incresingly evident, however, that the greatest beneficiaries of the Asad regime's economic policies were the large merchants and industrialists of Damascus. An emphasis on large-scale, capital-intensive industries favored Damascus operations and newly established enterprises in Ladhaqiyyah (Asad's province of origin) at the expense of the small manufacturers of the north-central provinces (especially Hamah). In agriculture as well, small-

[46]Dawisha, "Transnational Party," pp. 27–28; McLaurin et. al., *Foreign Policy Making,* p. 228.

scale farmers in Hamah, Homs, and Aleppo (the north-central provinces) were severely challenged by large government enterprises established in the northeast. Especially hard hit was cotton production, whose traditional predominance in the Syrian economy was superseded in 1974 by petroleum products. A severe reduction in the land devoted to cotton production contributed to large-scale unemployment among landless peasants and also hurt urban craftspeople in the north-central provinces.[47]

Economic reversals suffered by a variety of groups in Hamah, Homs, and Aleppo aroused discontent with the Asad regime and contributed to outbreaks of social unrest beginning in 1973. The socioeconomic underpinnings of the unrest do not, however, discount the authenticity of the religious symbolism employed by the dissidents. The overlap of socioeconomic and sectarian cleavages in Syria reinforces the predominance of sectarian identifications. Opposition to President Asad's economic policies unleashed latent Sunni resentment of an 'Alawi-dominated elite, even though some wealthy Sunni merchants and industrialists, especially in Damascus, were prospering under the regime.

The first serious instance of social unrest was precipitated by the issuance of a new Syrian permanent constitution in January 1973 which failed to designate Islam as the religion of the state. Rioting erupted in Hamah, Homs, and Aleppo, and demonstrators protested the "godlessness" of the Ba'th. While assailing secular Ba'thi ideology, they were also calling attention to the deviation of Syria's 'Alawi rulers from orthodox, Sunni Islam. In fact, a pervasive belief among the country's Sunni majority is that the 'Alawis are not true Muslims at all. Despite protestations by 'Alawi religious leaders that they uphold the tenets of Shi'i Islam, widespread suspicions persist that the sect's secret books include deviations from conventional Shi'ism. These suspicions undermined the Asad regime's legitimacy and underlay the intense popular reaction to the 1973 constitution. In response to the demonstrations, Asad amended the constitution to say that the President of

[47]Hanna Batatu, "Syria's Muslim Brethren," *MERIP Reports* 110 (Nov.-Dec. 1982): 18; Fred H. Lawson, "Syria's Intervention in the Lebanese War, 1976: A Domestic Conflict Explanation," *International Organization* 38, 3 (Summer 1984): 462–467.

the Syrian republic must be a Muslim, thereby also underscoring his own Muslim credentials.[48]

The social unrest of 1973 and subsequent years was identified with the increasing appeal of the Muslim Brethren (Ikhwan Muslimun), a fundamentalist Sunni group whose origins in Syria trace back to the 1930s. The membership of the Muslim Brethren consistently derived most heavily from urban artisans and small-scale traders. These groups have been characterized as "the most religiously oriented" members of Syrian society. Both before and since the Ba'th came to power in 1963, the Muslim Brethren was primarily a movement of the cities, in contrast to the rural appeal of the Ba'th Party. By the mid-1970s, economic grievances among the Brethren's natural constituency combined with a perception of the "deepening erosion of the status and power of the Sunni community" to channel activism through the Muslim Brethren's ranks.[49]

The response of the Asad regime to intermittent eruptions of unrest was swift and firm military repression. In reply to the 1973 riots against the constitution, Army units surrounded the city of Hamah, and state security forces acted against demonstrators in Homs. In July 1975, the Asad government accused "a number of members of the right-wing Muslim Brotherhood" of conspiring to overthrow the regime and arrested the alleged instigators. Three weeks later, demonstrations in Aleppo prompted mobilization of Army units.

In the most serious incident yet, rioting in Hamah in February 1976 led to large-scale arrests by armed units commanded by the President's brother, Rif'at al-Asad. He attempted to break the organizational structures of the dissidents, using not only the Defense Squadrons under his personal command, but also the Special Elite Forces and 500 regular Army troops. The publication of Syria's Muslim Brethren, known as *al-Nadhir,* retrospectively marked February 1976 as the starting date for their all-out struggle against the Asad regime.[50]

[48]Kerr, "Hafiz Asad," pp. 703–704; Van Dam, *Struggle for Power,* p. 112; Batatu, "Some Observations," p. 335.

[49]Batatu, "Syria's Muslim Brethren," passim.

[50]Lawson, "Syria's Intervention," pp. 463, 471–472.

Linkage Politics

Sporadic outbursts of small-scale violence in Syria in the early 1970s constituted danger signals to the Asad regime. Dissent was always quickly suppressed, and there were no indications of organized conspiracy posing a major threat to the military elite. Yet the necessity of resorting to force to quell popular opposition was an indication of the ultimate fragility of a regime resting on so narrow a base of support.

Upon reflection, one may be astonished that the government of President Hafiz al-Asad enjoyed as much stability as it did by the mid-1970s. Not only was power confined to the single political institution of the Army, but even within the military, members of one minority sectarian group held the key posts.

Yet, although the analyst can gain considerable insight into how and why certain actors rose to the helm in Syrian politics, the actual dynamics of decisionmaking remain obscure. One may identify a set of trusted advisers surrounding President Asad, or point to those primarily responsible for internal security, or note on which occasions the Ba'th Party was invited to vote on a given policy issue. Nevertheless, the secretive nature of Syria's authoritarian political system casts a shadow over the way in which policy is made.

Bearing this caveat in mind, one may still tread on firm ground in identifying linkages between Syrian domestic and foreign policy. Students of "linkage politics" are interested in the interplay between a state's internal and external environment. More specifically, "conflict linkage" focuses on the relationship between a state's domestic conflicts and conflict in the international system.[51]

Two variants of "conflict linkage" are worth noting in Syrian foreign policy prior to the Lebanese Civil War of 1975–76. The first highlights the significance of domestic constraints as an independent variable influencing foreign policy. Before Hafiz al-Asad came to power, Syria's short-lived military elites were so preoccupied with the domestic struggle for power that they were

[51]Yaacov Bar-Siman-Tov, *Linkage Politics in the Middle East: Syria Between External and Internal Conflict, 1961–1970* (Boulder, Col.: Westview Press, 1983), pp. 1–54.

incapable of pursuing activist regional policies. Beyond embracing pan-Arab ideology and supporting the Palestinian cause, Syrian leaders were in no position to give sustained attention to foreign policy.

The Asad regime, by contrast, achieved unprecedented domestic stability. By consolidating the support of a homogeneous military elite, drawing effectively on Ba'thi ideological appeal, and reaching out at least superficially for broader popular support, President Asad held the reigns of power longer than any of his predecessors. He then sought to assert Syria's regional leadership claim, beginning with increased influence over the neighbor with whom Syria traditionally enjoyed the deepest bonds.

An observer of Syria and Lebanon in the early 1970s might have noted that the centralization of power in Syria reached its zenith just at a time that Lebanon's delicate sectarian balance was beginning to come unhinged. By 1975, Syria appeared on the surface to be the picture of stability compared to its neighbor. Yet Syrian stability was ultimately premised on coercion, with latent societal discontent ready to be galvanized in the appropriate circumstances.

For this reason, a second variant of "conflict linkage" comes to mind. Conflict in a state's external environment may serve as an independent variable, generating internal conflict. The predominant sectarian overtones of Lebanon's civil strife were particularly ominous to the members of the sectarian minority at the helm in the Syrian state. Above and beyond the fear of "contagion," whereby Lebanon's strife might arouse the religious symbolism already voiced by Syrian dissidents, was the issue of Syrian public reaction to their government's involvement in the Lebanese Civil War. The controversial course pursued by the Asad regime in its high-cost intervention in Lebanon became a major factor in bringing Syria's latent communal tensions to the surface.[52]

[52]For further discussion of the "contagion effect" of the Lebanese Civil War, see pp. 236–237.

4

Lebanese Confessionalism

As Syria's leaders contemplated their foreign policy options, their Lebanese neighbor afforded inviting opportunities as well as peculiar dangers. Deep historic links created familiarity and multiple channels for exercising influence. Conversely, the openness of Lebanon's political system, in stark contrast to Syrian authoritarianism, was inherently unsettling to Syria's leaders.

Syrian apprehensions that the free-wheeling Lebanese political style harbored dangers to Syria's political stability were long-standing. From this perspective, the "fear of contagion" underlying Syria's defensive motives for containing Lebanese civil strife in 1975–76 can be better understood. Even when Lebanon's democratic system functioned without disruption, it offered Syrian dissidents a seductive model as well as a haven from prosecution by the Syrian regime.

Over the years, Lebanon frequently provided asylum for Syrian political exiles and refugees. Successful or abortive coups against Syrian regimes were planned in and launched from Lebanon. In 1952, the leaders of the Syrian Ba'th Party, Akram Hawrani, Salah al-Din Bitar, and Michel Aflaq, sought refuge in Lebanon. From there they plotted an attack on the Shishakli regime in Syria, which closed the border for twenty-four hours in protest. During the Suez Crisis of 1956, the discovery by Syrian intelligence of a Lebanese-based plot against the Syrian government provoked a period of friction between the two countries.

After Syria's secession from the United Arab Republic in 1961, the foreign ministers of Syria and Lebanon reached an agreement on mutual cooperation to curb political subversion. However, repeated Syrian charges of Lebanese sponsorship of subversion and sabotage prompted Syria in 1968 to impose higher duties and a tax on trucks engaged in the transit trade. After arbitration by the Arab League, the Lebanese government issued a warning to Syrian nationals residing in Lebanon, demanding that they refrain from any public statements or political activities. Only then did Syria remove the special taxes and duties.

Lebanon's free press was another source of anxiety to Syria. The Lebanese press provided a forum in which many shades of Arab political opinion found expression. Although there were newspapers identified with the Syrian branch of the Ba'th Party, others—sponsored by the Iraqi Ba'th or expressing independent positions—often published reports and documents damaging to Syrian authorities.[1]

Syrian perceptions of the Lebanese regime were therefore conditioned, from the moment of independence, by sensitivity to the unrestrained, unpredictable Lebanese political style. The most fascinating question in comparing Syria and Lebanon is why two countries with such similar social structures had such dramatically different political systems. The historic roots of Lebanon's distinctive experience go far to explain its unusual political system. Nevertheless, large segments of Lebanon's population did not accept the legitimacy of its formula of government. The growing disaffection among groups whose needs were not met by the political system precipitated the small-scale Civil War of 1958 and resurfaced in the full-scale Lebanese Civil War of 1975–76.

Communal Divisions

Lebanon resembles Syria in its multiplicity of sectarian minorities, despite differences in the relative size and geographic distribution of communal groups. The Sunni majority in Syria coexists with a variety of minority sects, most of them also Muslim. Syrian society is characterized by the salience of several "compact" minorities—

---

[1]Elizabeth Conroy, "Syria and Lebanon: The Background," in *The Syrian Arab Republic: A Handbook,* ed. Anne Sinai and Allen Pollack (New York: American Academic Association for Peace in the Middle East, 1976), p. 81; Itamar Rabinovich, "The Limits of Military Power," in *Lebanon in Crisis,* ed. P. Edward Haley and Lewis W. Snider (Syracuse, N.Y.: Syracuse University Press, 1979), pp. 56–57; Kamal Salibi, *Crossroads to Civil War: Lebanon, 1958–1976* (Delmar, N.Y.: Caravan, 1976), pp. 159–160.

the 'Alawis, Druze, and Isma'ilis—each of which form the majority of the population in a given region. The Sunni Muslim majority is scattered throughout the country, as are members of the Christian minority.[2]

By contrast, in Lebanon no single community forms a majority of the population. During the Ottoman period, relations between Maronites and Druze constituted the dominant communal cleavage. A major social transformation occurred with the creation of Greater Lebanon in 1920. In the newly added coastal towns of Beirut, Tripoli, Sidon, and Tyre, the population was largely Sunni Muslim, although there were also numerous Shi'is, Greek Catholics, Greek Orthodox, and Armenians. In the appended districts of the Biqa' in the east and the Jabal 'Amil in the south, the population was predominantly Shi'i Muslim, along with substantial Greek Orthodox and Greek Catholic communities. Overall, pronounced discrepancies existed between the social composition of Mount Lebanon and the rest of the country.[3]

According to the Lebanese census of 1932, the Maronites were the single largest communal group, at 29 percent of the total population. Other major Christian communities were the Greek Orthodox (9 percent) and Greek Catholics (6 percent). Among Muslims, the Sunnis had 22 percent and the Shi'is 20 percent. The Druze constituted 7 percent of the population, and all other sects were smaller.

Since 1932, the Lebanese government has refused to administer a new census. Muslims protested that the Maronite-dominated elite was refusing to acknowledge the emergence of a Muslim majority—a claim substantiated by the Christians' lower birth rates and higher rates of permanent emigration. By the early 1970s, when the total population of Lebanon was estimated at slightly over two million, analysts believed that Muslims outnumbered Christians and that among Muslims, Shi'is outnumbered Sunnis.[4]

---

[2]Albert Hourani, *Syria and Lebanon* (London: Oxford University Press, 1946), p. 137.

[3]Ibid, p. 129.

[4]David Smock and Audrey Smock, *The Politics of Pluralism: A Comparative Study of Lebanon and Ghana* (New York: Elsevier, 1975), p. 76.

Confessional Divisions in Lebanon, 1947

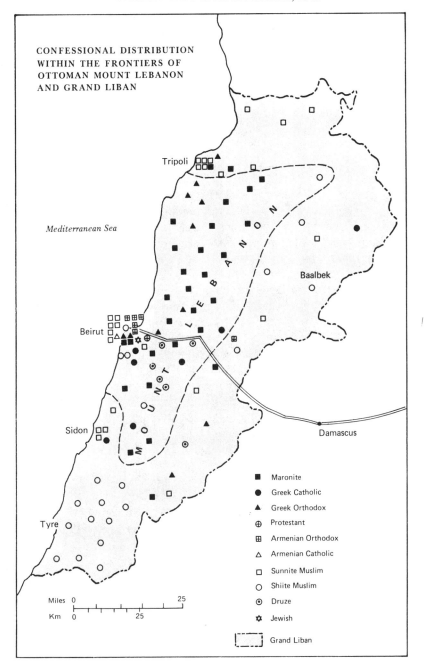

CONFESSIONAL DISTRIBUTION WITHIN THE FRONTIERS OF OTTOMAN MOUNT LEBANON AND GRAND LIBAN

Mediterranean Sea

Tripoli

Baalbek

Beirut

Sidon

Damascus

Tyre

■	Maronite
●	Greek Catholic
▲	Greek Orthodox
⊕	Protestant
⊞	Armenian Orthodox
△	Armenian Catholic
☐	Sunnite Muslim
○	Shiite Muslim
◉	Druze
✿	Jewish

Miles 0   25
Km 0   25

---- Grand Liban

Source: Walid Khalidi, *Conflict and Violence in Lebanon: Confrontation in the Middle East*, p. 30. Copyright © 1979 by the President and Fellows of Harvard College. Reprinted by permission of the Center for International Affairs.

The Confessional System

The emergence in Lebanon of a political system designed to achieve a balance between sectarian communities found no parallel in Syria. In part, this difference reflects precedents set in the Ottoman period, when the Mountain was the only part of geographic Syria with pre-democratic institutions. Both the dual *kaymakamate* of 1842 (partitioning the Mountain along sectarian lines) and the Administrative Council under the Organic Statute of 1861 (providing proportional sectarian representation) were important precedents. Sectarian representation was also the basis for allocating seats in the Representative Council under the French mandate. In each case, European influence was decisive in devising institutional mechanisms for dealing with societal pluralism.

No wonder, then, that in categorizing Lebanon's political system after independence, European typologies come to mind. Lebanon was categorized by Dutch political scientist Arend Lijphart as an example of a "consociational democracy"—comparable to Austria, the Low Countries, and Switzerland in Western Europe, as well as to Colombia and Uruguay (until 1967) in Latin America. A consociational democracy is defined as "government by elite cartel designed to turn a democracy with a fragmented political culture into a stable democracy." It is a system best suited to a country with deep cultural cleavages, which strives for stability through cooperation among leaders of rival subcultures.

Several conditions increase the chances that a consociational political system will achieve enduring stability. Elites must be committed to maintaining the system, and must be willing to accommodate the divergent interests of rival subcultures. Cooperation is ingrained over time as an operational code of interelite cooperation becomes habitual. Elite cohesion is more likely if there is a multiple balance of power among diverse subcultures, rather than a clear hegemony of one subculture or a dual balance of power between two groups of roughly equal size and influence. In either of the latter cases, elites might strive to achieve their aims by domination rather than cooperation. Incentives for cooperation are also enhanced if elites are wary of the perils of fragmentation or share a common fear of external threats to the country.

On the mass level, if the various subcultures have strong differences in outlook, conflict is more likely if they come into frequent contact than if they coexist with minimal mutual contacts. The more heterogeneous the group cultures, the more likely it is that close contacts will lead to strain and hostility, as opposed to the situation in an essentially homogeneous culture, where cross-cutting ties and affiliation may promote harmony and mutual understanding. For a consociational system, therefore, it is best that distinct lines of cleavage be maintained among the subcultures. Moreover, political cohesion within each subculture makes it easier for elites to compromise with each other without losing the allegiance of their own rank and file. While all these factors might stimulate the *will* of elites to cooperate, they also must have the *capability* of joint political action for the system to function efficiently. Fragmented societies have a built-in tendency toward immobilism, and therefore a relatively low total load on the decision-making apparatus maximizes the prospects for success.[5]

For a long while after independence, Lebanon fulfilled many conditions for a stable consociational system. Why, then, did the system eventually disintegrate and civil war erupt? Michael Hudson argues that the great difficulty in applying the consociational model to a new state is that it is intrinsically too static to accommodate the enormous social and political forces unleashed by social mobilization. Consociational government may be effective at conflict regulation in European states, where intergroup conflicts are old and of diminishing salience, but not in conditions of modernization such as characterized Lebanon in the late 1960s and early 1970s. When these developments generated a heavy load on the political apparatus, in both internal and external demands, the very structure of the consociational system impeded a positive response.[6]

The indigenous term for Lebanon's formula of government was *confessionalism,* referring to the allocation of political positions on the basis of "confessions," or religious sects. Confessionalism has been defined as "institutionalized separatism on a sectarian basis

[5] Arend Lijphart, "Consociational Democracy," *World Politics* 21 (1969): 207–222.

[6] Michael Hudson, "The Lebanese Crisis and the Limits of Consociational Democracy," *Journal of Palestine Studies* 5, 3–4 (1976): 112–114.

in the parliament, cabinet, and administration."[7] This principle was first formally embodied in the National Pact *(al-mithaq al-watani)* of 1943. This unwritten pact between the major religious communities was enunciated by Riyadh al-Sulh, Lebanon's first Prime Minister, in a speech delivered to the Chamber of Deputies on 7 October 1943. The National Pact provided that the President of Lebanon would always be a Maronite Catholic; the Prime Minister, a Sunni Muslim; and the President of the Chamber of Deputies, a Shi'i Muslim. Seats in the legislative and executive branches would be distributed according to a ratio of six Christians for every five Muslims, providing fixed proportional representation. The distribution of positions in favor of the Christians was a concession by Muslim leaders. Its intention was to reassure the Christian communities, who feared that, despite their majoritarian status in Lebanon itself, they might eventually be engulfed by the overwhelming regional Muslim majority.[8]

Confessionalism was only one dimension of competition between groups in Lebanese society. There were actually several balances of power at play in Lebanese politics, whose objectives were overlapping but not identical. These included competition between geographic interests, economic interests, secular ideological interests, and the personal interests of members of the political elite.[9]

Nevertheless, focusing on the balancing of interests *between* confessional groups may overemphasize the coherence *within* each group. As Albert Hourani points out, one important question to ask is: exactly who in each community benefits from its position in the political system? As consociational theory predicts, the confessional system was based on a network of alliances between political leaders, allowing each to exercise patronage among his own clients.

In actuality, the style of leadership varied in different communities and in different regions. Although the title *za'im* applied

[7]Michael Hudson, "Democracy and Social Mobilization in Lebanese Politics," *Comparative Politics* 1 (January 1969): 251.

[8]Walid Khalidi, *Conflict and Violence in Lebanon: Confrontation in the Middle East,* Harvard Studies in International Affairs, no. 38 (Cambridge: Center for International Affairs, Harvard University, 1979), p. 36.

[9]Malcolm Kerr, "Political Decision Making," in *Politics in Lebanon,* ed. Leonard Binder (New York: John Wiley, 1966), p. 191.

across the board to members of the political elite, three basic leadership categories can be identified. The "feudal" leaders were traditional lords dominating large estates in the countryside. Their power derived from their status as landowners, their use of "strong-arm men," and their ability to provide protection and patronage. This mode of leadership was most common among the Druze and Shi'is of Southern Lebanon, the Shi'is of the eastern Biqa' Valley, and the Sunnis of 'Akkar. "Populist" politicians in many northern Christian regions enjoyed less solid socioeconomic underpinnings, based on small land-holdings. These leaders could extend protection and patronage, but also had to offer their followers an ideology or program of action. Finally, Muslim leaders in the coastal cities combined patronage and ideological appeal with a third power resource. A group of "strong-arm men," or *qabadais,* operating in the popular quarters, played an important role in mobilizing and manipulating the urban masses.

These different *za'ims* did not share a consensus about the objectives that the Lebanese political system should serve. Despite basic agreement on the confessional "rules of the game," deeper consensus was lacking on the nature, or even the existence, of a Lebanese political society. Western observers often erred in assuming that, over time, the political tradition of the Christian parts of Mount Lebanon would spread to other sectors of the population. In fact, Sunni, Shi'i, and Druze elites continued to exercise authority in their communities through distinctive modes and adherence to divergent ideologies. Moreover, some groups "remained precariously inside or virtually outside" the system. These included Orthodox Christians, who played only a minor role in political life in contrast to the Maronites; and Shi'i Muslims, who lacked the leadership, organization, and resources to compete politically with the Sunnis.[10]

To the extent that Lebanon's government functioned by "elite cartel," conforming to a consociational model, the elites that participated most actively were the Maronite and Sunni *zu'ama* (the Arabic plural of *za'im).* Grievances over the allocation of power between these two groups, and by other groups that gained fewer

[10]Albert Hourani, "Ideologies of the Mountain and the City," in *Essays on the Crisis in Lebanon,* ed. Roger Owen (London: Ithaca Press, 1976), pp. 34–36.

spoils from the system, increased over time. Moreover, Lebanon's democracy was propped up by a basic fictional premise, that is, "the presumed stationary relative size of each major religious community."[11] While a consociational system is inherently prone to immobilism, the persistence of a fixed ratio of benefits while the composition and needs of Lebanon's population changed had explosive implications.

A full understanding of the functioning of Lebanon's confessional system must first evaluate the country's political institutions. The distribution of power among institutions and the means of achieving positions of authority set the rules of the game for Lebanon's "elite cartel." The increasing loads on the system may then be thematically evaluated. These included, first, a trend toward the consolidation of political blocs, raising new challenges to established institutions. Second, a process of socioeconomic change, accentuating the disparities in society, generated widespread discontent. Finally, a chronic ambivalence about Lebanon's foreign policy orientation in the Arab world was brought to a head by debate over the status of the Palestinian Resistance in Lebanon.

Political Institutions

According to the 1926 Constitution, the Lebanese Republic had a parliamentary system. The Chamber of Deputies, or Parliament, elected a President, who in turn appointed the Prime Minister. The Prime Minister then designated the members of the Cabinet, which was directly responsible to the Parliament. In actuality, however, a presidential system evolved, with all major appointments and most important executive decisions made by the President.

Deviation from constitutional guidelines derived from the subordinate role of the Lebanese Parliament. Members of the Chamber habitually sought a patron in the President or his Cabinet members. Parliamentarians depended on the executive for distribution of favors, and some aspired to be appointed as Cabinet members. After the one decisive act of electing the President, Chamber members were reluctant to defy the executive, and leg-

[11]J. C. Hurewitz, *Middle East Politics,* pp. 384–385.

LEBANON

- ● Town or Village
- △ Palestinian Refugee Camp

SYRIA

Bayt Millāt

△ Nahr al-Barīd
Tripoli ●
△ al-Baddāwī
al-Funaydiq

● Zghartā

Orontes River

al-Qā' ●

Shakkā △
KŪRA
Ihdin ●
CEDARS

● al-Batrūn

MEDITERRANEAN
SEA

Dayr al-Ahmar ●

● Jubayl

KISRAWĀN

Baalbeck ●
△ Wavell

Junieh ●
△ al-Dubayya
● Bikfayyā
THE MATN

Antilyās ●
Beirut ● al-Fanār
● Tarshīsh
Zahleh ●

Burj al-Barājina ●△
● al-Kahhāla
Shtūrā ●
B'abdā ●
● Aley

● al-Nā'ima
al-Dāmūr ●
● Harat al-Nā'ima
● al-Sa'diyyāt
● al-Jiyya
THE SHŪF

Lītānī River

SYRIA

Sidon ●
△ 'Ain al-Hulwa
● al-Miyya wa Miyya
Damascus

● Zahrānī

● al-Nabatiyya △

Lītānī River

Tyre ● al-Bass
△ Burj al-Shimālī
△ al-Rashīdiyya

GOLAN

Jordan River

ISRAEL

islative programs proposed by the Cabinet were usually adopted with little amendment or debate.[12]

Parliamentary assertiveness was also discouraged by the electoral process. Most electoral districts comprised eligible voters of more than one confessional group. Since each parliamentary seat was reserved for a member of a given sect, there was a strong incentive for interconfessional alliances between deputies. A mixed confessional slate of candidates could then present a single "list" to the constituency, and winning "lists" were often pledged to subsequent cooperation in the Chamber. Competition within Parliament for distribution of patronage was often sharpest among the members of a single sect.[13]

Candidates for the Chamber were heavily recruited among *zu'ama*. The socioeconomic basis of a *za'im's* influence, derived from landed properties or clannish enterprises in the towns, was increased through his ability to provide patronage while holding public office. Parliamentary seats were largely monopolized by two dozen prominent, wealthy families. A young politician aspiring to a parliamentary seat was often obliged to latch on to the coattails of a local *za'im,* joining his electoral list and pledging subsequent cooperation in Parliament. In some parliamentary elections, close to one-fourth of the members "inherited" parliamentary seats from older members of their families.[14] This practice bred widespread popular cynicism about the Lebanese political system.[15] On the other hand, the average percentage of members elected for the first time during seven parliamentary elections after independence was 44.3 percent. This substantial rate of turnover was accompanied by changes in occupational patterns among the members. From 1943 to 1964, there was a noticeable decline in the number of landowners and lawyers, and a rise in the number of businessmen and professionals.[16]

[12]Kerr, "Political Decision-Making," pp. 202–203; Smock and Smock, *Politics of Pluralism,* p. 116.

[13]Hurewitz, *Middle East Politics,* p. 383; Smock and Smock, *Politics of Pluralism,* pp. 118–120.

[14]Smock and Smock, *Politics of Pluralism,* p. 142.

[15]Hurewitz, *Middle East Politics,* pp. 382–383; Michael Suleiman, "Lebanon," in *Governments and Politics of the Contemporary Middle East,* ed. Tareq Ismael (Homewood, Ill.: Dorsey Press, 1970), pp. 238–239.

[16]Iliya Harik, "The Ethnic Revolution and Political Integration in the Middle East," *International Journal of Middle East Studies* 3 (July 1972): 320–321.

Political parties did not play a significant role in Parliament, with only 39 percent of the members of the Chamber identifying themselves as party members in 1972.[17] Each of the seventeen political parties in Lebanon was identified predominantly with one or two religious communities. Even parties casting their goals in ideological terms were confessional in composition, despite insistence that their membership was open.[18] Among the electorate, only 11 percent of the respondents in one survey were members of political parties. Whereas 32 percent supported a political party, the remaining 57 percent were neither party members nor supporters.[19]

Nevertheless, some parties lacking parliamentary influence had significant popular backing. A notable example was the Progressive Socialist Party (PSP), founded in 1949 by Kamal Junbalat. Despite its sweeping socialist, anti-establishment program, the party commanded small formal membership and had only ten deputies in Parliament. As a regional-sectarian grouping, however, the PSP and its leaders could count on strong loyalties among the Druze of the Shuf, who had lent their allegiance to the Junbalat clan for three or four centuries. The traditional clout of a feudal *za'im* coupled with the modern appeal of an anti-establishment politician lent Junbalat stature far beyond the influence of his party in Parliament.

There were also popular clandestine or semi-clandestine parties, such as the pro-Syrian and pro-Iraqi wings of the Ba'th Party and the Communists. Arab nationalist clubs and societies were officially beyond the pale, although Nasirist groups informally achieved a measure of tolerance. Finally, the Syrian Social Nationalist Party (mentioned in Chapter 2) was driven underground but continued to call for a Syrian-led union of the Fertile Crescent. Many clandestine parties were transnational in their aspirations, calling for the integration of Lebanon into a larger regional entity.[20]

Overall, the impact of political parties in Lebanon was fragmentary and divisive rather than integrative. The association of parties with sectarian groups reinforced both interconfessional and intraconfessional tensions. Lebanese parties were certainly not

[17]Smock and Smock, *Politics of Pluralism*, p. 121.

[18]Suleiman, "Lebanon," pp. 238–239.

[19]Smock and Smock, *Politics of Pluralism*, p. 121.

[20]Hurewitz, *Middle East Politics*, p. 383; Smock and Smock, *Politics of Pluralism*, pp. 123, 125.

agents of nation-building, like the Ba'th party in Syria, which became a legitimating agent for the regime, transcending sectarian identification.

Indecisiveness in the legislative branch of Lebanese government was paralleled in the Cabinet. When forming a Cabinet, the President selected members who balanced each other along several dimensions, foremost among them religious sect. Custom dictated appointment of an equal number of Maronites and Sunnis and a minimum of one representative of each of the other major confessions (Shi'is, Greek Orthodox, Greek Catholics, and Druze). The President also sought a balanced distribution among geographic regions, political parties, and ideological persuasions. The variety of relevant criteria made it easier to tolerate a troublesome Cabinet minister than to replace him, since a general reshuffling might be required to restore the overall balance. Despite this incentive for inertia, the average life span of Lebanese Cabinets was less than eight months. This ostensibly unstable situation was tempered by the high level of carryover in membership from one Cabinet to the next, since the inner circle of eligible members in Parliament (known as *mustawzirun*) was usually confined to bloc leaders or family notables whose identity was predictable. Cabinet ministers had little incentive to temper their differences on issues of policy, since each minister sought to retain credibility with his own clientele. Small wonder, then, that the Cabinet was the political institution in which immobilism was most conspicuous.[21]

If anyone had the wherewithal to exert decisive leadership, overriding the tendency toward immobilism in the Lebanese system, it was the President, whose role in appointing or dismissing the Prime Minister and Cabinet members enabled him to strive for a loyal administrative hierarchy and a subservient parliamentary majority. Only he, optimally in cooperation with his Prime Minister, could speak as a national leader transcending societal divisions and seeking intercommunal consensus. However, there were built-in constraints on the President's capacity for leadership. The fact that he was invariably a Maronite identified him as the spokesman of a single confession, suspect to other confessional groups. More-

---

[21]Kerr, "Political Decision-Making," pp. 192–200; Hurewitz, *Middle East Politics,* pp. 383–384; Smock and Smock, *Politics of Pluralism,* p. 113.

over, the President was constitutionally limited to a single six-year term of office, automatically giving him a "lame duck" image.[22]

In sharp contrast to the pivotal role of the Army in Syria, Lebanon's Army had no official political role and was intentionally kept small. The function foreseen for the Army was to serve as a neutral force, able to check any faction seeking to threaten the status quo. However, the logic of Lebanon's constitutional arrangements negated the creation of a superior force able to impose order in the face of determined opposition. Lebanon's annual security budget was estimated at only 2.2 percent of Gross National Product in 1956 and 3.3 percent in 1965. Its Army was less than one-fourth the size of the Jordanian Army, the next smallest in the Fertile Crescent. This "toy army" was simply not equipped for an external defense role.[23]

The Lebanese Army's domestic role was demonstrated during national elections, which as a rule were staggered over four successive Sundays so that adequate forces would be available if anything went amiss. Men were accustomed to go to the polls armed, and violent incidents were frequent. In the 1958 Lebanese Civil War (discussed below), the Army was successfully used as a buffer between contending domestic factions.

As a career army, the Lebanese Army depended entirely on the recruitment of volunteers. Attempts were made to recruit on a proportional basis among the confessional groups; and a rough balance was achieved among the Army's 10,000 men and approximately 200 officers by the eve of the 1958 Civil War. However, discrepancies in socioeconomic standing dictated that fewer members of the generally more prosperous Christian communities would enlist in the ranks every year. As a result, the number of Muslims recruited progressively grew, especially among deprived members of the Shi'i community. In the officer corps, by contrast, the Army command was disproportionately Christian, especially in the highest slots. The position of Commander of the Armed Forces was reserved for a Maronite, although the Cabinet position

[22]Hurewitz, *Middle East Politics*, pp. 380–384, 390; Kerr, "Political Decision-Making," pp. 203–204; Smock and Smock, *Politics of Pluralism*, pp. 110–111.

[23]Hurewitz, *Middle East Politics*, p. 391; Joseph A. Kechichian, "The Lebanese Army: Capabilities and Challenges in the 1980s," *Conflict Quarterly* 5, 1 (Winter 1985): 16.

of Minister of Defense was usually allotted to a Druze. The heavy representation of Christians in the Army command contributed to popular perceptions that the Army was fundamentally "pro-Christian"; whereas the Internal Security Forces, with more restricted domestic police functions, were widely perceived as "pro-Sunni."

In the first decades after independence, the Army was curiously qualified to check lapses in the functioning of other political institutions. It could serve such a role, however, only so long as its neutrality was sustained. By the eve of the Civil War of 1975–76, the credibility of the Army had declined to such a point that it was widely regarded as a partisan instrument of the Maronite President and his communal supporters within the Army command.[24]

Dynamic Political Processes

The distribution of power among Lebanese political institutions was not static. Over time, occupants of positions of authority attempted to increase their capabilities at each others' expense. Those who felt deprived by the system grew bolder in their challenge.

A major watershed was demarcated by the 1958 Civil War. In this crisis, diverse sources of strain in Lebanese society briefly came to a head. When the violence ceased, many observers voiced renewed confidence in Lebanon's political system. In fact, grievances were merely temporarily suppressed, and latent discontents erupted with greater force in the 1970s.

Tracing the evolution of political institutions, we may begin with the efforts of Lebanon's first two Presidents to expand the prerogatives of their office. During the administrations of Presidents Bishara al-Khuri (1943–52) and Kamil Sham'un (1952–58), presidential powers of appointment and patronage were exploited to build loyal followings in the administration and in Parliament. Charges of corruption and nepotism leveled against the Khuri administration were raised even more vocally against his successor. By exploiting parliamentary subservience, President Khuri secured

[24]Salibi, *Crossroads* pp. 53, 95; Kechichian, "Lebanese Army," p. 16 note 10; Hurewitz, *Middle East Politics,* pp. 391–395; Smock and Smock, *Politics of Pluralism,* pp. 130–131.

passage of an amendment to the Constitution, citing special circumstances to permit his re-election. President Sham'un was unable to duplicate his predecessor's performance, because the Sunni Prime Minister refused to ask Parliament for an analogous amendment.

In each case, the President's attempt to succeed himself drew criticism from both Christians and Muslims. A coalition of sectarian leaders of both faiths opposed Khuri's manipulated re-election, precipitating a national strike and forcing his resignation. Under Sham'un, opposition by Muslim and Christian leaders included denunciation by the Maronite Patriarch, Msgr. Paul Meouchy. The depth of antagonism to Sham'un was sufficient to precipitate a civil war because the issues at stake were far more weighty. Grievances were expressed largely in sectarian terms, with Muslims protesting Christian privileges not only in the political system but also in socioeconomic status and influence over the country's foreign policy. The prospect of Sham'un's re-election therefore became an issue that the President "could not really afford to win, because the opposition could not afford to lose."[25]

The crucial role of the Army in both 1952 and 1958 has been characterized as a "coup d'état by omission." When President Khuri called on Gen. Fuad Shihab, as Army Commander, to break the national strike demanding his resignation, Shihab's refusal left Khuri with no choice but to resign. Shihab was then named Prime Minister of a caretaker cabinet, remaining in control until the Parliament elected Sham'un. In 1958, Shihab again refused presidential orders to use the Army to suppress the Muslim rebels. One leader of the rebel forces was Kamal Junbalat, heading the mountain tribesmen in the Shuf, a center of Druze settlement southeast of Beirut. Another was Rashid Karami, a leader in the predominantly Sunni northern city of Tripoli. As the rebellion grew, Shihab played the role of mediator between the government and opposition, using the Army as an instrument of police control to keep the contending factions apart.[26]

Renewed optimism about the viability of the Lebanese system was widespread when Fuad Shihab assumed the presidency at the

[25]Kerr, "Political Decision-Making," pp. 206–207.

[26]Hurewitz, *Middle East Politics*, pp. 394–395; Khalidi, *Conflict and Violence*, pp. 37–39; Kechichian, "Lebanese Army," p. 17.

end of the Civil War. His policies were generally welcomed by the Muslims of the country, whereas many Christians felt that he made too many concessions at the expense of Christian prerogatives. One hallmark of the Shihab era was the President's strict control over the Army and Internal Security Forces. Although Shihab relinquished his role as Supreme Army Commander, he continued to use his influence in the Army as a source of leverage with Lebanese politicians. The most awesome reputation was reserved for the Deuxième Bureau, or Army intelligence bureau, whose influence reached a climax under the Shihab regime.

A concentration of power in the Deuxième Bureau was intended both to avert any renewed security challenge after the Civil War and to undermine the influence of the traditional oligarchs, or *zu'ama,* who were scornfully labeled *"fromagistes,"* or cheese-eaters, by Shihab. The Deuxième Bureau established contacts with a network of Sunni neighborhood strongmen, or *qabadais,* who had risen to prominence during the 1958 crisis. The regime also sponsored the growth of the Kata'ib (or Phalangist) Party as a nationwide Maronite political organization. The party's growth, in dramatic contrast to the small clientele of other political parties, threatened Maronite *zu'ama* who cultivated clan or village loyalties.[27]

The Shihab administration strove for civil service reform, seeking to assure equitable distribution of political and administrative responsibility among confessional groups. The 1926 constitution called for proportional distribution of government employment among confessions, but this provision was neglected and by 1958 the Maronite community alone filled 50 percent of government posts. Although Shihab did not devise a strict formula for allocating positions, the principle of *munasafah,* or fifty-fifty, provided guidelines for an equal number of positions for Christian and Muslim employees.[28]

The reforms were difficult to implement, however, in part because of disparities in the number of qualified applicants from

[27]Salibi, *Crossroads* pp. 2–14; Aziz al-Azmeh, "The Progressive Forces," in *Essays on the Crisis in Lebanon,* ed. Roger Owen (London: Ithaca Press, 1976), p. 63; Khalidi, *Conflict and Violence,* pp. 39–40.

[28]Kerr, "Political Decision-Making," p. 207, Smock and Smock, *Politics of Pluralism,* pp. 125–126.

different communities. Shi'i Muslims, in particular, were disadvantaged socially and politically and were unable to assume many public offices. Slots initially allocated for Shi'is were therefore taken over by Sunnis and Druze. Disparities arose among the Christian communities as well, with the more politically aggressive Maronites continuing to outweigh representation by Greek Orthodox and other Christian groups.[29] Other efforts at political and socioeconomic reform also ran into difficulty, because established patterns of administrative corruption and inefficiency were difficult to reverse. Moreover, the antagonizing of traditional leaders by Shihabist officials fueled their unwillingness to cooperate in implementing government policy. By the time Shihab's term drew to a close, reformist momentum had abated considerably.

During the administrations of Charles Hilu (1964–70) and Sulayman Faranjiyih (1970–76), domestic Lebanese politics became increasingly polarized. One noticeable change in the Lebanese political style was a consolidiation of political blocs in electoral politics. Other changes increasingly evident by the early 1970s were challenges to the role of the Lebanese Army and the emergence for the first time of an outspoken leadership in the Shi'i community.

Charles Hilu, a protégé of Shihab with no independent political base, was widely expected to adhere as President to the *nahj,* or method, as the Shihabist policies were dubbed. Instead, he tried to avoid close identification with his mentor by cultivating links with anti-Shihabist forces. However, Christian anti-Shihabists were eager to unify their ranks in opposition. In the 1968 parliamentary elections, the *hilf al-thulathi,* or Triple Alliance, was formed between three major Christian parties. The *hilf* included the growing Kata'ib Party, led by Pierre al-Jumayyil; the National Liberal Party under former President Kamil Sham'un; and the National Bloc sponsored by Raymun Iddih (Éddé). The coordinated effort paid off, and members of the *hilf* won a significant number of parliamentary seats at the expense of advocates of the *nahj.* In the 1970 presidential elections, the *hilf* selected as its candidate Sulayman Faranjiyih, a member of one of the leading clans of Zgharta, near Tripoli. He won by a margin of one vote over the Shihabist candidate, Iliyas Sarkis.[30]

[29]Salibi, *Crossroads,* p. 18.
[30]Ibid., pp. 22–23, 35–36, 47–51; Khalidi, *Conflict and Violence,* pp. 41–42.

Another move toward consolidation of political blocs was the establishment in 1969 by Kamal Junbalat of the Lebanese National Movement (LNM), a coalition of leftist and radical parties including his own Progressive Socialist Party. The LNM demanded thorough deconfessionalization of the Lebanese system, challenging the underlying rationale of the National Pact. In the 1972 parliamentary elections, an electoral coalition sponsored by Junbalat did not fare well against traditional *zu'ama* backing President Faranjiyih. LNM candidates attributed their losses to the Lebanese electoral system, which was in need of fundamental reform. They suggested that the sectarian distribution of seats in the Chamber should be abolished in favor of "social" or "popular" representation across sectarian lines. Other demands of the National Movement included an end to the principle of confessionalism in government employment; an amendment of the Constitution to redefine the division of responsibility among members of the executive branch; and a reorganization of the Army. In addition, the LNM called for removal of restrictions on naturalization, which made it impossible for members of some communities long resident in Lebanon to attain citizenship.[31]

Spokesmen of the Sunni Muslim establishment also demanded full participation by all confessional communities in Lebanese politics. However, Sunni leaders such as Sa'ib Salam, Rashid Karami, and Amin al-'Uraysi did not object to confessionalism in principle, as did Junbalat. Instead, they called for equitable application of the terms of the National Pact to enable Muslims to get their fair share of state benefits. During the Faranjiyih administration, an "outbidding game" occurred between the Sunni leaders and the LNM. The Muslim establishment focused on the issue of *musharakah,* calling for an equitable distribution of power between the President and his Sunni Prime Minister. Rashid Karami even announced his candidacy for President for the 1976 elections, asserting that the tradition of choosing a Maronite for President was merely a custom, without basis in the Constitution. Nevertheless, among Lebanese Muslims, the LNM gained support at the expense of the traditional leadership.[32]

---

[31]Salibi, *Crossroads,* pp. 61–62, 82–83, 112–113.
[32]Khalidi, *Conflict and Violence,* pp. 42–44; Salibi, *Crossroads,* pp. 62, 83.

Whether demands for reform were cast in terms of thorough deconfessionalization or of a more equitable distribution of power, conservative Christian leaders felt threatened. Members of the *hilf,* and especially the Kata'ib Party, which by 1974 had emerged as the foremost representative of the Christian establishment position, resisted both the demands of the Sunni establishment and the LNM. Ironically, Sunni leaders themselves felt threatened by the radicals, and might have become allies of the Christian establishment, maintaining the "elite cartel" of Lebanon's consociational system. However, Christian inclinations to put up their guard against all demands that would deprive them of privileges encouraged a rapprochement between the radicals and the Muslim establishment, of which the radicals were the prime beneficiaries.[33]

Opposition political coalitions continued to mushroom under the Faranjiyih regime. Faranjiyih initially selected as Prime Minister the staunchly anti-Shihabist Sa'ib Salam, an old friend and political ally. Salam headed a Cabinet composed of young technocrats, who had the advantage of being politically "untainted" but the corresponding disadvantage of lacking political experience. After accomplishing little in carrying out their reformist promises, the technocrats were replaced at the end of eighteen months with a Cabinet chosen according to traditional oligarchic criteria. Faranjiyih's conservative policies gave rise to increased opposition, and Sa'ib Salam resigned, casting his lot with Rashid Karami as well as Raymun Iddih, a Maronite political opponent of the President. The formation of the Tripartite Coalition *(al-tahaluf al-thulathi)* between these three powerful leaders in January 1975 substantially undermined the authority of the Faranjiyih regime.[34]

The increased polarization of the early 1970s was manifested in a rising challenge to the role of the Army and Internal Security Forces. During his presidency, Charles Hilu remained heavily dependent on the Deuxième Bureau, which maintained substantial political leverage. Soon after Faranjiyih came to power, he disbanded the Shihabist intelligence network, recruiting different Army intelligence officers considered loyal but lacking experience. The new Deuxième Bureau was then confronted with rising se-

---

[33]Salibi, *Crossroads,* pp. 83–84.
[34]Khalidi, *Conflict and Violence,* p. 42; Salibi, *Crossroads,* pp. 85–86.

curity threats which it was unable to contain. By 1974–75, political assassinations, abductions, murders, and bomb explosions became almost daily occurrences.

Simultaneous with the disbanding of the Shihabist Deuxième Bureau, Faranjiyih purged the Army command, liquidating its Shihabist core. The popular respect which the Army had enjoyed began to decline as the neutrality of its command came into question. The appointment of Gen. Iskandar Ghanim, a close friend of Faranjiyih, as Army Commander in 1971 aroused suspicions that the Army might be used as a partisan instrument of the Maronite President. These suspicions were borne out, in the view of Muslim and LNM spokesmen, by the use of the Army in 1973 in clashes with Palestinian guerrillas.[35]

Discontent over the role of the Army was one grievance articulated by an increasingly articulate Shi'i community in the early 1970s. Shi'is, the largest confessional group in Southern Lebanon, became targets of Israeli raids in reprisal for Palestinian commando attacks launched from the South. A new Shi'i leadership voiced the demand for protection by the Lebanese Army against these raids. Deprived socioeconomic status and lack of significant political representation gave the Shi'i community the deepest grievance against the Lebanese confessional system, and the accumulated discontent was ripe for mobilization.

Although the Shi'is were probably the largest single religious confession in Lebanon by 1970, they had previously lacked assertive leadership. The Imam Musa al-Sadr gradually emerged as the acknowledged spiritual and political spokesman of the community. A Shi'i Muslim Higher Council was first set up in 1969, despite strenuous objections by Sunni religious leaders. Previously, a Muslim Higher Council under Sunni control was charged with representing Shi'is and Druze as well. Sunni apprehensions about the creation of a separate Shi'i Council were partially allayed when Musa al-Sadr, who was elected as its head, expressed willingness to cooperate with both Sunni and Druze leaders. Sadr, a Persian of Lebanese origin who had come to Lebanon under the Shihab regime, gained renown as the leading Shi'i jurist in the country. He cultivated contacts with Christian Lebanese as well as members

---

[35]Salibi, *Crossroads,* pp. 57, 60, 95–96; Kechichian, "Lebanese Army," p. 19.

of other Muslim groups and was instrumental in lobbying successfully for the formation of the Shi'i Council.

Musa al-Sadr, officially designated as spiritual leader of his community, then became its political spokesman as well. Demanding military protection for Southern Lebanon against Israeli raids, he organized a nationwide general strike in May 1970 to dramatize the deteriorating situation in the South. Although Musa al-Sadr realized that the Lebanese Army was incapable of rendering the desired protection, he may have raised the issue to preempt popular support for radical spokesmen. Radical parties were becoming increasingly popular in the South, and Sadr hoped to divert this popularity to himself. Moreover, he hoped to be recognized as a regional spokesman for Southern Lebanon, not only for its predominant Shi'i community.

In response to Musa al-Sadr's challenge, the Lebanese government established a Council for South Lebanon, allocating funds for new projects in the South. These efforts barely scratched the surface, however. Tens of thousands of Shi'i residents of the South were fleeing because of the escalating violence, often congregating in shantytowns on the outskirts of Beirut. Then, on 17 March 1974, Musa al-Sadr addressed a mass rally of about 75,000 Shi'is in Ba'albek (a city in the eastern Biqa' Valley), announcing the creation of the Movement of the Deprived *(harakat al-mahrumin)*.

The new movement symbolized the radicalization of Sadr's own position and struck a responsive chord within his community. Under the slogan "arms are an ornament to men," Sadr declared his intention to set up training camps in the Biqa' Valley for Shi'is to defend their homes in the South against Israel. He threatened to march on Beirut with his followers, who would squat in the mansions of the affluent—Christian and Muslim alike. In sweeping terms, he attacked the Lebanese establishment as corrupt, oligarchic, and socially insensitive.

In mobilizing the Shi'i community and espousing the cause of social justice, Musa al-Sadr fed into a wave of discontent surging throughout Lebanon. Like the Sunnis, Shi'i Muslims were disillusioned with the traditional oligarchs of their community, and Sadr gave them a compelling cause to embrace. His success lent added strength to the Lebanese National Movement and to the Palestinian guerrillas, who were gratified by his accusing the Lebanese authorities, rather than the guerrillas, of responsibility for the distress in the South.[36]

Socioeconomic Disparities

The deprived status of the Shi'i community exemplified the overlap of vertical and horizontal cleavages in Lebanese society. The ascriptive (vertical) status of membership in the Shi'i confession was associated with the class (horizontal) status of socioeconomic disadvantage and further reinforced by regional concentration in the poorest part of the country. This presents a striking parallel to the intersection of communal, class, and regional identifications in Syria. An analogy may be drawn between the Shi'is' status in Lebanon and that of the 'Alawis in Syria before they rose to prominence in the ruling elite. The 'Alawis were among the poorest Syrians and were concentrated in the Ladhaqiyyah region. They lacked national political influence before rising through the Army to elite positions, just as Lebanese Shi'is lacked a leader of national stature prior to Musa al-Sadr.

The overlap of vertical and horizontal cleavages in society does not necessarily stimulate strong class consciousness; indeed, the opposite may occur. If ethnic or other vertical cleavages are the most important societal divisions, ethnicity may shape ideological orientation. When ethnic groups participate unevenly in modernization, "some ethnic communities include a full catalog of class distinctions; in other instances, the majority of a community's members fall into a single class category." In such a case, class consciousness cutting across communal lines remains muted, and social action based on socioeconomic grievances is difficult to mobilize and sustain.[37]

In Lebanon, vertical identifications remained paramount even after consciousness of social disparities was stimulated by rapid modernization. A high rate of urbanization began in the 1950s, and by the early 1970s, 58 percent of Lebanese lived in cities of

[36]Ibid., pp. 62–64, 78–79; Khalidi, *Conflict and Violence*, p. 42; Smock and Smock, *Politics of Pluralism*, p. 141.

[37]Cynthia Enloe, *Ethnic Conflict and Political Development* (Boston: Little, Brown, 1973), pp. 27–28, 36–37.

over 10,000 people. Beirut and its suburbs alone contained 45 percent of Lebanese citizens. Fifty-two percent of Lebanese had, by the early 1970s, migrated at least once in their lifetimes. Patterns of migration varied from one community to another. Substantial Christian migration occurred from villages to cities, including moves by Maronite peasants from northern Lebanon to Tripoli, and from central and Southern Lebanon to Beirut and Sidon. The growth of Shi'i suburbs, especially around Beirut, became increasingly pronounced after violence erupted in Southern Lebanon in the early 1970s.

Movement to multiconfessional urban centers did not necessarily decrease sectarian identifications. When villagers arrived in a city such as Beirut or Tripoli, their sectarian group often provided a major social network, determining their residential patterns, providing mutual assistance, and creating avenues of political participation. Certain groups developed strong ties in urban areas, such as the contacts between Palestinian refugees, most of whom were Sunni Muslim, and Muslim slum-dwellers in Beirut and other cities.[38]

Measured by conventional indicators of modernization, Lebanon's record was impressive on a national scale. In addition to rapid urbanization, the country could boast a literacy rate of over 75 percent by 1965. Its flourishing private enterprise system experienced dramatic economic growth, boasting the highest per capita income in the Arab world (estimated at $375 in 1965) despite being an oil-poor country.[39]

However, in terms of distribution of wealth, Lebanon's modernization was extremely uneven. Economic status and educational achievement varied widely among sects, with Christians as a whole faring better than Muslims. Moreover, overall Christian-Muslim dichotomies are misleading. For example, the extremely depressed condition of the Shi'is skews generalizations about the status of Muslims in general. Sunnis, by contrast, compared favorably in their circumstances with several Christian communities.

A study released by the Lebanese Ministry of Planning in 1961 substantiated Lebanon's extremely unbalanced regional develop-

---

[38]Salibi, *Crossroads,* pp. 7–10; Smock and Smock, *Politics of Pluralism,* pp. 92–93.

[39]Hurewitz, *Middle East Politics,* pp. 379–380.

ment. The study by the IRFED mission (an acronym for the Institut International de Recherche et de Formation en rue du Développement intégral et harmonisée) also reveals rough sectarian disparities, because communal groups often predominated in certain regions. Seventy percent of the localities in the central zone, including Beirut and Mount Lebanon, were classified as developed and only 5 percent as underdeveloped. By contrast, 46 percent of localities in the north were considered nondeveloped or underdeveloped, as were 35 percent of localities in the eastern Biqa' Valley and 30 percent in the South. The fact that Beirut and the Mountain ranked far ahead of the peripheral areas on every indicator of modernization fed sectarian grievances, since the peripheral areas were primarily Muslim and had only been incorporated into Lebanon since 1920.[40]

Nor were communal cleavages tempered by the growth of national occupational associations. Labor unions and professional organizations fostered ties across sectarian groups, but only in compartmentalized spheres of activity. Trade unions, for example, strove through the early 1970s to improve working conditions within the existing economic and social system, avoiding broader political issues. Professional associations were frequently dominated by Christians, mirroring all too well the conditions in society at large. The weak role of national associations was merely one indicator of a lack of significant class consciousness and class solidarities in Lebanon.[41]

Shortcomings in government provision of services to deprived sectors of society fed into sectarian grievances because of the overlap of vertical and horizontal cleavages. The government did sponsor public works and other social programs and the level of spending for these projects rose in the years after independence. However, a lack of systematic national planning combined with inefficient administration and pervasive corruption undermined the programs' impact. Entrenched commercial and landowning interests represented in the political elite guarded vested interests by obstructing any activist social programs.[42]

[40]Smock and Smock, *Politics of Pluralism,* pp. 96–98; Hudson, "Democracy and Social Mobilization," p. 256.

[41]Smock and Smock, *Politics of Pluralism,* pp. 99–103.

[42]Kerr, "Political Decision-Making," p. 210.

Muslim spokesmen complained repeatedly before the 1958 Civil War about the government's failure to administer a census since 1932. Lebanon's population had almost doubled since then, rising from the census's figure of 793,426 to an estimated 1,411,000 in 1956. Muslims, whose birth rate substantially exceeded that of Christians, were convinced that their proportion of the population had increased significantly. They wanted the government to modify the distribution of both political privilege and socioeconomic benefits accordingly.[43]

Socioeconomic grievances were a major source of rebel discontent in the 1958 war, although this discontent was channeled through sectarian groupings. Fuad Shihab recognized this social distress, and he launched ambitious projects designed to raise living standards in deprived Muslim areas. However, the plans proved impossible to implement in the face of administrative corruption and resistance from the traditional oligarchs who felt so threatened by Shihab's regime. After raising popular expectations, the Shihab regime's inability to fulfill them aroused more discontent than before.

A brief attempt at reformist policies at the outset of the Faranjiyih regime also ended in failure. The young technocrats of the Cabinet appointed in 1970 met firm opposition from the country's bourgeoisie, especially the business establishment, and from conservative interests in the political establishment. Faranjiyih's second cabinet simply canceled the ambitious projects. By 1972 the country, "despairing of the possibility of reform, was beginning to sink into an atmosphere of intense cynicism the likes of which had never before been experienced."[44]

Beginning in 1973, Lebanon experienced a rising wave of social dislocation and popular unrest. An increasingly high rate of inflation and conspicuous evidence of political and administrative corruption sparked labor demands and contributed to student activism. A student strike in Beirut soon after the October 1973 War over the possibility of an Arab political settlement with Israel was promptly followed by violent student demonstrations in Tripoli over the high cost of living as well as by student strikes and dem-

[43]Khalidi, "Conflict and Violence," p. 38, n. 32.
[44]Salibi, *Crossroads,* pp. 19–20, 55–61; see also Khalidi, *Conflict and Violence,* p. 39.

onstrations in other parts of the country. Coordination arose between student and labor protesters. Labor strikes in Beirut in January 1974 were followed in February by strikes of both students and workers over the high cost of living in Beirut, Sidon, and Tyre. Sporadic student unrest continued until the end of the academic year. The government's response was inconsistent, sometimes relying on the use of force and sometimes promising concessions which proved difficult or impossible to put into effect.[45]

One result of the spreading unrest was to accentuate the distance between traditional political oligarchs and their mass constituencies, especially in Muslim communities. Parties of the left held an ideological appeal for students and workers with which the *zu'ama* could not compete. Members of the Muslim establishment, who personally shared many interests with their Christian counterparts, felt increasingly pressured to embrace radical slogans demanding social justice as well as greater Lebanese support for Arab nationalist causes.[46]

Foreign Policy Orientations

Just as socioeconomic status was frequently correlated with religious sectarianism in Lebanon, so too was foreign policy orientation. From the very outset, Lebanese Muslims identified more fully with Arab nationalist ideology, whereas Lebanese Christians emphasized the country's distinctive status and its links with the West.

The differences were reflected in Lebanon's 1943 National Pact. In his speech to Parliament announcing the pact, Prime Minister Riyadh al-Sulh declared that "Lebanon is a homeland with an Arab face seeking the beneficial good from the culture of the West." This compromise language represented a middle ground between the Muslim demand for explicit reference to Lebanon as "an Arab country" and the preference of many Christians for avoiding explicit links to the Arab world. In essence, the National Pact entailed "Muslim renunciation of the aim of Arab union (their enosis com-

---

[45]Salibi, *Crossroads,* pp. 72–75.

[46]Frank Stoakes, "The Civil War in Lebanon, *World Today* 32 (January 1976): 9–10.

plex) in return for Christian renunciation of Christian (French) protection (their metropolitan complex)."[47]

Even at the time of Lebanese independence, a spectrum of foreign policy perspectives could be identified, varying from total identification with Arab nationalism to total identification with the West. Each of these views was primarily associated with certain sectarian communities. At one end of the spectrum was the view that the Lebanese were merely a branch of the Arab people, and that Lebanon possessed no distinctive mission of its own. A second view argued that although Lebanon should not have a special mission, it was burdened by history with a distinctive character that had to be overcome to perform its Arab role. Advocates of both views predominated in the Sunni, Druze, and Greek Orthodox communities. A third view was embraced by members of diverse sects who were suspicious of Sunni Muslim ambitions to gain dominant status in Lebanon. They held that Lebanon should have a special function, but in the limited sense of providing asylum for those who suffer discrimination in neighboring countries based on religious loyalties or racial origins.

Moving closer to the pro-Western end of the spectrum was a view held by Christians influenced by Arab nationalism but strongly tied to their religious roots. They believed that Lebanon should serve as a center from which Christian and, more generally, Western influences would be dispersed through the Arab world. Lebanon would therefore identify as an Arab country, but would expect special treatment and status among its neighbors. It would seek Western assistance, but avoid becoming a Western client ostracized by other Arab states. Finally, a position held primarily by Maronite Christians was that since Lebanon was largely Christian and more advanced than the surrounding countries, it should become a full participant in the Western Christian world, avoiding political association with the Arab world, although cultivating friendly ties.[48]

Major discrepancies in attitudes toward foreign policy persisted in the decades after independence. A survey taken in the early 1970s asked Lebanese to identify the country with which they had

---

[47]Khalidi, *Conflict and Violence,* p. 36.
[48]Hourani, *Syria and Lebanon,* pp. 132–135.

the most in common. Of the Muslim respondents, 40 percent mentioned Syria or another Arab state; whereas only 18 percent of the Christians mentioned an Arab country, with most mentioning European countries such as France or Switzerland. When confronted with proposals for political integration with other Arab states, Christians expressed deep fear of being consigned to minority status, whereas Sunni Muslims were most enthusiastic about such proposals because they would be identified with the majority community.[49]

The excitement generated by moves toward Arab unity under the leadership of Egyptian President Gamal 'Abd al-Nasir had a galvanizing effect on many Lebanese Muslims. The formation of the United Arab Republic between Egypt and Syria in February 1958 aroused Arab nationalist identifications that fueled Muslim discontent with Lebanon's Christian-dominated political system in the Civil War several months later.

Muslim sensitivities were jarred by President Kamil Sham'un's anti-Nasirist stands during the period of President Nasir's growing popularity. When Nasir led Arab opposition to the Western-sponsored Baghdad Pact of 1955, Sham'un offered to mediate between Egypt and Iraq, which had signed the Pact. The proposal was greeted with scorn by Egypt and its Syrian and Saudi Arabian sympathizers, who alleged that Sham'un secretly favored "defectionist" Iraq. Then, the Suez Crisis of 1956 precipitated a clash between Sham'un and his Sunni Prime Minister, who advocated diplomatic action in support of Egypt's position. Instead, Sham'un named a new cabinet that refused to join other Arab League members in breaking diplomatic relations with Britain and France because of their attack on Egypt. Shortly thereafter, in 1957, Sham'un endorsed the Eisenhower Doctrine intended to contain Communism and radicalism in the Middle East, a move that was widely perceived as a violation of the neutrality implicit in the National Pact.[50]

The charismatic appeal of President Nasir was deeply felt in Lebanon and manifested in the growth of Nasirist parties. In effect, Nasir achieved direct "plebiscitary" links with the urban Muslim

---

[49]Smock and Smock, *Politics of Pluralism*, pp. 134–136, 146–147.

[50]Hurewitz, *Middle East Politics*, p. 389; Khalidi, *Conflict and Violence*, p. 38.

population, to the point of undermining the influence of traditional Muslim *zu'ama*.[51] When the United Arab Republic (UAR) was formed, Lebanese Nasirists hoped that Lebanon might eventually join in the Arab unity endeavor.

The polarization of Lebanese public opinion over foreign policy issues by the eve of the 1958 Civil War makes it clear that the war was a culmination of internal and external loads on the Lebanese political system.[52] Moreover, Syria, as the northern partner in the UAR, was accused by the Lebanese government of actively supporting rebel forces in the Civil War. In addition to broadcasts by Radio Damascus and Radio Cairo encouraging the Muslim forces, Syria was accused of smuggling arms across the border, of sending armed forces to attack Lebanese custom posts, of training rebel forces on Syrian soil, and of providing material assistance to Kamal Junbalat and other rebel leaders.[53] Lebanese Foreign Minister Charles Malik formally articulated these charges at the United Nations on 6 June 1958. However, Muslim ministers and Foreign Office officials, when asked to join the delegation lodging the complaint, refused to participate. When the fighting in Lebanon persisted, President Sham'un appealed for American assistance under the Eisenhower Doctrine, and U.S. marines landed in Beirut.[54]

The selection of Fuad Shihab as President after the Civil War enabled Lebanon to return to its earlier tradition of neutrality in foreign policy. Shihab gained Muslim support and alienated many Christians by his verbal deference to Nasir. When Syria seceded from the UAR in September 1961, Shihab withheld support for the Syrian secessionist regime. However, shortly thereafter, on 31 December 1961, members of the Syrian Social Nationalist Party conspired with some young Army officers in an attempted coup d'état against Shihab. The President acted quickly to divert the coup and, with the support of Kamal Junbalat, insisted on the dissolution of the SSNP as a recognized opposition party.[55]

[51]Khalidi, *Conflict and Violence,* pp. 37–39.

[52]Hudson, "Lebanese Crisis," pp. 115–116.

[53]Conroy, "Syria and Lebanon," pp. 81–82.

[54]Hurewitz, *Middle East Politics,* pp. 389–390; Kerr, "Political Decision-Making," p. 207; Khalidi, *Conflict and Violence,* p. 38.

[55]Salibi, *Crossroads,* pp. 2–3, 11–13; Hurewitz, *Middle East Politics,* pp. 390–391; Kerr, "Political Decision-Making," pp. 207, 209.

By the mid-1960s, when efforts at Arab unity lost momentum, the new litmus test of Lebanon's Arab nationalist credentials was the degree of Lebanese support for the Palestinian cause. Since its small-scale participation in the Arab-Israel war of 1948–49, Lebanon had opted out of the Arab-Israel dispute, on the grounds of the country's military weakness and domestic divisions. Once the use of bases in Lebanon by Palestinian guerrillas increased after the June 1967 war, Lebanese governments had no choice but to address the problem. The polarizing impact of the Palestinian issue on domestic Lebanese politics will be addressed in the next chapter.

Syrian Influence in Lebanon

Syria's identification with the Palestinian Resistance Movement was a major reason for its increased political interest in Lebanon in the late 1960s. As Lebanon became a major center of guerrilla activity, Syria sought to enhance its influence over Palestinian groups operating in Lebanon.

Another Syrian political interest that gained significance in the 1970s was the cultivation of ties between the 'Alawi-dominated political elite in Syria and the Shi'i community in Lebanon. In 1973, Lebanese Shi'i religious authorities endorsed the Lebanese 'Alawis as part of their community. This act had important implications for Lebanese Shi'is, who gained confidence by identifying with the Syrian ruling group. Syria's 'Alawi rulers also gained credibility through affirmation of their Shi'i Muslim credentials. Some Syrian Muslims had cited Christian influences on 'Alawi religious practices to discredit their title to lead a Muslim-dominated state.[56]

Despite the continued absence of diplomatic ties between the two countries, Syrian-Lebanese relations improved at the official level in the 1970s. Fortuitously, the family of President Faranjiyih had close personal ties to the Asad family in Syria. Exchange of visits by senior officials began at Syria's invitation in 1970, and in January 1975 President Asad visited Beirut. A Border Commission, first established in 1967, was reactivated in 1970, and a Joint

---

[56]Rabinovich, "Limits of Military Power," p. 57.

Commission was established to resolve political and economic issues. Syria lifted transit restrictions on Lebanese goods passing through its territory and abolished the requirement for Syrians to secure travel permits if they wished to visit Lebanon. In 1974, Syria offered Lebanon military assistance against Israel.[57]

As opposed to political interests, Syrian economic interests in Lebanon declined over time. Under the French mandate, a customs union and use of a common currency by the two countries was a constant source of friction. Before independence, joint Lebanese and Syrian negotiations with France over future monetary policy ended with each going its own way. Lebanon signed an agreement with France, but Syria rejected it, after which Syria withdrew from the franc bloc and established independent exchange controls.

As for the customs union, divergent attitudes toward future economic policy made it impossible to achieve agreement. In early negotiations, Syria urged a common tariff policy to protect native industry and agricultural produce. Lebanon, eager to encourage a laissez-faire economic policy, was reluctant to agree to these measures. Moreover, the two countries' economies were basically competitive rather than complementary, removing incentives for cooperation in trade. President Bishara al-Khuri's decision to terminate the customs union in 1950, while popular with Lebanese Christians, generated tensions with Syria that required Arab League mediation. An economic agreement between the two countries in 1952 opened the the way for Syria intermittently to impose economic sanctions on Lebanon when political disagreements arose. One means was by raising the duties on goods that were shipped from Lebanon through Syria. Far more severe was the occasional closing of the Syrian border as an instrument of economic pressure against Lebanon.

By and large, however, the two economies developed in different directions. Syria's ambitious socialist schemes were repeatedly disrupted by political instability while Lebanon's private enterprise economy prospered. Lebanon was also more successful in attracting regional and other foreign capital — through its flourishing tourist industry, attraction of foreign capital to Lebanese banks,

[57]Conroy, "Syria and Lebanon," pp. 82–83.

and the growth of a transit trade of foreign goods from Lebanese ports to Iraq, Jordan, and the Gulf, as well as Syria. In addition, Lebanon provided employment to approximately 400,000 Syrian workers as of the early 1970s.[58]

Militarily, Syrian leaders were well aware of Lebanon's actual and potential significance. Both before and after the June 1967 war with Israel, Syria's line of defense was vulnerable to an Israeli force passing through Lebanese territory to attack Syria's "soft western underbelly." Syrian military planners also appreciated the potential value of Lebanon to a Syrian offensive strategy. By being able to station troops in Lebanon, Syria could activate an additional front against Israel, diverting to that front Israeli forces that otherwise might have been deployed against Syria.[59]

On the whole, therefore, Syria's interests in Lebanon increased since independence in the political sphere, remained important militarily, and declined only in the economic arena. Yet, in the words of one analyst, "[u]ntil the early 1970's, Syria was unable to acquire influence in Lebanon commensurate with the importance of its interests." In part, this was because Muslim leaders in Lebanon turned toward Egyptian President Nasir for guidance until his death in 1970. With the decline in Egypt's position as a regional power under President Anwar al-Sadat, the Asad regime strove to replace Egypt as the major regional center to which both Sunni and Shi'i politicians in Lebanon would turn for guidance and support. For instance, the Asad government sought to influence the outcome of the 1972 parliamentary elections in Lebanon as well as appointments to the Lebanese cabinet in 1973.[60]

Syrian interference in Lebanese politics was most conspicuous and most decisive, however, in sponsoring Palestinian guerrilla activities in Lebanon. Some analysts view this form of transnational influence as merely one prong in a revived "Greater Syria" strategy. They argue that Syria aspired to achieve increased influence over Lebanon, Jordan, and the Palestinian Resistance in order to

---

[58]Abdul Latif Tibawi, *A Modern History of Syria, Including Lebanon and Palestine* (London: Macmillan; New York, St. Martin's, 1969), pp. 379–380; Rabinovich, "Limits of Military Power," p. 56; Conroy, "Syria and Lebanon," pp. 80–81.

[59]Rabinovich, "Limits of Military Power," p. 57.

[60]Ibid., pp. 57–58.

advance its ambitions for regional leadership.[61] The accuracy of this assessment of Syrian policy, as well as the feasibility of pursuit of such goals by the Syrian regime, can best be evaluated by focusing on the Palestinian dimension of Syrian as well as Lebanese policy.

[61]Daniel Dishon, " 'Greater Syria': Reviving an Old Concept," in *The Syrian Arab Republic: A Handbook,* ed. Anne Sinai and Allen Pollack (New York: American Academic Association for Peace in the Middle East, 1976), pp. 83–85.

5

Palestinian
Transnational Linkages

The eruption of civil war in Lebanon as early as 1958 indicated the depth of popular grievances against the confessional system. Perhaps even in the absence of Palestinian guerrilla activities, civil strife would have occurred again by 1975. The discontent of those who were deprived by the Lebanese system had not disappeared; on the contrary, it was accentuated in the seventeen-year interval. Nevertheless, the nature and intensity of Lebanese civil strife in 1975–76 as well as the dynamics of the Syrian intervention cannot be understood without taking the Palestinian factor into account.

Writing in the Palestinian journal, *Shu'un Filastiniyyah*, Haythum al-Ayubi maintains that "the divisive factors found in the womb of Lebanese society before independence, and before the existence of the Resistance . . . were behind the tortuous split which hurt this society when the regime clashed with the Resistance. One cannot say that the Resistance caused the split, even if it was a factor which assisted in its exposure."[1] This assertion epitomizes the conclusion that the operations of the Palestinian Resistance played a catalytic, rather than a causative, role in precipitating the Lebanese Civil War.

Since the late 1960s, Palestinian guerrilla activities in Lebanon became the single most charged issue in the domestic political debate. Identification for or against the Resistance sharply polarized Lebanese politics. Guerrilla activities also encouraged intensified Syrian involvement in domestic Lebanese politics.

[1] Major Haythum al-Ayubi, "Tabi'ah al-Harb al-Lubnaniyyah" ("The Nature of the Lebanese War"), *Shu'un Filastiniyyah* no. 62 (January 1977):77. All translations from the Arabic are my own.

Palestinian Catalyst

Serving as a host to guerrilla operations is most likely to destabilize a regime whose authority structures are already weak. For this reason, both Jordan and Lebanon, whose political stability was precarious since independence, found that hosting Palestinian guerrillas had explosive domestic repercussions.[2]

For Lebanese to whom the legitimacy of the confessional system had long been questionable, support for guerrilla activities became a cause célèbre, promoting a consolidation of ranks among anti-establishment groups. For Lebanese privileged by the status quo, the Palestinian presence was a profound threat to their way of life. If the Lebanese state could not protect their interests, pro-establishment groups determined to take matters into their own hands.

Controversy over the role of the Lebanese Army became a critical focus of disagreement. Pro-establishment groups complained of the Army's weakness in meeting the challenge posed by Palestinian guerrillas to Lebanese sovereignty. The Kata'ib Party and other Maronite-dominated groups prepared their own militias for taking on the guerrillas. Anti-establishment groups, by contrast, faulted the Army with partisanship in clashing with the guerrillas rather than supporting their cause.

Much of the controversy stemmed from the problematic status of the Resistance as a transnational actor in Lebanon. The Palestinian cause is a pan-Arab cause and guerrilla organizations enjoy the support of many Arab regimes. Yet in Lebanon, the Palestinian issue also became a domestic issue, and the guerrillas became coalition partners with anti-establishment groups.

Because commitment to the Palestinian cause "has been the touchstone of true 'Arabism,' "[3] it became a symbol of the pan-Arab identification of Lebanese Muslims. For those who had long complained that Lebanon was artificially isolated from pan-Arab concerns, the Palestinian armed presence was a welcome means

[2]Fuad Jabber, "The Palestinian Resistance and Inter-Arab Politics," in William Quandt, Fuad Jabber, and Ann Mosely Lesch, *The Politics of Palestinian Nationalism* (Berkeley: University of California Press, 1973), p. 192.

[3]Ibid., p. 161.

of "Arabizing" Lebanese politics.[4] By contrast, those (primarily Christians) who were wary all along of Lebanon's Arab identification viewed the Palestinians as external intruders. Moreover, they were wary of the support received by the Palestinian organizations from other Arab regimes.

If the Palestinian Resistance had been a coherent actor, coordination with the Lebanese regime might have been more easily achieved. However, internal fragmentation was one of the most salient characteristics of the Resistance, a term connoting the loose umbrella framework for all guerrilla groups. Some guerrilla groups were circumspect about encroaching on Lebanese sovereignty; others openly embraced the slogans of Lebanese dissidents and vowed to help fulfill them. Some groups strove to maximize Palestinian autonomy vis-à-vis Arab patrons; others were identified totally with individual Arab regimes.

Syria was the Arab regime with the greatest influence over Palestinian guerrilla operations in Lebanon. Precisely because of the Palestinians' transnational status, Syrian support for the Resistance was both a lever for influencing domestic Lebanese politics and a mechanism for enhancing Syria's credentials in the Arab world.

Syrian Sponsorship of the Resistance

Syria's reputation as the prime champion of Palestinian guerrilla activities was earned long before the Lebanese Civil War of 1975–76. Syrian leaders were outspoken in their commitment to the pan-Arab goal of "liberating Palestine" from Israeli control. Although cast in purely ideological terms, Syrian support for the Resistance also reflected inter-Arab rivalries. The ongoing contest between Egypt and Syria for leadership in the Arab world decisively shaped the attitudes of each regime toward the Palestinian Resistance.

Moreover, despite unambiguous verbal declarations of support, Syrian ambivalence toward the Palestinians had been evident since guerrilla operations began in the 1960s. Sponsorship of commando operations in Jordan and Lebanon was coupled with reluctance to

[4]Hussein Sirriyyeh, "The Palestinian Armed Presence in Lebanon Since 1967," in *Essays on the Crisis in Lebanon,* ed. Roger Owen (London: Ithaca Press, 1976), p. 77.

permit operations on Syrian territory. Syria was unwilling to absorb the costs of Israeli retaliation, which might escalate into war. It was also averse to permitting autonomous Palestinian operations on Syrian soil.

In the mid-1950s, an incipient guerrilla movement was launched by Fath, a Palestinian organization operating in the Egyptian-controlled Gaza Strip. Proclaiming a doctrine of armed struggle, Fath explicitly sought to be a catalyst in drawing reluctant Arab regimes into confrontation with Israel. A decade later, in 1964, the Arab League sponsored creation of a rival organization, the Palestine Liberation Organization (PLO). Syria suspected that the PLO was an instrument to bring the Palestinian cause under Egyptian domination. In response, the regime of President Amin al-Hafiz initiated contacts with Fath's leaders.

While other Arab regimes viewed Fath's activities as "reckless adventurism" that could drag them into conflict with Israel at an inopportune time, Syria grasped the "opportunity to regain the initiative it had lost to Egypt in the Palestinian sphere."[5] However, the Hafiz regime was cautious in its support for commando, or *fida'iyyun* (fedayeen), activities. Syria encouraged al-'Asifah, the military arm of Fath, to infiltrate across the Jordanian-Israeli border rather than its own. Syria's covert, small-scale assistance was crucial, for without it "the fedayeen movement would probably have ceased to exist—temporarily, at least—in the first half of 1965."[6]

Overt support for Fath activities was offered by the left-wing Ba'th regime that came into power in Syria in February 1966, under Salah Jadid. In line with Jadid's espousal of a more determined stand against Israel, the regime officially supported a "popular war of liberation." On several occasions, Fath was permitted to launch operations from Syria's Golan Heights. However, Israel continued to attack Jordan in reprisal for guerrilla activities, regardless of their source. The cycle of guerrilla raids and Israeli reprisals escalated in early 1967, becoming a factor in triggering an Arab-Israel war (the Six Day War) in June.

From the point of view of the Resistance, even the overt support

[5]Jabber, "Palestinian Resistance," pp. 163–165.
[6]Ibid., p. 173.

of the Jadid regime was a mixed blessing. Yasir 'Arafat, Fath's leader, spent fifty-one days in a Damascus prison in 1966 after resisting Syrian attempts to assume direct control of the guerrilla movement.[7] Heavy dependence on a single Arab regime was bound to limit Palestinian autonomy, convincing Fath's leaders of the need to diversify their sources of support and to cultivate a mass popular following.

The Six Day War was a turning point for Palestinian aspirations and methods. Convinced of the futility of relying on Arab regimes to liberate Palestine, the Resistance determined to pursue on its own a heightened level of guerrilla operations. New guerrilla organizations proliferated, and a leadership struggle led to the dominance of Fath, as confirmed in a February 1969 meeting of the Palestine National Council, the legislative body of the movement. Fath thereby became the leading component of the PLO, which was reorganized as the umbrella organization of the Palestinian movement, and Yasir 'Arafat was elected chairman of the PLO Executive Committee.[8]

The proliferation of guerrilla organizations was accentuated by the efforts of various Arab regimes to influence the Resistance. In 1968, Syria created its own commando force, al-Sa'iqah, which was trained, armed, and financed by the Syrian government. Syrian leaders hoped that Sa'iqah's creation would contain the influence of other Palestinian groups in Syria. Fath, for example, did not have a significant influence in Syria once Sa'iqah was created and was obliged to move its training camps to Jordan.

Syria was even less hospitable to the Popular Front for the Liberation of Palestine (PFLP), which evolved from the Arab Nationalist Movement (ANM) of the 1950s. Blending in its ideology Marxism and 'Abd al-Nasir's doctrines of Arab unity, the PFLP called for social revolution throughout the Arab world as a prerequisite to the liberation of Palestine. In 1968, the group's leader, Georges Habash, spent seven months in Syrian jails, accused of plotting to topple the regime. In internal PLO debates, Fath could generally count on Sa'iqah's support in its struggle for leadership

[7]Ibid., p. 169.

[8]William Quandt, "Political and Military Dimensions of Contemporary Palestinian Nationalism," in Quandt, Jabber, and Lesch, *Politics of Palestinian Nationalism*, pp. 56–58.

against the PFLP. Sa'iqah upheld Fath's contention that the liberation of Palestine must precede the settling of ideological quarrels in the Arab world.

The creation and expansion of Sa'iqah also reflected an internal power struggle in the Syrian regime. Since mid-1968, the ruling civilian wing of the Ba'th Party under Salah Jadid was challenged by the military wing of the party under Defense Minister Hafiz al-Asad. By sponsoring expansion of Sa'iqah into a major organization of several thousand combatants in 1969, Jadid hoped to counterbalance the military's support for Asad. The latter, in turn, developed close ties to the leaders of the Palestine Liberation Army (the official military arm of the PLO) stationed in Syria.[9]

During 1968–69, the Resistance as a whole became less dependent on Syrian sponsorship, because of its increased freedom of movement on the Jordanian East Bank. However, the Resistance believed that "its actual *secure* base has always been in Syria, where such stronghold has taken a political rather than a territorial form." Guerrilla leaders realized that the regimes in Jordan and Lebanon, whose legitimacy was precarious, might view Palestinian operations as too threatening. Syria, by contrast, seemed to be a reliable sanctuary from Arab threats, as well as a vital source of supplies and a rear base.[10] Syria also sponsored Sa'iqah operations in Southern Lebanon, where by the end of 1969 Sa'iqah was the fastest-growing guerrilla organization.[11]

Lebanon: Reluctant Host

In seeking secure bases for guerrilla operations against Israel after the 1967 war, the Palestinian leadership adopted three criteria. The optimal host state would provide proximity to enemy territory, autonomous control of operations, and a large Palestinian population assuring a cushion of popular support.[12]

By these criteria, the East Bank of the Jordan was the guerrilla's first choice, and Southern Lebanon the second. Proximity to the

[9]Ibid., pp. 64–65; Jabber, "Palestinian Resistance," pp. 180–183, 194–195.
[10]Jabber, "Palestinian Resistance," p. 191.
[11]Quandt, "Political and Military Dimensions," p. 65.
[12]Jabber, "Palestinian Resistance," p. 190.

Israeli-occupied West Bank was best achieved along the lengthy border with Jordan, whereas Southern Lebanon had a shorter frontier with Israel that was well suited topographically to guerrilla activity. Neither host state would willingly allow autonomy for guerrilla activities. From 1968 to 1970, however, Jordan felt obliged to permit substantial autonomy, and the inability of Lebanese authorities to restrain the guerrillas ultimately allowed them even greater freedom in Lebanon. The third criterion, however, branded Jordan as a favored base. Whereas Jordan's Palestinian majority could be counted on by guerrillas for popular support, there was no reliable constituency in Lebanon. Anti-establishment political groups embraced the Palestinian cause, but the civilian population absorbing the costs of guerrilla operations became disenchanted with their presence.

The Palestinian presence in Lebanon originated with the first Arab-Israel war, in 1948. The influx of about 142,000 Palestinian refugees after that war, increasing the country's population by 10 percent, threatened to disrupt Lebanon's delicate confessional balance. Since about 90 percent of the refugees were Muslim, they could undermine the fiction of a persistent Christian majority. This is one reason they were not enfranchised. The majority were not integrated into the country's economy and were distributed among Lebanon's seventeen refugee camps.[13] Even when a segment of the Palestinian community was radicalized in subsequent years, most remained civilians uninvolved in guerrilla operations.

The destabilizing potential of the Palestinian presence in Lebanon was fleetingly evident during the 1958 Civil War. Palestinian civilians showed sympathy for the Muslim Lebanese rebels, and many participated in the fighting on an individual basis. Once order was reestablished, Lebanese authorities responded by placing the refugee camps under strict police control.

The Lebanese government was first obliged to take a position on Palestinian guerrilla activities when the Arab League created the PLO in 1964. Lebanon voted for the establishment of the PLO, but insisted that its military arm, the Palestine Liberation Army (PLA), could have no bases in Lebanon. Any Palestinian resident of Lebanon who wanted to join the PLA could do so only by

[13]Sirriyyeh, "Palestinian Armed Presence," p. 77.

leaving the country and renouncing the right to return. Lebanese authorities were concerned not only about Palestinian activities, but also about arousing the pan-Arab sentiments of Muslim Lebanese. The Lebanese Army was instructed to arrest any armed Palestinian trying to infiltrate across the border into Israel.[14]

Palestinian spokesman Haythum al-Ayubi explains that there was a fundamental and enduring contradiction between the perspectives of the Palestinian Resistance and the Lebanese authorities. The Palestinian strategy, seeking "the heating up of the region" with the goal of precipitating a war for the liberation of Palestine, was "an offensive strategy by nature." By contrast, the official Lebanese strategy was "defensive by nature," and based on "the absence of a link between domestic security and pan-Arab security, and satisfaction with self-preservation." As a result, although Palestinian guerrillas believed that they had an intrinsic right to pursue operations in any Arab land, the Lebanese regime "considered the Palestinians to be guests on Lebanese soil," subject to the rules imposed by Lebanese authorities.

The pretext used by Lebanese authorities for withholding support for guerrilla operations, Ayubi asserts, was Lebanon's military weakness. The rationale of the Lebanese authorities was that other Arab states, much stronger than Lebanon, had been unable to resist Israel in the June 1967 war. Therefore,

> the Resistance must limit its actions against Israel so that Israel would not use this as a pretext to realize its ambitions in Lebanon, especially since the Lebanese armed forces are too small to be able to prevent the Zionists from doing so. The strengthening of these [armed] forces would cost big sums and would weaken Lebanon rather than strengthening it, because it would be transformed into a confrontation state, and this would put it face to face with a power that it is unable to resist.[15]

Despite the lack of official sanction, guerrillas began to use Southern Lebanon as a major base for operations against Israel in October 1968. The Palestinian leadership recognized the need for

[14]Kamal Salibi, *Crossroads to Civil War* (Delmar, N.Y.: Caravan, 1976), pp. 9–10, 25–28.

[15]Ayubi, "Tabi'ah al-Harb," pp. 71–72.

a second major base in view of Israeli measures to obstruct infiltration across the Jordan River. Throughout 1968, Syrian authorities assisted the PLO leadership in establishing commando bases in Southern Lebanon, and developed special lines of supply connecting these bases with Syria. Simultaneously, political and organizational activities were extended by the Resistance to refugee camps on the outskirts of major cities. Refugee camps were gradually turned into "fortified arsenals," and increasing numbers of young Palestinians were trained for commando operations.[16]

What was the attitude of the Lebanese population toward guerrilla activism? Surveys showed that sectarian identification was the determining factor in Lebanese attitudes toward the Resistance. The average Muslim in Lebanon saw the Palestinian guerrilla presence as a form of security, believing that "[t]o let down the Palestinians . . . was tantamount to letting down the Muslim Lebanese cause."[17] A November 1969 public opinion poll showed that 85 percent of the Lebanese public favored commando operations in general, although only 62 percent supported operations from Lebanese territory.[18] For many Lebanese, identification with the Palestinian cause became a symbol of opposition to the Lebanese "establishment." Discontent with the regime derived from an assortment of grievances, but "the advent of the Palestinians upon the scene . . . [provided] a vividly visible symbol around which political positions aligned themselves."[19]

The community most directly affected by commando activities, however, became progressively less enthusiastic in its support. By setting up bases in Southern Lebanon, "the fedayeen broke one of their own rules." Almost no Palestinians lived in the border areas, where the majority of the population were impoverished Shi'i Muslims. Although initially sympathetic to guerrilla activities, the Shi'is became enraged when their villages were repeated targets of systematic Israeli retaliation. In January 1970, residents of the southern town of Nabatiyyah burned down an office belonging to Sa'iqah. Demonstrations were staged in several other towns to

[16]Salibi, *Crossroads*, p. 34.

[17]Ibid., p. 54.

[18]Jabber, "Palestinian Resistance," p. 193.

[19]Aziz al-Azmeh, "The Progressive Forces," in *Essays on the Crisis in Lebanon*, ed. Roger Owen (London: Ithaca Press, 1976), p. 65.

protest the commando presence. By July 1970, officials estimated that close to 23,000 southerners had fled to the Lebanese interior, causing widespread social dislocation.[20]

On a political level, the groups most threatened by the guerrilla presence were the traditional Maronite leaders and their constituencies. In their view, the Palestinian guerrillas were an intrusive group with no legitimate place in the Lebanese context. The guerrillas, rather than Israel, were held responsible for the dislocation caused by reprisals against Lebanese territory. Moreover, many Maronites felt "that the esteem in which most of the Muslim, urban, lower and middle income sectors of Lebanon held the Palestinians could only be construed as incipient treason against Lebbanon itself."[21]

The Cairo Agreement

Until 1969, Palestinian guerrilla operations in Lebanon occurred because Lebanese authorities did not have the wherewithal to prevent them. The impotence of the Lebanese state was symbolized by the weakness of its Army, which lacked the capability to prevent guerrilla infiltration.

Not all Lebanese agreed, however, that the Army should be trying to restrain the activities of the Resistance. After clashes between guerrillas and the Army in the spring of 1969, a new principle of *tansiq,* or "coordination," between the Army and the Resistance was set forth. This principle was embodied in the Cairo Agreement, the first official recognition by the Lebanese state of the legitimacy of Palestinian operations in Lebanon.

The Cairo Agreement was the outcome of a lengthy crisis, with important implications for domestic Lebanese politics as well as Lebanese-Syrian relations. The crisis was precipitated by an Israeli raid in reprisal for guerrilla attacks on Israeli civilians. On 28 December 1968, a band of Israeli commandos landed at Beirut International Airport, destroying thirteen Lebanese civilian airliners on the runways in a forty-five-minute surprise operation.

[20]Jabber, "Palestinian Resistance," pp. 190–191.
[21]Michael Hudson, "The Palestinian Factor in the Lebanese Civil War," *The Middle East Journal* 32 (Summer 1978): 267.

Protesters faulted the Lebanese Army with gross neglect of duty for not warding off the attack and voiced pent-up discontent with the Army's role in curbing Palestinian guerrilla activities. Demonstrators charged that the Army should be protecting the country against Israel, rather than restricting guerrilla operations. In the late 1960s, the Christian-dominated Army command had become increasingly determined to curb the guerrillas.[22]

The spring of 1969 witnessed a series of direct clashes between the Army and Palestinian guerrillas. In April, a Palestinian Armed Struggle Command (PASC) was formed between most of the commando organizations operating from Lebanon, Syria, and Jordan, and guerrilla activities accelerated in Southern Lebanon. On 14 April, an attempt by the Army forcibly to transfer a guerrilla emplacement set off a wave of pro-guerrilla demonstrations in several major cities. On 23 April, Lebanese security forces clashed with pro-guerrilla demonstrators, a number of whom were killed. Between May and October, violent Army-guerrilla clashes recurred in various parts of the country, especially in areas adjacent to Israel and Syria, where guerrilla bases were concentrated. Meanwhile, Palestinian organizations wrested control of all refugee camps in the country from Lebanese security forces.[23]

The atmosphere of crisis in Lebanon was intensified by official anxiety over Syrian support of the guerrillas. In an early instance of indirect intervention, Syria sent large contingents of Sa'iqah guerrilla forces into Lebanon. In May, Lebanese Army units clashed with Sa'iqah forces in the South. Clashes then recurred on a larger scale in October, and Syria announced that it was closing its frontier with Lebanon "in retaliation" for Lebanese attacks on Arab guerrillas. Two days later, Palestinian guerrillas from Syria attacked Lebanese customs and security posts on the Beirut-Damascus highway. The Lebanese Army accused Syria of supporting the guerrillas with rocket and mortar fire from across the border.[24]

Allegations that Syria was playing a provocative role in Lebanon were pressed by the Lebanese Kata'ib Party, which had become, by the late 1960s, the largest Maronite-dominated political orga-

[22]Salibi, *Crossroads*, p. 41.

[23]Ibid., pp. 39–42; Hudson, "Palestinian Factor," pp. 263–264.

[24]Naveed Ahmed, "The Lebanese Crisis: The Role of the PLO," *Pakistan Horizon* (Karachi) 29,1 (1976): 35–36; Jabber, "Palestinian Resistance," pp. 214–215.

nization in Lebanon. The party charged that Syria was inciting riots and demonstrations in Lebanon through its "infiltration," with the aim of promoting Ba'thi ideology. As Sa'iqah forces moving into Lebanon multiplied, the Kata'ib sent delegations to the Arab League and the United Nations to protest Syrian military operations. Pierre al-Jumayyil, leader of the Kata'ib Party, warned that the current crisis

> is not a Lebanese internal crisis but a difference between two independent and sovereign states in which one is openly attempting to interfere in the internal affairs of the other. The whole problem is clear; it is no longer the action of the fida'iyyun; it is our system, our regime, our institutions which are desired under the cover of the Palestinian commandos and the sacred cause of Palestine.[25]

As the events of 1969 unfolded, Lebanon experienced 214 days without a Cabinet. Immediately after the December 1968 Israeli raid on the Beirut International Airport, the Muslim Prime Minister resigned. His successor, Rashid Karami, was able to form only caretaker cabinets in the following months. Normalization was precluded by the inability of Lebanon's elites to reach consensus on the Palestinian guerrilla presence. Karami outlined two alternative options, either of which, he said, could polarize the country. The government might declare total support for commando activities in Lebanon, regardless of future consequences. Alternatively, Lebanon might insist on total elimination of commando bases and activities.

Arguing that either extreme position was unacceptable, Karami advocated the compromise principle of *tansiq*. This meant that Palestinian guerrillas and Lebanese military authorities would coordinate the scope, time, and place of commando actions against Israel. The Kata'ib initially rejected this formula, arguing for firmer restrictions on guerrilla operations. Fath also protested that the principle of *tansiq* contradicted its need for secrecy and also objected to any arrangement limiting its operations to specified portions of the country.[26]

---

[25]John Entelis, "Palestinian Revolutionism in Lebanese Politics: The Christian Response, *Muslim World* 62,4 (October 1972): 340–341.
[26]Ibid., pp. 337–348.

Only the intercession of Egypt's President Nasir achieved a truce, in November 1969, between the guerrillas and the regime. The fact that the Egyptian President was approached as a mediator between the guerrillas and the Lebanese regime reflected Nasir's widely acknowledged prestige in the Arab world. Nevertheless, in view of Syria's longstanding role as the major backer of the Resistance and its involvement in the recent crisis, excluding Syria from the negotiations was a significant omission.

The Cairo Agreement of 3 November 1969 became a vital instrument in defining the status of the Resistance in Lebanon. It was signed by Yasir 'Arafat, on behalf of the Palestinian Armed Struggle Command, and by the Lebanese Army Chief of Staff. The details of the agreement were not revealed at the time, but later became known, though subject to diverse interpretations. The accord formally embodied the principle of *tansiq,* calling for coordination between Palestinian guerrillas and the Lebanese Army.

The Cairo Agreement explicitly legitimated the Palestinian military presence in Lebanon, and in that sense was a major victory for the Resistance. However, representatives of the PASC were obliged to meet regularly with the Lebanese Army command for purposes of coordination. The PASC was to operate from fixed bases in Southern Lebanon, and the government was to exercise full sovereign rights over the area of the bases. The PASC pledged to control the actions of all members of its constituent organizations, to prevent any interference in Lebanese internal affairs.

Beyond the question of guerrilla operations in the South, the Cairo Agreement specified that Palestinian residents in Lebanon were free "to join the Palestinian revolution through armed struggle." The agreement acknowledged the right of the PASC to establish posts and armed units in the refugee camps, which had in any event already passed out of Lebanese police control. PASC command centers were also to regulate the storage of arms in the camps.[27]

[27]Itamar Rabinovich and Hanna Zamir, "Lebanon," in *Middle East Contemporary Survey,* ed. Colin Legum, Vol. I: *1976–77* (New York: Holmes and Meier, 1978), pp. 514–516; Sirriyeh, "Palestinian Armed Presence," p. 79; Salibi, *Crossroads,* pp. 42–43.

Jordanian Analogy

The Cairo Agreement resembled a series of accords concluded between the Palestinian Resistance and the Jordanian regime. The Hashimi Kingdom of Jordan was also a reluctant "host" to the guerrillas, and its armed forces also clashed with the Palestinian commandos. In Jordan, however, agreements on "coordination" were ultimately undermined when the Army decisively attacked the guerrillas and drove them out of the country. The reasons for the contrasting scenario lie both in the domestic Jordanian system and in the role of external actors.

On the surface, the Palestinian Resistance posed a more fundamental challenge to the regime in Jordan than in Lebanon. By claiming to constitute the "sole legitimate representative of the Palestinian people," the Resistance challenged the legitimacy of King Husayn's rule over the majority of Jordan's inhabitants. Palestinians comprise about two-thirds of the population of Jordan's East Bank, as well as the entire West Bank (which fell under Israel occupation in June 1967). Nevertheless, popular pressure obliged Husayn to permit guerrilla activities from Jordanian soil after the Six Day War. Intensive Israeli reprisals to these raids then undermined the regime's credibility, demonstrating Jordan's inability to respond effectively.

A series of clashes between the Resistance and the Jordanian Army in November 1968, January 1970, and June 1970 were followed by negotiated accords redefining the host-guest relationship. Critics of the Resistance charged it with establishing a "state within the state." Civil War finally erupted in September 1970, and the Resistance openly called for the King's ouster. Husayn then used the Army decisively to evict the Resistance from his Kingdom.

The strength of the Jordanian Army and its loyalty to the King was one of the major differences between regime-Resistance clashes in Jordan and Lebanon. In a ten-day encounter in "Black September" 1970, Palestinians, who constituted the majority of recruits in the Jordanian Army (although the officer corps was Beduin-dominated), obeyed orders to combat Palestinian guerrillas. A cease-fire accord negotiated in Cairo on 27 September merely ended the bloodiest phase of the fighting; clashes between guerrillas and the Army continued sporadically until the commando presence was decisively eliminated in July 1971.

Syria played an important role in the Jordanian Civil War, supporting the Resistance in its confrontation with Husayn's regime. On 19 September, the fourth day of the fighting, tanks from Syria crossed the border under the banner of the Palestine Liberation Army (PLA). The use of armored forces belied official disclaimers of direct intervention, although the PLA banner did symbolize limits to Syria's commitment. Variously estimated at sixty to three hundred tanks in strength, Syrian armored forces enabled the Resistance to withstand attacks by the Jordanian Army and to retain control of some areas in northwestern Jordan. Syria was the only Arab state to go to the assistance of the Resistance in any concrete way. By 23 September, Jordanian armor and air force units dislodged the Syrian-PLA tanks, forcing them to withdraw across the border.

The reverses suffered by the "PLA" forces reflected the partial, even half-hearted, Syrian commitment in support of the Resistance. The reason stemmed from the long-brewing rivalry between Salah Jadid and Hafiz al-Asad. Jadid, head of the civilian wing of the Ba'th Party, decided to intervene on behalf of the Resistance over the objections of Asad, his Minister of Defense. The latter insisted on a camouflaged armored intervention under PLA insignia and also refused to commit the air force, which was under his command. The ill-fated intervention brought matters to a head between the rival Syrian leaders. The coup d'état which brought Asad to the presidency on 20 November was "one of the more important side effects of the Jordanian civil war."[28]

Asad's role in discouraging open military backing for the Resistance in Jordan created an expectation that, once in power, his support for the Resistance would be more restrained than that of his predecessors. This was confirmed in the prompt improvement of Syrian relations with Jordan. Asad even offered to mediate between Husayn and the Resistance when clashes occurred in April and July 1971. The Syrian leader did, however, break relations

[28]Jabber, "Palestinian Resistance," pp. 191–192, 202–208; see also Quandt, "Political and Military Dimensions," pp. 126–127.

with 'Amman and close the border with Jordan after the King finally liquidated the guerrilla presence in Jordan.

In the Arab-Israel sphere, as well, Asad was more receptive to exploring diplomatic options than Jadid had been. In March 1972, he announced conditional acceptance of United Nations Security Council Resolution 242 (implying recognition of Israeli sovereignty), provided "the rights of the Palestinians were recognized." Moreover, Asad revamped the leadership of Sa'iqah, which had been subordinate to Jadid's control. He arrested several former leaders of the organization, replacing them with his own appointees and bringing Sa'iqah under Syrian Army command. As for the Palestine Liberation Army, which was technically accountable to the PLO, Asad had already secured an agreement making it militarily subordinate to the Syrian Army command.[29]

The Jordanian crisis abounded in repercussions and lessons for the Lebanese. On the regional level, Syria had both affirmed its commitment to the Palestinian Resistance and demonstrated the limits of that commitment. On the domestic level, the Jordanian analogy showed the importance of a strong and loyal Army in asserting sovereign control when a transnational actor exceeded its welcome as a guest. For Lebanon's weak Army, the analogy had ominous implications.

One direct outcome of the Jordanian civil strife was to drive thousands of Palestinian guerrillas who had been evicted from Jordan to join the guerrillas in Lebanon. Physically, this increased the scope of the guerrilla presence in Lebanon and the difficulty of controlling commando activities. Politically and psychologically, it increased the stakes for the guerrillas in preserving secure bases in Lebanon. Lebanon was now the only Arab country bordering Israel that permitted guerrilla operations, and the Resistance could not afford to forfeit that base.

From the guerrillas' perspective, the main question after Black September was how to avoid meeting the same fate in Lebanon. Reflecting on the Jordanian experience, Resistance spokesmen concluded that their failure to win over the mass population, both

---

[29]Mehmood Hussain, "The Palestine Liberation Movement and Arab Regimes: The Great Betrayal," *Economic and Political Weekly,* 10 November 1973, p. 2027; Kerr, "Syrian Intervention," p. 7; Quandt, "Political and Military Dimensions," pp. 129–132; Jabber, "Palestinian Resistance," pp. 208–215.

Palestinian and Jordanian, explained the King's ability to prevail. It would therefore be imperative to link up with their "natural" allies in Lebanon—the anti-establishment groups of the Lebanese National Movement—to assure mass support for their position.[30] As the attitudes of Lebanese authorities toward the Resistance became progressively more hostile, the Resistance "resorted to fortifying its camps and reinforcing its military forces and strengthening its alliances, so as to protect itself from a Lebanese strike in the Jordanian style."[31]

However, the Palestinian Resistance may have "incompletely applied" the lessons of the Jordanian Civil War. While striving to deepen their popular support in Lebanon, they did not reassure or cultivate the more flexible elements in the Maronite community. When Palestinian links to anti-establishment forces further polarized political sentiment, "Maronite opinion increasingly perceived the Palestinians as foreigners responsible for the collapse of Lebanon."[32]

Polarization and Militarization

The increased salience of the Palestinian issue in the Lebanese political debate reinforced the positions of extremist spokesmen on either end of the political spectrum. For members of the Kata'ib Party, the commando buildup in Southern Lebanon was thoroughly alarming. Kata'ib leaders only agreed to accept the 1969 Cairo Agreement for tactical reasons. The Kata'ib had been training their own militia, in anticipation of a showdown with Palestinian guerrillas in which the weak Lebanese Army could not be counted upon to assert state authority. By 1969, the Kata'ib militia was not yet prepared, in numbers and equipment, for confrontation with the guerrilla forces, and therefore accepted the Cairo Agreement on the condition that Palestinians fully respect Lebanese sovereignty. As it became clear that the Lebanese government was unable to enforce the Cairo Agreement's restrictions on commando activities, the Kata'ib militia began to take matters into its

[30]Hudson, "Palestinian Factor," pp. 265–266.
[31]Ayubi, "Tabi'ah al-Harb," p. 74.
[32]Hudson, "Palestinian Factor," p. 276.

own hands. In March 1970, for example, a clash erupted when armed Christians ambushed the funeral procession of a Palestinian commando officer being taken to Damascus for burial.[33]

Fragmentation within the Palestinian Resistance also impeded implementation of the Cairo Agreement. Although the PLO under the leadership of Yasir 'Arafat had committed itself to maintain discipline over its forces, some guerrilla organizations, such as the PFLP, did not always defer to PLO authority. Even members of Fath often engaged in trespasses under the cover of the agreement, leaving explanations to the PLO leadership.

When guerrilla operations met with escalating Israeli retaliatory actions, some Maronite spokesmen called for abolition of the Cairo Agreement. The PLO leadership vigorously objected, but agreed to compromise in implementing the agreement so long as its formal status was preserved. After a large-scale Israeli raid on the 'Arqub region of southeastern Lebanon in February 1972, 'Arafat pledged that all military operations against Israel from Lebanon would be suspended and that guerrillas would be withdrawn from specified areas. 'Arafat also took responsibility for preventing violations of the agreement by any guerrilla organizations. However, both Sa'iqah and the PFLP soon announced that they did not consider themselves bound by the agreement.[34]

In an incident reminiscent of the December 1968 airport raid, Israeli commandos landed in Beirut on 10 April 1973 and assassinated three prominent PLO leaders. As in the earlier episode, large popular demonstrations protesting the failure of the Army to forestall the Israeli raid precipitated a government crisis. Clashes then occurred between commandos and the Army. Once again, Syria infiltrated several hundred Sa'iqah militia, who crossed the border at several points and attacked Lebanese Army positions. Syria also closed its border with Lebanon and charged Lebanon with complicity in a foreign-inspired plot to liquidate the Resistance. Significantly, the Asad regime responded in this crisis the way the Jadid regime had done in 1969.

Finally, on 18 May, a new agreement was reached between Lebanese authorities and the PLO. The Malkert Agreement con-

[33]Salibi, *Crossroads,* pp. 44–46.

[34]Jabber, "Palestinian Resistance," pp. 212–213; Sirriyyeh, "Palestinian Armed Presence," pp. 79–80; Ahmed, "Lebanese Crisis," pp. 36–37.

firmed the continued validity of the Cairo accord, but spelled out and supplemented subsequent restrictions on guerrilla activities. The agreement called for the suspension of all commando operations from Lebanese territory; the prohibition of commando presence or military training in the refugee camps; and the exclusion of medium or heavy weapons from the camps. A Joint High Commission of the Lebanese Army command and the PASC was to resolve any problems or misunderstandings between the two sides.[35]

Despite formal reconciliation, enduring bitterness was generated by the May 1973 clashes. Palestinian guerrillas were now convinced that the Lebanese authorities were bent on their liquidation. Their sense of insecurity intensified after the October 1973 Arab-Israel War, when one Arab state after another joined in peacemaking efforts under American auspices. Many Palestinians feared that an Arab-Israel accord would be reached at their expense. They were further alarmed when 'Arafat and other PLO leaders seemed to be leaning toward a political solution. In the autumn of 1974, a formal split occurred in the leadership of the Resistance. The PFLP joined three small guerrilla organizations in forming the Front of Palestinian Forces Rejecting Capitulationist Settlements. The Rejectionists withdrew from the Executive Committee (the highest executive body of the PLO), while retaining membership in the Palestine National Council (the parliamentary organ).[36]

Weakened by internal divisions, yet spurred by an increasing sense of apprehension, the Resistance fortified its military position in Lebanon. By the beginning of 1975, Palestinian guerrilla groups had about 7,000 fully trained and well-armed men, plus 15,000 militia. The Resistance also strove for closer political coordination with the Lebanese National Movement, formed under the leadership of Kamal Junbalat in 1969. In cooperation with the Resistance, several groups affiliated with the LNM began to arm themselves and form their own militias.

[35]Salibi, *Crossroads,* pp. 66–69; Kerr, "Syrian Intervention," p. 7; Sirriyyeh, "Palestinian Armed Presence," pp. 80–81; Rabinovich and Zamir, "Lebanon," pp. 514–516.

[36]Israel Altman, "The Palestine Liberation Organization," in *Middle East Contemporary Survey,* ed. Legum, Vol. I: *1976–77* pp. 182–183; Salibi, *Crossroads,* pp. 69–76.

The bitterness and anxiety of the guerrillas was mirrored in the Maronite political camp. The Kata'ib justified establishment of military training camps for their militia as a reaction to the freedom granted to Palestinian guerrillas to carry arms. By the start of 1975, the membership of the Kata'ib Party rose to 80,000, including a 5,000–man, heavily armed militia supported by 20,000 irregulars.[37] Lebanon, in one analyst's words, was "turned into a powder keg with a fuse attached, and there was no telling when it would be made to explode."[38]

In April 1975, civil strife erupted in Lebanon. Syria immediately expressed concern about the fate of the Palestinian Resistance. The Syrian decision to intervene indirectly in January 1976 was aimed, at least in part, at forestalling the liquidation of the Palestinian presence in Lebanon. The Asad regime intervened initially via Palestinian guerrilla units, officially subordinate to PLO authority. Nevertheless, by June 1976, regular Syrian forces as well as Syrian-sponsored Palestinian units engaged in combat against Palestinian guerrillas in Lebanon. President Hafiz al-Asad was accused by Resistance spokesmen of perpetrating a Black September liquidation of the guerrillas reminiscent of King Husayn.

How complete a reversal was the Syrian shift of alignments in the Lebanese Civil War? The fluctuations in Syrian policy are perhaps most dramatically illustrated with respect to the Palestinian Resistance. Nevertheless, Syrian ambivalence about the guerrilla operations, and especially about the PLO's desire for autonomy, had long since been evident. When the Palestinians persisted in their alliance with the Lebanese National Movement despite Syrian objections, Syria felt obliged to bring them in line. Clearly, Syria had no intention of subordinating its broader regional objectives to the will of a transnational actor that might undermine their pursuit.

[37]*Quarterly Economic Review (QER) of Syria, Lebanon, Cyprus* (London: The Economist Intelligence Unit, 1975), 3rd quarter, p. 7; Sirriyeh, "Palestinian Armed Presence," p. 81; Salibi, *Crossroads*, pp. 54–55, 75–82.

[38]Salibi, *Crossroads*, p. 70.

III

INTERVENTION AND ESCALATION

6

Mediatory Phase

Syria's concern over the outbreak of civil strife in Lebanon in the spring of 1975 grew into an absorbing preoccupation as the Civil War progressed. Meanwhile, Syria's stakes increased as it tried to shape the outcome of the war by exercising leverage over domestic Lebanese parties and the Palestinian Resistance.

Modalities of Intervention

The modalities used by Syria to influence events in Lebanon followed a clear escalatory pattern. Syria's intervention evolved as a process with definable thresholds, corresponding to three principal phases. In the initial, mediatory phase (April to December 1975), Syria relied primarily on noncoercive, diplomatic means. In the second phase (January to May 1976), coercive means were used only indirectly, when Palestinian forces intervened in Lebanon on Syrian orders. Finally, direct intervention occurred in the third phase (June to October 1976).

The dynamics of the Syrian escalation reveal that intervention in Lebanon was an incremental process, rather than a discrete act whose intent was clearly formulated from the start. One indication of tentativeness in Syrian probes is that whereas certain modalities of intervention (i.e., diplomatic or military, direct or indirect) predominated in each phase, none of the phases was exclusively characterized by a single modality. In fact, each stage harbored signals of escalatory intent toward its successor. Conversely, mediatory attempts were never abandoned, even once direct military intervention was under way.

The decisionmaking process for Syria's intervention remains

opaque to outside observers because of the secretiveness and censorship of the regime. There is evidence, as President Asad's Adviser on Foreign Affairs, Adib al-Dawoodi, declared, that " . . . as the crisis worsened and the possibility of war increased, the evaluation process was widened and was made more rigorous."[1] However, while information on the size of the decisional unit and the identity of the participants in key Syrian decisions is revealing, the veneer of official consensus is never punctured by Syrian spokesmen. Wider consultations by President Asad may have been needed because the intervention was increasingly controversial within the elite and among the public at large, but allusions to such dissent are cryptic and rare. Therefore, in asking key questions about the Syrian intervention, it is best to counterpose official explanations with the actual record of Syrian behavior.

Was Syria's intervention invitational or penetrational? President Asad asserted in a 9 August 1978 interview:

> We entered Lebanon in response to requests and pleas for assistance, which came to us from hundreds of families, from thousands of Lebanese citizens, and from many [different] sides; and [we entered] with the approval of the legitimate authorities in Lebanon.[2]

Despite the consistent Syrian emphasis on Lebanese appeals, closer examination exhibits a complex and variable interplay between invitation and penetration. In the initial phase of the war, mediatory missions were sent essentially on the Syrian initiative, although they were generally welcomed by parties to the Lebanese strife. In January 1976, a series of overt appeals were addressed to Syria both by the Lebanese President and by members of the anti-establishment coalition. By contrast, when Syria's massive military thrust into Lebanon occurred in June 1976, it was clearly a penetrational intervention.

Should Syria be viewed as a neutral arbiter or as a partisan intervener in the Lebanese Civil War? Was Syria consistent in

---

[1]Cited in Adeed Dawisha, *Syria and the Lebanese Crisis* (New York: St. Martin's, 1980), pp. 179–180.

[2]Wadi' Skaf, ed., *Mawqifuna Min al-'Azmah al-Lubnaniyyah [Our Position Vis-à-Vis the Lebanese Crisis]* (Damascus: Institute of the Union of Studies and Consultation, 1979), p. 5.

objectives or opportunistic? Official spokesmen stress that Syria was an impartial arbiter, whose sole bias was directed "against any party which may try to destroy security and stability in Lebanon." They characterize Syria's position in Lebanon as "principled and steadfast," complaining that the position of many of the parties in Lebanon did change, but Syria's did not.[3] Well after the October 1976 cease-fire officially terminated Lebanon's Civil War, Information Minister Ahmad Iskandar Ahmad observed:

> The Syrian objectives in Lebanon today are the same as the Syrian objectives since the beginning of the Lebanese crisis, and since Syria sustained its initiatives and sacrifices to halt the slaughter between our Lebanese brothers. These objectives are the following:
>
> 1. Preventing partition—the partition of Lebanon, whatever this may necessitate by way of effort and sacrifices.
> 2. Establishing security and peace in Lebanon.
> 3. Protection of the Palestinian Resistance.
> 4. Helping our Lebanese brothers to reconstruct and develop their country.[4]

The foregoing list of objectives reflects two dominant foci of Syrian involvement in the war. In the domestic Lebanese arena, Syria was committed to averting the negative outcome of partition and to realizing the positive goals of stability and national reconciliation. With respect to the Palestinian Resistance, Syria was eager to preserve its image of champion and defender. What was the relative priority of the bilateral (Lebanese) and transnational (Palestinian) foci of Syrian policy? In Lebanon, did Syria favor the incumbents or insurgents as civil strife developed?

The record shows two distinct strands in Syrian policy and raises questions about the degree of synchronization between the two. On the diplomatic level, Syria tried to cultivate the image of an impartial arbiter throughout the Lebanese Civil War, pursuing contacts with pro- and anti-establishment Lebanese as well as the Palestinian Resistance. Syrian diplomacy consistently supported perpetuation of the Lebanese political system, with only minor institutional reforms, and preservation of the Cairo Agreement.

[3]Ibid., p. 4.
[4]Ibid., p. 24.

On the military level, however, Syria engaged in an abrupt and dramatic shift of alignments in the midst of the war. Its abandonment of traditional Palestinian and Lebanese anti-establishment allies in favor of the pro-establishment forces was a tactical maneuver. Refusing to countenance the complete victory of either coalition in the Lebanese strife, Syria broke ranks with its long-standing allies when they refused to heed its counsel.

With respect to the Palestinian Resistance, a dichotomy emerged between those factions Syria could control and those which it could not. The forces of Sa'iqah and the Palestine Liberation Army (PLA) forces based in Syria willingly carried out Syrian commands. On orders of President Asad, they first intervened in Lebanon to support the anti-establishment coalition, and subsequently fought against that same coalition, even combatting PLA units based in Lebanon! By contrast, both the PLO factions loyal to Yasir 'Arafat and the Rejectionist groups adhered to their alliance with the Lebanese insurgents against Syrian wishes. This stand infuriated the Syrian elite, prompting its military assault on the Resistance in Lebanon.

In the domestic Lebanese context, Syria's efforts during the initial, mediatory phase were directed at reviving immobilized Lebanese political institutions. When this proved difficult, Syria made several attempts at institutional innovation, sponsoring interim political bodies to resolve the crisis and restore order. Clearly, the escalation of Syria's involvement was reactive to increased polarization in the target state. As more extreme positions prevailed within the contesting Lebanese coalitions, the possibility of political compromise became more elusive. Maronites within the pro-establishment group openly sponsored partition of Lebanon and creation of a Christian mini-state; while Kamal Junbalat led the Lebanese National Movement in the call for revolutionary overthrow of the Lebanese system, rather than merely reform.

The most potent symbol—and accelerator—of Lebanese political polarization was the collapse of the Lebanese Army. From the earliest stage of the Civil War, there were signs of internal dissent in the Army, as well as challenges to its role by both individual militias and Palestinian guerrillas. Repeated disputes arose over the desirability of deploying the Army to check civil strife. The ultimate collapse of the Army in March 1976 painfully demonstrated the inability of the Lebanese state to solve its own problems. This development opened the door to deeper Syrian involvement—far deeper, indeed, than the Syrians themselves initially expected.

The complexity of tracing and analyzing the dynamics of the Syrian intervention stems from the various *axes* of ongoing conflict—Lebanese-Lebanese (subnational-subnational), Lebanese-Palestinian (subnational-transnational), Syrian-Lebanese (external-subnational), and Syrian-Palestinian (external-transnational). Although different axes of conflict were often activated simultaneously, the salience of issues and actors varied during different phases of the war. A chronological approach seems most useful in analyzing the interplay between Syrian initiatives and developments in the target state. Each of the three major phases will be further divided into brief time frames, within which developments will be treated thematically, based on the issues and actors involved.

During the initial months of the Lebanese Civil War, Syria's role was low-key, often unacknowledged, and usually played behind the scenes. Syrian diplomatic initiatives were reactive, following upon disturbing developments in Lebanon. By the end of this phase, however, Syria's diplomatic role became more conspicuous and overt and was accompanied by tentative coercive probes. Although Syrian military assistance was channeled to the Lebanese National Movement and the Palestinian Resistance, diplomatic initiatives were pointedly addressed to members of the pro-establishment coalition as well.

Socioeconomic Trigger

Syria sat on the sidelines during the early rounds of violence that sparked the Lebanese Civil War. The initial incident that triggered Lebanese civil strife was ostensibly a domestic, socioeconomic issue. The fishermen of the southern coastal city of Sidon and other coastal towns were angered when the government granted exclusive fishing rights along the coastline to the newly created Protein Company. This modern, high-technology company threatened the livelihood of a large portion of Sidon's primarily Muslim population. Resentment was exacerbated by the fact that former President Kamil Sham'un, the target of Muslim animosity during the 1958 Civil War and leader of the predominantly Maronite National Liberal Party, was Chairman of the Protein Company's board and owned a large percentage of its assets.

On 26 February 1975, the Lebanese Communist Party and other leftist parties organized a demonstration in Sidon, agitating for the revocation of the Protein Company's license. After the Army was sent in to break up the demonstration, a general strike was called by left-wing groups in Sidon and, later, in Beirut and Tripoli. Meanwhile, port workers disrupted operations along the entire Lebanese coastline, and the wave of strikes threatened to spread. Troops were sent to break up barricades around Sidon, and heavy fighting continued for several days. On 2 March, demonstrators accepted a cease-fire on the condition that the Army withdraw from the city. The Lebanese Cabinet, meeting in emergency session, arrived at a compromise proposal whereby the Protein Company would only be permitted to operate eighteen miles offshore, so as not to interfere with the small fishing boats closer to the coast.[5]

The "fisheries dispute" has been designated as the opening round of the Lebanese Civil War, marking "the point at which a significantly higher and sustained level of violence was manifested."[6] Most portentous for later developments was a controversy over the use of the Army to control civil strife. Issues raised included the appropriate channels of authority for ordering Army action; the propriety of the Army's role; and challenges posed to the Army's integrity by forebodings of internal dissent.

An intra-elite quarrel arose over authorization of Army use in the 26 February demonstration in Sidon. This decision ignored the instructions of the Sunni Prime Minister, Rashid al-Sulh. Instead,

---

[5]Kamal Salibi, *Crossroads to Civil War: Lebanon, 1958–1976* (Delmar, N.Y.: Caravan, 1976), pp. 92–93; Walid Khalidi, *Conflict and Violence in Lebanon: Confrontation in the Middle East,* Harvard Studies in International Affairs, no. 38 (Cambridge: Center for International Affairs, Harvard University, 1979), p. 44; *Quarterly Economic Review (QER) of Syria, Lebanon, Cyprus* (London: The Economist Intelligence Unit, 1975), 2nd quarter, pp. 8–9.

[6]Michael Hudson, "The Palestinian Factor in the Lebanese Civil War," *Middle East Journal* 32,3 (Summer 1978): 270.

the Maronite Army Commander, Gen. Iskandar Ghanim, assumed personal charge of the Army's conduct, maintaining contact with President Faranjiyih throughout the crisis. The Sunni establishment considered the use of the Army as an instrument of the Maronite presidency and the lack of deference to the Sunni premiership an intolerable affront. Prime Minister Sulh was faulted for having disgraced the Sunni community by accepting a slight to his authority by the Army commander. Sunni leaders demanded that he be replaced immediately by a more forceful leader.

On the substance of the Army's role, Sunni leaders complained that democratic liberties were violated when the Army fired on demonstrators in Sidon. Instead of firing on civilians, they argued, the Army should be defending Lebanon's border from Israeli raids. To assure that in the future the Army would perform its appropriate functions, they demanded a reorganization of the Army command into a Military Command Council whose membership would be equally divided between Christians and Muslims, although the commander-in-chief would still be a Maronite. The new council would then be answerable to the government as a whole, rather than to the Maronite President.

The Lebanese National Movement (LNM) joined in criticizing the use of the Army in Sidon, and Kamal Junbalat called for the immediate resignation of Chief of Staff Ghanim. However, a lack of coordination between the LNM and the Sunni establishment was evident in Junbalat's refusal to endorse their call for the Prime Minister's resignation. Instead, Junbalat persuaded other leftist leaders to support the Sulh government, presumably because he "did not wish to give his Sunni adversaries an easy political victory."[7] In the absence of a coordinated call for Prime Minister Sulh's resignation he was able to weather the storm, at least temporarily.

Meanwhile, members of the Christian establishment forcefully vindicated the Army's role in the Sidon incidents. Thousands of students joined demonstrations in support of the Army, held in predominantly Christian East Beirut. Responding to demonstrators' vilification of Muslim and leftist groups for demanding changes in the Army command, the Maronite leaders of the Kata'ib

---

[7]Salibi, *Crossroads*, p. 94.

and National Liberal parties rejected the Muslim proposal for a new Military Command Council.[8]

Hoping to defuse tensions over the Army's role, President Faranjiyih referred the issue of Army reform to a special committee for study. The government was particularly concerned by manifestations of tension within the Army in wake of the Sidon events. When Ma'ruf Sa'd, a populist Sunni leader, died on 6 March of wounds inflicted during the Sidon demonstration, intense fighting occurred between Maronite and Muslim recruits in the Lebanese Army. These clashes were an early indication of the Army's potential for internal disintegration.[9]

Controversy over the Army's role was further accentuated because of alleged participation by Palestinians in clashes with the Army. When troops were sent to remove barricades on the road to Sidon on 28 February, armed civilians who opened fire on the troops included Palestinians from the nearby camp of 'Ayn al-Hulwa. Christian political spokesmen seized on this participation as evidence of Palestinian interference in internal Lebanese affairs. They cited a coordinated Palestinian and radical plot to undermine not only the Army but the Lebanese political system as a whole. PLO leaders, however, vigorously denied any connection between the Resistance and the Sidon events.[10]

Shortly after calm was restored, Syria proposed a joint military and political command with the PLO. This suggestion, in March 1975, was presented as a sign of support for the Palestinian movement, but might alternately be viewed as an attempt to increase Syrian influence over Resistance decisions in view of recent tensions in Lebanon. Palestinian suspicions of Syrian intent surfaced when talks convened on 25 May about implementing the joint command came to naught. However, mere announcement of the proposal in March exacerbated Maronite apprehension about Syrian support for Palestinian participation in Lebanese affairs.[11]

[8]Ibid., pp. 92–94; Khalidi, *Conflict and Violence,* pp. 44–45; *QER of Syria, Lebanon,* 1975, 2nd quarter, pp. 8–9.

[9]Hudson, "Palestinian Factor," p. 270; Khalidi, *Conflict and Violence,* p. 44; *QER of Syria, Lebanon,* 1975, 2nd quarter, pp. 8–9.

[10]Salibi, *Crossroads,* pp. 92–94.

[11]Naveed Ahmed, "The Lebanese Crisis: The Role of the PLO," *Pakistan Horizon* 29:1 (1976):38; *QER of Syria, Lebanon,* 1975, 3rd quarter, p. 3.

Palestinian-Kata'ib Confrontation

The event most commonly identified with the start of the Lebanese Civil War was an outgrowth of escalating Christian-Palestinian tensions. On 13 April, men in an unidentified car fired at congregants outside a Maronite church in 'Ayn al-Rammana, a Christian suburb of Beirut. Three people, including the bodyguard of Kata'ib Party leader Pierre al-Jumayyil, were killed. In apparent retaliation, a bus filled with Palestinians from refugee camps around Beirut was ambushed later that day while passing through 'Ayn al-Rammana, and the passengers were shot. The assailants were presumed to be members of the Kata'ib Party.[12] Kata'ib-Palestinian armed clashes continued over the following weeks, despite a cease-fire agreement on 16 April.

The debate over responsibility for the 'Ayn al-Rammana incident raised the broader issue of the Palestinians' status in Lebanon. In a meeting between President Faranjiyih and Yasir 'Arafat on 14 May, the President complained that Resistance leaders had been specifically warned by the Lebanese Army to avoid driving vehicles through 'Ayn al-Rammana, so as not to offend the residents' sensitivities. He complained of repeated "excesses" by Palestinian guerrillas, attributing the most flagrant offenses to members of Rejectionist groups who refused to be bound by the Cairo Agreement.

In reply, 'Arafat emphasized that the Resistance was not "a political party in the Lebanese arena" and was determined to avoid interference in Lebanese internal affairs. He explained, however, that "we must be understood, for we are not an army in the disciplined sense, which can impose uniform behavior on all its elements." He then promised to do his best to oblige all elements of the Resistance to adhere to the Cairo Agreement.[13] 'Arafat had tried earlier to impose discipline, sending sorties of the PLO's military police to refugee camps on 15 April to restrain the Re-

---

[12]Salibi, *Crossroads,* pp. 97–98; Hussein Sirriyyeh, "The Palestinian Armed Presence in Lebanon Since 1967," in *Essays on the Crisis in Lebanon,* ed. Roger Owen (London: Ithaca Press, 1976), p. 82.

[13]Antwan Khuwayri, *Hawadith Lubnan, 1975 [The Events in Lebanon, 1975]* (Junyih: Al-Matba'ah al-Bulsiyyah, 1976), pp. 76–78.

jectionists from provocative acts. After accepting the 16 April cease-fire, he dispatched members of the Palestinian Armed Struggle Command to assist the Lebanese Security Forces in apprehending offenders.[14]

Leaders of the Resistance believed that the Kata'ib precipitated the 'Ayn al-Rammana episode to provoke the guerrillas and challenge their status in Lebanon. In a meeting with the Arab ambassadors to Lebanon on 14 April, Abu Iyad, second in command to Yasir 'Arafat in the PLO, asserted that the Resistance had exercised maximum self-restraint in recent years, despite the "invective and vituperation" of the Kata'ib. Palestinians even pursued a political dialogue with Kata'ib leaders, who then reneged on a pledge to publicize a document which said that "[t]he Resistance is not the cause of Israeli avarice and aggression." The recent events, Abu Iyad declared, were intended to spark a clash between the guerrillas and the Lebanese authorities. He expressed the hope that the Kata'ib perpetrators would be punished and order restored, but warned that if not, "we will not be responsible for the deterioration of the existing situation." Abu Iyad subsequently remarked that the Resistance had an interest in Lebanon's asserting its sovereign authority, because "with a strong state, one can reach an agreement."[15]

In view of weak Lebanese state authority, however, the Kata'ib may have had political motivations for provoking confrontation with the guerrillas at this stage. Perhaps the Kata'ib wished to prove that their cooperation was vital to any attempt to restore stability to Lebanon. By showing their capacity to bring about a breakdown of order, they wanted to convince the Muslim leadership, in particular, that they must be formally associated in power. In this respect, the Kata'ib stand had widespread support not only among Maronites, but among other Christian groups as well.[16]

The main axis of conflict in subsequent weeks continued to be Kata'ib-Palestinian. However, when violence spread after the initial 'Ayn al-Rammana outbreak, the National Liberal's militia, controlled by ex-President Kamil Sham'un, occasionally came to

[14]Ibid., pp. 31–32, 36; Sirriyyeh, "Palestinian Armed Presence," pp. 99–102; Hudson, "Palestinian Factor," p. 270.

[15]Khuwayri, *Hawdith,* pp. 23–24, 58.

[16]Salibi, *Crossroads,* pp. 98–100, 104–105.

the assistance of the Kata'ib. Exchanges in the Beirut vicinity involved the Muslim slums of al-Karantina and al-Maslakh, whose inhabitants included Sunni and Shi'i Lebanese, Kurds, and Syrian workers. Lebanese leftist parties called particular attention to the harassment of Syrian workers. Ba'thists, Nasirists, and Communists supported the Palestinians in clashes that spread from Beirut to Tripoli in the north and Sidon and Tyre in Southern Lebanon. Imam Musa al-Sadr, after meetings with Yasir 'Arafat and with the Sunni Mufti, Hasan Khalid, convened the Shi'i High Council on 19 April. The Council meeting, attended by seventy-seven influential Shi'is, declared its solidarity with the Resistance and called for fundamental political reform in Lebanon.[17]

Militiamen associated with the Lebanese National Movement also participated in clashes with the Kata'ib. The LNM's influence, however, was more decisive in the political than the military sphere. On 13 April, immediately after the 'Ayn al-Rammana incidents, a meeting of LNM leaders demanded the immediate dissolution of the Kata'ib Party and the exclusion of the two Kata'ib ministers serving on the Lebanese Cabinet. After a more broadly based LNM conference on 26 April, Junbalat declared that his front in Parliament would deny support to any government in which the Kata'ib Party participated.[18]

The significance of the LNM's measures stemmed from the history of political proscriptions in Lebanon. Since independence in 1943, individual political leaders or groups determined to avoid political dealings with each other. Never before had proscription been instituted, however, between two such broadly based groups.[19] Junbalat sought to rally political support for his stand, meeting with Raymun Iddih, the only Maronite leader who had publicly criticized the Kata'ib for the 'Ayn al-Rammana events. Instead of supporting the proscription, however, Iddih reminded Junbalat of the futility of attempts to proscribe President Sham'un during the 1958 Civil War, saying:

> In 1958, you had on your side all of the Sunni and Shi'i leaders and some of the Christian leaders, and the Maronite Patriarch himself,

[17]Khuwayri, *Hawadith*, pp. 44–45, 48; Salibi, *Crossroads*, p. 103; Dawisha, *Syria*, p. 85; *QER of Syria, Lebanon*, 1975, 3d quarter, p. 7.

[18]Salibi, *Crossroads*, pp. 98–102.

[19]Khalidi, *Conflict and Violence*, p. 47.

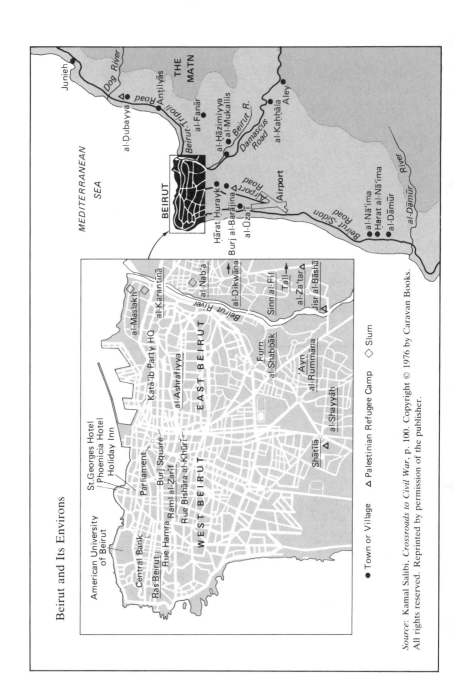

Beirut and Its Environs

Source: Kamal Salibi, *Crossroads to Civil War*, p. 100. Copyright © 1976 by Caravan Books.

● Town or Village   △ Palestinian Refugee Camp   ◇ Slum

for the act of isolating Sham'un, and despite this the isolation did not succeed. How, then, do you expect to succeed this time in isolating the Kata'ib, when you are alone?

In addition, Sunni leaders tried to discourage Junbalat from pursuing this political course, although they were reluctant to cross Junbalat by openly opposing proscription. President Faranjiyih, in turn, criticized Junbalat's stance and refused to accede to his demand for reprisals against the Kata'ib.[20]

Military Cabinet

The Cabinet crisis sparked by the proscription issue was exacerbated by further controversy over the role of the Army. In this instance, the dispute was over the nonuse of the Army, rather than its use. Both the Kata'ib and National Liberal Parties criticized the government of Prime Minister Rashid al-Sulh for not having sent in the Army during the initial clashes at 'Ayn al-Rammana. This was one justification used for Kata'ib resignation from the Cabinet, which precipitated the collapse of the Sulh government on 15 May. Sulh condemned the Kata'ib in his resignation speech and demanded either fuller Muslim participation in all levels of government or the formation of a nonsectarian government.[21]

President Faranjiyih responded to these developments in an unorthodox and unprecedented manner. On 23 May 1975, he appointed a military Cabinet under the premiership of Brig. Nur al-Din al-Rifa'i, a retired commander of the Lebanese Internal Security Forces. Rifa'i then selected the controversial Army commander Gen. Iskandar Ghanim as Minister of Defense; and all other Cabinet ministers except one were also military officers. Although the President was constitutionally authorized to designate any Sunni Muslim to form a government, subject to parliamentary approval, his move remains highly puzzling. After concurring in the partial deployment of the Army in the February fisheries dispute and then shying away from its use at 'Ayn al-Rammana, he abruptly embraced the extreme option of military

[20]Khuwayri, *Hawadith*, pp. 69–71; Salibi, *Crossroads*, pp. 105–106.
[21]*QER of Syria, Lebanon*, 1975, 3d quarter, p. 8.

government. While Faranjiyih's own political calculations are unclear, the political repercussions were unquestionably devastating. The President's move sparked a united and wide-ranging coalition in opposition, simultaneously alarming Syria sufficiently to prompt its first diplomatic initiative of the Lebanese Civil War.

Immediately after the military government was announced, a common front was established between the Lebanese National Movement and the Sunni establishment. Despite earlier disagreements between the two groups, Kamal Junbalat felt sufficiently provoked by the military government to contact Sa'ib Salam, his long-standing Sunni political rival. Cooperation with Salam was crucial because of the latter's partnership in the *tahaluf*, the tripartite alliance formed before the war between Salam, Rashid Karami (a Sunni politician), and Raymun Iddih (a Maronite politician). A joint statement was issued by the *tahaluf* and Junbalat on 24 May, expressing their determination to undermine the military Cabinet. They may have feared that the Cabinet was a first step toward full military rule, or that it was intended to groom General Ghanim as a successor to President Faranjiyih in 1976. The military Cabinet was endorsed only by Pierre Jumayyil of the Kata'ib and former President Kamil Sham'un, whose enthusiasm branded the Cabinet more starkly as an instrument of the Maronite presidency.[22]

Junbalat also made an overture toward the Palestinian Resistance, by instructing the LNM to promote cooperation with the Resistance "politically, popularly, and militarily." In one sense, the announcement of the military Cabinet deflected attention from the Palestinian role in the war, by highlighting differences among domestic Lebanese contestants. Nevertheless, the Resistance felt particularly threatened by the military Cabinet, since General Ghanim had often used the Army to curb its operations in the past. Displaying an ambivalent posture, the Resistance publicly declared its unwillingness to become involved in a domestic Lebanese matter, and asserted that it had no advance knowledge of the Cabinet's formation. Privately, however, Yasir 'Arafat initiated contacts with Egyptian President Sadat, in which he declared: "We

[22]Salibi, *Crossroads*, pp. 106–109; Khalidi, *Conflict and Violence*, p. 47; Khuwayri, *Hawadith*, p. 87.

were convinced that there was something cooking in the [Presidential] Palace, and here our apprehensions were realized." 'Arafat then alerted Syrian President Asad of the recent developments, asking his assistance in containing the situation. His overture was paralleled by Kamal Junbalat, who sent an envoy to Damascus for discussions with Syrian leaders.[23]

The Resistance had previously approached Syria when 'Arafat visited Damascus several days after the 'Ayn al-Rammana incident, on 18 April.[24] To what extent these overtures constituted an explicit request for Syrian involvement, and what type of involvement was desired, is unclear. Until the formation of the military Cabinet, Syria steered clear of public reactions to the Lebanese events, with the exception of press statements supporting the "rights of the Palestinian people." A decision by Syrian leaders on more active involvement in mid-March reflected apprehension over the formation of the military cabinet.[25] One analyst speculates that because of precedents for indirect Syrian intervention during clashes between Lebanese authorities and the Palestinian Resistance in 1969 and 1973, Syrian leaders may have felt pressured to intervene if the military Cabinet provoked similar clashes. Preferring to avoid this scenario, Syria decided to launch a diplomatic initiative instead.[26]

The decisionmakers who agreed on this approach became, in the following months, the core "ad hoc committee" for formulating Syrian policy toward Lebanon. In addition to President Hafiz al-Asad, the decisive voice on the committee, other members were Foreign Minister 'Abd al-Halim Khaddam (who also served as Deputy Prime Minister and as a member of the Regional and National Commands of the Ba'th Party); the Chief of the Air Force, Maj.-Gen. Naji Jamil (who was also Deputy Defense Minister and a member of the National Command of the Ba'th); and the Chief of Staff, Maj.-Gen. Hikmat Shihabi. This compact group represented the institutional interests of the Foreign Ministry and the armed forces as well as the Ba'th Party.[27] As Syria's mediatory

[23]Khuwayri, *Hawadith*, pp. 67–68.

[24]Ibid., p. 44.

[25]Dawisha, *Syria*, p. 87.

[26]Salibi, *Crossroads*, pp. 107–109.

[27]Dawisha, *Syria*, p. 70.

role persisted, Asad intermittently delegated Khaddam, often along with Jamil and/or Shihabi, to undertake diplomatic missions in Lebanon.

The team of Khaddam and Jamil that arrived at the Presidential Palace on May 24 had one explicit objective—to persuade Sulayman Faranjiyih to dismantle the military government. A more subtle, less clearly defined objective was to offer Syrian good offices in resolving the Lebanese Cabinet crisis and the underlying civil unrest. Already in this first diplomatic effort, the dual Syrian role of arbitrator and interested party came into play. The range of meetings by Khaddam and Jamil involved leaders of the Resistance, the LNM, the Sunni establishment, the Kata'ib, the National Liberals, and even the Maronite Patriarch. On the surface, the Syrians were merely trying to reconcile divergent Lebanese views; on closer examination, however, Syrian preferences emerge.

One account of a meeting between Foreign Minister Khaddam and Muslim leaders sheds light on Syrian perceptions of the Lebanese Army. Khaddam warned the Muslim spokesmen against irresponsible talk about the military Cabinet, "because this kind of talk will leave marks in the psychology of the military men, and . . . only Allah knows where it will lead." With more than a touch of irony, considering the Syrian experience, Khaddam cautioned that the Lebanese military might well be "susceptible to feelings . . . that have led to coups in more than one country." When some of the participants interrupted, saying that "[t]he Lebanese Army will split before it takes a united stand," Khaddam retorted: "I don't believe that. Rather, I dare say that the Lebanese military are quickly capable of uniting their ranks."[28] If Khaddam's statement truly reflected Syrian perceptions, this may have represented one of Syria's most serious miscalculations in evaluating conditions in the Lebanese target state.

How decisive was Syrian persuasion in leading to the resignation of the military Cabinet on 25 May, barely three days after its designation? On balance, the wellspring of domestic opposition was far more weighty. Indeed, President Faranjiyih reportedly told Junbalat, in the presence of Khaddam and Jamil:

[28]Khuwayri, *Hawadith,* pp. 90–91.

I formed the military government knowing that it would be refused. But what do you want me to do when the reigning Prime Minister, Rashid al-Sulh, refuses to assign work . . . and I find myself alone confronting tens of innocent killed and wounded falling daily in the streets of Beirut?

The President's defensive tone carried over to discussions about who would be a suitable Prime Minister for a new civilian government. On this issue, Faranjiyih solicited the views of Junbalat, who responded that the government should be turned over to "someone who preserves the dignity of the Muslims." In later negotiations, prior to the appointment of Rashid Karami as Prime Minister on 28 May, Junbalat insisted on further consultations with Muslim leaders, lest anyone say that Junbalat advanced his preference "under pressure."[29]

Junbalat's cryptic comment arouses speculation about the relative influence of Syrian "pressure" in the designation of Karami as Prime Minister. No doubt, the choice of Karami, long a bitter personal rival of Faranjiyih, was a humiliating setback for the President. Perhaps Karami emerged because of purely domestic considerations, as the sole candidate jointly acceptable to both the Sunni establishment and the LNM.[30] Alternatively, Karami may have been sponsored explicitly by the Syrians, because of his long-standing espousal of Syrian influence in Lebanon.[31] In fact, Karami remained a consistent advocate of Syrian policy throughout the Lebanese Civil War.

The precise impact of Syrian policy on the "military Cabinet" episode was less important than the setting of a precedent for Syrian mediation in Lebanon's domestic troubles. This precedent was activated in a second mediatory mission one month later. After receding into the background while Prime Minister Karami pursued four weeks of unsuccessful efforts to form a Cabinet, Syria was influential in finally working out a compromise formula. Syria also exhibited increasing concern about the deteriorating security situation in Lebanon, encouraging Lebanese and Palestinian sup-

---

[29]Ibid., pp. 89–94.
[30]Khalidi, *Conflict and Violence*, p. 47.
[31]Dawisha, *Syria*, p. 88.

port for a cease-fire and even engaging in a preliminary interventionist probe.

Widening Arena of Conflict

From the time of his appointment on 28 May 1975, Prime Minister Karami expressed determination to achieve a government acceptable to all parties in Lebanon. However, he had to come to terms with the political proscription of the Kata'ib by the Lebanese National Movement, as opposed to the insistence by the Kata'ib on their right to membership in any new Cabinet. Agreement only emerged after Foreign Minister Khaddam and Chief of Staff Shihabi, the Syrian envoys, again appeared at the Presidential Palace on 28 June. Khaddam suggested forming a temporary "mini-cabinet" of eight members, which would subsequently be enlarged to a full-size Cabinet. Kamil Sham'un was persuaded to represent both the National Liberals and the Kata'ib in a transitional Cabinet lacking members of either the Kata'ib or the LNM.

The "mini-cabinet" deviated from the expressed preferences of President Faranjiyih, who had wanted both Kata'ib and LNM members included. The designation of Kamil Sham'un as Minister of the Interior was also a painful concession for Prime Minister Karami, who had not been on speaking terms with Sham'un since the 1958 Civil War. Another compromise was struck over the division of responsibility for domestic security. Whereas Sham'un, as Interior Minister, had control over the Internal Security Forces, Karami was designated as Defense Minister (as well as Prime Minister), giving him formal authority over the Army. Once this accommodation was reached, the level of civil strife declined for two months.[32]

Syria maintained a low profile during this period, except for its decisive role in working out a Cabinet formula. The spread of violence in Lebanon prior to the Karami government's formation obviously aroused Syrian anxieties, prompting President Asad's revealing statement in mid-June that "i[t] is difficult to draw a line between Lebanon's security in its broadest sense and Syria's se-

---

[32]Khuwayri, *Hawadith,* pp. 106, 112–113; Dawisha, *Syria,* pp. 89–90.

curity."[33] In a similar vein, Foreign Minister Khaddam declared when he visited the Lebanese President:

> Lebanon and Syria are twin countries. . . . We are in a single front against the enemy [i.e., Israel]. Any internal problem which occurs in Lebanon might divert us from the basic battle.[34]

Implicit in these statements was an early articulation of Syrian fear of the "contagion effect" from Lebanese civil strife—a theme that would surface more frequently and vociferously later.

One reason for Syrian anxiety over the fighting in June 1975 was an incipient trend toward de facto partition of Lebanon. Syria's fragmented society was close enough to being Lebanon's "twin" for this development to be disturbing. The geographic scope of Lebanese civil strife, which had been concentrated in the Beirut vicinity from April until June, spread both east and north. In the eastern Biqa' Valley, an isolated Maronite village was assaulted by local Shi'i tribesmen in June. Further evidence of Shi'i military preparations was accidentally disclosed when an explosion occurred near Ba'albek early in July in a camp run by the Palestinian group, Fath. At this site, a group of Shi'is were being trained in planting land mines. The Shi'i leader, Musa al-Sadr, announced that the men killed in the accident were members of a new Shi'i organization called Amal (meaning "hope"), which was prepared in coordination with Fath to participate in the defense of Southern Lebanon. The revelation of Amal's existence aroused Christian apprehension about active Shi'i involvement, not in defending the South but rather in the next round of civil strife.

Late in June, tensions erupted in the northern, Sunni-dominated city of Tripoli. Shops and offices owned by Maronites from the adjacent, Maronite-dominated town of Zgharta, were targets of attack. As a result, many Maronites began to flee Tripoli, reinforcing a trend toward greater confessional homogeneity. Another indication of trouble in the north was the emergence in July of the "Zgharta Liberation Army," organized by the President's son, Tony Faranjiyih. Its significance derived from the status of the Faranjiyih clan in its native town and political base of Zgharta.

---

[33]Cited in Dawisha, *Syria*, p. 89.
[34]Khuwayri, *Hawadith*, p. 105.

The Faranjiyihs had an enduring political rivalry with the Sunni Karami clan, based in neighboring Tripoli. After Rashid Karami acceded to the Premiership, the Faranjiyihs wished to detract from his political victory and to be in a position to confront the Muslim militias of Tripoli. Second, the Maronites of Zgharta were disturbed by the growing popularity of the Kata'ib Party among Christians after the 'Ayn al-Rammana incidents. By sponsoring the Zgharta Liberation Army, the President's son wished to show that his clan, too, was prepared to defend the Maronite cause.[35]

Maronite spokesmen began to refer openly to the possibility of partitioning Lebanon if the conflict could not be resolved. At different junctures, the theme of partition sounded like a scare tactic by the Maronites; a fallback measure or emergency plan if all else failed; or a positively appealing contingency. By the time the Karami Cabinet was formed, some Maronite leaders had indicated that if they could not curb the guerrilla presence in Lebanon, they might be willing to "reconsider their position on many questions." This meant that the older, pre-mandatory boundaries of Lebanon might form a satisfactory basis for designating a separate Christian republic, comprising Mount Lebanon with the addition of the Christian sector of Beirut. Such references to *taqsim,* or partition, were distressing to Lebanese who felt a stake in the continued political integrity of Lebanon.[36]

The talk of partition and ongoing tensions in northern Lebanon precipitated an unconventional, but portentous, Syrian response in early July. In an obscure incident, a Palestinian guerrilla regiment from Syria briefly entered Tripoli, presumably to restore order. Some Lebanese commentators did not believe that the move was intended to avert partition, but rather to promote Syrian annexationist designs. According to one theory, Syria planned to absorb Tripoli and the surrounding 'Akkar region. This would occur if the Kata'ib provoked the PLO into open involvement in the Lebanese fighting, and then Syria intervened on the guerrillas' behalf. Syria could then absorb the eastern sections of the country, whose population was predominantly Muslim, while Israel in turn would occupy Southern Lebanon. This scenario would complement

[35]Salibi, *Crossroads,* pp. 116–121.
[36]Ibid., pp. 116–121.

the Maronite vision of establishing a Christian republic in the remaining territory of Mount Lebanon as well as Beirut.[37]

Lebanese fears and uncertainties about Syrian intentions were part of the charged political dialogue of the period. The weeks directly following the Karami Cabinet's formation were characterized by ongoing military preparations as well as efforts at political conciliation. There were fewer Maronite references to the desirability of partition, and the Kata'ib indicated willingness to cooperate in a truce. The party hoped that Karami would fulfill his pledge to enlarge the Cabinet as soon as circumstances permitted, so that its representatives might also participate. At its annual conference on 17 August, the Kata'ib Party adopted resolutions calling for "constructive dialogue" among the Lebanese and between Lebanese and Palestinians. The conciliatory tone of the proposals was not, however, backed up by concrete offers of political concessions.[38]

Mixed political signals also emerged from other domestic parties. President Faranjiyih asserted in a 22 August speech that the Constitution "was not sacred," implying that reforms might be contemplated. What he had in mind, however, would surely not satisfy the demands of the Lebanese National Movement, whose reform program, as released on 18 August, reaffirmed a commitment to thorough deconfessionalization of the Lebanese system.[39]

The status of the Palestinians in Lebanon was, as ever, a central issue in the political dialogue, despite the fact that the salience of the Palestinian dimension of the Lebanese conflict declined perceptibly from June through December 1975.[40] The slogans of Lebanese actors reflected divergent views of the priority that ought to be assigned to the Palestinian issue as opposed to purely domestic bones of contention. The Maronite position was "No reform before security," meaning that Palestinian actions in support of the LNM must be curtailed as a prerequisite to concessions on domestic reform. The Lebanese National Movement, by contrast, believed in "No security before reform." In the absence of conciliatory gestures by the establishment, they found the Palestinians to be

[37]Ibid., p. 118.
[38]Ibid., pp. 118–121.
[39]Khalidi, *Conflict and Violence,* p. 48.
[40]Hudson, "Palestinian Factor," pp. 270–271.

invaluable allies in promoting revolutionary change in the status quo.[41]

The Kata'ib position on this issue was articulated by the Party's chairman at a meeting with 'Abd al-Halim Khaddam and Hikmat al-Shihabi late in June. Pierre al-Jumayyil complained to the Syrian envoys that the fundamental mistake of the Palestinian Resistance was "their commitment to a specific party in Lebanon"—the LNM. He related that when the Kata'ib had attempted to enter a dialogue with the Palestinians, this aroused the anxieties of the Lebanese left. To undermine the incipient dialogue, Jumayyil charged, the left "created a wave of suspicion between us and the Palestinians, to the point where they portrayed us as if we wanted to destroy and demolish them." Foreign Minister Khaddam, in turn, displayed deference to both Jumayyil and Kamil Sham'un, saying that President Asad was well aware of their political weight and stature in Lebanon. He extended an invitation to both, as well as to President Faranjiyih, to visit Damascus when the Lebanese crisis was resolved. On 1 August, Prime Minister Karami did visit Damascus, amid Syrian proclamations of brotherhood and cooperation between the two countries in all spheres.[42]

Despite the posture of impartial arbitration which Khaddam took pains to project, Syria's policy at this juncture was more sympathetic to the Palestinian Resistance and the LNM. Syrian persuasion in facilitating the end of the military Cabinet and the designation of Karami as Prime Minister was appreciated by the Resistance. On 31 May, Yasir 'Arafat wrote to President Asad that the Syrian efforts assisted in "preserving Lebanese-Palestinian fraternity" and "confirmed Syria's vanguard role under your wise leadership."[43]

At the same time, Syria encouraged Palestinian restraint and support for Lebanese security. Syria may have promoted a declaration of noninterference by the Resistance in Lebanese affairs late in June. At a three-hour meeting with President Faranjiyih, Yasir 'Arafat reaffirmed the commitment by the PLO to abide by the 1969 Cairo Agreement and the 1973 Malkert Agreement. He then made a public declaration on Palestinian-Lebanese relations,

[41]Khalidi, *Conflict and Violence*, p. 48.
[42]Khuwayri, *Hawadith*, pp. 104–107, 132.
[43]Dawisha, *Syria*, p. 88.

broadcast on Lebanese radio and television on 25 June. 'Arafat declared unconditional support by the PLO for Lebanese sovereignty; promised noninterference in domestic Lebanese affairs, vowing not to support any Lebanese faction against another; and acknowledged the dependence of the Resistance on security and stability in Lebanon. The PLO's assurances may have facilitated the final compromises that led to formation of the Karami government several days later.[44]

In the domestic Lebanese violence that flared up in June and again in September 1975, Yasir 'Arafat officially sustained the posture of noninvolvement and even acted occasionally as a mediator between contending parties. The PLO leadership cooperated with Lebanese authorities in working out cease-fire agreements and sometimes jointly patrolled these cease-fires in coordination with Internal Security Forces. Nevertheless, the leadership of the Resistance was obviously torn between its pledge of noninterference and its proclivity to support Lebanese anti-establishment groups. Significantly, the Syrian-backed al-Sa'iqah guerrilla organization joined Fath during this period in furnishing military assistance to Muslim and leftist groups. This assistance entailed provision of arms, defense of some Muslim areas against Kata'ib attack, and backing for Muslim and leftist attacks against Kata'ib targets. However, the Popular Front for the Liberation of Palestine and other Rejectionist groups were relatively more involved militarily during this stage, directly participating in combat alongside the Lebanese National Movement and its allies.[45]

Prelude to Indirect Intervention

When the relative lull in fighting during the summer was shattered early in September 1975, Syrian involvement in the Lebanese crisis suddenly intensified. The outbreak of large-scale violence in northern Lebanon and Beirut sparked an increase in the level of Syrian mediatory activity, the seriousness with which it was pursued, and

[44]Sirriyyeh, "Palestinian Armed Presence," pp. 84–85; *QER of Syria, Lebanon,* 1975, 3rd quarter, p. 8.

[45]Hudson, "Palestinian Factor," pp. 270–271; Sirriyyeh, "Palestinian Armed Presence," p. 85.

the importance attached to the outcome. Syria also launched its first significant, albeit cautious, interventionist probe.

In an already familiar pattern, the eruption of violence in Tripoli early in September galvanized a domestic debate over whether the Army should be deployed. After heavy combat led to substantial destruction in Tripoli, about 3,000 Muslim militiamen marched five miles eastward to attack the Christian town of Zgharta. In an emergency Cabinet meeting on 9 September, Kamil Sham'un, in his capacity as Minister of the Interior, strongly argued for use of the Army. Rashid Karami, speaking as both Prime Minister and Minister of Defense, insisted that Army intervention would be acceptable only if the Army Commander, General Ghanim, was dismissed and replaced by another officer. In adopting this position, Karami was endorsing the view of the Sunni Muslim establishment over that of Kamal Junbalat. The LNM leader had informed Karami of his total opposition to deployment of the Army, for fear of setting a precedent that might later be used to suppress the LNM.

In a compromise agreement worked out on 10 September, Karami's view prevailed. General Ghanim, long highly unpopular among Muslims and Palestinians, was granted a leave of absence from the Army and replaced as Army Commander by Gen. Hanna Sa'id. The Army was to be deployed in a "zone of separation" between Zgharta and Tripoli, while security within each city remained the responsibility of the Internal Security Forces. This arrangement, Karami declared, would assure that "the Army and the Internal Security Forces are not an instrument of one party against another." Attempts to implement the agreement were doomed by charges that the Army could not be impartial. The Cabinet's compromise was accepted by the population of Zgharta but rejected by Tripoli spokesmen after a meeting sponsored by the LNM. On 14 September, the Army was accused of intervening against members of a Muslim political organization in Tripoli, killing twelve. Full-scale fighting then resumed.[46]

Further disputes arose over the possible use of the Army in

---

[46]Khuwayri, *Hawadith*, pp. 177–178; Salibi, *Crossroads*, pp. 123–125; *QER of Syria, Lebanon*, 1975, 4th quarter, pp. 7–8.

Beirut when violence erupted there. Kamal Junbalat had called for a general strike in Beirut on 15 September to protest the deployment of the Army in Tripoli. Then, on 17 September, the Kata'ib initiated a full-scale attack on downtown Beirut. The bombardment and destruction of the central sectors of the capital was ostensibly irrational and may have been intended to duplicate in Beirut the circumstances that prompted Army intervention in Tripoli. During escalating attacks in the capital and its environs, the Kata'ib were joined by other Maronite militias, including the National Liberals' militia, known as *al-Numur* (the Tigers), and an armed band called *Hurras al-Arz* (Guardians of the Cedars). Insistent calls by Christian spokesmen for Army intervention in Beirut met objections by Muslim establishment leaders that the Army could intervene only if its command structure was completely overhauled to provide greater Muslim authority. Meanwhile, the Lebanese National Movement was joined by the Palestinian Resistance in unconditional opposition to Army intervention.[47]

The Palestinian leadership was less circumspect in its position on Army deployment than it had been previously. On 18 September, the Lebanese Army command intercepted a telegram from Yasir 'Arafat to guerrilla leaders in Southern Lebanon, instructing them to obstruct any attempts by the Lebanese Army to move forces toward Beirut. Subsequent telegrams detailed measures by the Resistance and "armed Lebanese organizations supporting the Palestinian Revolution" (presumably the LNM) to set up barricades at key road junctures and to provision its forces with heavy arms (including rockets, cannons, and rocket-propelled grenades), to be able to confront Lebanese Army units.[48]

More in line with the official posture of the Palestinian leadership was participation by Palestinian units in efforts to restore stability in Tripoli. This process began one day after the deployment of the Army between Tripoli and Zgharta. After being contacted by Prime Minister Karami on 12 September, the PLO sent twenty men to Tripoli, including Zuhayr Muhsin. Significantly, Muhsin was both the head of the Military Bureau of the PLO and the head

[47]Salibi, *Crossroads*, pp. 125–127.
[48]Khuwayri, *Hawadith*, p. 203.

of Sa'iqah. After attending a meeting sponsored by the LNM, Muhsin decided to increase the number of Palestinian patrols deployed in Tripoli.[49]

The dual identity of Zuhayr Muhsin, answerable to Yasir 'Arafat as an official of the PLO and to Hafiz al-Asad as the head of Syrian-sponsored al-Sa'iqah, raised curious questions in the episode which followed. Muhsin informed Rashid Karami on 17 September that there were not enough Palestinian forces in northern Lebanon to reinforce the patrols operating in Tripoli. He then asked the Prime Minister: "Do you have any objection to using some elements of the Palestinian Liberation Army?" Karami accepted the suggestion, and the following day two Palestinian brigades (estimated at between 600 and 1,000 men) crossed the border from Syria. One brigade was composed of PLA forces and the other of both Fath and Sa'iqah members.

Questions immediately arose about Karami's unilateral decision, as Prime Minister and Minister of Defense, to accept Muhsin's offer. Karami had not consulted either President Faranjiyih or any other Cabinet member; and an emergency meeting was convened at the Presidential Palace as soon as word arrived that the Palestinian units had crossed the border. Faranjiyih quickly called President Asad, asking him to try to arrange the withdrawal of the Palestinian forces, "because this is a precedent that will create domestic dissension in Lebanon whose consequences can not be foreseen." After Asad's intercession, the PLA brigade withdrew from Tripoli that night, leaving its heavy arms behind. The other brigade of Fath and Sa'iqah forces remained and continued to patrol the city. Zuhayr Muhsin then declared:

> The batallion of the PLA which had entered the northern region withdrew to its barracks on Syrian soil on the instructions which it received from the leadership of the Resistance. This was after the circumstances which required its presence disappeared, and after security was restored in Tripoli.... This batallion had entered the region of Tripoli based on an agreement between the leadership of the PLO and the Lebanese Government represented by Prime Minister Rashid Karami.[50]

[49]Ibid., p. 184.
[50]Ibid., pp. 203–204, 208.

There are many unanswered questions about this preliminary instance of Syrian indirect intervention. As in the even more circumscribed probe of early July, the Syrian move was marked by tentativeness. Officially, Palestinian transnational authorities were assigned responsibility for initiating intervention by Palestinian brigades and then for agreeing to the PLA withdrawal. To what extent was Zuhayr Muhsin, however, following Syrian instructions in making the offer in the first place? How aware was Rashid Karami of what the offer entailed, and why didn't he consult President Faranjiyih? Finally, what was the relationship between Syria's involvement in this episode on 18 September and the intensive diplomatic initiative launched the very next day?

Committee for National Dialogue

The mystery shrouding the PLA intervention in Tripoli contrasts with fuller accounts of the week-long Syrian mediatory mission beginning on 19 September. The decision to initiate a more ambitious and higher-profile diplomatic effort was accompanied by wider consultations within the Syrian elite. The ad hoc committee of four that had made key decisions on Lebanon thus far (Asad, Khaddam, Shihabi, and Jamil) was now enlarged, bringing in seven additional members for consultations. Six held positions in either the National or Regional Commands of the Ba'th Party—including two Palestinians, one of whom was Sa'iqah Chief Zuhayr Muhsin. Two were prominent in the security apparatus—Muhammed al-Khuli, Chief of Security in the Air Force, also in charge of intelligence efforts in Lebanon; and the President's brother, Rif'at al-Asad, commander of the Defense Companies and also a member of the Ba'th's National Command.[51]

The desirability of gaining broader elite backing reflected increased Syrian stakes in the outcome of mediatory activities. When Khaddam and Shihabi arrived in Lebanon, their immediate goal was to achieve a durable cease-fire, and their long-term goal, to facilitate national reconciliation. By 20 September, a cease-fire was arranged in Beirut, after consultations including the President, the

---

[51]Dawisha, *Syria,* p. 91.

Prime Minister, the Maronite Patriarch, Maronite leaders Jumayyil and Sham'un, the Sunni Mufti (religious leader), Sunni leader Sa'ib Salam, LNM leader Junbalat, and Palestinian Resistance leaders 'Arafat and Muhsin. After these encompassing discussions, the cease-fire plan provided for joint patrols by the Resistance and Lebanese Internal Security Forces in the western, Muslim-dominated sector of Beirut. In the eastern, Christian-dominated part of the capital, security was entrusted entirely to the Internal Security Forces. After further meetings by Khaddam with the Political Bureau of the Resistance, in which Rejectionist elements were among those represented, a decision was taken initially to deploy four hundred men from various guerrilla organizations in West Beirut.[52]

The more complex task of striving for Lebanese national reconciliation sparked a concerted diplomatic effort culminating in creation of a Committee for National Dialogue. This institutional innovation, even more pointedly than Karami's mini-cabinet in June, was intended to rearrange the constellation of traditional Lebanese leaders to spur political accommodation. The Syrian envoys first sought agreement on the composition of a committee to draft a "working paper," defining the basic principles for national reconciliation.

In a week of intensive consultations spanning the entire Lebanese political spectrum, Khaddam was dubbed the "Syrian High Commissioner" by Lebanese observers. His discussions touched on both the substance of proposed reforms and the procedure for setting up a new committee. Muslim political and religious leaders as well as representatives of the Lebanese left demanded political reforms such as amendment of the Lebanese Constitution and electoral law and fuller sharing of power among sectors of the elite. Political reforms would be followed by social and economic reform, leading to true equality among all Lebanese. In another meeting, the Maronite Patriarch publicly declared his opposition to the partition of Lebanon, and Khaddam invited the Patriarch to visit Damascus.

A compromise on the composition of a committee authorized to sort out the demands of various parties was reached on 23

---

[52]*Al-Nahar*, 20 September 1975, p. 3; Khuwayri, *Hawadith*, pp. 206–207, 212.

September. In a meeting at the home of the Lebanese Mufti, Hasan Khalid, attended by Kamal Junbalat, Yasir 'Arafat, and other Resistance leaders, debate arose on the criteria for choosing members of the committee. Junbalat argued against membership based on confessional criteria, asserting that this "would sanctify political confessionalism at a time that the country was absorbed in a battle whose basis was political and social" —that is, based on broader political and social issues. He suggested, instead, representation of the three major ideological currents in the country—the Lebanese National Movement, the Kata'ib, and the liberal center. The compromise formula that Khaddam worked out favored the Lebanese left, in that six of the twenty members were identified with leftist parties—including one member of the Lebanese branch of the Syrian Ba'th Party. On the other hand, Khaddam was credited with persuading Junbalat implicitly to lift his proscription of the Kata'ib, by agreeing to sit on the same committee with Pierre al-Jumayyil.[53]

Khaddam characterized the formation of the Committee of National Dialogue *(lajnat al-hiwar al-watani)* as "a crowning [achievement] on the path of deepening confidence between the different [Lebanese] parties." On an official level, the Syrian role was profusely praised, with Rashid Karami conveying Lebanon's "thanks and estimation to sister Syria in the person of President Hafiz al-Asad." Kata'ib leader Pierre al-Jumayyil, pleased with his party's incorporation in the new committee, also expressed gratitude for the "faithfulness, brotherhood, and love" manifested by the Syrian President and his envoys. Reiterating the theme that "Lebanon and Syria were twins," he further explained:

> I believe that Syria and Lebanon complement each other, and that the misfortunes that befall Syria will inevitably befall Lebanon, and the misfortunes that befall Lebanon will befall Syria.

In his own remarks, Khaddam pointedly acknowledged that Syria considered its security threatened by events in Lebanon. He, too, declared that "[w]hen the painful events occurred in Lebanon, . . . [Syria] was struck with the same pain and worry, for whatever bad

---

[53]Khuwayri, *Hawadith*, pp. 215–216, 227–228, 230; Khalidi, *Conflict and Violence*, p. 49; *QER of Syria, Lebanon,* 1975, 4th quarter, pp. 3, 8.

things hurt Lebanon, hurt Syria to the same degree." He contended that the fighting in Lebanon stemmed from an external plot, aimed at "Arabizing the conflict in the Middle East—changing this conflict from an Arab-Israeli conflict to become an Arab-Arab conflict." The conspiracy in Lebanon was promoted by characterizing social tensions along sectarian, Muslim-Christian lines. In a revealing statement, Khaddam remarked:

> Naturally, when internal questions in Lebanon, which could exist in any country, are given a sectarian content, . . . this leads to the obliteration of patriotic identification and the accentuation of sectarian identification—all of which necessarily serves this scheme.[54]

Recognition that the confessional dimension of Lebanon's social conflict was accentuated during the Civil War reflected Syria's fear that Lebanon's troubles could be contagious.

Notwithstanding numerous expressions of gratitude for Syria's mediatory role, many Lebanese also had apprehensions about their neighbor's intentions. The Lebanese press alleged that an argument between President Faranjiyih and Foreign Minister Khaddam on 22 September nearly led to the abrupt termination of the Syrian mission. According to the magazine *al-Hawadith,* the President received intelligence reports of violations of the Beirut cease-fire by the Resistance and the Lebanese left, and suspected that Syria was surreptitiously encouraging these violations. The following exchange occurred:

> Faranjiyih: "I won't condone [the fact] that you let loose your elements to strike and burn and kill on the one hand, and then you come to negotiate with me on the other hand. Frankly, I can't negotiate with you under pressure."
>
> Khaddam: "It is not the Resistance and it is not al-Sa'iqah who violated the cease-fire. It is your groups in the Kata'ib and the [National] Liberals who violated the cease-fire and escalated the situation. If you wanted a cessation of the massacres, Beirut would not have burned."
>
> Faranjiyih: "Then you are accusing me of being implicated with the Kata'ib and the Liberals? Then why continue with the separate

---

[54]Khuwayri, *Hawadith,* pp. 239–241.

[i.e., bilateral] mediation? There is a Cairo Agreement between me and the Resistance. Am I the one who violated it? This agreement was signed in the framework of the Arab League. I will call on these states to bear their responsibility. If Syria wants to mediate, let her do it within the Arab League."

Khaddam: "Therefore we consider our mission concluded."[55]

The mutual accusations of partisanship in this dialogue—including allegations that Syria was not an impartial arbitrator and that the President was failing to stand above confessionalism—revealed deep underlying suspicions. The option of Arab League mediation will be discussed more fully below (Chapter 9); but in this instance a reconciliation occurred and Syria continued to pursue its critical role. According to the magazine *al-Sayad,* when Faranjiyih expressed dissatisfaction with Syrian mediation, Khaddam protested that "he came to Lebanon based on the request of the [Presidential] Palace and that the request was conveyed by the Imam Musa Sadr to the Syrian authorities." In this manner, the Foreign Minister tried to portray his mission as invitational.

What were the Lebanese apprehensions? According to one account, Syria was trying to draw Lebanon into a military alliance analogous to its partnership with Jordan. Others suggested that "the Palestinian state was to be established on Lebanese soil." Still others spoke of Syrian schemes for "Cyprusization"—that is, the partition of Lebanon. Each of these rumors, revealing the fear that Syrian good offices were merely a cover for its own ambitions and designs on Lebanon, was dismissed by Khaddam as attempts to "sabotage" Syria's efforts and reputation.[56]

Overall, the results of Syria's September mediatory mission were disappointing. The Committee on National Dialogue made no headway in resolving Lebanese tensions, because its members lacked the will to make the requisite political concessions. Beginning at the committee's first meeting, on 25 September, the Christian participants were dissatisfied with the group's composition and tone. Kamil Sham'un of the National Liberal Party complained that committee meetings were merely a tactic to avoid Army intervention, and then boycotted later sessions. Kamal Junbalat, in

---

[55]Cited in Khuwayri, *Hawadith,* pp. 219–222.
[56]Cited in Khuwayri, *Hawadith,* pp. 219–222.

turn, refused to address Pierre al-Jumayyil at the meetings, at least formally abiding by his proscription of the Kata'ib. By the final, ninth meeting of 11 November, the committee's meetings had deteriorated into a "dialogue of the deaf."[57]

Meanwhile, personal and political tensions between the President and Prime Minister came to a head by early November. Members of the Lebanese National Movement and Muslim establishment repeatedly urged Rashid Karami to be more assertive in dealing with Sulayman Faranjiyih. Early in October, Sa'ib Salam (the Sunni leader) and Raymun Iddih (the dissident Maronite leader) demanded the President's resignation as a prerequisite for resolving the crisis. As the level of domestic violence rose, Karami suspected that Faranjiyih, National Liberal leader Sham'un, and Kata'ib leader Jumayyil were deliberately undermining his efforts at reconciliation so as to prompt his resignation. In response, Karami announced that he had no intention of leaving office as long as Lebanon remained in turmoil.

Efforts to restore harmony between the President and Prime Minister, including both Syrian and Palestinian intercessions, finally yielded a pledge of cooperation on 14 November, followed by concurrent public announcements resolving to give priority to domestic reform. The emphasis on reform rather than security was intended as a concession to the Lebanese National Movement and was accompanied by an offer to include representatives of the LNM in the Karami Cabinet. However, Junbalat's group insisted that their own recipe for domestic reform—deconfessionalization—be accepted as a prerequisite to Cabinet participation.[58]

One ominous feature of the rise in domestic violence was the perceptible trend toward de facto partition. Toward the end of October, the Kata'ib penetrated sections of western Beirut overlooking the luxury hotels along the coast. In the fierce "Battle of the Hotels" that ensued, the LNM was locked in combat with the Kata'ib for control of the area. Soon, Beirut was dramatically split into two separate sectors, divided by a no man's land traversed only by armed men. Heavy fighting also occurred in Damur, south of Beirut, and in Zahleh in the eastern Biqa' Valley, late in Oc-

---

[57]Khalidi, *Conflict and Violence*, p. 49.
[58]*Ibid.*, pp. 49–50; Salibi, *Crossroads*, pp. 132–135; Khuwayri, p. 271.

tober. Throughout the country, substantial migration of Christians from Muslim-dominated areas, and of Muslims from Christian areas, occurred. Relations between sectarian groups were severely strained in communities that remained confessionally mixed. In most areas, real control was exercised either by the Maronite parties and their militias or by Muslim and LNM militias in occasional coordination with Palestinian guerrillas. Lebanese state authorities exercised tenuous control, even in neutral and buffer zones not clearly identified with any faction.[59]

Looking to Damascus

In an atmosphere of deepening pessimism over Lebanon's ability to solve its own problems, Lebanese leaders increasingly took the initiative in turning to Damascus. From late September 1975 until January 1976, Syrian diplomatic efforts were conducted quietly from the capital. Several important visits by Lebanese leaders to Damascus occurred, either at Syrian invitation or on their own initiative.

After an emergency meeting at the Presidential Palace in early October, Prime Minister Karami decided to visit Damascus, along with Yasir 'Arafat. According to the Lebanese magazine *al-Sayad,* Karami told President Asad and Foreign Minister Khaddam that he was confronted with three options. One was to deploy the Army—an alternative which he ruled out, because of his "desire not to inflame the fighting, and for the [sake of] the unity of the Army." Second, he could strive for national reconciliation, after stopping the fighting—but how could he bring that about, and what role was Syria willing to play? Third, if reconciliation failed, he could offer his government's resignation.

The Syrian response revealed much about Syrian perceptions of the Lebanese crisis and the means deemed desirable for its resolution. While assigning first priority to achieving an end to the fighting, the Syrian leaders emphatically opposed deploying the Army, declaring that this would be counterproductive. Asad and Khaddam then registered their personal confidence in Karami,

[59]Salibi, *Crossroads,* pp. 136–137, 140; Khalidi, p. 49.

declaring that "[w]e would consider your resignation a danger signal for the destiny of your country."

Turning, therefore, to the means of achieving Lebanese national reconciliation, the Syrian leaders asserted that the defense of the Palestinian Resistance was highest on their ladder of Arab priorities. In a pointed reference to Kamal Junbalat, they declared:

> We believe that the National Movement . . . should give priority in its patriotic and national struggle to the defense of the Resistance, and that it should place this as [its] first objective, before the realization of the demands for political, economic, and social reform of the Lebanese regime. For it is possible to realize some of these demands at the present time, and to continue the struggle to complete their realization during the coming years. However, this matter depends on the Lebanese National Movement itself.

This unusually frank articulation of Syria's closer identification with the Resistance than with the Lebanese left, and of its skepticism about the urgency of the left's full program of reforms, had significant implications for the future. Syria also indicated that its support for the Resistance was predicated on full implementation and respect for the Cairo and Malkert Agreements, while calling on all Lebanese parties including the Kata'ib to recognize the "Palestinian, Arab, and international legitimacy of the Palestine Liberation Organization."[60]

Immediately after the Damascus meeting to which he had been a party, Yasir 'Arafat directed the Resistance to assist in restoring stability in Beirut. He called on Palestinian Armed Struggle Command patrols in West Beirut to apprehend armed men, dismantle barricades, and strengthen adherence to the latest cease-fire. He also ordered an end to armed demonstrations in Beirut and withdrawal of all armed elements, calling upon the LNM to adhere to the new measures as well.[61]

When these efforts failed to avert unprecedented violence in the capital late in October 1975, Yasir 'Arafat led a delegation of Palestinian guerrilla leaders to meet Prime Minister Karami on 29 October and offer assistance in restoring order. Similarly, Foreign

---

[60]Cited in Khuwayri, *Hawadith,* pp. 291–292.
[61]Khuwayri, *Hawadith,* pp. 290–291.

Minister Khaddam called from Damascus to indicate Syria's willingness to advance any possible assistance. One result of these overtures was the formation, on 3 November, of a Higher Coordination Committee *(lajnat at-tansiq al-'ulya)* whose function was to investigate cease-fire violations and prevent such breaches from getting out of hand. The committee included representatives of the Army and the Internal Security Forces, as well as of Palestinian guerrilla groups.[62]

A temporary lull in the violence following creation of still another institutional mechanism did not endure. In a bold stroke, Syria invited Kata'ib chief Pierre al-Jumayyil to visit Damascus on 6 December. Whereas 'Arafat, Junbalat, and Musa Sadr, as leaders of partisan groups with which Syria traditionally identified, had visited Damascus repeatedly in previous months, the Syrian overture in singling out this extremist Maronite spokesman for high-level consultations sparked widespread surprise and concern in Lebanon.

The leading Lebanese daily, *al-Nahar,* relates that President Asad opened the six-and-one-half-hour meeting with the Kata'ib chief by expressing distress over recent events in Lebanon. He pledged that Syria was willing to offer "every possible service," and would pursue its diplomatic efforts in Lebanon, "if the matter was necessary and if it was asked to do so." Asad emphasized Syria's desire to be considered "a friend of all Lebanese without exception." Elaborating on Syria's objectives, Foreign Minister Khaddam expressed frustration over the complexity of Lebanon's problems. He revealed that since the beginning of the Lebanese crisis, top Syrian officials had spent at least three hours a day following Lebanese developments. Khaddam explained that there were really two crises in Lebanon—a Lebanese-Lebanese crisis and a Lebanese-Palestinian crisis. Asking rhetorically which of these issues should be addressed first, he left the question moot, saying: "[O]ne must begin with any solution, but one must arrive at a solution." As for Syria's involvement, Khaddam declared that Syria was not pursuing reactive strategies, but rather acting on the basis of its interests, and he advised Lebanon to do the same. One of the central causes of the crisis, he observed, was the weakness of the Lebanese state.

[62]Salibi, *Crossroads,* pp. 134–135.

Pierre al-Jumayyil readily agreed that the weakness of the Lebanese state caused great difficulties. He argued, in fact, that "it was incumbent upon Syria, if it really wanted to assist Lebanon—and it was the state most competent to do so—to restore to Lebanon its state." This unusual appeal was elaborated in Jumayyil's comment that "Syria was capable of exerting pressure on the various parties, in view of the friendships which linked her to them and [in view of] her weight [i.e., preponderant influence], and that she was capable of stopping the excesses." Explaining his party's own position, Jumayyil emphasized that it was not the presence of the Palestinian Resistance in Lebanon that the Kata'ib opposed, but rather the Palestinians' "excesses and their involvement in internal Lebanese matters."

Clearly attempting to persuade the Syrian leaders to shift the direction of their traditional Lebanese alignments, Jumayyil accused the Resistance and the LMN of having close ties with the "international left." He implied that Syrian support for these groups could be destabilizing and damaging to Syria's regional interests. As was his wont, Jumayyil also played on the "contagion" theme, warning that "the collapse of Lebanon would inevitably have direct repercussions for Syria." Khaddam concurred, asserting that "bloodletting in Lebanon would bloody Syria" as well.[63]

Whether or not Jumayyil influenced Syrian perceptions of Lebanese politics, his visit to Damascus certainly had political ramifications back home. Both Maronite extremists and members of the Lebanese Left were apprehensive about Syrian cordiality toward the Kata'ib leader. Even before Jumayyil left for Damascus on 6 December, violent incidents had flared up in various parts of the country, especially in Zahleh in the Biqa' and in Tripoli and Zgharta in the north. On the day of the visit, four members of the Kata'ib Party were ambushed and murdered in Maronite-controlled territory by unidentified assailants. In retaliation, about two hundred Muslim civilians were massacred by Maronite militiamen on "Black Saturday." Over the next few weeks, the cycle of violence escalated. An alliance of Muslim and left-wing groups, reinforced by Palestinian militiamen, were led by the Nasirite leader Ibrahim Qulaylat in a Beirut attack against Christian po-

---

[63]*Al-Nahar*, 7 December 1975, pp. 1, 8.

sitions. They dislodged Kata'ib forces from some of the large Beirut hotels and made advances against downtown Beirut. Forces aligned with the LNM then overran a Christian village in the Biqa' Valley, and the Kata'ib, in turn, attacked several Muslim villages near Beirut.[64]

The escalating violence of December may have been decisive in changing President Faranjiyih's attitude toward Syrian involvement in the Lebanese crisis. Walid Khalidi argues that whereas earlier mediatory attempts and interventionist probes had been launched as Syrian initiatives, the Lebanese President now "decided to turn in earnest to Damascus." Faranjiyih hoped that by inviting Syria into Lebanon, he could persuade the latter "to redress the balance in favor of the Maronites." Faranjiyih believed that if he agreed in principle to limited reforms in the Lebanese system while maintaining a strong military posture, he could count on Syria to keep the Lebanese National Movement and the Palestinians in line.[65]

This explanation of the transition from Syrian diplomatic overtures to Lebanese appeals for assistance probably benefits too much from the value of hindsight. Nevertheless, a qualitative change in the nature and scope of the Syrian intervention did indeed occur in January 1976. The degree to which Syrian escalation occurred in response to "invitations" by various Lebanese parties, rather than in promotion of Syrian designs, is a question that arose more sharply in the the next phase.

[64]Malcolm Kerr, "The Syrian Intervention in Lebanon: An Interpretation" (paper presented at the meeting of the Middle East Studies Association, New York, November 1977), p. 9; Salibi, *Crossroads,* p. 145; Khalidi, *Conflict and Violence,* p. 50; *QER of Syria, Lebanon,* 1976, 1st quarter, pp. 3, 7.

[65]Khalidi, *Conflict and Violence,* p. 50.

7

Indirect Intervention

The intermediate phase of Syrian involvement in the Lebanese Civil War marked a decisive transition from several points of view. A pronounced upward step on the ladder of escalation entailed a shift of emphasis from diplomatic initiatives to indirect intervention via Palestinian forces. Second, the Syrian decisionmaking process came into sharper focus as a larger number of officials became involved in handling the Lebanese crisis. Greater efforts were made to explain and justify Syrian involvement to a domestic audience. Finally, this was a crucial "swing" period in Syrian alignments with parties to the Lebanese conflict.

Syrian contacts with diverse Lebanese domestic actors and the Palestinians were already pursued in the first nine months of the war (April-December 1975). As the identity of actors and the salience of issues varied, Syria's moves were essentially reactive. The absence of coherent pro-establishment and anti-establishment coalitions presented both dilemmas and advantages for Syria. Agreement with one party might be undermined by its ostensible ally, to Syrian dismay. Alternatively, the Syrians might deal with one party to a coalition in the hope that it could persuade an ally to go along or possibly in the hope that rifts in the coalition would work to Syria's benefit.

Cohesiveness of Lebanese Coalitions

The Lebanese groups with which Syria traditionally identified were members of a loose, anti-establishment coalition. In the initial phase of the war, the PLO maintained its official posture of non-interference in domestic Lebanese affairs and did not wish to be considered a party to the conflict. The PLO's stance essentially paralleled that of Syria, as did Yasir 'Arafat's mediatory efforts at critical junctures. Rejectionist Palestinians, meanwhile, often fought alongside the Lebanese National Movement. In the second phase, the PLO overtly joined ranks with the LNM, thereby bridging the gap with the Rejectionists. Close Palestinian-LNM coordination eventually posed a severe challenge to Syria, which went to great lengths to undermine the alliance.

The Lebanese National Movement was a heterogeneous grouping of leftist-oriented parties. While sharing the goals of deconfessionalizing the Lebanese system and of achieving socioeconomic reform, these parties often lacked coordination or even worked at cross-purposes. The leadership of Kamal Junbalat was a crucial unifying force, with a prime base of support in his Progressive Socialist Party. Other parties in the LNM included the Communists, the Syrian Social Nationalist Party (SSNP), and the Lebanese branch of the Iraqi Ba'th Party. Other parties broke with the Lebanese National Movement during the second phase, when the LNM came into conflict with Syria. Those following the Syrian line were the Lebanese branch of the Syrian Ba'th Party, Musa al-Sadr's Movement of the Deprived, and the Working People's Party.

Even less clear-cut than LNM alignments was the position of the Muslim establishment during the war. Having already suffered disenchantment by grass-roots supporters, many of whom shifted allegience to the LNM, traditional Muslim leaders were at a loss about how to identify during the Civil War. A contrast in the positions of two Sunni leaders, Sa'ib Salam and Rashid Karami, arose in the first stage and intensified in the second. Karami, as Prime Minister, showed conditional willingness to cooperate with President Faranjiyih and maintained open lines of communication with Syria. Salam, on the other hand, issued a call for Faranjiyih's resignation in the first phase that he pressed with determination during the second. He was an early critic of Syrian conduct in Lebanon. Despite the long-standing predominance of the secular leadership in the Muslim communities, both the Sunni Mufti, Hasan Khalid, and the Shi'i Imam Musa al-Sadr played increasingly articulate political roles during the Civil War.

The variety of spokesmen and orientations among anti-establishment groups contrasted with relatively greater coherence in the pro-establishment, Maronite-dominated coalition. Rivalries and differences of view did exist among the leaders of what came to be known as the Lebanese Front. Its three principal leaders were Pierre al-Jumayyil of the Kata'ib Party, Kamil Sham'un of the National Liberals, and President Sulayman Faranjiyih, whose partisan following derived from his base of support in Zgharta. A fourth, less prominent leader of the Lebanese Front was Father Sharbal Kasis, head of the Conference of Maronite Monastic Orders. Each of these men counted on the allegiance of a distinct group of supporters as well as a private militia. Each had his own views on how much reform of the Lebanese system might be tolerable to assure the survival of the Republic. Once Syria shifted its alignments to achieve close cooperation with the Maronites, contacts with the President were either reinforced or supplanted by Syrian meetings with other pro-establishment leaders.[1]

Maronite Offensive

The second phase of Syrian involvement in the Lebanese war was triggered by a Maronite offensive that brought the PLO directly into the conflict. On 4 January 1976, the Kata'ib initiated a siege of two Palestinian refugee camps, Tall al-Za'tar and Jisr al-Basha, on the eastern outskirts of Beirut. The camps were strategically located along the exits from East Beirut, commanding the main road to the central Matn region. Since September, access to this road had been blocked by Palestinian forces in the two camps, primarily members of Rejectionist groups. The Kata'ib viewed the blockage of their lines of communication to the hinterland as a formidable military threat, and the camps themselves as alien enclaves in a Maronite sphere of control. By 13 January, the Kata'ib besieged another Palestinian camp north of Beirut, al-Dubayya, a majority of whose inhabitants, ironically, were Maronite Palestinians.

Strategic considerations also figured in the attack by both Kata'ib

[1]Walid Khalidi, *Conflict and Violence in Lebanon: Confrontation in the Middle East,* Harvard Studies in International Affairs, No. 38 (Cambridge: Center for International Affairs, Harvard University, 1979), pp. 67–84.

and National Liberal forces on the Muslim slums of al-Karantina, al-Maslakh, and al-Nab'a. These quarters controlled access to the coastal road linking East Beirut to the heavily Maronite regions to the north. The strategy took into account the prospect of partition, in which case the Maronites would consolidate their hold on the vicinity of East Beirut. Maronite militias were charged with particular brutality in the "Karantina massacre" of 18 January, in which the Muslim quarter was invaded and razed to the ground, leading to approximately 1,000 Muslim and Palestinian deaths.[2]

In response to the siege of the Palestinian camps, the PLO abandoned its official stance of noninterference in the Civil War. Once the siege of Tall al-Za'tar and Jisr al-Basha was under way, Yasir 'Arafat announced that the Resistance would use force and sustain any costs necessary to break the siege. The second-in-command of Fath, Abu Iyad, declared that the Resistance would oppose any efforts to partition Lebanon. Having already suffered the partition of Palestine, he said, the Palestinians would resist the further setback to their cause that the partition of Lebanon would entail.

The Kata'ib offensive against the Palestinian camps may well have been intended to draw the Resistance more openly into the Lebanese struggle. On 13 January, the Maronite leadership, significantly including President Faranjiyih, held a summit meeting at the Presidential Palace. They announced that the Lebanese war was now a struggle between Lebanese, especially Christians, on the one hand, and Palestinians, both Muslim and Christian, on the other, and declared their determination to combat the perceived Palestinian threat.[3] This characterization overlooked, or failed to anticipate, the progressively closer coordination between the Resistance as a whole and the Lebanese National Movement. While Rejectionist Palestinians had fought alongside LNM militias in the past, PLO-Fath units were now prepared to do so. After

[2]Kamal Salibi, *Crossroads to Civil War: Lebanon, 1958–1976* (Delmar, N.Y.: Caravan, 1976), pp. 149–154; Khalidi, *Conflict and Violence,* p. 51.

[3]Michael Hudson, "The Palestinian Factor in the Lebanese Civil War," *The Middle East Journal* 32 (Summer 1978):271–272; Hussein Sirriyeh, "The Palestinian Armed Presence in Lebanon Since 1967," in *Essays on the Crisis in Lebanon,* ed. Roger Owen (London: Ithaca Press, 1976), pp. 85–86; Salibi, *Crossroads,* pp. 150–151.

the siege of the refugee camps began, Palestinian officials met with Kamal Junbalat and other Muslim and leftist leaders, including Prime Minister Karami, and agreed on coordination to check Maronite moves toward partition.

The principal target of the counteroffensive by the LNM and Palestinians was the Maronite coastal town of Damur, south of Beirut. This town was the base of support of Kamil Sham'un and its strategic significance was enchanced by its proximity to the Shuf, Kamal Junbalat's home region. Fighting also broke out in other parts of the country, as Muslims and Palestinians in Tripoli fought the Maronites of Zgharta; a siege was waged on the Christian town of Zahleh in the Biqa'; Shi'i and Palestinian forces surrounded a Maronite town near Ba'albek; and Sunni forces attacked Christian villages in the northern 'Akkar region. Prime Minister Karami appealed urgently for a cease-fire and for an end to the siege of Damur and of the Palestinian refugee camps. When the violence escalated instead and he was unable to ward off the razing of al-Karantina and al-Maslakh on 18 January, Karami announced his resignation.[4]

PLA Intervention

As the polarization between the contending Lebanese coalitions increased, so did Syrian concern and involvement. In the early weeks of January, both "invitational" and "penetrational" dimensions characterized the Syrian role. President Faranjiyih was reportedly in "continuous contact" with Syrian President Asad once the siege of the Palestinian refugee camps began on 4 January. The two leaders agreed that Faranjiyih would visit Damascus shortly to discuss an overall Lebanese settlement.[5] In the first official indication that Syria would intensify its involvement in Lebanon, Foreign Minister Khaddam asserted that "this is a very sensitive situation in relation to us in Syria, and in relation to the presence of the Palestinian Resistance there." Therefore, he proclaimed:

[4]Salibi, *Crossroads,* pp. 152–154; Khalidi, *Conflict and Violence,* p. 51; Hudson, "Palestinian Factor," p. 271.

[5]Salibi, *Crossroads,* p. 155.

We have made it clear, in a decisive manner, that we would not permit the partition of Lebanon. Any initiative for partition would mean our immediate intervention. For Lebanon was part of Syria, and we would restore it with any attempt at partition.

Moreover, Khaddam specified that he was referring not only to the areas of Lebanon detached from Syria in 1920, but to Mount Lebanon as well — "for Lebanon will either be unified or it will be restored to Syria."[6]

In actuality, Syria's behavior in early January was limited to small-scale, indirect probes, similar to those of the previous July and September. In two instances, Syria militarily supported the Palestinian-LNM counteroffensive. Palestinian reinforcements from Syria joined in the siege of the Christian town of Zahleh in the Biqa' Valley. Likewise, Syrian-sponsored Sa'iqah guerrillas assisted Sunni forces in attacking Christian villages in the northern 'Akkar region.[7]

A more complex scenario emerged, however, when the LNM-Palestinian offensive against Damur ran into trouble. Having diverted forces to Beirut and other zones of combat, the Lebanese National Movement was not equipped to pursue its siege of Damur against Maronite resistance. Palestinian forces were of limited assistance, since most of them were still deployed in the South, close to the Israeli border. Kamal Junbalat became increasingly anxious, and in a meeting at the home of the Sunni Mufti, Hasan Khalid, in 'Aramun, he joined other LNM and traditional Muslim leaders in initiating an appeal for Syrian assistance.[8]

Syrian President Hafiz al-Asad later cited the appeal of the 'Aramun summit as evidence that Syria's intervention in Lebanon was purely invitational. In an unusual and highly revealing speech delivered on 20 July 1976, President Asad explained the Syrian rationale in responding to the LNM's appeal. Asad relates that in mid-January, Lebanese Muslim and leftist leaders sent urgent "signals of distress" to Syria, due to the military collapse of LNM-Resistance forces. The members of the 'Aramun summit urged

---

[6] *Al-Nahar,* 8 January 1976.
[7] Salibi, *Crossroads,* p. 153.
[8] Khalidi, *Conflict and Violence,* p. 51.

Syrian Foreign Minister Khaddam to request President Asad to contact President Faranjiyih and try to stop the fighting.

Asad portrays himself as reluctant to comply with the request, not because of unwillingness to make the effort, but because he considered the demand unreasonable. He explains that the LNM and the Resistance had more weapons at their disposal than the entire Lebanese Army, let alone the Kata'ib and National Liberals. He therefore told Khaddam that "they must hold out" and that he would not contact Faranjiyih. However, Asad relented after Khaddam repeatedly called him to describe the desperation of the appealers, who feared that after the fall of al-Karantina and al-Maslakh, the Kata'ib's next move would be to occupy West Beirut. Asad called Faranjiyih on 18 January and arranged a cease-fire for that night, but the agreement did not hold and fighting escalated instead. At this point, Asad met with "some of our comrades in the leadership" to determine what might be done "to rescue the situation." Having already supplied arms and attempted mediation, the Syrians decided that "nothing remained but direct intervention."[9]

Who were the "comrades" that took this decision? At this point, Asad formed a special ad hoc cabinet to participate in all important decisions involving Lebanon. The nine-member group, under Asad's chairmanship, included prominent representatives of the Army, Air Force, and intelligence service, the Prime Minister, the Foreign Minister, the leader of Sa'iqah, and the two senior representatives of the Regional Command of the Ba'th Party. The representation of all key centers of power in the Syrian political system reflected the enhanced importance attached to developments in Lebanon.[10]

The outcome of deliberations by the Syrian elite was a decision for a higher level of commitment in Lebanon. Asad explains the decision to intervene "under the banner of the Palestine Liberation Army," but later mentions that Syria moved in the PLA "and other forces" whose identity is not specified. He asserts that when

[9]Hafiz al-Asad, Text of speech delivered on 20 July 1976 (in Arabic), Al-Ba'th, Periodic Publication, no. 10, 4 August 1976, pp. 2–3.

[10]Adeed Dawisha, "Syria in Lebanon: Asad's Vietnam?" Foreign Policy 33 (Winter 1978–79): 140–141.

the PLA began its entry into Lebanon, no one was aware that this was occurring. The autonomy of the Syrian decision is underscored by his remark that

> We did not consult with them [i.e., the Palestinian Resistance] and we did not consult with the nationalist parties, and naturally not one of them was prepared to discuss with us any measures [that they took]. The important thing is that they requested us to carry out what [i.e., whatever] would rescue them.[11]

The approximately 3,500 men that entered Lebanon from Syria were primarily affiliated with the Yarmuk Brigade, one of the PLA units stationed in Syria. They were responding to a Syrian command to move forward, although officially all PLA units were subject to the direct command of Yasir 'Arafat. Whereas the issue of PLA loyalties would later arouse acrimonious Syrian-Palestinian dispute, in this instance the PLA intervention clearly furthered the goals of the PLO in Lebanon and of the Lebanese National Movement. Most of the PLA forces from Syria were initially concentrated in the Biqa' Valley, but the presence of these reinforcements enabled 'Arafat to draw on his forces in Southern Lebanon for the siege against Damur.

The indirect Syrian intervention quickly shifted the Lebanese military balance to favor the anti-establishment coalition. By 20 January, Damur and the surrounding Maronite villages fell and were plundered, and Kamil Sham'un's own home was devastated on 24 January. The LNM pursued its attacks on Zahleh in the Biqa' and on a Maronite town near Ba'albek, while Muslim and Palestinian forces from Tripoli assaulted neighboring Zgharta.[12] Deep pessimism arose in Maronite circles, for East Beirut and the northern sector of Mount Lebanon were the only remaining areas squarely under their control. With these exceptions, it appeared that "the whole country fell now under Palestinian military occupation and, indirectly, under Syrian control."[13]

[11]Asad, Speech of 20 July 1976, p. 4.
[12]Khalidi, *Conflict and Violence*, p. 51; Hudson, "Palestinian Factor," p. 272.
[13]Salibi, *Crossroads*, p. 158.

Constitutional Document

Expressing satisfaction with the outcome of the PLA intervention, Syrian Foreign Minister Khaddam announced on 1 February 1976 that proponents of partition had failed dismally. For this he credited Syrian efforts, explaining that "if the PLA had not intervened, Lebanon would now be devouring itself and be destroyed." Moreover, Khaddam predicted that the fighting would not resume, "because new circumstances will be imposed."[14] He was alluding to Syrian diplomatic activities that complemented its military initiative. The sequence paralleled that of the previous September, when the arrival of Palestinian units in Tripoli was followed by a week-long Syrian diplomatic mission. In January, the PLA intervention dovetailed the arrival on the next day of a three-man Syrian mediatory team composed of Khaddam, Chief of Staff Hikmat Shihabi, and Air Force Commander Naji Jamil. They headed straight for the Presidential Palace at B'abda to assist in negotiations for a cease-fire accord.[15]

The circumstances surrounding the mediatory mission are related differently in Syrian and Lebanese accounts. President Asad asserts that when he called Sulayman Faranjiyih on 20 January, the Lebanese President immediately exclaimed, "There are Syrian forces entering Lebanon!" Asad recalled their conversation the previous day and the urgency of the situation that had prompted Syrian intervention. Stressing Syria's commitment to the Palestine Resistance, Asad remarked that "there is a red line in relation to the Palestinians that we will absolutely not permit anyone to cross." The conversation resulted in an agreement to send a Syrian delegation to Lebanon. With a note of exasperation, Asad recalls the "many discussions, receptions, meetings, and encounters" that took place before a cease-fire agreement was finally achieved.[16]

The impression conveyed by the Lebanese daily *Al-Nahar* is that Syria was intimately involved in deliberations for a cease-fire even before the PLA intervention. The newspaper reports that the 19 January phone conversation between Faranjiyih and Asad

[14]*Al-Nahar*, 1 February 1976.
[15]Salibi, *Crossroads*, p. 155.
[16]Asad, Speech of 20 July 1976, p. 4.

"touched on the possibility of a Syrian intervention to secure the cease-fire." By asserting that "Asad agreed in principle" to this proposal, the article implies that Faranjiyih solicited the Syrian military move. The two presidents then discussed specific cease-fire provisions in a later conversation that day.[17] The arrival of the Syrian delegation was also instrumental in alleviating the political impasse triggered by the resignation of Prime Minister Karami. In view of Karami's close contacts with Syria, his resignation may have been an important factor prompting Syria's indirect intervention. Karami left himself room for political maneuver by not submitting his resignation in writing to the President, as tradition would dictate. Faranjiyih, in turn, chose to ignore and then to refuse the resignation. Once a cease-fire was worked out with Syrian assistance on 21 January and a Syrian-Lebanese-Palestinian Higher Military Committee was appointed to supervise its implementation, Karami agreed to withdraw his resignation.[18]

The Syrian mediators then set forth to devise a program to reform the Lebanese political system. Foreign Minister Khaddam discussed the outlines of a modified confessional system with various Lebanese parties, lobbying to gain their acceptance of the plan. The resulting Constitutional Document (referred to by some Lebanese as the "Damascus Agreement") might be considered a written, revised version of the National Pact of 1943.

The Constitutional Document provided for modifications of Lebanese political institutions to favor Lebanon's Muslim majority. The President, Prime Minister, and President of the Chamber of Deputies would continue to be Maronite, Sunni Muslim, and Shi'i Muslim, respectively, preserving an essential tenet of confessionalism. However, in accordance with the long-standing Muslim call for *musharakah,* or more meaningful participation in government, the Prime Minister would be elected by the Parliament, rather than appointed by the President. The number of deputies in Parliament would be raised from 99 to 110, of whom one-half would be Christians and one-half Muslims. This new distribution would supersede the traditional six-to-five ratio favoring the Christians, but would not correspond to the country's Muslim majority.

[17]*Al-Nahar,* 20 January 1976, pp. 1, 4.
[18]Ibid.; Khalidi, *Conflict and Violence,* p. 52.

In a sphere of reform advocated since President Shihab's administration (1958–66), the Constitutional Document called for civil service appointment based on merit rather than sect. The Shihabist formula of an equal number of Christian and Muslim appointees was applied to top-level government positions, and all other appointments were to be made on grounds of merit alone. Institutional innovation is evident in creation of a special High Court empowered to try the President, Prime Minister, and other top officials, introducing greater accountability to the executive branch. A High Economic Council would be in charge of planning and development, although no substantive socioeconomic measures were proposed.[19]

In his July 1976 speech, Asad hails the Constitutional Document as a major victory for all Lebanese. He takes pride in the fact that the document explicitly refers to Lebanon as an Arab state. However, he singles out two groups with vested interests in obstructing the reform plan. The first was the "stratum of leaders and *za'ims*" who benefited from confessionalism and feared a loss of privileges if the system were dismantled. Although they had paid lip service to the goal of abolishing confessionalism in the past, they were "struck with shock" when this became a viable possibility. Second, members of the numerous Lebanese militias earned their livelihood through the fighting, and feared that if security was restored after acceptance of the reform plan, they would be unemployed.[20]

From the perspective of Lebanese, the views expressed by leading politicians displayed considerable variation. Moreover, the positions of some individuals shifted over time. These fluctuations were associated with evolving perceptions of the domestic balance of power and of the reliability and usefulness of the Syrian connection.

The most positive endorsements of the Syrian proposals came from the pro-establishment coalition. Having witnessed the repercussions of Syrian military support for their rivals, Maronite leaders hoped that by embracing the Constitutional Document they would persuade Syria to support them instead. The prime exponent

[19]Malcolm Kerr, "The Syrian Intervention in Lebanon: An Interpretation," paper presented at the conference of the Middle East Studies Association, New York, November 1977, pp. 9–10; Khalidi, *Conflict and Violence*, p. 52.

[20]Asad, Speech of 20 July 1976, pp. 4–5.

of this view was President Faranjiyih, who traveled to Damascus on 7 February to crystallize the Syrian proposals before presenting them to the Lebanese Chamber of Deputies on 14 February. Lebanese commentators called particular attention to a press release announcing that Syria would guarantee implementation of the Cairo Agreement, thereby transforming "Lebanese-Palestinian relations into tripartite relations in actuality."[21]

One early opponent of Syria's diplomatic and military role who subsequently modified his position was Kamil Sham'un of the National Liberal Party. In his capacity as Minister of the Interior, he announced, upon hearing of the PLA intervention, that "forces of the Syrian Army have entered Lebanese soil . . . [and] this intervention threatens this part of the Middle East with a new war." When asked why he equated the PLA forces with the Syrian Army, Sham'un replied:

> It is very hard to differentiate between the Syrian Army and those military formations which are commanded by a number of Syrian officers and in whose ranks an additional number of Syrian officers fight unofficially. Let us not forget that all of the equipment and military supplies are given by Syria. . . . It is perhaps less official than aggression by the Syrian Army, but the result is exactly the same.

Despite this initial critique, Sham'un felt obliged to declare by 24 January that "I have accepted the Syrian initiative to restore peace." Under pressure from other Maronite leaders, he withdrew his initial contention that Syria had become a party to the Lebanese dispute and could not therefore serve as an impartial arbiter. Sham'un insisted, however, that the crucial outcome of Syrian diplomacy must be the enforcement of the Cairo and Malkert Agreements. For he believed that "if the Syrians want to help in restoring peace, it is within their capacity to do so because all of the Palestinian organizations are under Syrian protection."[22]

The most outspoken and consistent Maronite critic of deepening Syrian involvement in Lebanon was Raymun Iddih of the National

---

[21]*Al-Nahar*, 8 February 1976.
[22]*Al-Nahar*, 20 January 1976, 25 January 1976; Salibi, *Crossroads to Civil War*, pp. 155–159.

Bloc Party. He went so far as to declare that "Lebanon, as a result of the criminal behavior of some Christian leaders, has become subject to a Syrian mandate." Iddih suggested that in order to "calm the justifiable fears of many Lebanese," Syria ought to announce "that it does not aim to intervene in Lebanon's internal affairs, . . . that Syria has no regional ambitions in Lebanon, and that it does not aim to occupy [Lebanon's] land." With respect to the Constitutional Document, Iddih stated that if President Faranjiyih went to Damascus "to thank President Asad for restoring security, I can only support him; but if he is going to ask permission of the President of the Syrian state for instituting this or the other reform, . . . then I object."[23] In his position, Iddih remained on the fringe of Maronite opinion and of pro-establishment sentiment in general.

Traditional Muslim political figures by and large endorsed the Constitutional Document, while stating that they would have preferred more encompassing political reforms. The most enthusiastic advocate of the "Damascus Agreement" was the Imam Musa al-Sadr, who emerged during this phase as an outspoken supporter of Syria's policies in Lebanon. Sadr expressed a "great deal of optimism" and complete satisfaction with the Constitutional Document — a somewhat ironic stance since the accord provided no tangible political or socioeconomic benefits to the deprived Shi'i community. Among prominent Sunni politicians, Sa'ib Salam was reserved in his support for the accord, complaining that "it legitimized confessionalism, and that those who were responsible for the ordeal could not make a new Lebanon."

By contrast, Prime Minister Rashid Karami actively endorsed the Syrian proposals.[24] One commentary on Karami's position suggests that the Prime Minister had long believed that Syria must play a critical role in resolving the Lebanese crisis. This was not because of the distinctiveness of the Syrian proposals for reform, whose broad outlines resembled those advocated by many Lebanese politicians. Rather, Karami believed that a Lebanese solution "is lacking . . . in the power of implementation . . . because of the paralysis of the state apparatus and its weakness and frag-

---

[23] *Al-Nahar,* 24 January 1976, 25 January 1976.
[24] *Al-Nahar,* 31 January 1976, 16 February 1976.

mentation." As a result, "there was no alternative to accepting the Syrian intervention to fill the vacuum of authority."[25]

An incipient break between many traditional Muslim politicians and Kamal Junbalat arose as the latter began to express reservations about Syria's diplomatic initiative. Junbalat had participated, along with prominent Muslim leaders, both in the first 'Aramun summit (on 19 January) that solicited Syrian assistance as well as in a subsequent meeting at 'Aramun, on 30 January, with the Syrian delegation to Lebanon. His initial posture of welcoming Syrian involvement turned gradually to ambivalence and then to hostility. This process coincided with changing perceptions of Syria's fidelity in supporting the LNM's stand in the Lebanese conflict.

Kamal Junbalat appeared to be satisfied with the entry on 19 January of PLA forces in support of LNM-Resistance forces in Lebanon. That very night he traveled to Damascus and met with President Asad, later to report that "the trip was very, very successful." During that meeting, Asad and Khaddam enumerated the major points forming the basis of the Syrian reform proposals. When the delegation led by Khaddam arrived in Lebanon and presented its suggestions in detail, Junbalat asserted on 22 January that "we agree with the Syrian initiative and with the suggestions which were bestowed by the noble Syrian delegation in order to solve the crisis in Lebanon." In a more nuanced appraisal the next day, Junbalat declared that "the suggestions of course might not please us fully, because true political reform can only be achieved by implementing the phased program of the parties [the LNM]." Nevertheless, he highlighted the positive aspects the Syrian proposals, through which, he declared, "we will progress one step toward the abolition of the confessional regime."[26]

The first indications of friction between Junbalat and the Syrians appeared early in February. Declaring that he was no longer optimistic and that he would adopt a "wait and see" attitude, Junbalat asserted: "The partial reform which is sought by the Syrian solution, which is a common denominator and no more, must be rendered in a legal, constitutional text . . . because we want firm foundations for the reform that is demanded." The Syrian dele-

---

[25]*Al-Nahar,* 1 February 1976.
[26]*Al-Nahar,* 21 January 1976, 23 January 1976, 24 January 1976.

gation, in turn, told Junbalat on 2 February that he should leave it to the Lebanese authorities to define the means for implementing the reform proposals, and that it was inappropriate for any domestic party to become involved in technicalities of the agreement.[27] Junbalat's sentiment may have reflected suspicion that Syria was moving closer to the pro-establishment coalition, which had embraced its initiative.

The implications of Junbalat's incipient falling-out with the Syrians were far-reaching. Largely because of his objections, the Constitutional Document was never enacted by the Lebanese Parliament. Moreover, the associated Syrian diplomatic goal of promoting a widened, "national unity" cabinet foundered as discussions deadlocked. In domestic Lebanese terms, the seeds for the attenuation of the Lebanese National Movement were laid when Musa al-Sadr as well as the Lebanese branch of the Syrian Ba'th Party and the Union of the Forces of the Working People embraced the Syrian initiative. These groups ultimately parted company with Junbalat as his split with Syria deepened. Henceforth, the LNM consisted only of Junbalat's Progressive Socialist Party, the Nasirists, the Syrian Social Nationalist Party, the Communists, and the Lebanese branch of the Iraqi Ba'th Party.

Junbalat's shift of attitude toward Syria was eventually mirrored in the position of the Palestinian Resistance. The Palestinian leadership, while officially welcoming Syrian mediatory efforts from the outset, increasingly shared Junbalat's suspicions of Syrian intent. Mainstream PLO spokesmen were initially restrained in their criticism of Syria, leading to considerable inconsistency in public pronouncements by Palestinian leaders. On the one hand, Nayif Hawatmih, leader of the leftist Democratic Front for the Liberation of Palestine (DFLP), endorsed Syria's mediatory role, saying:

> Specific agreements have been reached which give practical implementation to the Cairo Agreement.... Syria exercises the role of guarantor of the proper execution of these agreements, and at the same time guarantees [that]...the Lebanese state...should not violate it and should not encourage any aggression on the part of the Kata'ib and their associates against the Resistance.[28]

[27]*Al-Nahar*, 3 February 1976.
[28]*Al-Nahar*, 29 January 1976.

On the other hand, many members of Palestinian Rejectionist groups found restrictions on guerrilla operations posed by the Cairo Agreement unduly confining even before the Civil War. Now that refugee camps were under siege and many Palestinians suspected a Maronite plot to liquidate the Resistance, limits on Palestinian military actions were particularly galling. A PFLP publication openly rejected Syria's mediatory proposals, declaring that "the only acceptable Syrian position . . . is complete support of the Lebanese National Movement and the Palestinian Resistance." The group warned that "any attempts at guardianship, containment, and hegemony" would "threaten the fall of the Syrian regime and the collapse of its role, not only in Lebanon but also in Syria itself and throughout the Arab world."[29]

Despite evidence of growing antagonism to Syria within the Resistance, President Asad's account insists that Syria's mediation fully met Palestinian demands. He relates that as soon as a cease-fire agreement was achieved in January, he consulted the leaders of the Resistance to find out what they wanted, before pursuing Syrian mediatory efforts. A PLO delegation to Damascus headed by Yasir 'Arafat listed demands including the freedom to exercise all rights under the Cairo Agreement (presented by Asad as a set of prerogatives rather than restrictions); the right to guarantee the security of the refugee camps; responsibility for Palestinian affairs outside the camps; and confirmation of the principles of noninterference with the Palestinian presence in Lebanon. Asad comments that "I would say that what was demanded was not necessary in its entirety for the sake of preserving the Resistance and allowing it to play its role against the likely enemy [i.e., Israel]." Nevertheless, President Faranjiyih agreed to these demands without deleting a single letter from the written formulation of the Palestinian leaders.

Subsequent Palestinian objections are attributed by Asad to the fact that "the Resistance is now fighting for the goals of others." Instead of keeping Palestinian priorities in mind, the Resistance allowed itself to become the tool of "forces inside Lebanon and on the world scene that want to use the Resistance for their tactical or strategic objectives."[30] Asad's portrait reveals the backdrop to

[29] *Al-Nahar,* 21 February 1976.
[30] Asad, Speech of 20 July 1976, p. 4.

Syria's disillusionment with its traditional Lebanese allies, as the LNM and Palestinian leadership undermined Syrian mediation and prestige in Lebanon.

Lebanese Army Breakdown

Syria's annoyance over opposition to the Constitutional Document turned to alarm when the Lebanese Army disintegrated in March. Already in January, an LNM statement charged the Army with partisanship for having "supported the isolationist forces [the Kata'ib and National Liberals] in imposing the . . . siege over Tal al-Za'tar." An LNM delegation warned Prime Minister Karami that "the Army is threatened with splitting upon itself if it is deployed in the arena [of combat]," and Karami promised to do his utmost to assure Army neutrality.[31] Then, in the midst of the LNM attack on Damur, the Air Force bombarded LNM supply lines over the objections of the Prime Minister. Shortly thereafter, a Sunni officer, Lt. Ahmad al-Khatib, announced the formation of the Lebanese Arab Army (LAA). In a formal break with the Lebanese Army, Khatib and several dozen soldiers who followed his lead set up their headquarters in the Biqa' Valley.[32] In reaction, the Syrian security apparatus briefly apprehended Lieutenant Khatib, bringing him before a military court in Damascus. Syrian spokesmen portrayed Khatib's actions as "directed against Syria and aimed at obstructing its efforts to end the fighting in Lebanon."[33]

Attempting to stem the deteriorating situation, Syria initiated the mechanism of a joint Syrian-Lebanese-Palestinian Higher Military Committee to supervise the cease-fire accord of late January. Many Lebanese parties aired grievances before the committee. In one instance, a delegation of the Kata'ib Party petitioned the Higher Military Committee to substitute patrols by the Lebanese Army and Internal Security Forces for patrols by PLA forces, especially in East Beirut. On another occasion, Kata'ib leader Pierre al-Jumayyil requested the committee to supplement PLA

[31]*Al-Nahar*, 10 January 1976.
[32]Salibi, *Crossroads*, pp. 153–154; Hudson, "Palestinian Factor," pp. 271–272.
[33]*Al-Nahar*, 29 January 1976.

forces with a voluntary, "official, nonpartisan militia" to which the Kata'ib would willingly contribute.[34] In February, the Lebanese government decided to buttress the committee's authority by relegating to it "command of all armed forces present on Lebanese soil, including Internal Security Forces, the Lebanese Army, and the PLA."[35]

All of these efforts came to naught. On 10 March, dissident Muslim troops precipitously seized their barracks, proclaiming loyalty to Ahmad al-Khatib's Lebanese Arab Army. Faced with mounting desertions, the Army High Command debated how to respond. Hesitancy by some senior officers contrasted with demands by Maronite officers of middle and junior rank for drastic measures against Khatib and his followers. Syrian officials on the scene urged an amnesty for the Army rank and file, after which Syria would arrest Khatib and his principal supporters.[36] When the Lebanese President refused to accept this proposal, Syria officially complained of a "lack of comprehension" by President Faranjiyih of the seriousness of developments and his failure to take "the necessary measures to contain the new moves and prevent a clash." Frustrated by the Lebanese lack of responsiveness, the Syrian mediatory team returned to Damascus; several hours later, a coup d'état was attempted.[37]

The proclamation of a coup on 11 March by Brig. Aziz al-Ahdab, a Sunni officer of the Beirut garrison of the Lebanese Army, reflected the Army's fragmentation rather than a concerted move by the military. Ahdab had few followers in the Army, lending a comic opera quality to his move. Brigadier Ahdab insisted from the outset that he did not aspire to govern, but rather "to compel the politicians to elect a new President." He characterized his coup as "a device to create in the country an atmosphere of national unity around the Army."[38]

Far from fostering Army unity, the abortive coup added momentum to the "battle of the barracks," in which Maronite and Muslim soldiers each seized garrison towns and heavy equipment

[34]*Al-Nahar*, 20 February 1976, 25 February 1976.
[35]*Al-Nahar*, 28 February 1976.
[36]Khalidi, *Conflict and Violence*, 53–54.
[37]As cited in *Al-Nahar*, 2 April 1976.
[38]*Al-Nahar*, 14 March 1976.

belonging to the Army. Within weeks, the Lebanese Army (estimated at 19,000 men on the eve of its collapse) splintered into
several components. A majority of officers remained loyal to the
High Command during the coming months. Of the rank and file,
about half simply went home, while the others joined the combatants. There were two major alternatives to remaining loyal to
the Lebanese Army. One was to join Khatib's Lebanese Arab
Army, which gained control of most of the barracks, located primarily in heavily Muslim areas. Another option was to join individual militias, such as the right-wing Christian militias led by the
Maronite colonels Antoine Barakat and Fuad Malik.[39]

For Syria, the disintegration of the Lebanese Army had profound repercussions. There was no longer any indigenous Lebanese force capable of preserving order, let alone of implementing
a comprehensive set of national reforms. Whereas the small-scale
entry of PLA forces had previously sufficed to tip the Lebanese
military and political balance, a higher-profile military involvement
would now be necessary to sustain or enhance Syrian influence.
Even the Higher Military Committee for Syrian-Lebanese-Palestinian security coordination ceased to function after the Ahdab
"coup."

Syrian spokesmen charged that the formation of the LAA and
the Ahdab coup attempt were orchestrated by Lebanese politicians
(primarily Kamal Junbalat) to subvert Syria's mediatory efforts.
An official Syrian statement of 1 April asserts that by 8 March,
mediators had reached a preliminary agreement on the composition of a Lebanese government of national unity. This progress
was deliberately obstructed by "the activity of a number of politicians to push some military circles, so as to embarrass the President and place him in a predicament, and to push the country
afterwards toward a new crisis and an explosion of the fighting."[40]

Several analysts confirm that the Lebanese National Movement
as well as the PLO were implicated in the military developments
of early March. Michael Hudson contends that both the formation
of the LAA and the Ahdab coup "enjoyed the blessing if not the
actual instigation of Fath."[41] In Walid Khalidi's view, Kamal Jun-

[39]Khalidi, *Conflict and Violence*, pp. 67–68.
[40]As cited in *Al-Nahar*, 2 April 1976.
[41]Hudson, "Palestininan Factor," p. 272.

balat was stalling in negotiations with Syrian Foreign Minister Khaddam over formation of a unity government "in anticipation of the Army mutiny."[42] On 15 March, Junbalat held a meeting with Lt. Ahmad al-Khatib of the LAA, aimed in Junbalat's words "only at coordination to remove the President of the Republic, no more." This political objective, which was the announced goal of the Ahdab coup, was also embraced as the common objective of the LAA and the LNM.[43]

A broad political consensus soon crystallized around the call for Faranjiyih's resignation. On 13 March, two days after Brigadier Ahdab voiced this demand, the Chamber of Deputies met in emergency session and by a two-thirds majority called on the President to resign. However, Faranjiyih refused to abide by the resolution, declaring that he was constitutionally empowered to complete his term of office. Attempting to oblige Faranjiyih to step down, LNM forces and units of the Lebanese Arab Army jointly launched an attack on the Presidential Palace. Under personal duress, President Faranjiyih appealed to Syria for assistance. Syria responded by striking a bargain with Faranjiyih, whereby the President agreed to a constitutional amendment arranging the early election of his successor, six months before the end of his term on September 1976. In exchange, Syria pledged to use the troops at its disposal to protect the Presidential Palace.

In carrying out its side of the bargain, Syria drew not only on PLA units already deployed in Beirut, but also on Syrian Army regulars posing as members of Sa'iqah, the Syrian-sponsored Palestinian guerrilla organization. Despite the efforts of these forces to block the approaches to the palace, strikes by Khatib's long-range artillery on 25 March obliged the President to flee, seeking refuge in the Maronite-controlled area of Mount Lebanon, northeast of Beirut.

The attack on the Presidential Palace was only one prong of a joint offensive by the LNM and the Lebanese Arab Army. They succeeded in dislodging the Kata'ib from the long-contested hotel area in Beirut, and attacked the heartland of Maronite territory in Mount Lebanon, north of the Beirut-Damascus highway. This

---

[42]Khalidi, *Conflict and Violence,* p. 53.
[43]*Al-Nahar,* 16 March 1976.

offensive yielded control of important road junctions and partial disarmament of the population, but not direct occupation of the area under attack.[44]

Syrian Shift of Alignments

Despite evidence of involvement by Palestinian militiamen in the LNM-LAA military offensive in March, the PLO leadership remained cautious in its public posture. Yasir 'Arafat attempted to avoid unduly antagonizing Syria, which continued to supply the arms of the anti-establishment forces. Accordingly, 'Arafat undertook the role of mediator between the LNM and Syria.[45] However, this mediatory mission did not meet with Syrian satisfaction. Asad relates that three or four days after the Ahdab coup, 'Arafat asked him to try to persuade President Faranjiyih to resign. Asad told 'Arafat that he found this request strange, that it "was not a fundamental issue for the Lebanese masses," and that Ahdab's coup "had no relation to the Lebanese national interest." Nevertheless, Syrian delegations were sent to Lebanon and achieved an agreement on amending the Lebanese Constitution to provide for early elections.

Asad expresses indignation that even after this effort was made, calls for Faranjiyih's immediate resignation were accompanied by renewed fighting. 'Arafat then requested Asad to hold a meeting with Kamal Junbalat. Asad queried, "Why should we meet with him, when he insists on renewing the fighting?" When 'Arafat responded that Junbalat's bellicose statements were "merely for public consumption, as is the Lebanese style," Asad agreed to meet the LNM leader.[46]

Asad's account of the seven-hour meeting with Junbalat on 27 March 1976 reveals that the event marked a turning point in the Syrian President's attitude toward the Lebanese conflict. Until that time, Syria continued to support its traditional allies in Lebanon, although with diminished enthusiasm. After the meeting, a shift

[44]Khalidi, *Conflict and Violence*, pp. 54–55; *Quarterly Economic Review of Syria, Lebanon, Cyprus,* 1976, 2nd Quarter, p. 11.

[45]Hudson, "Palestinian Factor," p. 272; Khalidi, *Conflict and Violence*, p. 55.

[46]Asad, Speech of 20 July 1976, pp. 5–6.

in alignments reflected Asad's assessment that Syria's interests no longer coincided with those of the anti-establishment coalition.

In Asad's account, Junbalat emerges as an ungrateful and unreasonable recipient of Syrian favors. At the outset of the meeting, Asad reminded Junbalat that despite generous Syrian political and military support, his forces were unable to hold out in January and Syria was obliged to intervene on their behalf. Intervention was followed by a political initiative that secured for the Palestinian Resistance all of the guarantees it wanted, and realized 90 to 95 percent of the reforms demanded by the LNM in the Constitutional Document. Although Junbalat disputed this evaluation of the Syrian reform plan, Asad says that the Lebanese leader raised no fundamental objections. He complained, for example, that many clauses of the agreement were ambiguous, to which Asad responded that the broad guidelines would be elaborated upon in later regulations and laws, and "at that point, you will explain what you want." Asad then accused Junbalat of supporting Ahdab's coup along with its objective of the President's resignation. Even after Syria accommodated this demand and reached an agreement on the subject, "you yourselves exploded the situation." In the past, Asad remarked, "we believed that we were traveling with you along a single line and toward a single goal," but now he demanded that Junbalat provide an explanation.

Junbalat claimed that his principal objective was to realize a secular state in Lebanon. Asad objected, saying that in meetings with the Lebanese Mufti, the Shi'i Imam Musa al-Sadr, and other Muslim leaders, they vehemently opposed secularization as antithetical to Islam. The only response Junbalat offered to the Muslim religious leaders' view was, "Don't worry about them, they do not represent anything!" To this Asad remarked that the issue was not one of representation but rather of religious principles and must therefore not be taken lightly. At this point, Junbalat showed his true colors, blurting out:

> Let us teach them a lesson! The matter must be resolved militarily. They have governed us for 140 years; we want to get rid of them now!

The issue, Asad concludes, was merely one of revenge and reprisal, based on grudges harbored against the Maronites for over a century. Junbalat was voicing the grievances of a traditional Druze chief, camouflaged as progressive and revolutionary ideals. As the meeting came to an end, Asad was convinced that Junbalat was determined to fight and warned him: "Do not rely on our support."[47]

An abrupt shift in Syria's public posture occurred after the Asad-Junbalat showdown. On 1 April 1976, the Information Office of the Syrian Ba'th Party released a searing personal attack on Junbalat. Referring to him as the "spurious king of the left," the Party contends that Junbalat's ideological pretensions were merely a mask for his ambition to become President of Lebanon. Sparked by an "historical complex" related to the subordinate role of the Druze in the Lebanese political system, Junbalat would allegedly be willing to see 20,000 Lebanese killed and partition take place, so as to emerge as leader of the truncated state. Junbalat is thereby identified as a partner in an international conspiracy, backed by the United States and Israel, aimed at Lebanon's partition. Moreover, the statement declares, "the battle is aimed at Syria's regime" and at its initiative in Lebanon. Nevertheless, after Junbalat's meeting with President Asad, "the last veil has fallen from the face of the imposter," and his downfall is declared to be imminent.[48]

Subsequently, President Asad expounded further on the shift in Syria's policy. In his first speech to the nation on his Lebanese policy, delivered on 12 April, Asad asserts that "we are against any party which insists on continuing the fighting." He assails those who are "traders in politics and not politicians, traders in revolution and not revolutionaries, traders in progressivism and not progressives." Syria is determined to stand up against those responsible for the bloodletting "out of nationalist and Arab principle and out of the principle that the Palestinian cause is the pivot of the Arab struggle." Although doing so imposes additional burdens on Syria, Asad prepares his people to assume an increased level of commitment:

> We in this country, Muslims and Christians, are prepared to move into Lebanon and to protect every oppressed person without regard

[47]Asad, Speech of 20 July 1976, p. 6.
[48]As cited in *Al-Nahar,* 1 April 1976.

for his religious affiliation. . . . [W]e in this region [i.e., Syria] possess complete freedom of movement, and we are able to take the positions which we believe in without anyone being able to prevent us from taking those positions.[49]

In the first week of April, Kamal Junbalat charged that 17,000 Syrian soldiers were massed along the Lebanese border, sarcastically observing that "we hope they would enter to help the National Movement." He said that Asad had threatened to cut off arms and ammunition to the LNM and the Palestinian Resistance, and was already beginning to impose a blockade on several key ports. Junbalat warned the Syrians that they were making fundamental miscalculations. In the first place, he contended that "it is not possible, in any circumstances, for there to be a clash between the National Movement and the Palestinian Revolution, which is part of that movement." Second, "our Syrian brothers have a mistaken picture with respect to the balance of forces in Lebanon — only one-third of the Maronites are with the isolationists Pierre Jumayyil and Kamil Sham'un."[50] Junbalat's comment reinforces the observation that interveners often err by miscalculating the balance of forces between parties to civil strife in the target state.[51]

On the ground, forces of Sa'iqah as well as some Syrian regulars crossed the border into Lebanon on 9 April 1976. Syrian armor, passing through the border town of Masna'a, advanced along the strategically vital Beirut-Damascus highway, providing support to beleaguered Christian forces at Zahleh in the Biq'a Valley and setting up a garrison farther to the west at Shtura. A naval blockade of the northern port of Tripoli and the southern ports of Sidon and Tyre, crucial sources of supply to the LNM, cwas begun in earnest. After these rapid maneuvers, the Syrian forces froze their advance and a cease-fire was declared on the same day.[52] This Syrian military probe, including regular units, was a precursor to the direct military intervention which would occur in June 1976,

[49] As cited in *Al-Nahar,* 13 April 1976.

[50] *Al-Nahar,* 1 April 1975 and 5 April 1975.

[51] Ted Gurr, "The Relevance of Theories of Internal Violence for the Control of Intervention," in *Law and Civil War,* ed. John N. Moore (Baltimore: John Hopkins University Press, 1974), pp. 73–75.

[52] Khalidi, *Conflict and Violence,* p. 55, *QER of Syria, Lebanon,* 1976, 2nd quarter, pp. 3–4, 11.

just as the PLA probes of July and September 1975 foreshadowed the indirect intervention of January 1976.

Responding to these developments, Kamal Junbalat charged that 5,000 to 6,000 soldiers had entered Lebanon, including the Syrian 91st Armored Brigade. He condemned "the Syrian Army which entered under the veil of al-Sa'iqah," demanding its immediate withdrawal. The LNM leader distinguished between the illegitimacy of the Sa'iqah-Syrian Army move, which had not been requested by Lebanese authorities, and the legitimacy of the previous, authorized entry of the PLA in January.[53] Other Lebanese spokesmen, however, gave the Syrians a much more favorable reception. After Hafiz al-Asad's 12 April speech, Lebanese President Faranjiyih praised the "courageous stand" of Syria, motivated by "noble brotherly sentiment" and "Arab solicitude for the unity, independence, and flourishing of Lebanon." Kata'ib leader Pierre al-Jumayyil praised Asad's "historic speech," which served to "tear away the blinders from every eye" in exposing Junbalat's true colors.[54]

After its open break with Junbalat, Syria launched a major effort to disrupt the alliance between the Palestinian Resistance and the LNM. In his 12 April speech, Asad warned "our brothers in the Palestinian leaderships that they should be conscious and should be alert to the danger of the conspiracy" with which he identified Junbalat.[55] Later, in his 20 July address, Asad recalled that he had summoned 'Arafat for a meeting on 28 March, the day after Junbalat's visit. At that point, Asad criticized the involvement of Palestinian guerrillas in the Lebanese fighting, saying that "I cannot imagine what connection there is between fighting by Palestinians on the highest mountains in Lebanon and the liberation of Palestine." He drew an analogy to the Jordanian Civil War of 1970, when guerrillas made a similar mistake in adopting the slogan "Palestine will be liberated by way of 'Amman." 'Arafat then promised Asad that the Resistance would withdraw from the Lebanese fighting.[56]

In the weeks following his meeting with Asad, 'Arafat intensified

[53] *Al-Nahar,* 11 April 1976.
[54] *Al-Nahar,* 13 April 1976.
[55] As cited in *Al-Nahar,* 13 April 1976.
[56] Asad, Speech of 20 July 1976, pp. 7–8.

his mediatory role, striving to tone down the conflict between Syria and Junbalat. On 1 April, he welcomed Syria's "great efforts" to achieve a cease-fire, emphasizing "the strategic relationship which ties the Lebanese National Movement and sister Syria and the Palestinian revolution in confronting all conspiracies." Ten days later, Abu Iyad lamented the "dangerous and terrible test" which this strategic relationship was facing, while contending that "I cannot believe that a single Syrian soldier could fire a bullet at an Arab individual in this country."[57]

An important meeting between Syria and the Palestinian leadership was held on 15 April, leading to a seven-point accord. To Syria's satisfaction, the Resistance agreed to a "united position against any party that would begin a resumption of the combat activities." Palestinian leaders expressed support for the Syrian diplomatic initiative as well as opposition to the partition of Lebanon. The Syrian-Palestinian-Lebanese Higher Military Committee, which had ceased functioning after the Ahdab coup, was reinstated. It was instructed to supervise enforcement of the cease-fire until the election of a new Lebanese President, who would then institute security measures as he deemed appropriate. However, President Asad later complained that "this agreement never saw the light in terms of execution."[58]

Presidential Elections

Syria's options in Lebanon were closely tied, at this point, to the outcome of elections for a successor to President Faranjiyih. On 9 April 1976, the same day that Syrian armor penetrated Lebanese territory, the Lebanese Parliament was convened. The Chamber unanimously adopted a constitutional amendment providing for the early election of a presidential successor. Although Faranjiyih initially refused to be bound by the resolution, pressure by Syria and by prominent Maronite leaders induced him to relent. Elections were set for 1 May.

The candidates for election, although both Maronite, appealed

[57]*Al-Nahar,* 2 April 1976, 11 April 1976.
[58]Asad, Speech of 20 July 1976, pp. 7–8.

to different constituencies. Iliyas Sarkis, narrowly defeated by Far-anjiyih in his candidacy for the presidency in 1970, was favored by the Kata'ib and the National Liberal Party, as well as by Prime Minister Rashid Karami. By contrast, Raymun Iddih, whose crit-icism of Kata'ib activities early in the war had alienated the Ma-ronite leadership, was strongly favored by the anti-establishment coalition. Iddih was also an early critic of Syria's role in Lebanon, whereas Sarkis was expected to be pliant to Syrian influence. The official Syrian position, enunciated in the newspaper *al-Ba'th*, was that the election of the Lebanese President "is an internal Lebanese matter," and Syria would not interfere.[59] However, a Kata'ib del-egation returning from Damascus noted Syrian support for Sarkis, adding that Asad was committed to pursuing the Syrian initiative and was "prepared to use all means, political and otherwise, to arrive at this objective."[60] Speaking on behalf of the Syrian regime, Sa'iqah leader Zuhayr Muhsin acknowledged that "there has been much talk recently . . . about pressures being exercised by Syria on delegates, and threats to some politicians here and there for the sake of the victory of a specific candidate." Muhsin roundly denied the charges, insisting that Syria was committed to "full respect for the democratic game."[61]

The Lebanese National Movement, protesting that Syrian in-terference precluded a fair election, engaged in fighting late in April that forced the election's postponement because Parliament could not be convened in secure circumstances. An agreement was reached to hold the elections on 8 May, under the protection of Syrian-sponsored PLA and Sai'qah troops. According to one ac-count, reluctant deputies "were herded politely at gunpoint by the Sa'iqah guerrilla organization to cast their vote for Sarkis."[62] The parliamentary session was boycotted by pro-Iddih deputies led by Kamal Junbalat and Sa'ib Salam, and Sarkis was elected to the presidency by 66 of the 69 votes cast (out of a potential total of 99).[63]

Political commentators noted that those who had voted for Sar-

[59]As cited in *Al-Nahar*, 29 April 1976.
[60]*Al-Nahar*, 7 May 1976.
[61]*Al-Nahar*, 1 May 1976.
[62]*QER of Syria, Lebanon*, 1976, 3rd quarter, p. 11.
[63]Khalidi, *Conflict and Violence*, pp. 55–56.

kis did not represent either a geographic or a popular majority of the political map of Lebanon. Kamal Junbalat went so far as to say that Sarkis's backers represented only 20 percent of the population. Significantly, deputies from regions geographically adjacent to Syria overwhelmingly voted for Sarkis, despite the strength of anti-establishment political sentiment in their districts. Sarkis's election was widely viewed as the culmination of the latest phase of the Syrian initiative, whereby Syria's promotion of its favored candidate demonstrated "its ability to control security and to impose its respect."[64]

The Palestinian Resistance was cautious in its posture toward the presidential election. While its implicit support for Iddih's candidacy was obvious, open confrontation with Syria over the issue was avoided. Abu Iyad pledged that the future Lebanese President would receive full support from the Resistance. Moreover, he said that the Cairo Agreement was no longer an issue, because "we are prepared in the presence of a balanced Army and a balanced government to accept that there be no agreements between us and the Lebanese government."[65] In the aftermath of the election, commentators remarked that because of the lack of Palestinian support, the LNM failed to block the election by force. Moreover, the LNM could not preserve the coalition between traditional Muslims and the left. Iddih, who unwillingly was identified as the candidate of the left, could not split the Christian-right coalition. Overall, Kamal Junbalat was the greatest loser of the election, because the integrity of the anti-establishment coalition was damaged while relations with Syria worsened.[66]

Once the election was over, President-elect Sarkis expressed hopes of building the political consensus lacking at the electoral session of Parliament. Contending Lebanese groups spelled out terms for cooperation with the Sarkis regime. Spokesmen for the LNM indicated, first, that they would assess Sarkis's commitment to political reform and, in particular, to the abolition of political confessionalism. Second, they insisted that security should be a Lebanese matter, without involvement by any external deterrent force, Syrian or non-Syrian.

[64]*Al-Nahar,* 9 May 1976.
[65]*Al-Nahar,* 26 April 1976.
[66]*Al-Nahar,* 9 May 1976.

The Kata'ib, by contrast, wanted to pursue the Syrian diplomatic initiative and sustain the Syrian-sponsored deterrent force. Their rationale was that "the Lebanese war might not end except through a force that surpasses the force of the combatants, and ... Syria alone is able and determined to advance this force."[67] The growing closeness between the Kata'ib Party and Syria began to draw public attention, prompting Pierre al-Jumayyil to exclaim: "The Kata'ib cannot be accused by anyone of being agents for Syria or anyone else, especially by those who [previously] insisted on accusing us of enmity to Syria."[68]

Hopes generated by the prospect of a new administration soon soured into disillusionment when President Faranjiyih announced that he did not intend to resign until the formal conclusion of his term in September. Syria may have acquiesced in Faranjiyih's unwillingness to resign, because it indirectly benefited from having a known figure in office and possibly also from having the domestic Lebanese situation unresolved. Kamal Junbalat, referring to Faranjiyih as "Syria's man," said that "they wish to delay the resignation of Faranjiyih, so that they may infiltrate and may be everywhere, in preparation for stirring up problems in the country."[69]

A new wave of violence, which began with the LNM's attempt to subvert the Presidential election, continued through May. The anti-establishment forces waged a serious battle for control of the Beirut port, and the struggle for control of Maronite bastions in Mount Lebanon was resumed with active participation by Lieutenant Khatib's Lebanese Arab Army. Kamal Junbalat acknowledged close coordination with the LAA, saying that "they [the LAA] are in a common front, and the National Movement is the political leader for the Lebanese Arab Army." Lieutenant Khatib's forces, originally concentrated in the Biqa' Valley and in northern Lebanon, took over additional military outposts in central and Southern Lebanon. By May, the LAA had gained control over security, communications, and provisions in the South. Former Lebanese Army officers acted under LAA auspices to set up a "Lebanese Arab Customs" force and a "Lebanese Arab General

[67] *Al-Nahar*, 12 May 1976.
[68] *Al-Nahar*, 7 May 1976.
[69] *Al-Nahar*, 15 May 1976.

Security" force, regulating customs ana immigration at the Lebanese borders.

Syria's response to the LNM-LAA initiative was to reinforce its land-and-sea blockade against the alliance, curtailing arms, ammunition, and provisions. In one incident, an Algerian ship bound for Sidon with arms for the anti-establishment forces was diverted to the Syrian port of Ladhaqiyyah and obliged to unload its cargo. Syrian-sponsored PLA and Sa'iqah forces also sought to control strategic positions in Lebanon, reportedly engaging in a campaign of assassinations against members of the anti-Syrian press and of the Iraqi Ba'th Party in Tripoli.[70]

In May, a controversy arose over the use of Palestinian forces to serve Syrian policy objectives. Kamal Junbalat had already distinguished between the legitimate role of PLA forces that had entered Lebanon in January and the illegal entry of regular Syrian forces, "under the veil of al-Sa'iqah."[71] During May, both Sa'iqah and PLA units took a more active role in hostilities. Sometimes they served as a buffer between contending forces. On other occasions Syrian-sponsored Palestinian units engaged in fighting on the side of Christian forces, becoming involved in gun battles with the anti-establishment coalition. As a result, exchanges occurred between PLA and Sa'iqah units on the one hand and Rejectionist and PLO guerrillas on the other.[72]

A new initiative to mediate between Syria and the Palestinian Resistance was undertaken by Shi'i Imam Musa al-Sadr. A spokesman for the Imam stressed that "We have embraced the Syrian initiative . . . out of free will," and that Musa al-Sadr's mediation was aimed at overcoming "the conspiracy . . . aimed at widening the gap of the dispute between the Resistance and Syria." After meeting in Damascus with President Asad and Yasir 'Arafat on 7 May, Musa al-Sadr announced that "the views of Asad and 'Arafat were completely in harmony on matters of security." An emergency Islamic summit at the home of the Lebanese Mufti in 'Aramun then delegated Musa al-Sadr to visit Damascus again to "strengthen the relationship between Syria and the Resistance."[73]

[70]*QER of Syria, Lebanon,* 1976, 3rd quarter, p. 13; *Al-Nahar,* 15 May 1976.
[71]See above, p. 200.
[72]Sirriyyeh, "Palestinian Armed Presence," p. 86.
[73]*Al-Nahar,* 8 May 1976, 10 May 1976, 14 May 1976.

Efforts at mediation were doomed because Palestinian leaders were increasingly incensed over the use of PLA units in Tripoli. The Resistance issued a public statement on 13 May containing a "warning to the leadership of the Palestine Liberation Army against drawing the PLA without the knowledge of the political leadership into battles with the Patriotic and Progressive Forces [i.e., the LNM]." Abu Iyad also criticized the PLA's military command, saying that "its officers and soldiers are members of this people, [but] the leader at its head does not represent the Army as a whole." On 14 May, Yasir 'Arafat demanded that PLA units stationed in Tripoli "should withdraw completely from the lines of confrontation." The order was ignored.[74]

An editorial in *Al-Nahar* revealed that the Resistance had already expressed its apprehension to Syria over "a basic question," that is, "from whom does the PLA take its orders when it is outside Syrian soil?" Syria's response was that "when the PLA is outside Syrian soil, its leadership submits to Yasir 'Arafat, and when it is within its [Syrian] soil, it submits to the Syrian leadership."[75] As early as April, growing controversy between Syria and the Resistance precipitated demonstrations at the Palestinian refugee camp of al-Yarmuk, outside Damascus. In reprisal, the Syrian Army surrounded the camp, imposed a curfew, and imprisoned many Palestinian militants. The secret police harassed PLO members and the mass media launched a campaign criticizing "ungrateful Palestinians." The charged atmosphere made it difficult to maintain operation of PLO headquarters in Damascus, and 'Arafat decided to move them to Beirut.[76] Syrian-Palestinian relations reached a new low when 'Arafat was denied transit through Syria on his way to Libya on 26 May.[77]

Invitational Intervention?

By the end of the transitional phase of its commitment in the Lebanese Civil War, Syria recognized its failure to disrupt the

[74]*Al-Nahar,* 14 May 1976, 15 May 1976, 16 May 1976.
[75]*Al-Nahar,* 16 May 1976.
[76]*QER of Syria, Lebanon,* 1976, 3rd quarter, p. 3.
[77]Khalidi, *Conflict and Violence,* p. 58.

alliance between the Resistance and the LNM. At this point, a domestic Lebanese debate surfaced over authorization for the entry of Syrian-sponsored Palestinian forces. In essence, Lebanese politicians were disputing whether Syria's intervention to date should be viewed as "invitational" and, if so, who bore responsibility for issuing the invitation. The debate is highly revealing of shifts in attitude toward Syria's role among parties to the Lebanese civil strife.

One theory advanced by Kamal Junbalat was that Syria had encouraged the Kata'ib to increase the level of violence in Lebanon, to provide a pretext for their deepening commitment. Abu Iyad similarly argued that "discussion of a 'security vacuum' was aimed at . . . precipitating the intervention of foreign forces." In Junbalat's view, Syria's key mistake lay in relying on an alliance with the Kata'ib and some traditional Muslim leaders, "to use them to face the National Movement." He singled out Prime Minister Rashid Karami as a "sychophant" who had sunk to the lowest level in "fawning" before the Syrians. Junbalat exclaimed:

> May God forgive Rashid Karami, who committed a deadly sin. . . . For he agreed personally to the entry of the Syrian forces, despite the fact that this is absolutely not within his prerogatives. For a political decision must be taken in the Council of Ministers [i.e., Cabinet] in every matter of this sort, and this was not done.[78]

Responding to these charges, Prime Minister Karami cited the declaration by the Imam Musa al-Sadr, after discussions with Syrian leaders, that Syrian forces entered Lebanon in January in direct response to the request of the Islamic summit at 'Aramun. Significantly, Karami and other participants in the debate refer consistently to the entry of Syrian, rather than PLA, forces. Karami elaborated:

> The Syrian forces came in compliance with the appeal of the 'Aramun summit, and not through a particular appeal on my part. President Asad announced this to the Imam al-Sadr . . . [saying] that these forces are at the disposal of the 'Aramun summit, and they

---

[78] *Al-Nahar,* 16 April 1976, 26 April 1976, 18 May 1976.

are prepared to take the position requested of them, whether it be negative or positive.

The impression that Syrian-sponsored forces in Lebanon would remain answerable to the Islamic leadership was, however, contradicted in another statement by the Shi'i Imam. He cited President Asad as saying that once President-elect Sarkis took office and achieved national reconciliation, "there will no longer be any need for non-Lebanese forces." If, however, the need did persist, then "their use is contingent upon the new President and officials in Lebanon."[79]

The Lebanese debate was further complicated when former Prime Minister Sa'ib Salam brought up the issue of the initial Syrian indirect intervention in September 1975. He recalled that at a meeting of the Committee for National Dialogue in November 1975, Raymun Iddih had asked Prime Minister Karami whether Syrian forces entered based on his personal request or that of the Cabinet, and Karami had replied that the request was authorized by the Cabinet. Iddih confirmed this account of the proceedings, but Karami denounced it as a fabrication, and other participants in the Committee for National Dialogue said that they had no recollection of the exchange.[80]

In a critique of the ongoing debate, Kata'ib leader Pierre al-Jumayyil remarked on the shifts in positions of many Lebanese politicians in recent months. He asserted that in January 1976, Sa'ib Salam and other participants in the 'Aramun summit had taken the initiative in "requesting Syrian military assistance so that it would provide support to one group of Lebanese against [another] party." Those who had advocated partisan intervention on their behalf were now turning against Syria, "when [its] initiative became a sincere attempt to stop this squalid war."[81] A similar note was conveyed by the Syrian newspaper al-Ba'th, in a terse commentary on the Lebanese debate:

> The parties who insist on defaming Syria's position and on continuing the battles were the first who requested the Syrian intervention in the past.[82]

[79] Al-Nahar, 16 May 1976, 17 May 1976.
[80] Al-Nahar, 19 May 1976, 20 May 1976.
[81] Al-Nahar, 19 May 1976.
[82] As cited in Al-Nahar, 15 May 1976.

8

Direct Military
Intervention

The entry of 12,000 Syrian Army troops into Lebanon in the first
week of June 1976 dramatically contrasted with the tentativeness
of Syria's previous commitment in Lebanon. After the reassessment of early 1976, involving a shift in the direction of its alignments and an incremental rise in its commitment, the Syrian elite
plunged decisively into direct military engagement.

Once President Asad and his advisers decided on this course,
they did not await invitations by parties to the Lebanese strife.
This phase of Syrian intervention and escalation was penetrational
in its designs and implementation. Nevertheless, miscalculations
about the costs involved in achieving more ambitious objectives
obliged the Syrian elite to make tactical readjustments. The large-
scale Syrian military offensive suffered initial reversals, only to be
subsequently revived at a still higher level of military commitment.

Penetrational Intervention

The immediate precipitant for Syrian military intervention was an
attack on two Maronite villages in northern Lebanon by maverick
units of the Lebanese Arab Army late in May 1976. Residents of
the villages sent a telegram to President Asad, appealing for Syrian
assistance. In a subsequent justification of Syria's response, Prime
Minister Karami suggested that Syria's intervention was "motivated by nationalist and humanist sentiments, in response to the
request of a group of citizens who were in a state of despair and
fear, prompting them to appeal for assistance to sister Syria."[1]

[1] *Al-Nahar,* 3 June 1976 and 7 June 1976; Malcolm Kerr, "The Syrian Intervention

The authenticity of the Lebanese appeal was immediately questioned. On 1 June, Kamal Junbalat charged that "the Syrians pressured one of the officers in the north to commit aggression against two towns." This attack was contrived to generate a pretext for Syrian response, and "no one asked them to intervene."[2] Maronite leader Raymun Iddih also discounted the claim by Syrian Foreign Minister Khaddam that Syria had intervened based on the request of Lebanese authorities and a large segment of Lebanese public opinion. Iddih challenged Khaddam to name the Lebanese authorities who issued the appeal and "to announce who are those who represent public opinion." He also urged President Faranjiyih to announce publicly whether he had invited the Syrian forces, contending that "if neither he nor his government requested the entry of the Syrian Army, then [what is the reason for] his silence and the silence of his government about this flagrant transgression against the sovereignty of Lebanon?"[3]

A full-fledged debate was soon under way in Lebanon about the propriety of the Syrian intervention, along with speculation over its possible course. Supporters of the intervention argued that it would be limited in goals and duration. The role of the Syrian forces would be confined to preserving security in troubled areas and regulating the entry of weapons into the country. Once security was achieved, a roundtable discussion between domestic Lebanese parties could lead to a political settlement. Lebanon would reach an agreement with Syria limiting the duration of the Syrian military presence, subject to renewal at the request of the Lebanese authorities and parties to the Lebanese conflict.[4]

The most enthusiastic proponents of this view were members of the Maronite coalition, the Lebanese Front. At a summit conference on 5 June, the Lebanese Front endorsed the Syrian intervention without qualification, citing statements by Foreign Minister

---

in Lebanon: An Interpretation," paper presented at the conference of the Middle East Studies Association, New York, November 1977, p. 13; Walidi Khalidi, *Conflict and Violence in Lebanon,* Harvard Studies in International Affairs, no. 38 (Cambridge: Center for International Affairs, Harvard University, 1979), pp. 58–59.

[2]*Al-Nahar,* 2 June 1976.
[3]*Al-Nahar,* 5 June 1976.
[4]*Al-Nahar,* 3 June 1976.

Khaddam reiterating Syrian commitment to the independence and territorial integrity of Lebanon. Kata'ib Party leader Pierre al-Jumayyil called for a "security accord with a Syrian guarantee in preparation for a political solution."[5]

For his part, President Faranjiyih insisted that he did not know beforehand of Syria's plan to intervene, and President-elect Sarkis also denied foreknowledge. Faranjiyih justified the intervention as a necessary means for implementing the Constitutional Document, with first priority to the Cairo Agreement. The Lebanese daily *Al-Nahar* took issue with Faranjiyih's justification, indicating that the Syrian-sponsored Constitutional Document was never passed by the Lebanese Parliament, and that the President was therefore not authorized to implement it. Moreover, "if it is imperative that the Cairo Agreement be implemented, the [Constitutional] Document does not call for its implementation through a Syrian military invasion, but rather through dialogue and mutual understanding."[6]

Opponents of the Syrian intervention argued that a Lebanese political solution could not be achieved "under the shadow of the Syrian forces." They viewed the presence of the Syrian Army as an attempt to impose a "Pax Syriana," under the guise of instituting the Constitutional Document. In these circumstances, the Lebanese National Movement would be stripped of strength at the negotiating table, preventing a genuine dialogue. Even if agreement was reached, Syria would be heavily involved in selecting a new Lebanese Cabinet and rebuilding the Army, leading to an extended Syrian military presence of a year or more.[7]

In the wake of the Syrian intervention, Sunni leader Sa'ib Salam's earlier reservations about Syria's role changed to open criticism. Salam claimed that "from the first moment," he had warned against direct involvement in Lebanon by the Syrian Army. In the absence of any request for the operation by Lebanese constitutional authorities, this was "a violation of the sovereignty of Lebanon and a dangerous precedent which might befall any Arab country." Instead of restoring stability, Salam warned, Syrian intervention would precipitate an escalation of Lebanese civil strife. Then, "the pretext for which the Syrian Army entered, which is

[5]*Al-Nahar,* 6 June 1976.
[6]*Al-Nahar,* 2 June 1976, 10 June 1976.
[7]*Al-Nahar,* 3 June 1976.

stopping the fighting . . . would have led to the opposite . . . , increasing its escalation and widening its scope." Finally, Salam cautioned that the negative consequences "might hurt Lebanon and might also hurt Syria." Expressing concern for the interests of "sister Syria," Salam urged it not "to fall into a field of quicksand in Lebanon."[8]

From the perspective of the Lebanese National Movement, there was no doubt that Syria planned a total assault on its forces and those of the Palestinian Resistance. The LNM's response was to formalize a Central Military Command with the Palestinian Resistance and the Lebanese Arab Army, to confront "the danger of the Syrian invasion." Henceforth, the LNM-LAA Palestinian forces were referred to collectively as the "joint forces."

In a parallel vein to Salam, an LNM statement of 1 June declared that "this intervention has become the main complicating element in the Lebanese crisis." The LNM argued that Syria was intent on "a scheme of effective occupation" whose ultimate goal was to achieve the partition of Lebanon, as advocated by the "isolationists" (i.e., the Lebanese Front). Kamal Junbalat asserted that Syria wished to divide Lebanon into a number of "ministates."[9]

The charge of Syrian designs for partition was articulated most forcefully by Raymun Iddih, the outspoken Maronite critic of Syria's intervention. Iddih recalled the warning by Syrian Foreign Minister Khaddam on 7 January 1976 that "Lebanon was part of Syria, and we would restore it with any attempt at partition."[10] What Syria really wanted as a result of its intervention, he charged, was to annex the Biqa', Tripoli, and the 'Akkar (the region north of Tripoli, linking the Lebanese coast to the Biqa'), as its ultimate "share" once Lebanon was partitioned.

Iddih called on the local population of these regions to resist the Syrian intervention. He also charged that another intended outcome of the partition plan—the creation of a Christian homeland in Mount Lebanon (from Zgharta to the Beirut-Damascus highway) was unacceptable. Iddih contended that "the majority of Maronites and the majority of Christians in Lebanon do not consent to establishing a Christian national patrie," although the

[8]*Al-Nahar,* 2 June 1976, 4 June 1976.
[9]*Al-Nahar,* 2 June 1976, 5 June 1976, 7 June 1976.
[10]See above, p. 181.

leaders of the Lebanese Front were conspiring with Syria to achieve that objective.[11]

Abortive Syrian Offensive

While one may speculate whether the ultimate objective of Syria's intervention was to facilitate a political settlement or to promote partition, its immediate objective was certainly not realized. The Syrian elite hoped that their large-scale offensive would deal a crushing blow to the wayward Palestinian Resistance and Lebanese National Movement, to force them to stop contesting Syria's will in Lebanon. Having failed to achieve acquiescence to its preferred political solution by the LNM or to disrupt the alliance between the LNM and the Resistance through political leverage, Syria determined to pursue the same outcome through coercion.

The Syrian offensive began on 31 May 1976, when Syrian troops headed toward the two Maronite villages in northern Lebanon that were attacked by the Lebanese Arab Army. By the following day, Syrian troops and armor entered the Biqa' Valley, rising in number to approximately 6,000 by 5 June. Once inside Lebanon, the troops followed three axes in their advance, heading toward Tripoli in the north, along the main Beirut-Damascus highway in the center, and toward Sidon in Southern Lebanon. However, Syrian forces were obliged to halt before reaching their destinations either in Sidon or in Beirut. After encountering stiff resistance, the number of Syrian forces was doubled to 12,000 by 7 June.[12]

When Syrian armored columns initially advanced along the Beirut-Damascus highway, they expected their heavy equipment to intimidate Palestinian and LNM militiamen. Instead, the latter made effective use of anti-tank weapons provided by Syria earlier in the war. Syrian forces were temporarily halted at Sofar, in the central sector of the Beirut-Damascus highway, and only with the doubling of their number on 7 June were they able to proceed. The contingent heading toward Sidon reached the environs of the city later the same day but was unable to penetrate farther after

[11]*Al-Nahar*, 5 June 1976, 29 June 1976.
[12]Kerr, "Syrian Intervention," p. 13; Khalidi, *Conflict and Violence*, pp. 58–59.

an ambush by Palestinian and Lebanese Arab Army troops incapacitated a Syrian armored reconnaisance squadron.[13]

In his 20 July 1976 speech, President Asad attempts to discount the impression that Syria suffered a military reversal in its June offensive. Asad recounts that in moving toward Sidon, a detachment the size of a company preceded the advancing Syrian brigade. This vanguard unit was "applauded by the people along the length of the road, in every village and town; and roses were thrown upon it in every place." When the unit reached Sidon, the soldiers descended from their mechanized vehicles to circulate among the people, "exchanging welcomes and embraces with them as if they had come [back] to their families after a long absence." Suddenly, however, the soldiers and the native population were fired upon by "armed elements of the organizations"—the Palestinians and LNM—resisting the Syrian advance.

At pains to explain why Syrian forces were unable to withstand the attacks, Asad declares that Syria consciously chose not to exercise its full range of military options. If Syria had so desired, it could easily have responded militarily with "resolute and crushing measures." However, Syria was convinced that the problem in Lebanon was not primarily a military problem, and that "the conspiracy is much greater than these little ones who carry out these small treacherous actions." Believing that the underlying issues could not be resolved by military means, Syria instructed every soldier to strike only in self-defense and "within the narrowest limits."

Moreover, Asad contends that the Syrian forces in Lebanon consisted of infantrymen lacking artillery, armor, or other means of support. Moreover, the Syrian Air Force "has not fired a single shot or released a single bomb or a single missile in any place in Lebanon." Although strictly military logic would have dictated that Syria provide rapid support for its forces, political considerations dictated restraint. However, Asad insisted that "naturally, we are confident in the competence of our troops, and no one can surpass specified limits in harming them."[14]

Syrian humiliation at being unable to overcome unexpectedly

[13]Khalidi, *Conflict and Violence*, p. 59; *Quarterly Economic Review* (QER) *of Syria, Lebanon*, 1976, 3rd quarter, p. 13.

[14]Hafiz al-Asad, Text of speech delivered on 20 July 1976, pp. 9–10.

heavy resistance by Palestinian and LNM forces was deepened by defections from Syrian ranks. Most conspicuous were defections among PLA and Sa'iqa forces that had entered Lebanon earlier under Syrian auspices. This notably took place in Beirut, in reaction to a confrontation on 6 June between advancing Syrian forces and Palestinian-LNM militiamen in the Biqa' Valley. After the Syrians were erroneously reported to have used their Air Force for attacks in the Biqa', violent clashes erupted in Beirut between Palestinian-LNM militiamen and Sa'iqah-PLA forces already stationed by the Syrians in the capital. As Palestinians fought Palestinians, many of those associated with Syria switched allegiance, contributing to the ease with which the Sa'iqah-PLA forces in Beirut were disarmed. Even more threatening to the Syrian elite was dissent among regular Syrian forces. Individual pilots and unit commanders refused to participate in the Lebanese operation, and after entering Lebanon some officers defected to join Palestinian and LAA ranks. The offenders were quickly punished, however, and incidents of dissent remained limited.[15]

In a conscious effort to precipitate dissent within the Syrian Army, the LNM issued a statement on 4 June directed at "the brave Syrian Arab fighter." Presenting each Syrian with "the opportunity to think about what you are being pressed to do," the LNM queried:

> Don't you ask yourself: Why do [the Lebanese] masses greet you by digging trenches? . . . Does it make sense that you should enter today to suppress the Lebanese Arab masses and . . . the Palestinian Resistance and to support the isolationists?

In an analogous appeal, the Rejection Front of the Palestinian Resistance called upon political forces close to the Syrian regime to

> announce their outrage about the conspiracy of striking at the Resistance and the National Movement, and to resist it . . . for those

---

[15]Fred H. Lawson, "Syria's Intervention in the Lebanese Civil War, 1976," *International Organization* 38, 3 (Summer 1984): 477; Khalidi, *Conflict and Violence,* p. 59; *Quarterly Economic Review (QER) of Syria, Lebanon,* 1976, 3rd quarter, p. 13.

forces which participate in power bear a historic responsibility if they remain silent.[16]

The spectacle of Palestinians loyal to Yasir 'Arafat fighting Palestinians loyal to Hafiz al-Asad alongside Syrian Army units prompted recriminations between Resistance leaders and Syria. Yasir 'Arafat flatly charged that Syria was attempting to liquidate the Palestinian Resistance.[17] Abu Iyad sarcastically added that "we are against the liquidation of the Palestinian Resistance in the name of defending the Palestinian Resistance." He asserted that the Syrian objective was "to cut the Palestinian Resistance down in size," so as "to achieve what the Jordanian Army failed to achieve" in 1970.

Elaborating on Palestinian grievances against Syria, Abu Iyad explained that the PLO had always believed that Syria and the Resistance had a "strategic relationship." The PLO was the first to welcome the Syrian initiative in Lebanon. Although Syria acted as an arbiter in the conflict, "we always considered her to be at our side and at the side of the National Movement." When speculation began after the attempted coup by Brigadier Ahdab in March about the prospect of Syrian intervention, "we warned, with full brotherliness . . . against a Syrian military intervention." However, Syria decided to "stand in the face of [a] great victory which was realized by the National Movement and by the Palestinian revolution," preventing them from gaining the upper hand in the Lebanese conflict.

Abu Iyad served notice that "we are part of the Lebanese National Movement" and would remain united with them in resisting the Syrian intervention and in demanding full withdrawal of Syrian forces from Lebanon.[18] In a separate action, the leaders of the Rejection Front of the Resistance called for the expulsion of Sa'iqah from the Resistance movement. Sa'iqah's expulsion was necessitated by "its flagrant stand against the will of the Palestinian masses, and its use of the Palestinian identity in a way that serves the enemies of [the Palestinian] cause."[19]

[16]*Al-Nahar,* 4 June 1976, 5 June 1976.
[17]Khalidi, *Conflict and Violence,* p. 59.
[18]*Al-Nahar,* 1 June 1976, 17 June 1976.
[19]*Al-Nahar,* 4 June 1976.

President Asad, in his July 1976 speech, takes issue with the Palestinian right to pass judgment on Syrian conduct. He claims that the Palestinian leaders were the only ones who came forth and said that "Syria does not belong in Lebanon." If, by contrast, the President, Prime Minister, or President of the Chamber of Deputies of Lebanon asked Syria to refrain from entering or to depart, Syria would acknowledge their right to do so and would consider complying. However, Lebanon is not Palestine, and the Palestinians therefore lacked any legal or moral premise for demanding Syrian withdrawal from Lebanon.

Moreover, Asad charges the Palestinian leadership with ingratitude, asserting that Syria entered Lebanon in the first place in order to rescue them. Now, PLO spokesmen were asking Syria to leave Lebanon, not for the sake of Palestine, but rather "for the sake of others, for the sake of anything other than Palestine." Syria, however, as the "heart of Arabism," would not be provoked into abandoning the sacred Palestinian cause, which "is our cause and not the cause of individuals, particularly if those individuals act in a way which is harmful to this cause." Syria's right to discern what would best promote the Palestinian cause was underscored by its numerous sacrifices on behalf of Palestine, unparalleled by any other Arab country.[20]

Other Arab countries did, however, begin to take an active interest in the fate of the Palestinians and in the overall Lebanese conflict after Syria's massive intervention occurred.[21] An emergency meeting of Arab foreign ministers was convened on 6 June, and on 9 June the Arab League decided to establish a 2,500-man inter-Arab force. The task of the force was to separate the Lebanese combatants, replace the Syrian forces, and implement a cease-fire accord.

Although the formation of an inter-Arab force might be considered a reversal for the Syrians, in practice this was not so. In the first place, Syrian and Palestinian (PLA) units were to be assigned to the force, in addition to units recruited from various Arab states. No guidelines were elaborated for the relative size of the Syrian component, nor was a date set for the withdrawal of

---

[20]Asad, Speech of 20 July 1976, pp. 10–11.
[21]For fuller detail, see Chapter 9.

regular Syrian forces. What happened in practice was that after acceptance of the cease-fire accord, Syrian soldiers donned white helmets representing a new pan-Arab function, and only token units were sent by other Arab states.

Arab mediation was also at play when Libyan Prime Minister 'Abd al-Salam Jallud negotiated a Syrian-Palestinian accord on 21 June. Under the terms of the cease-fire, Syrian forces were to withdraw to the Biqa' Valley. The Palestinian-LNM alliance, in turn, was to give up the Sa'iqah positions they had taken over at the outset of the Syrian intervention and to return Syrian officers and men that they had taken prisoner. Palestinian spokesmen soon complained that, although they had kept their side of the bargain, the Syrians had failed to withdraw their forces as promised and remained poised on the heights of Mount Lebanon and dug in around Sidon.[22]

Refugee Camps under Siege

Palestinian bitterness against Syria was deepened by the conviction that Syria's intervention had tilted the military balance in favor of the pro-establishment coalition, enabling a new Maronite military offensive. The Kata'ib and National Liberals launched a major attack on 22 June 1976, directed against Beirut slums controlled by the LNM as well as Palestinian refugee camps.

The strategic rationale of the Maronite offensive, as in earlier Beirut attacks, was to remove hostile enclaves impeding communications between East Beirut and the Maronite-controlled territories to the north and east. The refugee camps' defenders therefore suspected that the Maronite campaign was a prelude to partition of the country. Ironically, most of the inhabitants of Jisr al-Basha, which fell to its attackers on 1 July, were Maronite Palestinians. In Tall al-Za'tar, which withstood a siege for many more weeks, only about 17,000 of the 30,000 inhabitants were Palestinian. Most of the others were Shi'i refugees who had fled from Southern Lebanon to seek employment in the eastern suburbs of

[22]Kerr, "Syrian Intervention," pp. 13–14; Khalidi, *Conflict and Violence*, p. 59; *QER of Syria, Lebanon* 1976, 3rd quarter, pp. 4, 13–14.

Beirut, which had the highest concentration of light industries in the country.[23]

Yasir 'Arafat accused Syria of complicity in the siege of Jisr al-Basha and Tall al-Za'tar, although much of the evidence he cited was indirect. Syrian pressure against the Palestinian-LNM forces in many parts of the country drained the latter's energies and potential, preventing them from mounting an effective defense of the camps.

After Syria's military reversals in early June, Syrian leaders changed their tactics. A continued thrust against urban centers such as Sidon, Tripoli, or Beirut would have led to heavy Syrian casualties, with uncertain military results. Instead, a strategy of attrition against the anti-establishment coalition was pursued throughout the country. One means of harassing and starving out the Palestinian-LNM coalition was to tighten the blockade of their supplies that had commenced in April. The Syrian Navy patrolled the northern half of the Lebanese coast, preventing the unloading of supplies at Tripoli, whose harbor was under LNM control. Meanwhile, Israel engaged in a naval blockade of the southern half of the Lebanese coast with apparent Syrian acquiescence, forestalling the unloading of supplies at Sidon and Tyre.[24]

Moreover, Syrian armed units concentrated in the Biqa' Valley blocked lines of communication between anti-establishment strongholds in the north and south of the country. The hold of Syrian forces over the Biqa' was further consolidated, reinforcing suspicions by many Lebanese of Syrian designs for annexation of the area. From their Biqa' stronghold, Syrian forces widened their attack on anti-establishment positions in other areas. Early in July, a Syrian armored offensive dislodged their opponents' forces from the hills surrounding Farayya in the northern Kisrawan region. Advances were also made in Mount Lebanon and around Sidon, and Syria joined pro-establishment forces in repeated bombardment of Tripoli in the north. Nevertheless, the Kata'ib voiced reservations about the extent of Syrian support for their cause. They complained that the Syrian blockade of arms and supplies to the anti-establishment forces was not as complete as it could

---

[23]Khalidi, *Conflict and Violence,* pp. 59–60, n. 72.
[24]For a fuller discussion, see Chapter 10, especially p. 285.

have been. They also suspected that Syria was deliberately permitting loopholes in the blockade, so that the military balance would not shift completely in favor of one side, compromising Syria's tactical flexibility.[25]

Palestinian-LNM forces tried to regain the initiative and relieve the pressure on the besieged Tall al-Za'tar camp by staging an assault near Tripoli on 8 July. In response, a Maronite counteroffensive was directed against local villages near Tripoli sympathetic to the Lebanese National Movement. Some of these villages were inhabited primarily by Muslims and others by Greek Orthodox, many of whom identified with the Syrian Social Nationalist Party.

The ability of the Palestinian-LNM coalition to function effectively in the north was impeded by a decline in its military potential. Aside from diminished access to supplies, there were also signs of disintegration in the Lebanese Arab Army. As the military balance shifted to favor the pro-establishment coalition, several LAA units gave their allegiance to a new Syrian-sponsored force called the Vanguards of the Lebanese Arab Army. After this split occurred in the Lebanese Arab Army, units retaining allegiance to the initial force maintained their hold only in the major cities of the South, in addition to a strong presence in Beirut.[26]

Positions Harden

As the military balance increasingly favored the pro-establishment coalition, a hardening of political positions and escalation of political rhetoric by Lebanese contestants occurred. Early in July, Kata'ib spokesmen asserted that no cease-fire could be achieved unless the Palestinians were disarmed. After the fall of the Jisr al-Basha camp and success in the Maronite offensives in the north, Bashir al-Jumayyil, son of the Kata'ib leader and military commander of the party's forces, called for the "liberation" of all Lebanese territory from the hold of the Palestinian-LNM alliance.

---

[25]Kerr, "Syrian Intervention," p. 14; QER of Syria, Lebanon, 1976, 3rd quarter, pp. 13–14; 1976, 4th quarter, pp. 6, 11–15.

[26]Khalidi, Conflict and Violence, p. 60; QER of Syria, Lebanon, 1976, 4th quarter, pp. 12–13.

By 5 August, Tony Faranjiyih, son of the Lebanese President and commander of Maronite militiamen in the north, also called for the "full liberation" of the country.

For his part, Kamal Junbalat maintained that the Lebanese National Movement perceived Syria as the main obstacle to national reconciliation in Lebanon. Early in July, he asserted that a cease-fire accord was only possible if Syria withdrew from Lebanon. A month later, he contended that "all doors to an agreement" were closed and that Syria must be confronted by every possible means. To consolidate the LNM's position, Junbalat created a Central Political Council in mid-July, to administer the areas under LNM control. As in the earlier establishment of a parallel administrative mechanism by the Maronites, the Council was intended to promote political cohesion among LNM parties and to enhance the efficiency of social mobilization and military logistics. Another objective was to counter suspected Syrian incitement of divisions between the Lebanese National Movement and the traditional Muslim leadership, by appealing more effectively to the clientele of the Muslim leaders.[27]

The sharpening of Junbalat's antagonism with the Syrians was not, however, duplicated by his Palestinian coalition partners. Under extreme duress from the ongoing siege of the Tall al-Za'tar camp, the Palestinian leadership opted for a more conciliatory course. On 11 July, Yasir 'Arafat appealed to all Arab countries to engage in a mediatory effort, and Libyan mediation did result in a partial withdrawal of Syrian forces from Sidon the next day. Then, on 22 July, the PLO Executive Committee opened direct negotiations in Damascus, two days after a new Syrian offensive began against Palestinian-National Movement positions in the mountains east of Beirut.

The Syrian-PLO negotiations led to an ostensible reconciliation between the two parties, culminating in a joint communiqué on 29 July. In addition to an agreement to conclude the fighting, an ambiguous pledge of "noninterference" in Lebanon's internal affairs was included. Palestinians could construe the clause as a call for Syrian withdrawal from Lebanon, while Syria could interpret

---

[27]Khalidi, *Conflict and Violence*, pp. 60–61; *QER of Syria, Lebanon*, 1976, 4th quarter, p. 13.

it as an admonition to the PLO to cease its alliance with the Lebanese National Movement. The PLO explicitly pledged to adhere to the 1969 Cairo Agreement, and an astonishing phrase went so far as to praise Syria's role "in defense of the Palestinian cause." On 30 July, a Lebanese-Syrian-Palestinian committee was formed to assist in implementing the agreement.

Reactions to the PLO's change of heart were extreme on both sides of the Lebanese political spectrum. Most disappointed were members of the LNM, who felt a sense of betrayal on the PLO's part. Rejectionist Palestinian organizations shared the LNM's reaction. From the opposite vantage point, Maronite leaders were dismayed by the possibility of Syrian-Palestinian reconciliation, to their own disadvantage. They intensified the siege of Tall al-Za'tar and assaulted the shantytown of al-Nab'a on the outskirts of East Beirut, inhabited primarily by Shi'i Muslims identified with the LNM. These military developments undermined the already fragile Syrian-Palestinian accord. On 6 August, Maronite militiamen gained control of the al-Nab'a shantytown, and on 12 August, Tall al-Za'tar finally succumbed after a fifty-three-day siege. In view of these occurrences, any prospects for implementing the Syrian-Palestinian agreement collapsed.[28]

After the fall of Tall al-Za'tar, the Lebanese combatants fought for control over Mount Lebanon over a two-month period. In particular, the salient that Palestinian-LNM forces had captured in the Dhur Shuwayr area was contested. This salient fell within Maronite-controlled territory north of the Beirut-Damascus highway. In mid-August, Syria backed the Maronite demand that anti-establishment forces withdraw unconditionally from the salient. In response, Palestinian and Lebanese National Movement spokesmen insisted that they would only withdraw if Syrian forces withdrew simultaneously from Sofar, in the central sector of the Mountain, and retreated to the Biqa' Valley.

When Syria refused this quid pro quo, the "Battle of the Mountain" erupted in full force. Syrian forces further consolidated their position by occupying Hammana, northeast of Sofar, on 13 August. They thereby achieved firmer control of the line of communications between the contested salient north of the Beirut-Damascus high-

---

[28]Khalidi, *Conflict and Violence,* pp. 60–61.

way and the LNM sanctuary in the Shuf area south of the highway. With Syrian cover, Maronite militiamen opened an offensive on 16 August aimed at dislodging anti-establishment forces from the Dhur Shuwayr area.

The fighting in the Mountain was complemented by a Syrian siege of two Palestinian refugee camps near Tripoli. In Beirut, as well, fighting intensified in response to the skirmishes in the Mountain. In persistent targeting of residential quarters and civilian institutions in the capital, both sides now relied on howitzers and rockets in addition to heavy mortars.

In unsuccessful efforts at Syrian-Palestinian negotiation in early September, Syria was represented by Air Force Commander Naji Jamil and the PLO by Abu Iyad. Abu Iyad claimed that the PLO softened its stance during these negotiations, agreeing to unilateral withdrawal from the contested salient in return for binding assurances that Syria would not attack Palestinian and LNM forces in Lebanon. Despite the omission of insistence on reciprocal Syrian withdrawal, Syria refused the offer.[29]

On the political level, Syria's priority was to assure that Iliyas Sarkis acceded to the presidency without mishap. From Syria's perspective, there may have been some advantages to President Faranjiyih's stubborn refusal to resign before his term expired on 23 September. Faranjiyih was a familiar figure to the Syrians, and his presence on the scene while their military involvement deepened gave them more leeway in consolidating their position. Nonetheless, the transition toward the new President's term was crucial, and one reason for the pressure applied by Syria on Palestinian-LNM forces in the Dhur Shuwayr salient may have been to induce them to accept Sarkis's leadership.

As the date of Sarkis's intended inauguration approached, however, the security situation raised doubts as to whether the event could be arranged. Continued combat in the Mountain salient was accompanied by escalating artillery and rocket barrages in Beirut. In an attempt to ameliorate the situation, President-elect Sarkis seized the initiative in arranging a series of meetings with interested parties. A 17 September encounter with Yasir 'Arafat proved inconclusive. Over the next two days, however, unannounced visits

<hr />

[29]Ibid., pp. 61–62.

by Sarkis to both Damascus and Cairo yielded one constructive decision. The site of the inauguration was moved from Beirut to the city of Shtura in the Biqa' Valley, where Syrian military control assured security for the event.

On 23 September, Sarkis was inaugurated under the protection of the Syrian Army at Shtura. The investiture was boycotted by Kamal Junbalat as well as defeated candidate Raymun Iddih and Sunni leader Sa'ib Salam. All told, sixty-seven of the ninety-nine members of the Chamber of Deputies attended the ceremony.

In his inaugural address, Sarkis proclaimed that the Syrian military presence in Lebanon was in response to the invitation of the Lebanese government. He asserted that Lebanon's sovereignty was sacred and pledged that the country would never undergo partition. Attempting to conciliate the Lebanese National Movement, he promised "to champion any changes which . . . may contribute to the national welfare." Finally, Sarkis expressed commitment to the Palestinian cause, while emphasizing that the Palestinians must adhere to the 1969 Cairo Agreement.

Sarkis's inauguration was probably "the last remaining hope for a psychological turning point" in the Lebanese Civil War. Although Yasir 'Arafat declared an immediate cease-fire at the time of the inauguration, his goodwill gesture was dramatically undermined several days later. On 26 September, Rejectionist Palestinian guerrillas opposed to Fath's relatively conciliatory line attacked the Semiramis Hotel in Damascus. The hotel was soon recaptured by the Syrians and three of the Palestinian assailants were publicly hanged. Officially, Syria held Fath responsible for the attack, going so far as to demand the replacement of Yasir 'Arafat as leader of the PLO.[30]

Race against Time

An increasing source of pressure on Syrian decisionmakers was evidence of wider Arab interest in influencing Lebanese developments. On 15 August, two days after the fall of Tall al-Za'tar,

[30]Khalidi, *Conflict and Violence*, pp. 62–63; see also Kerr, "Syrian Intervention," pp. 14–15.

Saudi Arabia and Kuwait called for a summit meeting of the Arab League in mid-October. Libyan Prime Minister Jallud then suggested that an Arab League peacekeeping force should be substituted for all of the combatants in the battle zone, including Syria and the Palestinians. Syria was now confronted with a "race against time."[31] To assure its preferred military and political outcome in Lebanon, Syria would have to act quickly before other Arab states constrained its options.

Two days after the Semiramis attack, the Syrians shifted gears from facilitating Sarkis's transition to power and launched a military offensive. In coordination with Maronite militias, Syria attacked Palestinian-LNM positions in the Dhur Shuwayr salient, dislodging them within one day, on 28 September. This operation did not involve high casualties, except in the town of Salima, where rightist militias were accused of committing massacres against the local Druze population. Afterwards, the Syrian Army prevented the Maronites from occupying towns in the area, insisting on doing so itself. When the operation was over, Syria had control of the major strategic roads of the Matn region surrounding the contested salient. The anti-establishment forces were obliged to regroup along the Beirut-Damascus highway, primarily in the towns of Bhamdun and Alay.[32]

The Syrian offensive came as a surprise to many Lebanese observers, prompting speculation about Syrian motives. The prevalent expectation in Lebanon had been that Syria would initiate a partial miltary withdrawal in exchange for reciprocal Palestinian-National Movement withdrawal from their positions. This could lead to the military collapse of the anti-establishment forces in the Mountain and subsequently throughout the country, permitting Syria to bargain from a position of strength at the forthcoming Arab summit. Instead of pursuing a phased military withdrawal as a prelude to political dialogue, Syria used military means to compel the Palestinian-LNM forces to abandon their positions. *Al-Nahar* questioned whether Damascus had given conscious priority to a military showdown, abandoning all hope for political settlement. Damascus may have been discouraged from political dialogue

[31]Kerr, "Syrian Intervention," pp. 14–15.
[32]Khalidi, *Conflict and Violence,* p. 63; Kerr, "Syrian Intervention," pp. 15–16.

by Maronite leaders, who informed President Sarkis that there was no point in pursuing dialogue "with a party that does not understand the language of dialogue but only the language of force." Continued emphasis on diplomatic means, they argued, was bound to perpetuate a situation of "no war-no peace," which would serve neither the interests of the new Lebanese regime nor those of Syria. Maronite leaders reportedly cautioned the Syrians that procrastination in Lebanon might have deleterious implications in Syria. Perhaps the attack on the Semiramis Hotel was an ominous forewarning of other incidents. Unless a decisive military move was pursued in Lebanon, a similar move "might be transferred to Syria, and the flame of the fire of the Lebanese war would be extended to it." Syrian authorities may also have calculated that they could not leave their forces entrenched in Lebanon on the verge of winter. Moreover, the large number of Lebanese refugees in Syria was creating social problems.

Aside from fears of "contagion" from Lebanese social strife, Syria may have been influenced by practical concerns over fulfilling its objectives in Lebanon. Maronite leaders informed Damascus that they favored any outside force that could decisively settle the Civil War, and might appeal to Arab peacekeeping forces interspersed with international forces to replace the Syrians. Taking this consideration into account, Syria then "decided to settle [the matter], if only partially, fearing that they would have to withdraw; and decided to advance, fearing that they would have to retreat."

Lebanese observers who took a sanguine view of Syrian intentions concluded that Damascus would pursue a "partial and limited" military showdown with well-defined objectives. Instead of obstructing President Sarkis's efforts to reach a political settlement, the Syrians would promote a conducive atmosphere for these efforts. Once the objectives of the operation were reached, Sarkis would be able to form a Cabinet to concentrate on reconstruction and growth, rather than being preoccupied with security problems. Thus, "a military settlement would clear the way for a political settlement."

Palestinian and LNM spokesmen, however, had a different perception of Syrian motives. In their view, the Syrian surprise attack against their positions in the Mountain was intended to undermine the political dialogue begun by Sarkis. After all, merely five days had passed since the new President's inauguration, hardly enough time to judge his efforts as a failure or a success or to justify recourse to a military alternative. These observers believed that Damascus was eager to present the forthcoming Arab summit conference with a fait accompli, so that no one would feel obliged to strengthen the Arab peacekeeping forces with other Arab elements. In addition, Damascus may have wanted President Sarkis to form a Cabinet corresponding to new political and military realities—that is, one in which the Lebanese National Movement would have no role.[33]

Opportunities for dialogue did not materialize, despite a brief reprieve in the fighting after Syria's 29 September mountain offensive. Early in October, Syria again tried to persuade Palestinian leaders to abandon their alliance with the LNM and to withdraw their forces from the towns of Bhamdun and Alay along the Beirut-Damascus highway. The Palestinians, in turn, insisted that Arab peacekeeping forces be interposed between Palestinian-LNM forces and those of Syria before any withdrawal occurred.

At this juncture, a representative of the Arab League, Hasan Sabri al-Khuli, convened meetings among representatives of Syria, Lebanon, and the PLO. At the conclusion of the discussions held on 9 and 11 October at Shturah in the Biqa', the mediator announced "agreement in principle" on phased withdrawal by Syria and the Palestinians from their mountain positions, as well as other steps that might lead to an overall settlement. However, the Syrian government did not publicly acknowledge any progress in the Shtura talks, and effectively precluded a third negotiating session by launching a military offensive instead. A conscious choice was made by the Syrian leaders, who

> apparently preferred to resort to military action, at least for a limited
> further period, rather than accept a mediated agreement which
> would leave them having failed to assert their ascendancy over the
> leftist-Palestinian front in Lebanon, or over what had come to be
> their own right wing clients.[34]

With less than a week to go before the Arab summit that was called for 18 October, Syria launched a final punitive offensive.

[33]*Al-Nahar,* 29 September 1976.
[34]Kerr, "Syrian Intervention," pp. 16–17.

An assault against Bhamdun on 13 October succeeded in dislodging the anti-establishment forces, but the Syrians met strong resistance and had to inflict heavy casualties before the town fell seventy-two hours later. The Syrian Army then prepared to move toward Alay, the regional headquarters of both the Palestinians and the Lebanese National Movement, and toward Sidon in the South. Before the Syrians could reach their objectives, however, the Arab League convened a hasty meeting to impose a cease-fire accord.[35]

Arab Summit

The timing and composition of the Arab League summit aroused considerable debate. A meeting of Arab Foreign Ministers on 4 September 1976 designated 18 October as the intended date for a summit meeting of Arab heads of state. However, Egypt suggested that the full-scale plenary summit be preceded by a preparatory mini-summit. Syria responded that if a preparatory meeting was held, Lebanon and the PLO should be left out. As the date of the summit approached, Syria was particularly eager to see the Palestinians excluded, in view of its determination to have 'Arafat deposed as the leader of the PLO. Once the Syrian military offensive of 13 October was launched, Syria announced that President Asad would not attend a mini-summit, but would send Foreign Minister Khaddam instead.

It was Saudi Arabia that exerted the necessary influence to convene a mini-summit capable of taking binding decisions. Distressed by the pace of Syria's mountain offensive, Saudi Arabia on 15 October issued a call for a mini-summit at its capital, Riyadh, the following day. President Asad was persuaded to attend, and a special Saudi plane was sent to bring Yasir 'Arafat from Lebanon. Lebanese President Sarkis was also invited, as were representatives of Egypt and Kuwait. This forum then worked out a series of agreements to resolve the Lebanese crisis, which were ratified by the full plenary summit of the Arab League in Cairo on 25 and 26 October.[36]

[35]Khalidi, *Conflict and Violence,* pp. 63–64.
[36]Kerr, "Syrian Intervention," pp. 17–18; Khalidi, *Conflict and Violence,* p. 64.

The resolutions of the Riyadh and Cairo summits addressed two central issues—creation of an Arab Deterrent Force to restore security in Lebanon and elaboration of a framework for Lebanese-Palestinian relations. In the realm of domestic security, the cease-fire accord concluded on 16 October was to take hold in all areas of confrontation by 21 October. All Lebanese and Palestinian armed groups were to withdraw to positions occupied before the outbreak of the Civil War, and all heavy weapons were to be confiscated.

To enforce these security measures, the Arab League decided to transform the 2,500-man peacekeeping force created in June into a 30,000-man Arab Deterrent Force (ADF). The ADF would officially be under the command of Lebanese President Sarkis, who would determine the size of Syria's contribution relative to other Arab states. In practice, the failure of the Arab League to designate the composition of the ADF at the outset assured continued Syrian predominance. The allocation of $90 million by the Arab League for the ADF in effect amounted to a subsidy for an enduring Syrian military presence in Lebanon.

The Arab League resolutions gave prominent attention to the future Palestinian role in Lebanon. The Palestinians were to adhere strictly to the terms of the 1969 Cairo Agreement, and to withdraw to the areas in Southern Lebanon assigned to them under that accord. The PLO renewed its commitment to respect Lebanon's sovereignty and to refrain from intervening in the country's internal affairs.

Responsibility for assuring Palestinian compliance with the Cairo Agreement was assigned to the ADF, and thus implicitly to Syria. In addition, a committee composed of Syrian, Saudi, Egyptian, and Kuwaiti representatives was designated to supervise implementation of the Cairo Agreement within forty-five days after the ADF's formation. Whereas conformity to the 1969 Agreement imposed curbs on Palestinian activity, the PLO did score an important gain at the Arab summit. President Asad was persuaded to abandon his campaign to depose Yasir 'Arafat as the leader of the organization, and the two were formally reconciled at a meeting in Damascus on 20 October.[37]

---

[37]Kerr, "Syrian Intervention," pp. 18–20; Khalidi, *Conflict and Violence,* pp. 64–

On the issue of domestic Lebanese reconciliation, however, the Arab summit resolutions had very little to offer. The Arab League called for convening a political dialogue as soon as possible, but suggested no guidelines for discussion. In fact, none of the leaders of Lebanese political factions was invited to Riyadh or Cairo, and they viewed the summit resolutions as a Palestinian-Syrian, rather than an intra-Lebanese, accord. Initially, both pro- and anti-establishment spokesmen opposed the accords and expressed unwillingness to cooperate with the ADF.

By 14 November, however, when Syrian troops painted their helmets green and moved into their new positions as an Arab Deterrent Force, no resistance was mounted. One explanatory factor is sheer exhaustion; after the loss of over 65,000 lives and the breakdown of fifty-five previous cease-fire agreements, the Lebanese were in no position to resume hostilities without outside assistance. Moreover, efforts had been made to achieve acquiescence of the major domestic parties.

The most strenuous opposition to the ADF, ironically, was voiced by Maronite leaders who objected to the presence of Syrian troops in Maronite territory. President Sarkis held intensive meetings with the leaders of the Lebanese Front—ex-President Faranjiyih, Pierre al-Jumayyil of the Kata'ib Party, Kamil Sham'un of the National Liberal Party, and Father Sharbil Kassis of the Maronite Monastic Orders—and gradually persuaded them to agree to the new arrangement. Convincing the anti-establishment forces was largely the domain of Fath, which exacted compliance from LNM and Palestinian Rejectionist groups. The latter at least derived consolation from the entry of "Arab" troops into Maronite territory. As for President Sarkis, he called on all Lebanese to greet the ADF "in love and brotherhood."[38]

65; Sam Younger, "After the Cairo Summit," *World Today* 32 (December 1976): 439; Itamar Rabinovich and Hanna Zamir, "Lebanon," in *Middle East Contemporary Survey*, Vol. I: *1976–1977,* ed. Colin Legum (New York: Holmes and Meier, 1978), p. 507.

[38]Lawrence Whetten, "The Military Dimension," in *Lebanon in Crisis,* ed. P. Edward Haley and Lewis W. Snider (Syracuse, N.Y.: Syracuse University Press, 1979), pp. 82–83; Khalidi, *Conflict and Violence,* p. 65.

Taking Stock

The designation of the Syrian-dominated ADF to supervise implementation of the Arab summit accords underscored the fact that Syria could "hardly be regarded as an external actor in Lebanese politics." It had achieved military predominance and made substantial political inroads into both major coalitions in Lebanon. Nevertheless, one is struck by Syria's inability to elicit fundamental political concessions from members of either coalition.[39]

Ironically, although Syria had consistently emphasized its commitment to forestalling the partition of Lebanon, by the October 1976 cease-fire, de facto partition had taken place. The eastern Biqa' Valley had fallen under effective Syrian domination; Christian control was secured over parts of Mount Lebanon, Beirut, and the northern littoral, with a political center at the town of Junyih; other parts of the country including Tripoli and parts of Beirut, Mount Lebanon, and the southern littoral were controlled by the LNM, Muslims, and Palestinians; and Southern Lebanon experienced a "political and administrative vacuum." Meanwhile, the Lebanese state had atrophied as a central source of authority.[40] President Asad reiterated Syria's unhappiness with this outcome in a 31 September 1978 interview, saying:

> We were trying throughout . . . and we are still trying to reach the objective for which we entered, which was to put a final end to the fighting and [to achieve] the extension of state authority over all of Lebanese soil.[41]

The official Syrian emphasis on consistency of objectives in its Lebanese intervention, however, belies a clear pattern of escalating stakes and commitment. Ascending the ladder of escalation generated its own momentum, as it did in other cases of

---

[39]Itamar Rabinovich, "Limits of Military Power," pp. 55, 71–72.

[40]Ibid., p. 66.

[41]Wadi' Skaf, ed., *Mawqifuna Min al-'Azmah al-Lubnaniyyah* [Our Position vis-à-vis the Lebanese crisis], (Damascus: Institute of the Union of Studies and Consultations, 1979), p. 5.

intervention in civil wars. The distinctive feature of the Syrian involvement was a reluctance to allow either Lebanese coalition to prevail decisively. The desire to achieve political accommodation and restore security was coupled with an increasingly pronounced bid for Syrian supremacy as an orchestrator of Lebanon's political future.

Syria's tactical maneuvering between the major political coalitions in Lebanon was evident in all three phases of its commitment. Although Syria's initial mediatory efforts promoted the claims of its traditional, anti-establishment allies in Lebanon, the substance of Syrian reform proposals was modest enough to win pro-establishment approval. Syria's indirect intervention was initially intended to tip the military balance in favor of anti-establishment forces, but several months later worked to benefit the opposing coalition.

Nevertheless, neither mediation nor indirect intervention sufficed to achieve political accommodation or to restore security to Lebanon. The logic of escalation took hold as further commitment seemed necessary, not merely to promote the original objectives, but also to justify the investment that had already been made. The major escalation entailed in direct military intervention on behalf of the pro-establishment coalition in June transformed the contest to one in which regular Syrian forces and Palestinian guerrillas were the major combatants on Lebanese soil. The military reversals that Syria underwent in that campaign stalled the escalation momentum, compelling recourse to a strategy of attrition that led to military stalemate throughout the summer.

By contrast, the Syrian mountain offensive of late September to mid-October was well planned and executed from the military point of view. Nevertheless, this drive against Palestinian-LNM positions was abruptly halted by the 16 October cease-fire. In order to explain Syrian willingness to cease the escalatory momentum at that point, several considerations must be taken into account. The first question is whether, by halting, Syria was necessarily falling short of its objectives. It may be that "a total military victory in Lebanon was against the grain of Syrian policy." The marriage of convenience with the Christian militias of the Lebanese Front might have become too close for comfort, and the alienation of anti-establishment forces too pronounced. Nor did Syria desire to liquidate the Palestinian Resistance forces, but rather to make them more answerable to Syrian influence.[42]

Another relevant factor was the problem of sustaining the costs, on both the elite and societal level, of escalated commitment in Lebanon. A tone of defensiveness appeared in official Syrian statements as involvement in Lebanon deepened. Due to indications that the Lebanese adventure was increasingly unpopular, Syrian spokesmen were obliged to rationalize their policies in progressively more explicit detail. President Asad's 20 July 1976 speech, already cited at length, is perhaps the most elaborate official formulation. At the outset, Asad acknowledges to his countrymen that "perhaps I should have discussed this subject a while ago, but I delayed the discussion."

The first reason cited for the delay was Asad's confidence in the intuition and broad comprehension of events of the Syrian citizen, precluding the need for further official explanation. Secondly, Asad "relied on the confidence that is granted toward me," as a popular delegation of authority to the leader. Third, Asad claimed to uphold a national consensus, saying, "I relied on my sense that I was expressing the inner thoughts of every one of you in all of the decisions that I took in the face of these events." Finally, conveying a sense of ultimate accountability, he asserts that "if I felt for one moment that the confidence of this people in me had been shaken, I would not remain in power for a single second."[43]

The apologetic note on which Asad began his remarks reflects awareness of popular discontent with the Lebanese Civil War. In general terms, discontent stemmed from frustration over Syria's failure to achieve concrete results in pursuit of clearly defined objectives. More pointedly, what hit home for most Syrians was the mounting costs of the operation and the social dislocation associated with it.

Asad frequently referred to the burdens assumed by the Syrian people in his comments on the Lebanese intervention. Syrian costs were sometimes justified in terms of commitment to Palestine:

[42]Rabinovich, "Limits to Military Power," p. 70; Kerr, "Syrian Intervention," pp. 18–20.

[43]Asad, Speech of 20 July 1976, p. 1.

> Syria's sacrifices are clear and radiant: she has sacrificed with her sons and her economy, with the land, with everything, so that the Palestine cause would continue.[44]

Other references noted the depth of Syria's devotion to Lebanon:

> We do not find that anyone in the world sacrifices for Lebanon's sake as we do in Syria. . . . Syria is the one that offered efforts and sweat and blood, while the world—including the friends of Lebanon—were content with advice to Lebanon.[45]

However, Asad acknowledged the negative impact of sustained sacrifices in a 1978 interview:

> I want to say frankly that we are offering continuous sacrifices of various kinds in Lebanon, and it is in our own interest in Syria not to continue in offering these sacrifices.[46]

Some of the social costs associated with the Lebanese intervention were epitomized in the refugee issue. Asad explained that on the eve of the Lebanese Civil War, there were about one-half million Syrians living in Lebanon who were employed as businessmen, doctors, lawyers, workers, and in other occupations. As a result of the war they returned to Syria, and this influx was supplemented by one-half million Lebanese and 150,000 Palestinian refugees. Asad underscored the impact of over one million people entering a country whose inhabitants number less than nine million by drawing a contrast with India. When India absorbed ten million refugees from Bangladesh, this constituted only one-fiftieth of the country's population and yet created a great problem. How much greater was Syria's problem, absorbing refugees comprising one-ninth of its total population![47]

In view of the heavy burden imposed by the Lebanese intervention upon the Syrian economy — estimated at up to $1 million

[44]Ibid., p. 11.
[45]Skaf, ed., *Mawqifuna*, p. 10.
[46]Ibid., p. 9.
[47]Asad, Speech of 20 July 1976, pp. 1–2.

a day—[48] one may speculate whether economic costs were an ongoing factor in the calculations of Syrian decisionmakers. A contrary theory is advanced by Fred Lawson, who argues that Syria's leaders expected intervention in Lebanon in June 1976 to resolve Syria's own economic difficulties. In identifying "a precise linkage between domestic social conflict [in Syria] and the nature and timing of Syria's military intervention in the Lebanese civil war," Lawson cites evidence of increasing economic dislocation in Syria by the early months of 1976. A rising inflation rate of close to 30 percent and a shortage of foreign exchange were accompanied by specific agricultural and industrial setbacks in Syria's volatile north-central provinces.[49] The outbreak of civil strife in Lebanon compounded these difficulties by disrupting access to the port of Beirut and to Lebanese financial institutions, as well as triggering an Iraqi cutoff of oil-transit operations through Syria.[50] If these trends continued, social unrest might be precipitated; by contrast, a military move into Lebanon "could provide Syria's rulers with significant additional resources that they could use to their own domestic political advantage." By stabilizing the Lebanese conflict, Lawson contends, the Asad regime sought to gain access to "the capital held by Lebanese financial institutions, the light manufactures produced by Lebanese companies, and the facilities of the port at Beirut."[51]

Lawson's argument is unconvincing because of a series of implicit assumptions about the perceptions and expectations of Syrian decisionmakers. One premise is that military intervention would permit Syria to restore stability in Lebanon at low cost, or at least that forseeable economic gains would exceed any financial burdens involved. A related premise is that the Lebanese conflict was, in Syria's view, amenable to quick solution, thereby restoring Syrian access to Lebanese facilities and capital. Both premises are contradicted by the sober, incremental pattern of Syrian commitment

[48]Alasdair Drysdale, "The Asad Regime and Its Troubles," *MERIP Reports* no. 110 (Nov.-Dec. 1982): 5.

[49]See pp. 77–79.

[50]See p. 257.

[51]Fred H. Lawson, "Syria's Intervention in the Lebanese Civil War, 1976: A Domestic Conflict Explanation," *International Organization* 38, 3 (Summer 1984): 465–470, 474–475, 479.

in Lebanon and by the clear indications to Syrian leaders, especially after the collapse of the Lebanese Army in March 1976, that Lebanon's political crisis was deep and enduring. No evidence is available about whether economic costs were seriously weighed before Syria's military intervention in June. However, it is reasonable to assume that Syrian leaders anticipated financial burdens associated with intervention, while probably underestimating their magnitude. President Asad and his advisers presumably concluded that the political stakes in Lebanon overshadowed any potential expenses entailed.

Yet arguing that intervention in Lebanon was not an anticipated panacea for Syria's economic problems does not discount the elite's concern with ramifications of their Lebanese commitment for Syria's domestic politics and social equilibrium. Indeed, anxiety over the contagion effects of Lebanese civil strife beset Syrian decisionmakers throughout the Civil War, as attested to by their own statements. Recognition of this ongoing concern does not, however, enable the analyst to posit "a precise linkage between domestic conflict [in Syria] and the nature and timing of Syria's military intervention" in June 1976, as Lawson claims. If anything, the evidence suggests that Syria's backing for its traditional allies in Lebanon until April 1976 was more palatable to major political constituencies and to public opinion at large in Syria than was the shift of alignments preceding the large-scale intervention in June. It was Syrian backing of the Maronite-dominated establishment in Lebanon that highlighted the sectarian overtones of the war, calling into question for a great many Syrians the Islamic and pan-Arab convictions of their rulers.

Political opposition to Syria's policies in Lebanon reflected two major foci of discontent. Many members of the Ba'th Party, in both its military and civilian wings, found Syria's switch of alliances during the war distasteful. On ideological grounds and based on patterns of past allegiance, they objected to engaging in combat against Palestinian, Muslim, and leftist groups. The direct clash between Syrian forces and Palestinian guerrillas, in particular, was "a policy without precedent, and shocked and alienated wide segments of Syrian opinion."[52]

[52]Hanna Batatu, "Syria's Muslim Brethren," *MERIP Reports* No. 110 (Nov.-Dec. 1982): 20.

Syrian alignments in Lebanon also aroused the deeply ingrained Sunni Muslim distrust of the 'Alawi minority, ascribing the Asad regime's foreign policy to its minoritarian composition. On this basis, they "saw its [i.e., the regime's] decision to support an essentially Christian camp against an essentially Muslim one as the natural extension of Syria's domestic politics."[53] Clearly, President Asad's sensitivities about his sectarian background colored his insistent emphasis on his Muslim credentials. In criticizing Kamal Junbalat's alleged vindictiveness, for example, he said:

> If I am a true Muslim, and I am a Muslim with God's help, then I must be against this orientation, against revenge and reprisal.[54]

On a larger scale, the Syrian regime was worried about societal parallels with Lebanon and the possible "contagion effect" of civil strife. Some of the regime's Sunni critics "saw parallels between their underrepresentation in an 'Alawi-dominated state and that of Lebanese Muslims in a Maronite-dominated state."[55] The fear of contagion was explicitly expressed by the editor of the Syrian government's newspaper, *al-Thawrah,* on 21 May 1977, when he warned that Syria's enemies acted in underhanded ways "to inject into our country part of what happened in Lebanon."[56] In fact, economic dislocations, increased sectarian tensions, and strains within the ruling elite were manifested as the intervention in Lebanon unfolded. Several plots, including an abortive coup attempt in April 1976, were discovered and contained by the regime, and were followed by numerous arrests in the Army and the Ba'th civilian party apparatus.[57] However, serious manifestations of political dissent, including a series of assassinations against political leaders and outbreaks of social unrest, did not come to the surface until after the cease-fire of October 1976 brought the Lebanese Civil War to a formal conclusion.

Perhaps, then, the mounting domestic costs of the Lebanese

---

[53]Rabinovich, "Limits to Military Power," pp. 64–65.

[54]Asad, Speech of 20 July 1976, p. 6.

[55]Drysdale, "The Asad Regime and Its Troubles," pp. 4–5.

[56]As cited in Rabinovich, "Limits to Military Power," p. 72.

[57]Nikolaos Van Dam, *The Struggle for Power in Syria,* 2nd ed. (London: Croom Helm, 1981), p. 92.

operation help explain Syria's willingness to consider a partial decommitment in the wake of the October 1976 cease-fire accord. However, one cannot overlook the fact that, regardless of specific Syrian objectives in Lebanon and domestic political concerns, the timing of the cease-fire accord was designated at an Arab summit conference. How important were other Arab states in influencing the course and outcome of Syria's intervention in Lebanon? What were the broader inter-Arab, Arab-Israeli, and superpower rivalries at play? Fundamentally, how much freedom of maneuver did Syria have in striving to assert its leadership status in the Arab world?

IV

REGIONAL AND GLOBAL CONSTRAINTS

9

Inter-Arab Rivalries

By the eve of its intervention in the Lebanese Civil War, Syria's regional stature had reached an unprecedented level. No longer a state with a chronically unstable political system, vulnerable to the foreign policy designs of stronger neighbors, Syria could now conduct an assertive foreign policy. The Asad regime, after consolidating domestic support, established a network of ties in the Fertile Crescent, earning recognized status as a subregional power.

When Syrian leaders committed themselves to resolving Lebanon's domestic turmoil, they hoped for an outcome that would enhance Syria's regional stature. The reputation of serving as a successful mediator, championing the Palestinian Resistance, and exercising leverage over parties to the Lebanese strife could elevate Syria's leadership credentials. Whereas tangible attributes might suffice to label Syria as a subregional power, subjective recognition of Syria's status by other Arabs was vital to achieve enduring leadership.

There is no evidence that the Syrian elite expected their country's influence to extend beyond the Fertile Crescent and encompass the entire Arab world. Realistically, this goal was not within reach in the foreseeable future, regardless of the outcome of the Lebanese conflict. Nevertheless, influence over the Palestinian Resistance was sought by every Arab state aspiring to leadership. Moreover, consolidation of Syrian influence in its immediate vicinity would make it a desirable coalition partner to many other Arab states.

Syria's experience in Lebanon revealed the limits of Arab consensual norms in restraining penetrational behavior by a determined state. Until its full-scale confrontation with the Palestinian Resistance, Syria's freedom of maneuver was not meaningfully curbed by other Arab states, either collectively or unilaterally. The ultimate Arab efforts to restrain Syria also reflected evolving criteria of Arab leadership. Whereas Egypt's earlier decisive influence was tied to geostrategic attributes and the charismatic personality of its ruler, by the mid-1970s it was the influence derived from oil wealth that enabled Saudi Arabia to summon the interested parties to a summit ending the Lebanese Civil War.

Arab Leadership Aspirations

How literally should one construe the ideology of Arab nationalism, with its ideal of Arab unity, as a norm governing the actions of Arab states? Alternatively, does this ideology merely provide a rationale to legitimize attempts at domination by some members of the regional system? In effect, both ideological and realpolitik considerations enter into aspirations for leadership by individual Arab States. The would-be leader may embrace the symbols of Arab nationalism as a means of asserting influence over less vigorous or stable regional actors.

The ideal of Arab unity has long appealed to popular Arab sentiment. Arab elites exploit this compelling symbol both to gain domestic legitimacy and in their rivalry for leadership with each other. States lacking domestic stability have found Arab nationalist goals especially appealing. The Fertile Crescent states of Syria, Lebanon, Jordan, and Iraq, with no historical tradition as separate political entities, each experienced fundamental "national identity" problems. Identification with the extended Arab nation filled a "void of loyalties" on the popular level.

Yet the country best able to achieve leadership by embracing pan-Arab ideals enjoyed relative domestic stability. Only Egypt, with a historically well-defined national identity, could assume the role of a regional great power, while the influence of other Arab states was confined to their immediate neighbors. In addition to Egypt's central geostrategic position, integrated administration, and skilled human resources, the charismatic appeal of President Gamal 'Abd al-Nasir enhanced Egypt's leadership role from 1954 to 1970.[1]

[1]Malcolm Kerr, "Regional Arab Politics and the Conflict with Israel," in *Political*

Nasir captured the Arab imagination by embracing the popular causes of anti-colonialism and revolutionary socialism. He was not, however, a dogmatic ideologue, and indeed pragmatism was a central feature of his leadership skills. Somehow, while never quite prevailing completely over his Arab rivals, he was repeatedly able to seize the initiative, with enormous resilience in bouncing back from defeats. There was, however, no lack of rivalry or resistance to Nasir's leadership role. One set of opponents included states whose own leadership aspirations were thwarted by Nasir. At different junctures, these included Syria, Iraq, Saudi Arabia, and Algeria. Other states were content to remain minor powers, but feared that Egyptian hegemonic ambitions might encroach on their sovereignty. The growth of Nasirist movements in several Arab countries, including Lebanon, aroused anxieties among local elites. Repeatedly, however, the outcome was similar: "the Egyptian cause [was] too strong in each case to be driven away once and for all, but [had] nothing at hand to bring it firmly to power either."[2]

A gradual decline in Egypt's leadership stature after Nasir's death may be traced to deeper historical roots. Throughout Egypt's modern history, "cycles of Pan-Arabism alternated with isolationist periods." The October War of 1973 provided Nasir's successor, President Anwar al-Sadat, with an opportunity to move out of Nasir's shadow. For Sadat, the October War was not intended to rejuvenate pan-Arabism, but rather to awaken Egyptian patriotism and the "vision of an Egyptian Egypt." Egypt retreated into regional isolation after the war, deviating from the Arab consensus by moving toward a separate peace with Israel and strengthening its bond to the West.[3]

Syria's Opportunity

The decline of Egypt's pan-Arab standing, undermining its status as a "regional great power," provided more leeway for others to

---

Dynamics in the Middle East, ed. Paul Hammond and Sidney Alexander (New York: American Elsevier, 1972), pp. 33–39; idem, *The Arab Cold War,* 3d ed. (London: Oxford University Press, 1971), p. 1.

[2]Kerr, "Regional Arab Politics," pp. 41–42.

[3]Fouad Ajami, "The Struggle for Egypt's Soul," *Foreign Policy* 35 (Summer 1979): 3–30, passim.

seek an enhanced regional role. For Syria, two preconditions had to be fulfilled before this goal could be achieved. On the regional level, rivals for power had to be contained, at least in the immediate subregional arena of the Fertile Crescent. Domestically, Syria needed sufficient inner stability to seek coalition from a position of strength.

In the early years of Syrian independence, neither condition was met. The slogans of "Greater Syria" and "unity of the Fertile Crescent," first articulated in the 1940s, represented unity schemes directed at Syria from the outside.[4] Both proposals were espoused by Hashimi rulers, who came to power in Transjordan and Iraq with British assistance. These rulers traced their lineage to the Sharif Husayn of Mecca, who cooperated with the British in organizing an Arab revolt against Ottoman rule during World War I in exchange for promises of Arab independence after the war.

Two of the Sharif's sons were disappointed in their royalist ambitions. Faysal had proclaimed himself King of Syria in 1918 and was recognized as King of a united Syria, Lebanon, Palestine, and Transjordan in July 1919 by an all-Arab congress. However, he was evicted from his throne by the French army in the summer of 1920. At the peace conference at Paris, he nevertheless secured British backing for his candidacy for the Iraqi throne, to which he formally ascended in October 1921. Meanwhile, his brother 'Abdallah recruited a private army to march on Syria and confront the French. On the way, he passed through British-mandated Palestine east of the Jordan River, setting up a central administration in 'Amman. 'Abdallah's claim to rule Transjordan—that is, the other, or eastern side of the Jordan River—was recognized by the British in 1922, on the condition that he renounce the objective of conquering Syria from the French.

There were thus two frustrated claims to Syria within the Hashimi family. Both 'Amman and Baghdad attempted during World War II to rectify wrongs committed in Syria. 'Abdallah aspired for the merger of Syria and Transjordan, as a first step in the reunification of a "Greater Syria" which would ultimately include Lebanon and Palestine as well. He articulated this plan in all-Arab

[4]Daniel Dishon, "The Lebanese War—An All-Arab Crisis," *Mid-stream* (January 1977): 28.

gatherings beginning in 1943, and once Transjordan achieved independence in 1946, the "Greater Syria" plan became a cardinal principle of its foreign policy.

The Iraqi claim, however, was more influential in its impact on Syria's post-independence politics. After Faysal's death, perennial Prime Minister Nuri al-Sa'id designed an active regional policy in close coordination with Britain. Sa'id's Fertile Crescent Plan, officially presented to the British in 1942, called for the union of Syria, Lebanon, Palestine, and Transjordan into one state. The state of "Greater Syria" would immediately join Iraq in a newly created Arab League, whose membership would then be open to other Arab states.

Neither of these schemes ultimately came to fruition, largely because of the fact that by 1941 the Hashimi family had lost its influence in the Arab nationalist movement. Many Arab nationalists were suspicious of the close coordination between Nuri al-Sa'id and the British, and neither Syrians nor Iraqis were enamored of 'Abdallah's meddling in their internal affairs. The principal source of effective opposition to further expansion of Hashimi influence was, however, Egypt, which emerged in 1945 as the recognized leader in the newly created Arab League.[5]

The establishment of the League of Arab States reduced both the feasibility and appeal of unity schemes restricted to the Arab east. For one thing, the League Charter included carefully worded safeguards of the sovereignty of individual member states. As a result, it was more difficult for Iraq or Transjordan to propose merger with Syria and the transformation of its government from a republic to a monarchy. On the political level, Egypt's leadership role in the Arab League enabled the Egyptian monarchy under King Faruq to curb Hashimi ambitions.

In the coming years, Iraq was the principal challenger to Egypt's leadership role, and the focus of their contention was Syria. To cite Patrick Seale:

> . . . [the] tacit premise underlying the Arab policies of both Egypt and Iraq was that Syria held the key to the struggle for local primacy.

[5]Patrick Seale, *The Struggle for Syria: A Study of Post-War Arab Politics, 1945–1958* (London: Oxford University Press, 1965), pp. 6–15.

Whoever controlled Syria or enjoyed her friendship could isolate her, and need bow to no other combination of Arab states.[6]

Egypt's overriding objective was to assure that no single power in the Fertile Crescent would be strong enough to challenge its leadership. This principle guided not only the Egypt of King Faruq, but also the successor regime of Gamal 'Abd al-Nasir.[7] This continuity highlights the underlying geopolitical considerations of Egypt's efforts to curb Iraqi ambitions in Syria, although Nasir cast his objectives in ideological terms. Essentially, "what the Egyptians constantly sought in Damascus was not outright union, but only that Syria should keep Iraq at arm's length."[8]

In fact, it was Syria that initiated an appeal for union with Egypt in 1958. The Syrian Ba'th Party, whose influence had increased since 1954, aspired to union with Nasir's Egypt as a precedent to more comprehensive Arab unity. Nevertheless, endless quarrels with other political parties in Syria revealed by 1958 that the Ba'th could not achieve a controlling voice within the Syrian elite. In these circumstances, "the Syrians, in a great burst of political desperation and popular enthusiasm, delivered themselves body and soul to Nasser, after finding themselves unable to set their own house in order."[9] When Syrian army officers accompanied by Ba'thi politicians approached Nasir early in 1958 suggesting political union, the Egyptian President initially objected that the road was dangerously unprepared. The Syrians, however, agreed to accept union on Nasir's terms, and the United Arab Republic was created in February 1958. The centralization of the UAR became a vehicle for Egyptian domination, and Syrian resentment of the heavy-handed Egyptian role culminated in the secession of September 1961.[10]

After the UAR experience, no Syrian government was willing to contemplate union with Egypt without safeguards against Egyptian domination. Nevertheless, from 1961 to 1966, Syrian elites were defensive about the fact that their country precipitated the

[6]Ibid., p. 2.
[7]Ibid., pp. 1–4, 16–23.
[8]Kerr, *Arab Cold War,* pp. 2–5; idem, "Regional Arab Politics," pp. 43–44.
[9]Kerr, "Regional Arab Politics," p. 46.
[10]Kerr, *Arab Cold War,* pp. 11–25.

secession, and were overshadowed by Nasir's regional stature. The almost simultaneous coups d'état that brought the Ba'th Party to power in Iraq and Syria in February and March of 1963 revived active deliberations on Arab unity. Through close coordination, the two Ba'thi regimes achieved a common negotiating position with Nasir. When they failed to secure his agreement to a satisfactory federal scheme, Iraq and Syria entered negotiations for a union of their own. However, in November 1963 the Iraqi regime fell, merely nine months after it came to power. The regime led by the 'Arif brothers from 1963 to 1968 had closer ties to Egypt than to Syria, and the Ba'thi regime that came to power in 1968 was led by a different faction of the party than that which ruled in Syria. In any event, pervasive internal instability in Iraq since the fall of the monarchy precluded a sustained bid for Arab leadership.[11]

In Syria, by contrast, when the radical faction of the Ba'th assumed control in February 1966, Salah Jadid was no longer unduly deferential to Nasir or apologetic about the UAR experience. Striving for regional influence on autonomous grounds, Jadid made it clear that Syria rejected Egyptian leadership, and sought to "outdistance Nasir in militancy on nationalist and revolutionary issues," including the Palestinian cause.[12] The regime of President Hafiz al-Asad continued to champion the Palestinian cause as a vehicle for gaining regional influence. For Asad, however, support for the Palestinians was merely one facet of a more ambitious strategy. By achieving influence in Jordan and Lebanon as well as with the Palestinian Resistance, Asad hoped for a firm base of subregional power in the Fertile Crescent that would eventually enable Syria to supersede Egypt's regional stature.

Auspicious developments on several planes enabled Hafiz al-Asad to move toward his foreign policy objectives. The decline in Egypt's regional stature after Nasir's death was due in part to Anwar al-Sadat's inability to duplicate his predecessor's charismatic appeal and in part to the specific policies he chose to pursue. While Egypt and Syria, with Saudi financial backing, achieved an effective coalition in 1973 to wage the October War against Israel,

---

[11]Kerr, "Regional Arab Politics," pp. 44–45.
[12]Kerr, *Arab Cold War,* pp. 42–43; idem, "Regional Arab Politics," pp. 47–48.

there was soon a falling-out between the wartime partners. Asad especially resented being treated by Egypt as a "junior partner" during the war. His subsequent suspicion that Egypt would accept a separate peace agreement with Israel, from which Syria would derive no benefit, reinforced Asad's determination to achieve an autonomous regional stature. The consolidation of a new Arab bloc, excluding and possibly opposing Egypt, would provide Syria with the opportunity to serve as the "senior partner," at least in its immediate vicinity.[13]

A rapprochement between Syria and the Hashimi regime in Jordan was particularly significant. On the eve of his seizure of power from Jadid in November 1970, Defense Minister Hafiz al-Asad limited the scope of the Syrian intervention in the Jordanian Civil War by refusing to use the Syrian Air Force against King Husayn's forces (see Chapter 5). The Asad regime signaled its intention of improving relations with Jordan by only selectively implementing the economic blockade decreed by several Arab states against the King after his eviction of the Palestinian Resistance from the country in 1971. A formal rapprochement between Syria and Jordan occurred after the October War of 1973. King Husayn was eager to end his country's isolation by cultivating Syrian friendship, and agreements for economic, cultural, and limited military cooperation were concluded between the two countries in 1974–75.[14]

Lebanese Arena for Inter-Arab Contention

Lebanon was a key focus of Syria'a new foreign policy activism in the early 1970's. The context of increased Syrian influence in Lebanon must be understood in terms of Lebanon's long-standing sensitivity to the vagaries of inter-Arab politics. In view of deep divisions among Lebanese on foreign policy, Lebanon's regional environment impinged heavily on the country's domestic political processes. Vulnerability to external forces was accentuated by Leb-

[13]Dishon, "Lebanese War," p. 27.

[14]Paul Jureidini and Ronald McLaurin, "The Hashemite Kingdom of Jordan," in *Lebanon in Crisis,* ed. P. Edward Haley and Lewis W. Snider (Syracuse, N.Y.: Syracuse University Press, 1979), pp. 149–153; Dishon, "Lebanese War," p. 28.

anon's "anonymity" as a nation. The ambivalence of Muslim Lebanese over whether to consider themselves primarily Arab, Muslim, or Lebanese, and that of Christian Lebanese over whether to retreat into the Mountain or engage with their Arab neighbors, made for a fragmented political culture. Lebanon's political system was also permissive of external disruption because of its relatively liberal policies, allowing a variety of Arab organizations and movements to find expression within the country. Often referred to as a "microcosm of the Arab world," Lebanon's status as a center of intellectual activity was reflected in the fact that 55 percent of the students in its universities were non-Lebanese.[15]

At the time the National Pact was formulated in 1943, strong bonds existed between the Lebanese ruling elite and other Arab leaders. Sunni Muslim politicians especially enhanced their domestic prestige through ties to Arab heads of state, and they shared in the conservative outlook of most Arab elites at the time. Moreover, willingness to refrain from undue interference in each others' affairs was reflected in the loose confederal basis of the Arab League. Indeed, special guarantees of "respect for the independence and sovereignty of Lebanon within its present frontiers" were included in the Alexandria Protocol, at the League's founding conference in 1944. Lebanon had considerable leeway in pursuing a foreign policy based on official neutrality in inter-Arab disputes and a passive role in the Arab-Israel conflict.[16]

By the time the United Arab Republic was established in February 1958, however, the pan-Arab and socialist appeals of Nasir had struck a responsive chord among many Lebanese Muslims. Lebanon's Arab orientation was one issue sparking rebel grievances in the 1958 Lebanese Civil War, just as charges of intervention by the UAR heightened Christian anxieties. The issue became less politically charged once President Fuad Shihab (1958–64) pursued a cautious policy of detente with Nasir. Shihab's successor, Charles Hilu, agreed at an Arab summit conference in October 1964 to participate in a United Arab Command of the countries

[15]Walid Khalidi, *Conflict and Violence in Lebanon*, Harvard Studies in International Affairs, no. 38 (Cambridge: Center for International Affairs, Harvard University, 1979), pp. 93–96, 101.

[16]Ibid., pp. 99–100; Lewis Snider, "Inter-Arab Relations," in *Lebanon in Crisis*, ed. Haley and Snider, p. 179.

bordering on Israel. Hilu insisted, however, that no Egyptian, Jordanian, or Syrian troops be permitted to enter Lebanon unless formally invited by the Lebanese government. In addition, Lebanon declared that it would not engage in offensive operations, but would defend itself if attacked.[17]

The operations of Palestinian guerrillas in Lebanon created new opportunities for inter-Arab entanglement. Originally, Arab governments agreed at the Khartum summit of August 1967 that Palestinian guerrilla activities against Israel should be staged from Egypt, Syria, and Jordan, but not from Lebanon. By the time the Cairo Agreement of November 1969 was negotiated between the Lebanese government and the Palestinian Resistance, however, the Arab consensus on Lebanon's right to neutrality had vanished. One provision of the accord went so far as to "emphasize that the Palestinian armed struggle is in the interest of Lebanon as well as of the Palestinian revolution and all Arabs."[18]

The polarizing impact of Palestinian guerrilla activities on domestic Lebanese politics was accentuated by a curious cast of Arab characters. Most incongruous, on the surface, was the assistance provided by conservative Arab regimes to the Maronite leadership in opposing the guerrilla presence. When Sulayman Faranjiyih, the more conservative candidate, was elected President in 1970, Saudi Arabia and other states of the Gulf "did not hide their satisfaction at the election of a strong President in Lebanon who could bring the commando movement there under control." Although these states were providing substantial financial assistance to the PLO, they were afraid that, if unbridled, the movement could become a "spearhead of radicalism" in the region that could ultimately threaten their own regimes.[19]

Even the Egyptian regime quietly applauded Faranjiyih's election. Then, in February 1974, the Egyptian Arab Socialist Union (the sole political party) invited Pierre al-Jumayyil and a delegation of the Kata'ib Party to visit Cairo. During meetings with party and government officials, the Kata'ib were assured that "Egyptian socialism was not for export." It is conceivable that regional backing

[17]Salibi, *Crossroads to Civil War*, (Delmar, N.Y.: Carvan, 1976), pp. 24–26; Khalidi, *Conflict and Violence*, p. 100.

[18]Snider, "Inter-Arab Relations," p. 180.

[19]Salibi, *Crossroads*, p. 51.

for the Maronite hard-liners contributed to their self-confidence and to the feeling that there was no need to compromise with their domestic political challengers.[20]

The political losers in the conservative Arab regimes' decision to support the Maronite position were not only the Palestinian Resistance, but also the Sunni Muslim establishment. They lost heavily in the dwindling political asset of support in Arab capitals. Sunni leaders were also hurt by the tendency of left-wing Arab regimes to criticize traditional Lebanese oligarchs, preferring to back overtly anti-establishment Lebanese groups instead. The reduced authority and regional clout of the Sunni establishment, whose cooperation with the Maronite elite was a vital pillar of the Lebanese system, was a major factor in the system's collapse in the 1975–76 Civil War.[21]

In this context, any Syrian attempt to increase its influence in Lebanon required tackling a network of inter-Arab rivalries superimposed on the Lebanese scene. By the early 1970s, Syria "gradually replaced Egypt as the external center—demanding allegiance and extending support—for both Sunni and Shi'i Lebanese politicians."[22] Syria also maintained contacts with members of the Christian elite before the 1975–76 Civil War (as noted in Chapter 4). However, the most vital axis for Syrian influence over Lebanese politics was its close involvement with the activities of Palestinian guerrillas.

Ambivalence over Arabization

As Syrian involvement in the Lebanese crisis unfolded, other Arab governments lacked both the capacity and the will for counterintervention. As early as October 1975, Saudi Arabia and Kuwait began to advocate collective action by the Arab League. However, Arab ability to act in concert was undermined after Egypt signed a second disengagement accord (Sinai II) with Israel in September, whose reverberations hardened the lines of cleavage between Arab

[20]Ibid., p. 97; Mohammed Mughisuddin, "Egypt," in *Lebanon in Crisis,* ed. Haley and Snider, p. 140.
[21]Khalidi, *Conflict and Violence,* pp. 99; Salibi, *Crossroads,* pp. 72–73.
[22]Rabinovich, "Limits of Military Power," p. 58.

"moderates" and "rejectionists." Syria could flaunt its support of the Palestinians in contrast to Egypt's oblivion to their interests. As long as Syria's intentions in Lebanon were unclear, and its mediation was apparently welcomed by Lebanese parties, the Asad regime enjoyed freedom of maneuver without undue concern over reactions by other Arab actors.[23]

In the second phase of the Syrian involvement (January-May 1976), however, the anxieties of many Arab states were aroused. The February reform plan sponsored by Syria was widely viewed as a "Pax Syriana," designed to consolidate Syria's influence in Lebanon; while Syria's indirect intervention marked its escalated commitment to influencing the outcome of the fighting. Arab states who feared Syria's regional ambitions and were determined that Syria should not become "a regional power of more than middle rank" sensed that a response was vital.[24]

In addition to the *intensity* of Syria's involvement, the *direction* of its policy stirred concern. The February reform plan was deemed too moderate, and Syria's subsequent switch of alignments was thoroughly distressing, for Arab advocates of anti-establishment groups in Lebanon. Several states therefore encouraged and even incited opposition to the February plan within Lebanon, although only Iraq went so far as to threaten counterintervention during this phase.[25]

When Syria intervened directly in June, individual Arab countries reinforced ties to domestic Lebanese groups and factions of the Palestinian Resistance so as to undermine Syrian objectives. However, unilateral counterintervention never materialized. Instead, a collective Arab response crystallized for the first time, through the mechanism of the Arab League.

The accomplishments of the Arab League merit critical scrutiny. Was this regional organization invoking "collective security," echoing the ideals of the United Nations, to save one of its members from perceived external aggression? Alternatively, was the Arab League similar to the Concert of Europe, preserving a balance of power among its members by designing a counterweight

[23]Snider, "Inter-Arab Relations," pp. 182–190.
[24]Dishon, "Lebanese War," p. 29.
[25]Rabinovich, "Limits of Military Power," p. 63; Snider, "Inter-Arab Relations," pp. 193–194.

to hegemonic aspirations by one? When the League in June 1976 set up an "Arab Security Force," transformed and enlarged by October 1976 into an "Arab Deterrent Force," how effectively was Syria being constrained? Indeed, were the peacekeeping efforts either intended or empowered to replace the Syrian forces, or did they merely provide pan-Arab legitimation for the Syrian presence?

Aside from Lebanon itself, the actor with the greatest stake in the answers to these questions was the Palestinian Resistance. A change of heart by the Palestinian leadership over the desirability of "Arabizing" the Lebanese crisis reflected the vagaries of the Palestinian-Syrian relationship. The PLO joined Syria in the initial phase of the Lebanese Civil War in opposing "Arabization" of the crisis. So long as Syria supported its traditional anti-establishment allies, the PLO preferred to minimize the overt role of other Arab actors. Once Syria switched alignments, however, the PLO became the leading advocate of Arabization, calling on the Arab states individually and collectively to fulfill their pan-Arab responsibilities and prevent the liquidation of the Resistance in Lebanon.

At the outset, the PLO joined Syria in boycotting an emergency session of the Arab League on the Lebanese crisis on 15 October 1975. By January 1976, when the Palestinian refugee camp of Dubay fell into Maronite hands, Yasir 'Arafat sent cables to Arab heads of state, charging Lebanese Army complicity with the Maronites in attacking the camp. Arab ambassadors in Lebanon then met with Prime Minister Rashid Karami and with President Sulayman Faranjiyih to discuss the issue.[26] Arab assistance was subsequently sought in internal Resistance affairs. On 12 April, 'Arafat cabled Egyptian President Sadat that Syria was attempting to "liquidate the PLO and to set up Zuhayr Muhsin, commander of the Syrian al-Sa'iqah, as leader of the Resistance." Suspicion that Syria was trying to achieve hegemony over the Resistance, and to replace 'Arafat as leader of the movement, led the PLO to disqualify Sa'iqah as an authentic Palestinian organization, and to dismiss Zuhayr Muhsin as head of the PLO's Military Department.[27]

---

[26]Maruis Deeb, *The Lebanese Civil War* (New York: Praeger, 1980), pp. 106, 108.

[27]Mughisuddin, "Egypt," p. 144; Abbas Kelidar and Michael Burrel, Lebanon, *The Collapse of a State,* Conflict Studies, no. 74 (London: Institute for the Study

It was the PLO that initiated the call for an emergency meeting of foreign ministers of the Arab League members on 8 June 1976. 'Arafat condemned Syria's intervention and its measures against the Resistance, threatening to follow the example of Angola and call in outside forces. The Palestinian leader implored the Arab League to take immediate, decisive measures against Syria. The conference then voted for "the formation of symbolic Arab security forces under the auspices of the Secretary General of the League of Arab states to preserve security and stability in Lebanon, and the movement of these forces . . . to begin their work and replace the Syrian forces." This clause was the major provision of a draft proposal adopted by the Arab League, which subsequently decided on the composition of an Arab Security Force to supervise a cease-fire in Lebanon. The intended membership included units from Syria, Palestine (i.e., the Resistance), Saudi Arabia, the Sudan, Libya, and Algeria.[28]

Immediately after the Arab League meeting, 'Arafat visited five Arab capitals to seek support in implementing the resolutions.[29] Forerunners of the force, including small units from Libya, Algeria, and the Sudan, began to arrive in Beirut on 10 June. Deployment of forces to their assigned positions was impeded by the attitude of the Maronite-dominated Lebanese Front. Its spokesman rejected the Arab League resolutions on the grounds, first of all, that the legitimate Lebanese authorities had been excluded from Arab conferences discussing the situation in Lebanon. Second, they argued that a commission formed by the Arab League to facilitate implementation of its resolutions held most of its meetings with representatives of the Lebanese National Movement and the Palestinian Resistance, rather than pro-establishment groups. Finally, they objected to deployment of Palestinians alongside other members of the Arab Security Force. Emphatically, Kamil Sham'un, head of the National Liberal Party, declared that he considered the sending of the Arab forces tantamount to intro-

---

of Conflict, 1976), p. 15; Israel Altman, "The Palestine Liberation Organization," in *Middle East Contemporary Survey*, Vol. I: *1976–1977,* ed. Colin Legum (New York: Holmes and Meier, 1978), p. 185.

[28]Antwan Khuwayri, *Al-harb fi Lubnan, 1976* [The war in Lebanon, 1976], 3 vols. (Junyih, Lebanon: Al-Matba'ah al-Bulsiyyah, 1977), II, pp. 369–371.

[29]Deeb, *Lebanese Civil War*, p. 113.

ducing new enemy forces into Lebanon, pledging that "we will resist them with all our strength."[30]

The Palestinian Resistance complained that Arab governments were delaying in sending their units. A foreign ministers' meeting on 30 June resolved to expedite the sending of troops, without noticeable results. 'Arafat then cabled Egyptian President Sadat early in July urging an expansion of the tasks of the Arab Security Force. Its members, 'Arafat argued, should be assigned to positions around the besieged Tall al-Za'tar refugee camp, and should stop the Syrians from shelling Palestinian camps near Sidon and Beirut. No concrete measures were adopted, however, and when Tall al-Za'tar finally fell on 12 August, 'Arafat deplored the "silent Arab regimes" who had allowed this to occur.[31]

Finally, the Arab foreign ministers resolved to convene a summit conference in the third week of October to discuss the situation in Lebanon. As Syria mounted offensives against the Palestinians and the LNM in late September and mid-October, 'Arafat again cabled Arab heads of state. He accused Syria of wanting to present the rest of the Arabs with a fait accompli based on its advances in Mount Lebanon. Saudi Arabia then acted on 15 October to advance the summit meeting to the next day.[32]

A foreign ministers' meeting on the eve of the Riyadh summit disputed the chain of command of the proposed Arab Deterrent Force. 'Arafat demanded that the ADF be directly answerable to the Arab League, where he could at least be assured of a hearing. The Kuwaiti delegation, however, suggested that the ADF be under the command of the Lebanese President, which in the current circumstances would assure greater Syrian influence. The latter view prevailed, and President Sarkis became the nominal commander of the force.[33]

The Palestinians did succeed, therefore, in promoting Arabization of the Lebanese crisis through the Arab League; expediting the convening of the Riyadh summit; and assuring reaffirmation of the 1969 Cairo Agreement and the leadership position of Yasir 'Arafat in the Resistance through Arab involvement. On the other

[30]Khuwayri, *Al-harb,* II, pp. 384–385.
[31]Deeb, *Lebanese Civil War,* pp. 114–116.
[32]Ibid., pp. 117–118.
[33]Khuwayri, *Al-harb,* II, pp. 693, 703.

hand, the Arab Security Force and ADF were too little and too late for containing the Syrian intervention, and the predominant Syrian composition and role in commanding the peacekeeping forces further undermined their multinational character.

Rivals for Syrian Favor

Just as collective Arab involvement placed few constraints on Syrian freedom of action in Lebanon, unilateral measures by Arab states were limited in their effects. Aside from the choice of whether to become involved through collective or individual modalities, each Arab state had to define its orientation toward contestants in Lebanon's civil strife. For those who had prior links to domestic Lebanese actors or to the Palestinian Resistance, involvement in the Civil War often meant extending aid to traditional allies. Other Arab states, however, were clearly more concerned with curbing Syrian influence in Lebanon than with the outcome of the Civil War. For them, tactical alliances with Lebanese actors were made or broken in response to Syrian shifts of alignments.

Even outside Arab League auspices, however, affiliations among Arab states governed attempts to influence Syrian behavior. Tacit recognition of Syria's growing regional influence governed attempts by members of rival Arab coalitions to lure Syria into their ranks. Failing that objective, each group sought to curb Syria's ambitions.

One coalition that wavered between courting Syria's allegiance and obstructing its objectives in Lebanon was comprised of "Rejectionist" states—that is, those opposed to a peace agreement with Israel. Within this group, Libya was joined by Algeria in repeated attempts to win Syrian favor by undertaking a mediatory role in Lebanon. Although Iraq intermittently joined the others in striving for a broad Rejectionist coalition including Syria, its policies were primarily aimed at undermining Syria's growing influence.

Iraq, having finally achieved substantial domestic stability by the mid-1970s, was eager to pursue a more active regional policy. In contrast to its earlier struggle with Egypt for control over Syria, Iraq now found itself contending with Syria for influence in the

Fertile Crescent. The rivalry for leadership was coupled with an ongoing ideological polemic between regimes governed by competing factions of the Ba'th Party, each of which claimed more authentic pan-Arab and socialist credentials.[34]

From the outset of the Lebanese Civil War, Iraq encouraged anti-Syrian groups — including Rejectionist Palestinians and leftist groups in the Lebanese National Movement who were traditional recipients of Iraqi support, as well as tactically cultivated allies. In August 1975, the PLO leadership initiated communications with Baghdad, which had been disrupted since Iraq endorsed the split of Rejectionist Palestinian groups from the rest of the Resistance in 1974. In the autumn of 1975, Iraq unsuccessfully urged Lebanese President Faranjiyih to replace Rashid Karami, who was backed by the Syrians, with Taki al-Din Sulh, its own candidate for Prime Minister.[35]

With indications of deeper Syrian involvement in Lebanon, Iraq pursued more vigorous symbolic and concrete countermeasures. In March 1976, Iraq threatened to send troops into Syria if the Syrian Army intervened in Lebanon on a large scale. In April, Iraq stopped the flow of oil through a pipeline traversing Syria, depriving Syria of the transit royalties. More significantly, Iraq reneged on an agreement to supply oil to the Syrian refinery at Homs at pre-1973 prices, and then cut off the supply of oil altogether. In addition to economic warfare, Iraq reportedly encouraged the growth of domestic opposition within Syria to the government's policies in Lebanon.[36]

Nevertheless, Iraq joined in a Libyan-Algerian effort in spring 1976 to lure Syria into joining a Rejectionist coalition. The incentives included a promise of $600 million in financial assistance; the stationing of an Iraqi contingent backed by air support on the Syrian side of the Golan Heights, facing Israel; and an end to Iraqi economic warfare. In exchange, Syria would have to forswear any ambition to exclusive influence in Lebanon; avoid reconciliation with Egypt and renounce any efforts toward a peace accord with Israel; and agree to reunion of the Ba'th factions in Syria and Iraq.

---

[34]Khalidi, *Conflict and Violence,* p. 85.

[35]Mughisuddin, "Egypt," p. 139; Snider, "Inter-Arab Relations," pp. 184, 189.

[36]Snider, "Inter-Arab Relations," pp. 193–194; Dishon, "Lebanese War," p. 29, n. 14; Rabinovich, "Limits to Military Power," p. 65.

Iraq claimed that Syria accepted this plan in May but then went back on its word, rejecting the option of reconciliation with Iraq and choosing a course of collision instead.[37]

Once Syria intervened directly in Lebanon, Iraq was the only country to opt out of the Arab League's mediatory strategy and pursue unilateral reprisals. Early in June, redeployment of an Iraqi Army contingent to Syria's eastern border prompted Syrian complaints at the Arab League's foreign ministers' conference of "suspicious Iraqi maneuvers."[38] By autumn 1976, Iraq had infiltrated into Lebanon several thousand troops, who joined the Palestinian Resistance and LNM in direct combat with the Syrians. Finally, in the 25 October Arab League summit in Cairo, only Iraq objected to the decision that the Arab Deterrent Force be composed primarily of Syrian forces already in Lebanon.[39]

Iraq's hostile, competitive tone contrasted with persistent attempts at conciliation by the Libyan regime. Since coming to power in September 1969, Libyan President Mu'ammar al-Qaddafi had supported anti-establishment groups in Lebanon. Portraying himself, rather than Anwar al-Sadat, as the legitimate heir to Gamal 'Abd al-Nasir's revolutionary leadership, he took a special interest in cultivating Nasirist organizations in Lebanon. The growing tension between Egypt and Libya since the October War of 1973 fueled Qaddafi's determination to forge a Rejectionist front opposing Egypt's policy of accommodation with Israel. He was particularly eager to avert reconciliation between Syria and Egypt, or between Egypt and the Palestinians.[40]

Early in the Lebanese Civil War, Libya opposed Arab League mediation, boycotting the October 1975 foreign ministers' meeting, as did Syria and the PLO. Libya's posture was not based on principled opposition to the Arabization of the Lebanese crisis, but rather on suspicion that Saudi Arabia was promoting the meeting to effect Syrian-Egyptian reconciliation. Similar considerations prompted Libya's objections to a meeting scheduled for May 1976 in Riyadh, attended by the prime ministers of Saudi Arabia, Kuwait, Syria, and Egypt. Syria decided at the last moment to cancel

[37]Dishon, "Lebanese War," p. 29.
[38]Khuwayri, Al-harb, II, p. 385.
[39]Snider, "Inter-Arab Relations," pp. 193–194.
[40]Khalidi, Conflict and Violence, pp. 85–86.

the meeting, just days after a visit to Damascus by Libyan Prime Minister 'Abd al-Salam Jallud. Jallud may have lobbied successfully against Syrian participation in the meeting, offering financial incentives for Syria to join the Rejectionist coalition instead. Nevertheless, Syria was suspicious of any alignment in which Iraq was a partner, and could not easily overlook the fact that Iraq and Libya were the principal financiers of anti-Syrian groups in Lebanon. According to some press reports, Qaddafi was providing as much as $1 million daily to Lebanese anti-establishment forces. There were, therefore, sufficient reasons for Syria to be wary of casting its lot with the Rejectionist coalition.[41]

Even after President Asad agreed to pursue Arab League-sponsored summitry in June, Libyan efforts at mediation continued. On the eve of the June foreign ministers' conference, Libyan Prime Minister Jallud and the Algerian Minister of Education arrived in Damascus. As mediators between Syria and the anti-establishment forces in Lebanon, they arranged a short-lived cease-fire accord.[42] Libya and Algeria then pledged that each would send a symbolic unit to help Syrian forces restore stability in Lebanon even before the formation of a collective Arab Security Force, and they later contributed units under its auspices. In the final months of the war, Prime Minister Jallud's diplomatic efforts, often in conjunction with an Algerian partner, focused on promoting reconciliation between Syria on the one hand and LNM groups on the other.[43]

The frustration of Libyan hopes of being a principal coalition-builder in the Lebanese crisis was largely due to successful efforts by its Saudi rival. Saudi policies aimed at fashioning a "moderate" Arab coalition were pursued consistently throughout the Civil War. However, Saudi attitudes toward the Lebanese contestants were deeply ambivalent and resulted in inconsistent behavior. The Saudi dilemma has been characterized as follows:

> On the one hand they viewed the Maronite establishment as a bulwark against the forces of radicalism and the left. On the other, there was the spontaneous sympathy of public opinion in Saudi

[41]M. Graeme Bannerman, "Saudi Arabia," in *Lebanon in Crisis,* ed. Haley and Snider, pp. 128–129.

[42]Deeb, *Lebanese Civil War,* p. 113.

[43]Khuwayri, *Al-harb,* II, pp. 371, 386–387.

Arabia and Kuwait and sectors of their ruling elites with the Lebanese Muslims and the Palestinians.

The Saudi elite was thus torn in opposite directions by conservative ideology and sectarian bonds.[44]

The inner tension in Saudi policy resulted in limited support for groups in each of the competing coalitions early in the Lebanese Civil War. Presumably, by providing assistance to "moderate" elements on both sides, the chances of reconciliation might increase. While supporting Christian groups and individual members of the Muslim establishment such as Sa'ib Salam, Saudi Arabia also assisted "moderate" groups within the Resistance. From a PLO perspective, Saudi aid was a welcome counterweight to Syria's attempts at greater control over the movement.[45]

A gradual shift in Saudi policy led to the cessation of assistance to Maronite groups early in 1976. Saudi anxieties were aroused by Christian advocacy of Lebanon's partition as early as November 1975, and reinforced by large-scale Christian massacres of Muslims in December. The Maronite offensive against Palestinian refugee camps in January 1976 may have been decisive in prompting a shift in Saudi policy. Withdrawal of Saudi support fed into a sense of isolation on the part of the Lebanese Front, and a change in their attitude toward Arabization of the Lebanese crisis. Whereas pro-establishment groups had welcomed the Arab League meeting of October 1975 (at a time that the PLO and Syria opposed it), by early 1976 Christian spokesmen regarded the Arab League as a hostile forum.[46]

The ironic contradictions in Saudi policy were vividly reflected in the flourishing arms trade in Lebanon, for which the Saudis were a major source of financing. As Anthony Sampson argues in *The Arms Bazaar,* "This war provided a ghastly example of how easily weapons can get out of hand and establish their own anarchy." By financing both Christians and Palestinians, "oil turned into bullets on both sides." Saudi Arabia financed the Syrians, who initially armed Palestinians. Then, Palestinians directed the same

---

[44]Khalidi, *Conflict and Violence,* pp. 86–87.

[45]Bannerman, "Saudi Arabia," pp. 117–121; Altman, "Palestine Liberation Organization," p. 196.

[46]Bannerman, "Saudi Arabia," pp. 125–127.

weapons at Syrian tanks after the Syrians changed sides.[47] Kamal Junbalat bitterly observed on the eve of the October 1976 Riyadh summit that "the situation is now in the hands of the Arab oil states, for they are the ones who are supporting the forces entangled in the Lebanese conflict and supply them with weapons and money."[48]

In its attitude toward the Syrian intervention in Lebanon, Saudi Arabia wavered between support for Asad and attempts to restrain him when the direction of Syrian policy became objectionable. One incentive for supporting the Asad regime was Saudi concern that Syria's domestic stability might be undermined as a consequence of involvement in the Lebanese war. Conflict between Syria and the Palestinians might lead to Asad's overthrow and replacement by a more "radical," Rejectionist leadership that would join Iraq in undermining conservative regimes throughout the region. Saudi Arabia therefore wished to buttress Asad, while prodding him toward a negotiated resolution of the Lebanese crisis.[49]

Financial assistance to Syria was the principal lever of Saudi influence. King Khalid visited Damascus in December 1975, and may have been consulted about the deployment of PLA units to Lebanon in January. When Iraq cut off the flow of oil to Syria, Saudi Arabia compensated for the deficits, transporting oil to Syria through the Transarabian Pipeline. In view of increased costs associated with direct military intervention, financial vulnerability may explain Syria's willingness to overcome its opposition to Arabization and attend the June foreign ministers' conference at Saudi urging. Threats of financial penalties may also have influenced Asad to attend the Riyadh summit in October 1976, when its date was moved forward at the initiative of Saudi Arabia. Once Asad went along with the Arab League's formula for the Arab Deterrent Force, he was assured that its expenses would be paid by the oil-producing Arab states.[50]

On the diplomatic level, Saudi efforts were consistently aimed at reconciliation between Syria and Egypt. In addition to averting

[47]Anthony Sampson, *The Arms Bazaar* (New York: Viking, 1977), pp. 18–23.

[48]Khuwayri, *Al-harb*, III, p. 682.

[49]Khalidi, *Conflict and Violence,* pp. 86–87.

[50]Bannerman, "Saudi Arabia," pp. 125–131; Rabinovich, "Limits to Military Power," p. 70.

a negative outcome by keeping Syria out of the Rejectionist bloc, Saudi Arabia wished to revive the coalition it had previously sponsored during the October War of 1973. The Syrian-Egyptian coalition disintegrated because of divergent attitudes toward accommodation with Israel, culminating in a rancorous split over the Sinai II accord of September 1975. In the Saudi view, Egyptian-Syrian accommodation was an essential prerequisite for resolving the Lebanese crisis and assuring a responsible Syrian foreign policy.[51]

When Saudi Arabia and Kuwait urged Syrian attendance at the initial Arab foreign ministers' conference of October 1975, Syria objected that instead of discussing Lebanon, the ministers should discuss Sinai II, "because it forms the background to the Lebanese developments." Again, when a meeting was scheduled in Riyadh in May 1976, Syria demanded that President Sadat disavow Sinai II as a condition for reconciliation, while Sadat was willing to attend only if Lebanon was the exclusive topic for discussion. After the June meeting of Arab League foreign ministers, Saudi Arabia finally succeeded in sponsoring the quadripartite conference it had hoped to host in May. The meeting in Riyadh from 22 to 24 June, however, led merely to symbolic concessions by each side to cease verbal attacks against the other—pledges that were rapidly ignored.[52]

The Egyptian-Syrian meeting in June was more important in its negative than its positive results, in that Syria had at least been lured away from participating in the Rejectionist coalition and had begun a dialogue with Egypt. By the time of the October Riyadh summit, the participants were willing to avoid any reference to Sinai II, and concrete measures of reconciliation included Egyptian willingness to reopen the Syrian embassy in Cairo and resume the exchange of ambassadors with Syria.[53] The refurbished Syrian-Egyptian-Saudi coalition of 1976 was qualitatively different than that of 1973. In the reformulated version, the principal architect of alignment was Saudi Arabia rather than Egypt; and

---

[51]Rabinovich, "Limits to Military Power," p. 70; Khalidi, *Conflict and Violence,* pp. 86–87.

[52]Bannerman, "Saudi Arabia," pp. 124–129.

[53]Khuwayri, *Al-harb,* II, pp. 702–703.

Syria emerged as much more of an equal, rather than a junior, partner.[54]

If Asad found the prospect of reconciliation with Egypt galling until Saudi pressure finally prevailed by October 1976, Sadat's own hesitation about rapprochement was motivated by other considerations. Having endured widespread Arab condemnation after Sinai II, Sadat derived great satisfaction from Arab criticism of Syria's Lebanese policies. Moreover, by adopting a reactive policy in Lebanon through support for whichever coalition was currently opposed to Syria, Egypt could detract from Syria's regional standing and possibly enhance its own.

Egypt's low profile in Lebanon in 1975–76 contrasted to 'Abd al-Nasir's active behind-the-scenes role in the 1958 Civil War. The reasons derived from the decline of Egypt's regional stature in general, and its influence in Lebanon in particular. In the early months of the war, Egypt discreetly backed the pro-establishment coalition, especially the Kata'ib Party. However, Egypt suspended its assistance to the Kata'ib and criticized their actions in January 1976, after the Maronite offensive against the Palestinian refugee camps and nearby Muslim districts. In this respect Egypt's Lebanese policy paralleled that of Saudi Arabia, its principal financier and foreign policy ally in the region. An early advocate of Arabization, Egypt was the first state to propose an inter-Arab peacekeeping force for Lebanon. When President Faranjiyih rejected the proposal, Sadat condemned the "corrupt right-wing leaders" of Lebanon for insensitivity to their country's real needs.[55]

Beyond verbal pronouncements, Egypt sponsored small-scale indirect intervention in Lebanon. Sharing the PLO's desire to avert Syrian domination of the Resistance, Sadat welcomed Palestinian overtures for assistance. Late in January, the 'Ayn Jalut brigade of the Palestine Liberation Army (PLA), which was trained and stationed in Egypt, was transported to Lebanon to fight alongside the PLO. As Syria's shift of alignments became apparent in the following months, Egypt seized the opportunity to appear as a benefactor of the PLO. When Yasir 'Arafat cabled Sadat on 12

[54]Dishon, "Lebanese War," pp. 30–31.

[55]Mughisuddin, "Egypt," pp. 133, 137, 142–144; Khalidi, *Conflict and Violence,* p. 84; Snider, "Inter-Arab Relations," p. 188.

April complaining of Syria's anti-Resistance activities, Egypt's reply was that it would not "allow any action conducive to the liquidation of the Palestinian Resistance, and that Egypt fully supports the Lebanese progressive elements led by Kamal Jumblatt."[56]

After Syria intervened directly in Lebanon, Sadat closed the Syrian embassy in Cairo and recalled Egypt's ambassador from Damascus. Sadat also permitted the reopening of the Voice of Palestine, a Palestinian broadcasting station closed the previous September after it had condemned Sinai II. In September, Egypt proposed that Palestine, as represented by the PLO, be admitted to full membership in the Arab League, instead of remaining a "non-voting member." While this suggestion conformed to Sadat's long-term advocacy of the formation of a Palestinian government-in-exile, it was at this point specifically intended to buttress Yasir 'Arafat's leadership of the Resistance, in response to Syrian maneuvers to replace him.[57]

Viewing Egyptian conduct during the Civil War in its broader regional context, three prominent themes merit further comment. First, Egyptian alignments in Lebanon were incongruous with the overall direction of Egyptian foreign policy. Vocal Egyptian support for the Palestinian position in Lebanon in 1976 contradicted the bitter recriminations between the two since Sinai II. In one appraisal, whereas Syria and the PLO were strategic allies who experienced a tactical falling-out during the Lebanese war, Egypt and the PLO were merely tactical allies during that conflict.[58]

Even more curious was the assistance provided by Egypt to Iraq, perhaps the most strident Rejectionist state, during the Civil War. Iraq, which had no direct land access to Lebanon, sought means to transport reinforcements to its anti-Syrian protégés there. Sadat obligingly established an "airbridge" with Baghdad, enabling Iraq to send "volunteers" to Lebanon via Egypt. In January, Iraqi-

---

[56]Abbas Kelidar and Michael Burrel, *Lebanon, the Collapse of a State: Regional Dimensions of the Struggle,* Conflict Studies, no. 74 (London: Institute for the Study of Conflict, 1976), p. 15; Khalidi, *Conflict and Violence,* p. 84; Altman, "Palestine Liberation Organization," p. 196; Mughisuddin, "Egypt," pp. 143–144.

[57]Deeb, *Lebanese Civil War,* p. 113; Altman, "Palestine Liberation Organization," p. 196.

[58]Mughisuddin, "Egypt," p. 137.

trained members of the Qadisiyyah Brigade of the PLA were thereby sent to Lebanon. In summer 1976, Iraq again availed itself of the Egyptian connection to send regular troops to the Lebanese battlefield.[59]

Second, the Sinai II accord affected the inter-Arab climate of the Lebanese war not only by increasing Egypt's sense of isolation and causing it to reach out for Lebanese allies, but also by arousing Syrian suspicions of Egypt's manipulative role. As early as 25 September 1975, Syrian Foreign Minister Khaddam linked the Lebanese crisis directly to the signing of Sinai II, while an official Syrian statement in April 1976 complained that the Lebanese crisis was being escalated by "outside powers" who wanted to divert attention from the "unpopular" Sinai accord.[60] Although one may question whether Syrian leaders actually believed that Egypt was inciting hostilities in Lebanon, tensions over Arab-Israel diplomacy undoubtedly increased polarization in the inter-Arab arena.

Third, Syrian-Egyptian sparring over Lebanon surely reflected Egyptian anxieties over Syria's regional leadership ambitions. For example, Sadat told a Kuwaiti correspondent in August 1976 that Syria was striving for pan-Arab leadership and "as a consequence" had become "embroiled" in Lebanon. A Syrian spokesman complained that Egypt was seeking to bring matters in Lebanon "to a head" in order to "exhaust" Syria and "to check Syria's national [i.e., pan-Arab] role."[61] Having lost, at least temporarily, its own ability to play a leadership role, Egypt hoped at least to curb its rival's ability to do so.

Greater Syria?

Syria's ability to act in Lebanon without counterintervention by Arab rivals attested to the fluid distribution of power in the Arab world. Other Arab states implicitly, if grudgingly, acknowledged the Syrian stake in Lebanon as well as Syrian ability to exert

[59]Kelidar and Burrel, *Lebanon,* p. 15; Khalidi, *Conflict and Violence,* p. 84; Snider, "Inter-Arab Relations," p. 193.

[60]Snider, "Inter-Arab Relations," pp. 188–189; Mughisuddin, "Egypt," pp. 137, 143.

[61]Dishon, "Lebanese War," p. 30.

leverage over the Palestinian Resistance. There were limits to the costs other Arab actors were willing to incur in challenging determined Syrian policies in its immediate environment. Nevertheless, other Arab leaders pondered the scope of Syrian regional ambitions. Was Asad merely bent on restoring stability in Lebanon or would he embrace encompassing Arab unity schemes advancing Syria's role as the projected leader?

Arab commentators recalled historical precedents in speculating on Syrian motivation. The East Jerusalem daily *al-Quds* observed on 21 June 1976:

> Some say that the Syrian leaders want to revive the Greater Syria plan, provided it is "made in Damascus"—having always rejected it in the past when it was "made in Amman" or "made in Baghdad."[62]

Syrian spokesmen hesitated to embrace the concept of "Greater Syria" overtly, both because its earlier royalist connotations conjured up schemes directed at Syria by ambitious neighbors, and because of reluctance to arouse the anxieties of Syria's contemporary neighbors. However, the concept was alluded to indirectly. Since Syria began to pursue a more active regional policy in the early 1970s, the notion of "geographic Syria" occasionally surfaced in official sources, alluding to an historic entity embracing Lebanon and Palestine (including Jordan). On 8 March 1974, President Asad declared:

> It will be useful to remind the Israeli leaders that Palestine is not only part of the Arab homeland but is also a principal part of southern Syria. . . . Palestine will remain part of our liberated Arab homeland and of our Syrian Arab country.[63]

Vague allusions to the past did not suffice, however, to rationalize Syria's Lebanese policy both at home and abroad. Especially after its direct intervention in Lebanon and confrontation with the Resistance in June 1976, the concept of Greater Syria was evoked by the Syrian elite as a legitimizing notion. Syria relied on the

[62]Quoted in Dishon, "Lebanese War," p. 28, n. 8.
[63]Quoted in Dishon, "Lebanese War," p. 28.

concept to justify its military presence in Lebanon as well as its claim to assert authority over the Palestinian movement. On this basis, Syria claimed to discern the interests of the Palestinians better than did their own leaders.[64]

What did the Greater Syria concept imply about Syria's future aspirations? By the summer of 1976, unofficial spokesmen in the Syrian press spoke of consolidating their country's subregional influence. The option advocated by one commentator on 22 September was

> a federation of the countries of the Arab East together with Syria and Jordan . . . It is the right of the Palestinians and our right and duty that the Palestinians return to their land and that their return be based on an understanding that Palestine is Southern Syria.[65]

Another, less specific proposal, outlined by an organ of the Ba'th Party on 5 October, called for "creating a nucleus of confrontation," referring to a "confrontation zone [which] should embrace Syria, Jordan, the PLO, and Lebanon."[66]

Whether Syria's regional goals were cast in terms of a proposed federation, a "nucleus of confrontation," or a zone of influence, the intended components were always the same. Indeed, they were always identical geographically to the contours of the earlier Greater Syria scheme, except for ambiguity as to how much of Palestine could feasibly be incorporated. Arab apprehensions over Syria's ambitions were aroused not only by Asad's policies in Lebanon and toward the PLO, but also by the unfailing cooperation he received from Jordan's King Husayn.

It was highly ironic that Jordan, the target of intervention by Syria when it experienced civil strife in 1970, became the sole Arab apologist for Syria's subsequent intervention in Lebanon. Jordan's involvement in the Lebanese Civil War was minor, but several incidents exemplified its support for Syria. In summer 1976, Iraqi redeployment of troops toward the border with Syria appeared ominous. With thousands of Syria's best troops engaged in Lebanon, Jordan performed a valuable service by redeploying its own

---

[64]Rabinovich, "Limits to Military Power," p. 69.
[65]Quoted in Rabinovich, "Limits to Military Power," p. 69.
[66]Quoted in Dishon, "Lebanese War," p. 28.

troops to support Syrian forces facing Iraq. On the political and diplomatic level, King Husayn sought to explain Syria's Lebanese policies to interested third parties, particularly in the later stages of the war. Most significantly, Husayn reassured American officials that Syria's intervention in Lebanon would pose no threat to Israel.[67]

Jordan's role as Syria's lone advocate did not, however, counteract the otherwise solid front of disapproval for Asad's Lebanese policies by the October 1976 Riyadh summit. Inter-Arab rivalries and attempts at drawing Syria into opposing coalitions had precluded collective action until June 1976. But the attempts, however ineffective, to establish Arab peacekeeping forces to replace Syrian forces revealed widespread suspicion of Syrian intentions. While Arab disunity allowed Syria substantial time and space for maneuver in Lebanon, outer limits were set on how the Syrian presence could be defined. Lip service, at least, had to be paid to Lebanese sovereignty and to the autonomy of the Palestinian Resistance. As long as Syria respected these formal demands of the Arab consensus, its freedom of action remained substantially unconstrained.

[67]Jureidini and McLaurin, "Hashemite Kingdom," pp. 158–159.

10

Prospect of Israeli Counterintervention

Syria's options in defining its Lebanese commitment were more continuously and effectively constrained by Israel than by Arab opponents. Next to Syria, Israel was the state with the most at stake in the outcome of the Lebanese conflict.

Like other external actors, Israel's behavior during the Lebanese Civil War was reactive to Syria. Israel was at first primarily concerned with the *direction* of Syrian alignments, fearing that Syrian support for traditional allies in Lebanon would strengthen the PLO's capabilities against Israel. Once Syria shifted alignments, Israel's main priority was to limit the *intensity* and geographic scope of Syria's military presence within range of Israel's northern border.

Even in the absence of Syrian intervention, Israel had substantial interest in the outcome of the Lebanese Civil War. Victory for anti-establishment forces allied with the Resistance posed an unacceptable security threat, in Israel's view. Israeli threats of counterintervention were, however, directed at Syria rather than at parties to the Lebanese strife. Covert Israeli assistance to proestablishment groups was coupled, over time, with overt assistance to parties in Southern Lebanon, as a form of indirect Israeli intervention.

The credibility of Israeli deterrent threats influenced Syria's penchant for a cautious, incremental escalation of its Lebanese commitment. The priority assigned to Southern Lebanon by Israel for security reasons set that region off limits to the Syrian intervener. Moreover, the intricate interplay between the Arab-Israeli and inter-Arab components of Syria's regional environment affected calculations by Syrian decisionmakers throughout the Lebanese Civil War.

The Eastern Front

Syria's perceptions of the prospects for either war or peace with Israel were conditioned, after the October War of 1973, by the growing gap between Syrian and Egyptian strategies. As Egypt moved toward a separate peace with Israel, Syria worried that Egypt's removal as a "confrontation state" would not only limit Syrian military options, but its diplomatic options as well. Syria dreaded the prospect of a succession of interim agreements between Egypt and Israel in which the interests of other Arab actors were ignored.

However, if Syria became the recognized leader of a subregional Arab bloc, its options would improve dramatically. Military coordination with Jordan, Lebanon, and the PLO might permit a credible military option against Israel even without Egyptian participation, as well as a stronger bargaining position in negotiations. The concept epitomizing Syria's leadership aspirations in the Arab-Israeli sphere was the "Eastern Front." Depending on the climate of Syrian-Iraqi relations, the Eastern Front concept might or might not assume Iraqi participation. However, the core membership of the proposed Eastern Front directed against Israel was identical to that of the proposed Greater Syria in the inter-Arab sphere.[1]

President Asad's proposal in March 1975 of a Syrian-Palestinian joint military command may have been a response to a recent breakdown of Egyptian-Israeli talks under American auspices, which Syria had vigorously opposed. Although the joint command with the PLO did not go into effect, there were unconfirmed reports in June that Syria and Jordan concluded an agreement for policy coordination under a joint military command. The first official Syrian reference to the inclusion of Lebanon as a member of the Eastern Front was made by Foreign Minister 'Abd al-Halim Khaddam on 9 September 1975. Khaddam announced that Syria

[1]Itamar Rabinovitch, "The Limits of Military Power," in *Lebanon in Crisis*, ed. P. Edward Haley and Lewis W. Snider (Syracuse, N.Y.: Syracuse University Press, 1979), pp. 57–59; Lewis Snider, "Inter-Arab Relations," in ibid., pp. 185–186.

was planning the establishment of a defensive line from Ras al-Naqurah on the Lebanese coastal border with Israel to the Gulf of 'Aqabah in southern Jordan. The timing of the announcement reflected both the status of Egyptian-Israel negotiations and the resumption of fighting in Lebanon.

Syria linked the Lebanese fighting in September 1975, after a relative lull, to the signing of the second Egyptian-Israeli disengagement accord (Sinai II) on 1 September. Syrian sources charged that Israel and the United States had conspired to reignite Lebanese strife to divert attention from Sinai II; to goad the Lebanese Army to attack Palestinian guerrillas in Southern Lebanon; and to undermine the Syrian-Palestinian alliance to undermine the Eastern Front strategy.[2]

Although Lebanon was a "confrontation state" only in the 1948 Arab-Israeli war, Syria had long recognized its neighbor's potential military significance in both a defensive and offensive capacity. Syria's line of defense was vulnerable to an Israeli attack across Lebanese territory directed at its "soft western underbelly." However, if Syria could station troops in Lebanon, it would gain substantial offensive leverage against Israel. Syria would then be in a position to activate an additional front, and could oblige Israel to divert troops toward the Lebanese border that would otherwise be deployed on the Syrian front.[3]

Syria's own status as a "confrontation state" underwent several changes prior to the Lebanese Civil War. The Arab-Israeli war of 1948 occurred two years after Syrian independence, when Syria was governed by a civilian elite. After the adoption by the United Nations in November 1947 of the Partition Plan to create a Jewish as well as an Arab state in Palestine, the Arab League sponsored creation of an Arab Liberation Army to prevent Palestine's partition. The military committee of the force was headquartered in Damascus, and approximately one-fourth of the Syrian officer corps joined. Many officers who participated in the Arab Liberation Army subsequently became important political figures in Syria, and for them the 1948 war was a traumatic, politicizing experience.

---

[2]Snider, "Inter-Arab Relations," pp. 183–190.
[3]Rabinovich, "Limits of Military Power," p. 57.

Although the military accomplishments of the Arab Liberation Army in Palestine from November 1947 to May 1948 were not impressive, its "volunteers" were the only force other than local Palestinians to resist the Partition Plan. When Israel declared independence in May 1948, Syrian regular forces joined those of Egypt, Jordan, Iraq, and Lebanon in attacking the new state. As a result of the disorganized condition of the Syrian Army, only 5,500 of its 8,500 troops were in fighting units, and only 1,500 of these were mobilized in the unit sent to fight the Israelis. This unit was inexperienced, poorly equipped, and short of ammunition, and mounted only several brief thrusts before its collapse. Arab defeat in the 1948 war was a shameful experience for Syria's Army officers, and junior officers assigned blame for the defeat to their superiors in the military establishment and to the corrupt social structure of the country. When this group of junior officers rose to positions of leadership in Syria's military elite, memories of the 1948 defeat "served to harden their attitudes to Israel ever since."[4]

Syria's inability to frame an effective posture toward Israel after the 1948 defeat was symptomatic of broader Arab dilemmas. Three fundamental difficulties plagued Arab leaders in designing policies toward Israel through the late 1960s. First, due to insufficient military and economic capabilities, the Arab states could not prevent Israel's establishment or even its confinement to the boundaries of the Partition Plan, sustaining severe territorial losses in the June 1967 Arab-Israeli War. Second, Arab leaders had trouble defining their long-run objectives against Israel, because "the Arabs have been unable to decide whether their policy should aim at destroying the Israeli state or only at the limited objective of containing it." Third, internal Arab divisions impeded definition of realistic and coherent objectives toward Israel. In effect, "each Arab regime has been so internally insecure and, in the atmosphere provided by the pan-Arab idea, so exposed to criticism by its neighbors that its leaders have tended to shrink from taking unorthodox positions in the ritually symbolic question of Palestine and Israel." Arab elites sought domestic popularity and regional prestige in strident

---

[4]Michael Van Dusen, "Syrian Politics and the Future of Arab-Israeli Relations," in *World Politics and the Arab-Israeli Conflict,* ed. Robert O. Freedman (New York: Pergamon, 1979), pp. 256–259.

anti-Israel positions, using the issue in outbidding and competition with their rivals.[5]

Syria's long-term domestic instability accentuated the salience of the third variable. Pan-Arab, Palestinian, and anti-Israel slogans were unifying symbols for a fragmented polity. The predominance of members of the 'Alawi minority in the Syrian elite by the mid-1960s encouraged orthodoxy on Arab-Israel issues. 'Alawi leaders hoped to enhance the regime's legitimacy among the Sunni Muslim majority by establishing credentials on a cause embraced by Sunnis throughout the Arab world, especially by championing the claims of the predominantly Sunni Palestinians.[6]

Syria refused to join Egypt and Jordan in endorsing United Nations-sponsored Security Council Resolution 242 after the June 1967 War on grounds of commitment to the Palestinian cause. The 22 November 1967 resolution coupled its call for withdrawal of Israeli forces from territories occupied in the war with assurance of respect for "the sovereignty, territorial integrity, and political independence of every state in the area." Aside from the implicit acknowledgment of Israel's right to a secure existence, Syria objected to the fact that the only allusion to the Palestinians was a call for the "just settlement of the refugee problem." Palestinian national rights must be guaranteed, Syria argued, before lasting peace could be achieved in the Middle East.

Nevertheless, President Hafiz al-Asad moved toward conditional acceptance of Security Council Resolution 242 in March 1972. A significant change of tone was reflected in Asad's statement that Syria would embrace the resolution provided that Israel withdrew from all areas captured in 1967 and recognized Palestinian "rights" as an essential element in any peace settlement.[7] After the relatively effective military performance of the Syrian and Egyptian Armies in the October 1973 War, Asad participated in peacemaking with Israel on a limited scale. In May

---

[5]Malcolm Kerr, "Regional Arab Politics and the Conflict With Israel," in *Political Dynamics in the Middle East*, ed. Paul Hammond and Sidney Alexander (New York: American Elsevier, 1972), pp. 53–62.

[6]Van Dusen, "Syrian Politics," pp. 251–252.

[7]Fred Khouri, "The Arab-Israeli Conflict," in *Lebanon in Crisis*, ed. Haley and Snider, pp. 161–162.

1974, a disengagement agreement between Israel and Syria provided for a limited Israeli withdrawal from the Golan Heights in
exchange for Syrian acceptance of a United Nations peacekeeping force.

Asad's participation in Henry Kissinger's "step-by-step" diplomacy was an unprecedented departure from Syria's earlier
belligerent posture toward Israel. Syrian suspicions were
aroused, however, by negotiations toward a second Egyptian
disengagement agreement with Israel in the absence of Israeli
concessions toward Jordan or the Palestinians. Explaining Syria's attitude in his 20 July 1976 speech, Asad significantly remarks
that Syria refused to negotiate "despite the fact that negotiation
would have restored a portion of our occupied land, and under
conditions that were acceptable, if we had followed that path."
The Syrian refusal was based on concern lest the Palestinian Resistance be isolated and its cause aborted. Asad believed that
even in the best of circumstances, the Arab states would be
obliged "to give everything to the enemy when we arrived at the
1967 lines, and the Palestinian cause would have been
liquidated."[8]

Syrian sources frequently emphasized that Syria placed its
commitment to the transnational Palestinian cause over "narrow" Syrian state interests. Syrian spokesmen cited other sacrifices for the Palestinian cause, including willingness to sustain
Israeli retaliation for Palestinian guerrilla activities. Asad noted
that 50 percent of the Syrian planes downed by Israel before the
October War were engaged in defending positions of the Palestinian Resistance. Within one day, thirteen Syrian planes were
downed over Southern Lebanon. In another instance, five
hundred Syrian soldiers became martyrs when Israel attacked a
guerrilla base inside Syria.[9] Despite these Syrian claims, the record shows that Syria consistently diverted Palestinian guerrilla
operations, first to Jordan and then increasingly to Lebanon.[10]
One major reason was to escape Israel retaliation against Syria
and the possibility that the cycle of guerrilla raids and reprisals
might escalate into an Israeli-Syrian war.

[8]Hafiz al-Asad, Speech delivered on 20 July 1976, p. 11.
[9]Ibid.
[10]See Chapter 5.

Israeli Reprisal Policy

Apprehension over Israeli reprisals was a major factor discouraging Syria as well as Egypt from permitting Palestinian guerrillas to operate on their territory. Yet the states that did serve as hosts to the PLO were even less capable of absorbing the repercussions for their countries' external security and domestic stability. Did Israeli leaders, in framing their reprisal policy, anticipate the political consequences for states which were targets of the reprisals?

Israeli reprisals included attacks on both military and civilian targets in states hosting Palestinian guerrillas. These attacks ranged in scope from small-scale to brigade-size operations, and made use of conventional ground assaults, artillery salvos, air strikes, and commando raids.[11] The rationale for selecting the stragegy of reprisals was based on three considerations. First, Israel viewed violent behavior by Arab states, in committing or condoning attacks against Israel, as a form of delinquency. Arab governments were therefore held responsible for guerrilla actions emanating from their territory. Second, Israeli leaders believed that the Arabs were implacably hostile to Israel's existence and bent on its destruction if ever that were feasible. Therefore, the Arab threat had to be met with a decisive military response rather than political measures. Third, domestic pressures arose in Israel as a beleaguered population reacted to guerrilla raids with anxiety and frustration, pressing the government for reprisals as an outlet for collective tensions.[12]

In the language of strategic theory, Israel's reprisal strategy exemplified "coercive diplomacy," intended to affect an opponent's will rather than to impose a military solution. This stragegy was most often used in the mode of "negative compellance," that is, an attempt to persuade the target nation to stop taking certain actions. Israel wanted to oblige Arab governments to cease per-

[11]Barry M. Blechman, "The Impact of Israel's Reprisals on Behavior of the Bordering Arab Nations Directed at Israel," *Journal of Conflict Resolution* 16 (June 1972): 155.

[12]Daniel Kurtzer, "Palestinian Guerrilla and Israeli Counterinsurgency Warfare: The Radicalization of the Palestine Arab Community to Violence, 1949–1970" (Ph.D. dissertation, Columbia University, 1976), pp. 163–171.

mitting infiltration across their borders, by convincing them that the costs of doing so were prohibitive. Realistically, however, Israel did not expect a complete cessation of hostile activities, but rather their curtailment—so that the reprisal was really a "means of communicating to the Arab governments the tolerable limits of conflict." Israel's policy was based on two assumptions about the reactions of Arab states—first, that they would be willing to incur the political costs of curtailing guerrilla activity; and, second, that they would be capable of forcing the guerrillas to abide by the government's will.

In its goal of negative compellance, Israel's reprisal policy was relatively effective on a short-term basis. Measurement of the dependent variable—Arab behavior—in the time frame of ten to twenty days after a reprisal occurred reveals that hostile acts against Israel were significantly less frequent than in comparable time frames when reprisals had not occurred. However, even this short-term decline in hostile Arab behavior did not universally hold—especially in states that were internally weak. With the increase of guerrilla activity emanating from Jordan and Lebanon after the June 1967 War, Israeli reprisals did not reliably achieve negative compellance vis-à-vis the host states.

On a tactical level, therefore, Israel's reprisal policy had limited effectiveness in achieving negative compellance over the short term. On a strategic level, no decrease whatever in Arab violence could be discerned over the long term. The impact of reprisals generally "decayed" over time, and by thirty days after a reprisal, no noticeable change was evident in ongoing Arab behavior. This finding held even though Israeli reprisals against a given state had a cumulative effect of proving Israel's determination, and reprisals against the target state increased in intensity over time. Moreover, if another goal of coercive diplomacy is supposed to be "positive compellance"—that is, persuading the target government to take (rather than refrain from) certain actions—reprisal policy was even less successful. Israel achieved no cooperative behavior by its neighbors through its reprisals.[13]

Israeli reprisal policy not only fell short of its intended effects on the behavior of Arab host states, but it may also have been

---

[13]Blechman, "Impact of Israeli Reprisals," passim.

counterproductive in its impact on the Palestinian community in these states. As a counterinsurgency strategy, the political aim of the reprisals was to discourage guerrilla operations. However, especially after the June 1967 War, "the more 'successful' Israel was [militarily] in its strategy, the more successful al-Fatah (sic) became as a guerrilla threat." An unintended consequence of Israel's reprisal policy was radicalization of the Palestinians, facilitating mobilization and recruitment efforts by guerrilla organizations. Resentment of Israeli retaliation and the casualties it caused may have goaded Palestinians to a higher level of violence over the long run.[14]

Perceptions by Lebanese, Palestinians, and other Arabs of Israel's reprisal strategy often assumed conspiratorial Israeli intentions. As opposed to the preceding interpretations—which assumed that the goal of reprisals was to deter guerrilla operations, but that the strategy fell short of its objectives—Arab commentators attributed manipulative designs to the Israelis. In one view, Israel escalated its retaliatory strategy against Lebanese targets in the hope of precipitating a showdown between the Lebanese Army and the Palestinian guerrillas comparable to the Jordanian confrontation of 1970–71. Israel allegedly calculated that if the Lebanese authorities were either unwilling or unable to take on the guerrillas, polarization over the issue would accentuate cleavages in Lebanese society and reinforce trends toward Maronite separatism. Domestic strife could then lead to Lebanon's partition, giving Israel the option of asserting de facto control over Southern Lebanon, or even annexing the South if the Lebanese state totally collapsed.[15]

Allegations of Israeli territorial designs on Southern Lebanon trace Israel's ambitions to the pre-independence period. Some early Zionist spokesmen lobbied for inclusion of Southern Lebanon up to the Litani River within the borders of the Palestine mandate, referring to the Litani River as the "natural and historic border" between Lebanon and Israel. Israel's water shortage has

[14]Kurtzer, "Palestinian Guerrilla and Israeli Counterinsurgency Warfare," pp. 190–198, 264–268.

[15]Khalidi, *Conflict and Violence in Lebanon,* Harvard Studies in International Affairs, no. 38. (Cambridge: Center for International Affairs, Harvard University, 1979), pp. 90–91.

been cited as a second source of interest in the Litani River. Israelis argued that the river's natural basin extended to their border and that Southern Lebanon was often "overflooded," wastefully allowing much of the Litani's water to flow out to the sea. Suggestions were made that Israel be permitted to use this water and compensate Lebanon for doing so.

Moreover, Israel is charged with encouraging and even inciting Maronite separatist inclinations. At the 1919 Paris Peace Conference, Zionist delegates reportedly contacted the Maronite Patriarch of Lebanon and urged him to proclaim a Maronite "homeland" in Mount Lebanon, instead of acquiescing in the proposed French mandate over Greater Lebanon. In a letter by Israel Prime Minister Moshe Sharet in 1954, the latter declared:

> I shall agree completely to giving all possible assistance to any Maronite uprising aiming at partitioning [Lebanon] even if such uprising has no chance of success. It will, if nothing else, shift attention from the Arab-Israeli conflict.... We should encourage the Maronites' aspiration to independence and avoid having their aspiration die down.

When domestic tensions rose in Lebanon in the early 1970s, members of the Maronite elite perceived a common interest with Israel in curbing guerrilla activities. In one assessment, the Israeli raid in the center of Beirut in April 1973, leading to the assassination of three prominent Palestinian leaders, could not have occurred without at least the tacit cooperation of high Maronite officials such as the Commander of the Army and the Chief of the Security Forces.[16]

Syrian President Asad reiterates many of these themes in his 20 July 1976 speech. Israel, he says, has historically aspired to the partition of Lebanon. This was not due to Lebanon's military importance, since Lebanon was a fragmented community that could not possibly present any threat to Israel. Instead, Israel's motives were political and ideological. First, Israel prefers the establishment of small, sectarian states in the region, so that it may be

---

[16]Hasan Sharif, "South Lebanon: Its History and Geopolitics," in *South Lebanon,* ed. Elaine Hagopian and Samih Farsoun, Special Report, no. 2 (Detroit: Association of Arab-American University Graduates, 1978), pp. 19–24.

stronger by comparison. Second, the partition of Lebanon would undermine the credibility of calling for a "secular, democratic state" in Palestine. If Lebanon were partitioned, Israel could argue: "If Arabs cannot live with each other, how can they live with the Jews?"

Third, Asad contends that Israel wants Lebanon partitioned so that it will no longer have to confront the charge that Zionism is a racist ideology, since Israel accepts immigrants on the basis of religion. If Lebanon were split along sectarian lines, Israel could argue that "either both [Lebanon and Israel] are racist, or neither is racist." Finally, the Syrian President charges that Israel would relish Lebanon's partition as a stab at both Arab nationalism and Islam. Arab nationalism would appear as a weak bond indeed if the Arabs of Lebanon were unable to coexist after so many years of interaction. Islam would appear as a narrow-minded religion whose adherents were incompatible even with members of the same nation. In sum, Asad maintains that the partition of Lebanon "is a conspiracy against Islam, and a conspiracy against Arabism, for the benefit of the enemy, of Zionism, and of 'Israel.' "[17]

Defining the "Red Line"

Once Syria contemplated intervention in the Lebanese Civil War, Israel's possible reaction had to be taken into account. The prospect of Israeli counterintervention affected both the scope and timing of Syria's actions. A subtle process defining the outer limits of tolerable Syrian behavior was associated with the concept of a "red line" beyond which Syria was warned not to pass.

Parallels may be drawn between the definition of the "red line" and Israel's earlier reprisal policy. In each case, coercive diplomacy was used to demarcate for the adversary the tolerable limits of conflict. As opposed to reliance on military response in the reprisal policy, the "red line" was defined primarily through nonmilitary signals, backed by repeated threats of force.

The signals communicated by Israel were of two kinds. On the interstate level, Israel wished to discourage a significant Syrian

[17]Asad, Speech on 20 July 1976, p. 2.

military presence in Lebanon, facilitating Lebanon's incorporation into an Eastern Front strategy. On the transnational level, Israel worried about how Syria's role in the Lebanese Civil War might affect future Palestinian operations. Contradictions between Israel's goals on the interstate and transnational level emerged after Syria's shift of alignments in the war. With Syria locked in combat with the Palestinian guerrillas in Lebanon, the tensions between short-range and long-range consequences that had long beset Israel's reprisal policy again faced Israeli policymakers. In the short term, it was in Israel's interest to allow Syria to attack Palestinian positions in Lebanon; in the long term, however, a substantial Syrian presence in Lebanon could contribute to an effective Eastern Front strategy. Moreover, one could not predict how long Syria and the PLO would remain at odds.

The nuances of the Israeli position were carefully noted by the Syrian elite. They recalled the precedent for Israel's firm deterrent posture during the Jordanian Civil War of 1970–71. In September 1970, after Palestine Liberation Army units crossed from Syria into northern Jordan to assist the Palestinian Resistance in its struggle with King Husayn, Israel began to mobilize its forces, moved four hundred tanks to the Golan Heights, and placed its Air Force on alert. Israel warned of its intention to intervene directly in Jordan if this was necessary to support King Husayn, and the warning influenced the Syrian decision to order withdrawal of the "PLA" forces within five days of their initial penetration.[18]

Once the Lebanese Civil War began, Syria persistently declared that Israel had no right to intervene in Lebanon, but that Syria was prepared to meet the challenge if it arose. President Asad reported telling the American Ambassador to Syria as early as October 1975:

> In our position on the events in Lebanon, we do not take into account what "Israel" might do—not at all. If our brothers in Lebanon wanted to avail themselves of our military capabilities, we would put everything they wanted at their disposal, in any part of Lebanon—from the extreme north to the extreme south. . . . At any time that "Israel" strives to confront us, we do not feel any con-

[18]Henry Brandon, "Jordan; the Forgotten Crisis: Were We Masterful . . . ," *Foreign Policy,* 10 (Spring 1973): 164–169.

straint, and we will be prepared to resist "Israel," not only on Syrian soil, but anywhere within the Arab homeland.[19]

Despite the confident tone of this pronouncement, there are numerous indications of Syrian caution in considering Israel's response to its intervention in Lebanon. Asad himself related that when the Lebanese National Movement appealed for assistance in January 1976, he consulted with his closest advisers about "the dangers of intervention and the possibility of war between us and Israel." When they responded that war was "an actual possibility, but not inevitable," they decided that "in that case we must enter and save the Resistance."[20] This episode implies that had war with Israel appeared inevitable, Syria might have reevaluated its strategy.

Israel's own calculations over how to respond to Syria's commitment in Lebanon underwent several major shifts. During the initial, mediatory phase of Syrian involvement (April-December 1975), the official Israeli posture was restrained. The one significant exception was a major raid by the Israeli Air Force against Palestinian guerrilla targets early in December. With the announced intention of deterring anticipated guerrilla raids against Israel, targets were struck near Tripoli, where military bases for guerrillas were situated near refugee camps, and in Nabatiyyah, the site of the command post for Southern Lebanon of the Syrian-sponsored Sa'iqah guerrilla organization. The air strike followed several months in which Israel hesitated to conduct reprisals and an Israeli spokesman complained that "the terrorists have come to believe that they can do anything they please on all fronts, and that the domestic situation in Lebanon would prevent Israel from responding to them." Israel's Cabinet, led by the governing Labor Party, expressed consensus over the air attack.[21]

The first explicit warning that Israel would respond militarily in the event of large-scale Syrian intervention in Lebanon was made by Israel Prime Minister Yitshaq Rabin on 31 October 1975. When Syria intervened indirectly on 18 January, Syrian leaders presum-

[19]Asad, Speech on 20 July 1976, p. 13.
[20]Ibid.
[21]*Ha-Arets*, 3 December 1975, 5 December 1975. All translations from the Hebrew are my own.

ably believed that PLA and Sa'iqah units would be less objectionable to Israel than regular Syrian units.[22] Israel withheld official
comment on whether the units that crossed into Lebanon were
actually guerrilla units. Defense Minister Shim'on Peres emphasized, instead, that the presence of a large number of guerrilla
forces in Lebanon and the possible entry of the Syrian Army into
Lebanon were two problems with direct repercussions for Israel's
security. He warned that "if Syria invades Lebanon, Israel will
undertake the necessary defensive measures."[23]

By the time Syria actually intervened in June 1976, however,
circumstances in Lebanon had changed so dramatically that Israel
felt obliged to redefine its position. Prime Minister Rabin explained
that Israel "would not wish to disturb anyone who was crushing
'Arafat's terrorists," and that he was "not shedding a single tear"
over the Syrian-PLO clashes. Defense Minister Peres asserted that
intervention by Israel would merely benefit the PLO, by shifting
attention from inter-Arab struggles to the Israeli challenge. Peres
argued, moreover, that Syria was not striving for hegemony over
Lebanon, but merely seeking a cease-fire accord.

Despite these sanguine appraisals, Israel was apprehensive over
the intensity of the Syrian military penetration. Foreign Minister
Yigal Alon alluded to the "red line" that Syria must respect, reiterating that Israel was reserving all options for defending its
security interests along its northern border. In the popular mind,
the "red line" was identified geographically with the Litani River,
south of which Syria was warned not to conduct military operations. However, Prime Minister Rabin emphasized the qualitative
connotations of the "red line," as an Israeli guideline for gauging
Syrian behavior. The criteria that would govern Israel's response
were enumerated by Rabin as follows: the objectives of the Syrian
military forces and against whom they are operating; the geographical locale they are controlling and its proximity to Israel's borders;
the strength and composition of the operating force; and the duration of its stay in a given locale.[24]

The concept of the "red line" was applied flexibly in practice.
For instance, when Syria's offensive against the Palestinians in

---

[22]Rabinovich, "The Limits of Military Power," p. 60.
[23]*Ha-Arets,* 21 January 1976.
[24]Ibid., 2 June 1976, 3 June 1976, 16 June 1976.

Lebanon encountered stiff resistance early in June, some Syrian units penetrated south of the Litani River to confront guerrillas and units of the Lebanese Arab Army. Israeli security personnel did not reveal particular anxiety about Syria's deviation from the presumed location of the "red line." They explained that Syrian military activities above the border area dubbed as "Fatahland" by the Israelis was limited in scope, aiming primarily at securing an axis of movement in the direction of Sidon. If anything, Palestinian spokesmen may have exaggerated the scope of Syrian operations in the hope of provoking an Israeli response that would divert the Syrian attack from them.[25]

Reviewing the overall security situation at the end of June, Israeli military analyst Ze'ev Schiff perceived two major dangers confronting Israel. One was the possibility of Syrian military entrenchment in Lebanon, followed by the enlargement of the Syrian forces, their movement southward, and the erection of an offensive-defensive infrastructure in Lebanon. Schiff differed with other Israeli military experts who believed that Syrian military expansion into Lebanon would have the advantage of splintering the Syrian Army and weakening it along the principal Golan Heights front against Israel. On the contrary, he was convinced that Syrian military objectives in Lebanon were integrally bound to the strategy of the Eastern Front. In the event of war, Israel would have to be prepared to confront Syria with its extended Lebanese front, as well as Jordan, the Palestinians, and possibly Iraqi forces.

The second danger lay in potential resumption of Palestinian guerrilla activities from Southern Lebanon once the Civil War ceased. Syria's attitude might be ambivalent on this score, because pursuit of an Eastern Front strategy would be vulnerable to disruptions by unpredictable guerrilla activity. On the other hand, attempts to freeze Palestinian operations would encounter political resistance. Syria might seek a compromise in allowing sporadic guerrilla activity while seeking to transfer some of its own forces to the South, but this formula would meet Israeli opposition. One issue over which consensus exists in Israel, Schiff asserted, is the determination that Fatahland not be reactivated as a base of operations against Israel.[26]

[25]Ibid., 14 June 1976.
[26]Ibid., 27 June 1976.

"The Good Fence"

Israel's prime preoccupation in Lebanon, during the Civil War as before, derived from the security dimension of the Palestinian guerrilla presence. Israel's attitude toward the Syrian commitment was therefore primarily focused on its direction, and only secondarily on its intensity. Nevertheless, Israel did have an intrinsic interest in the domestic outcome of Lebanese strife, despite official downplaying of this issue.

Israeli spokesmen consistently avoided expressing support for either of the contending coalitions in Lebanon, on the grounds that this was an internal Lebanese matter. However, Israel's sympathy for the pro-establishment coalition was evident early in the war, and covert Israel assistance to pro-establishment groups was reported. In Southern Lebanon, Israel's involvement was more overt and pronounced, especially after Syria's direct intervention. Israeli assistance to Christian villages in the South, under the "Good Fence" policy, signified indirect Israeli intervention in the Lebanese conflict.

By the summer of 1975, Israel extended substantial support to two of the leading pro-establishment groups—the Kata'ib, led by Pierre al-Jumayyil, and the National Liberals, led by Kamil Sham'un. Israel ties to Sham'un were particularly close, because he was viewed as the leader most capable of withstanding the growing Syrian influence in Lebanon. Other Christian-dominated groups that avoided ties with Israel included the followers of President Sulayman Faranjiyih as well as the Greek Orthodox community.[27]

Since the early months of the war, Israeli spokesmen had expressed concern about the fate of the Lebanese Christian community. Israeli assistance to pro-establishment groups consisted primarily of arms transfers and subsidies for arms. Whereas the Lebanese National Movement and the Resistance received arms early in the Civil War from Syria and other Arab states, pro-establishment groups were obliged to seek weapons abroad or to import them by sea. Dany Sham'un, son of the National Liberal

[27]Snider et al., "Israel," p. 92, n. 3.

Party leader and commander of the group's "Tiger" militia, boasted during the war that there was never any problem getting the weapons one wanted, as long as one had the funds:

> We bought Russian guns through Bulgaria, which we fixed up through Western Europe. . . . And we could buy Israeli weapons through Europe. . . . Of course most of the weapons came from governments, not from private dealers; the idea that private dealers can arrange a war is really Victorian.

When asked about his source of funds, however, Sham'un, like other Christian spokesmen, was reticent. With estimates of arms acquisitions by pro-establishment groups during the war ranging from $200 to $600 million, it was obvious that funding by outside sources was forthcoming, and Israel was one of the leading contributors.[28]

By spring 1976, direct Israeli military supplies flowed to Maronite forces through the port of Junyih, the Christian stronghold north of Beirut. Israeli naval operations along the Lebanese coast, including the use of patrol boats to cover unloading of military supplies at Junyih, was one facet of tacit cooperation between Israel and Syria in their support for pro-establishment forces in the final phase of the war. Both countries attempted to cut off supplies and munitions to the Palestinians and the Lebanese National Movement. Syria had closed off the port in Sidon from the time of its assault on the city in June until Syrian forces withdrew in mid-July. From then until the end of hostilities, Israel reportedly sustained a "loose maritime blockade" on all southern ports, especially Sidon and Tyre, while Syrian vessels monitored the flow of supplies along the northern coast.[29]

The sum total of Israeli assistance to pro-establishment groups was estimated by Western sources at $100 million, including $35 million in direct aid and the cost of sustaining the naval blockade and patrols along the Lebanese coast.[30] Although Israel never acknowledged this military assistance during the Civil War, in August 1977 Prime Minister Menachem Begin candidly declared:

---

[28]Anthony Sampson, *The Arms Bazaar* (New York: Viking, 1977), pp. 18–21.
[29]Sharif, "South Lebanon," pp. 24–26.
[30]Khalidi, *Conflict and Violence*, p. 91.

We are helping the Christians of Lebanon; we are giving them military assistance. This is not a secret and should not be a secret. The public opinion in the U.S.A. and in the Christian world must know that were it not for our assistance to the Christian minority in Lebanon they would have been liquidated long ago and for good.[31]

Israel's attempt to promote its security interests was most conspicuous and most openly acknowledged with respect to Southern Lebanon. Once a limited overlap of objectives arose between Syria and Israel in support of pro-establishment forces, Lebanon fell into two incipient spheres of influence. Essentially, Syrian and Israeli policies were mirror images of each other. In northern and central Lebanon, Syria intervened directly while Israel offered covert assistance to the groups it favored. Below the Litani River, Israel became progressively more actively involved while Syrian interference remained largely covert.[32]

For most of the Lebanese Civil War, Southern Lebanon was not embroiled in combat. While the fighting was concentrated in Beirut and Mount Lebanon, guerrillas left the South to participate in combat alongside the Lebanese National Movement. Guerrilla raids across the border with Israel came to a virtual halt; and Syrian caution in remaining north of the "red line" insulated the South from ongoing hostilities. Thus this region, about 15 percent of whose population of 400,000 was Christian, while the majority were Shi'i Muslim, was able to avoid the religious and factional confrontations of the rest of the country.

When the Lebanese Army disintegrated in March 1976, most Army units in the South joined the anti-establishment Lebanese Arab Army. However, the men of Qlay'ah, a small Maronite town of about 3,000 inhabitants near the Israeli border, refused to declare allegiance to the LAA, taking refuge in their village and appealing to Israel for assistance. Their action was an isolated incident at the time, and other Christian border villages did not follow their example. At about the same time, Israel Defense Minister Shim'on Peres extended an offer of humanitarian assistance to the Lebanese population. He declared that Israel was

---

[31]Quoted in Sharif, "South Lebanon," p. 24.
[32]Snider et al., "Israel," p. 95.

willing to receive any Lebanese refugees wishing to escape the miseries of the Civil War.[33]

Israel's "Good Fence" policy was officially articulated in June with a similar humanitarian rationale. In the interim, conditions deteriorated sharply in the South as the impact of the blockade on southern ports required rationing of supplies, but no administrative authority was available to assure equitable distribution. An Israeli newspaper acknowledged that only extreme deprivation persuaded the population of the South to turn to Israel:

> The decision by the villagers of southern Lebanon to accept Israeli help was a hard decision to make; they would not have taken such a decision were it not for the blockade hardship and the fear of hunger and extermination.[34]

In mid-June, Israel announced the opening of the first border clinic near the fence demarcating its border with Lebanon. Medical assistance became a major feature of Israel's Good Fence policy, and Israeli hospitals and border clinics reported caring for over 9,000 patients by October 1976. Other services and provisions extended by Israel included food, burnable fuels, drinking water, school facilities, agricultural consultants, two-way trade, and employment opportunities for some Lebanese. Observers ascribed a variety of motives to Israel in its Good Fence Policy. In the view of one Arab analyst, the "nonmilitary aims" of the policy included an effort to provide a model of cooperative relations between Israel and its neighbors, analogous to the "open bridges" policy that had encouraged commerce between the Israeli-occupied West Bank and Jordan since the June 1967 War. Second, Israel hoped to create conditions that would make it impossible for Palestinian guerrillas to return and resume operations in Southern Lebanon. Third, Israel wished to consolidate its influence among the population of the South, and especially among the Christians. Fourth, Israel strove "to use trade and humanitarian assistance as acceptable alibis for Lebanese-Israeli collusion, so that Lebanon could pre-

[33]Sharif, "South Lebanon," p. 25.

[34]*Al ha-Mishmar,* 12 December 1976, quoted in Sharif, "South Lebanon," p. 27.

pare the ground for military activity or for expansion of Israeli influence as far north in Lebanon as possible."[35]

Israeli spokesmen, by contrast, emphasized their "human responsibility" to extend assistance to their neighbors above and beyond political considerations. Prime Minister Rabin disclosed that he had refused to meet with representatives of Lebanese villages who wished to do so, because Israel was committed not to interfere in Lebanon's internal affairs. In October 1976, Defense Minister Peres denied media reports that Israeli soldiers participated in combat in Southern Lebanon and that Israeli ships had detained vessels on behalf of pro-establishment Lebanese forces. Peres asserted that the permanent border between Israel and Lebanon would be respected and that Israel did not "gaze longingly at lands in Lebanon." On the other hand, Israel shared with the residents of Southern Lebanon an interest in preventing guerrilla organizations from achieving control of the South and resuming their operations. Peres maintained that "[a]s long as there is a war of terror against Israel, there is a war against the terror, without compromise and without cease-fires."[36]

The period of June-October 1976 marked the inception of Israeli indirect intervention in Southern Lebanon. Israel's support for the beleaguered Christian villages near its border took the form of humanitarian assistance, but also represented the cultivation of proxies to promote Israeli objectives in the South. In particular, the sympathetic presence of Christian militiamen in the South could serve as a buffer against Palestinian infiltration and the resumption of operations against Israel.

Interlocking Conflicts

In an interview after the formal end of hostilities, President Asad expressed his views about those who had cooperated with Israeli objectives in Lebanon:

> Israel will not find many agents for its purposes in Lebanon. . . . We believe that those who deal with Israel in Lebanon are a minority

[35]Sharif, "South Lebanon," pp. 27–28.
[36]*Ha-Arets,* 24 October 1976, 27 October 1976.

that is ostracized and rejected by the Arab homeland and the Arab people. . . . It is not, of course, surprising to us that Israel should try to impose its hegemony on a part of Lebanon, by exploiting Lebanese elements who have deviated from the patriotic Lebanese path.

However, when asked whether Lebanon might be transformed into a broader theater of conflict, thereby igniting an Arab-Israeli war, Asad declared emphatically that "the Arab-Israeli conflict is not and will never be linked to Lebanon." He explained that although Israel's ambitions for expansion extended to Lebanon as well as other parts of the Arab homeland, the ongoing Lebananese crisis must be resolved as a purely Arab issue.[37]

Nevertheless, Israeli policies during the Lebanese Civil War were integrally linked to a range of Arab-Israeli dialogues and disputes. Specifically, three sets of constraints limited Israel's freedom of maneuver during the Lebanese crisis. First, the momentum toward a peace agreement with Egypt might be jeopardized by unacceptable Israeli conduct in Lebanon. Second, Israel had to take the reactions of the major Arab confrontation states (especially Syria and Jordan) into account as it tried to demonstrate its strength of will in Lebanon without sparking an Arab-Israeli war or foreclosing future options for a comprehensive peace settlement. Third, Israel had to be sure that its conduct in Lebanon did not exceed the limits of toleration set by the United States.[38]

A curious pattern during the Lebanese Civil War witnessed Israel setting outer limits on Syrian conduct in Lebanon, while the United States constrained Israel's freedom of maneuver. This triangular exercise of influence was further epitomized in the intermediary role played by the United States, as it conveyed signals back and forth between Israel and Syria, defining the nature of the "red line" and relaying assurances of benevolent intent or warnings of the consequences of pursuing a given strategy. In the absence of direct channels of communication between Israel and Syria, the United States provided a critical unofficial link between the two states.

[37]Wadi' Skaf, ed., *Mawqifuna Min al-'Azmah al-Lubnaniyyah* [Our position vis-à-vis the Lebanese Crisis], (Damascus: Institute of the Union of Studies and Consultations, 1979), pp. 8–9.

[38]Snider et. al., "Israel," pp. 108–110.

Far from serving as a neutral avenue of communication, or even as an "honest broker" between Israel and Syria, the United States was an interested party on the sidelines during the Lebanese conflict. The United States had recently begun to cultivate bilateral ties with Syria and, in doing so, challenged long-standing Soviet influence in that country. Although Lebanon itself was not central to the Middle East policies of either the United States or Soviet Union, the escalating Syrian intervention in the Lebanse Civil War caused substantial concern to both superpowers.

11

Superpowers on the Sidelines

Many observers of the Syrian intervention in Lebanon speculated that either the Soviet Union or the United States was orchestrating Syrian behavior. A more accurate portrait would depict each of the superpowers as either baffled, anxious, frustrated, or alternatively pleased with Syrian conduct at different junctures. Syria, in turn, consistently gave priority to the pursuit of its regional objectives. The Asad regime enjoyed sufficient freedom of maneuver vis-à-vis the superpowers to deflect their attempts at influencing its policies in Lebanon.

Channel of Communications

Despite relative Syrian autonomy from superpower leverage, the American connection was valued as a means of deterring Israeli counterintervention. Having resumed diplomatic relations with the United States barely a year before the Lebanese Civil War, Syria remained wary of American motives and especially of the American commitment to Israel.

Ambivalence over dealings with the United States is reflected in President Asad's own accounts of two meetings in which the United States warned of potential Israeli counterintervention. On 16 October 1975, the American Ambassador informed Asad that Israel "would view the intervention of foreign military forces as a very great threat, so that whatever the United States might say to Israel, it will go ahead and intervene." Asad replied that the Lebanese war was an internal Arab problem in which Israel had no right to intervene. Syria would frame its policies in Lebanon in accordance with its Arab commitments, without taking Israel's reaction into account.

The second contact occurred on 14 April 1976, several days after Syria had introduced a limited number of regular forces into Lebanon. The United States warned Syria not to proceed any further, declaring that "Israel would feel obliged to take special steps and measures if Syria trespasses that point." An American message expressed concern lest Syria interpret the absence of official Israeli reaction as acquiescence in Syria's conduct—which "would contradict what we have continually been conveying to Damascus during recent weeks." Asad rejected the American warning categorically, saying that "Syria is not prepared now and will not be prepared in the future to accept any warning from any party in the world." The dimensions of the Syrian commitment in Lebanon—including the size and positions of the Syrian forces—would be determined, he maintained, exclusively with reference to "the interest of the Lebanese people."[1]

The tone of Asad's statement is as revealing as the content. Whereas the Syrian President conveys impatience with American warnings, he implicitly acknowledges a two-way channel of communications whereby Israel would also be informed of Syria's intent. The United States was encouraging restraint on Israel's part—a useful function from Asad's perspective. However, the United States urged Israeli caution not to suit Syria's preferences, but rather to promote its own regional objectives in the Middle East.

The United States was eager to sustain its activist peacemaking role, which was launched through Secretary of State Henry Kissinger's "step-by-step" diplomacy after the October 1973 War. When the Lebanese Civil War began, negotiations were under way between Egypt and Israel for a second disengagement agreement in the Sinai. The United States worried that any unilateral Israeli intervention in Lebanon might disrupt ongoing peacemaking endeavors or even trigger a new round of Arab-Israel hostilities.[2]

Long-standing American misgivings about the efficacy and wis-

[1]Hafiz al-Asad, Speech delivered on 20 July 1976, pp. 12–13.
[2]Robert Stookey, "The United States," in *Lebanon in Crisis,* ed. P. Edward Haley and Lewis W. Snider (Syrcuse, N.Y.: Syracuse University Press, 1979), pp. 233–234.

dom of Israel's reprisal policy against Southern Lebanon found renewed expression in December 1975. After a major Israeli raid against Palestinian positions in Nabatiyyah and near Tripoli, Egypt requested an emergency meeting of the United Nations Security Council. Although the United States opposed a Security Council resolution condemning the raids, President Gerald Ford sent a message to Israel Prime Minister Yitshaq Rabin urging advance consultation before such operations.[3]

U.S. State Department spokesmen referred to the entry of PLA forces into Lebanon in January as a strictly Palestinian intervention, expressing the view that direct Syrian intervention in Lebanon was unlikely in the foreseeable future. The United States refrained from endorsing Israel's warning that it would take "the necessary defensive measures" if direct Syrian intervention followed. American officials advised Israel to phrase its warnings to Syria with the utmost caution, while privately conceding that Israeli warnings were responsible for Syrian restraint. When the State Department officially warned against all forms of "external intervention" in Lebanon, Israeli commentators complained that the statement implied that Syria and Israel posed equal threats to the country's integrity. This posture was particularly annoying to Israel in view of Henry Kissinger's private acknowledgment that there was no danger of a unilateral intervention by Israel in Lebanon unless Syria first engaged in a large-scale direct or indirect intervention.[4]

Once Syria did intervene directly, American officials noted that Israel's reaction was "extremely restrained." The pervasive view in Washington was that Israel would reconcile itself to the Syrian presence in Lebanon. Nevertheless, Kissinger reminded Israeli Ambassador Simha Dinitz that the United States expected Israeli consultations before deciding on any unilateral measures in the Lebanese crisis.[5] In order to avert miscalculations on the part of either Israel or Syria as the Syrian advance continued, the United States became an active communications channel between the two countries. This function was especially important in defining the "red line" which represented, for Israel, the outer limits of tolerable Syrian penetration. The Syrian government reportedly in-

---

[3]Ibid., pp. 235–236; *Ha-Arets*, 4 December 1975, 5 December 1975.
[4]*Ha-Arets*, 23 January 1976.
[5]Ibid., 2 June 1976, 16 June 1976.

formed the United States that its forces would refrain from advancing close to the Lebanese-Israeli border and would restrict their operations to the north of the Litani River as much as possible. Although Israel eventually became more flexible in its definition of the "red line," Israel conveyed warnings through the United States that a major Syrian military presence or large-scale reinfiltration of guerrillas in Southern Lebanon would not be tolerated.[6]

Precedents for American Commitment

American efforts at restraining Israel's behavior during the 1975–76 Lebanese Civil War contrast sharply with the close coordination between the two countries during the 1970 Civil War in Jordan. In that crisis, the United States had encouraged Israel to develop a credible military operation for intervention to save King Husayn from being overthrown by Palestinian guerrillas with Syrian support. In this joint strategy, Israel would intervene both by air and by ground, if necessary, while the United States pledged to neutralize Egyptian or Soviet reactions.

The American preference for indirect intervention, through coordination with its Israeli client, rather than a direct American attempt to assist King Husayn, reflected both military and political considerations. Policymakers at the Pentagon were convinced that the United States lacked capabilities for effective ground intervention in Jordan, and were uncertain of the success of an American air attack. Politically, the negative Arab reactions expected if the United States intervened made it preferable to rely on Israel instead. Moreover, officials argued that it was better to keep Israel closely involved in an American "game plan," to avert the possibility of unilateral Israeli intervention against the Palestinian guerrillas in Jordan.[7]

A lack of sufficient local military capabilities might have also ruled out direct American intervention in Lebanon in 1975–76, if

[6]Ibid., 15 October 1976, 31 October 1976; Stookey, "The United States," pp. 238–239.

[7]Alan Dowty, "The U.S. and the Syria-Jordan Confrontation, 1970," *Jerusalem Journal of International Relations* 3 (1978): 172–196, passim.

the United States had considered that option. However, the American stake in the political survival of King Husayn found no parallel in the Lebanese case. At no point did Lebanon play a central role in America's policies in the Middle East. Ironically, however, the one case of direct U.S. military intervention in the region occurred during the Lebanese Civil War of 1958.

President Kamil Sham'un of Lebanon was the only Arab leader to endorse the Eisenhower Doctrine, through which the American President offered in March 1957 to assist any Middle East state threatened by international communism. When Sham'un invoked the Eisenhower Doctrine after the outbreak of civil strife in May 1958, American officials indicated that the United States was willing to respond to the threat posed to Lebanon's independence by Nasirism. The United States perceived President Nasir as a menacing force in the region linked to Soviet objectives. However, the United States disassociated itself from the Lebanese President's own political ambitions. Since one of the precipitating causes of the Civil War was Sham'un's attempt to seek a second term of office in defiance of the Constitution, the United States made it clear that its troops would not be used to help him achieve that goal. The event that sparked American action was the coup d'état against the pro-Western Hashimi monarchy in Iraq on 14 July. Concern over spreading regional instability prompted the Sixth Fleet to move closer to the Lebanese coast, and on 15 July, 1,700 hundred Marines landed on Lebanese beaches. At its maximum, the American presence amounted to over 14,000 troops, about 8,000 associated with the Army and 6,000 with the Marines.

The American military intervention in Lebanon was followed by a concerted mediatory effort. The American Ambassador, Robert McClintock, who personally disapproved of the Marines' landing, immediately met with Lebanese Army Commander Fuad Shihab to avert clashes between the Lebanese Army and the Marines. The Marines were then peacefully escorted to designated areas by the Lebanese forces, and subsequent careful deployment of U.S. forces averted their involvement in hostilities. On balance, the American military presence had a calming effect on the Lebanese crisis, facilitating mediatory efforts by a special American envoy, Richard Murphy. Talks by Murphy with Lebanese leaders achieved the political compromise leading to Fuad Shihab's election as President on 31 July, and American troops withdrew completely by 28 October.[8]

Low American Profile

As a legacy of the American intervention in 1958, Lebanese generally assumed a persistent American affinity for the Maronite community in Lebanon. Although the United States insisted that it had sought to preserve Lebanon's integrity rather than the presidency of Sham'un or the confessional system which sustained Maronite privilege, the popular recollection was different. In the early stages of the 1975–76 Lebanese Civil War, the United States again disavowed favoritism for Maronite claims or clients, and embraced proposals for reform of the confessional system.

Initially, the United States was pleased by the election of President Sulayman Faranjiyih in 1970 and his firm commitment to upholding Lebanese government authority in the face of domestic disorder. However, in view of Faranjiyih's reluctance to relinquish Christian prerogatives, the American Embassy sought closer ties to other leaders, especially Prime Minister Karami and the relatively liberal Maronite leader Raymun Iddih. After the outbreak of the Civil War, Secretary of State Kissinger addressed a letter to Prime Minister Karami in November 1975, supporting Karami's efforts to end the violence and reach political accommodation.

Despite this gesture, the Lebanese crisis held low priority for American policymakers during its early months. Only when Syrian military intervention appeared probable early in 1976 did Henry Kissinger devote attention personally to the crisis. The State Department's Bureau of Intelligence and Research began to prepare daily reports on Lebanon, distributed only to Kissinger and several top aides. The flow of information and continuity of contacts with Lebanese parties was disrupted, however, because of frequent changes in the American diplomatic mission. When Ambassador G. McMurtrie Godley left Lebanon early in 1976 because of illness, he was not replaced until 21 April. His successor, Francis E. Meloy,

---

[8]William Quandt, "Lebanon, 1958, Jordan, 1970," in *Force Without War,* ed. Barry Blechman and Stephen Kaplan (Washington, D.C.: Brookings, 1978), pp. 225–248.

Jr., was ambushed and murdered on 16 June. A permanent successor was not named until after President Sarkis took office late in September.

These circumstances underscored the low-key American role, especially during the initial months of the war. In its one serious mediatory effort, the United States sent L. Dean Brown as a special envoy to hold discussions with the Lebanese parties in April 1976. Brown endorsed the Syrian-sponsored proposal for constitutional reform, urging adherence to a cease-fire and arrangements for election of a successor to President Faranjiyih. Kamal Junbalat credited Brown with helping achieve the cease-fire on the eve of the 8 May presidential elections, and Brown consulted intensively with spokesmen for various factions. He pledged that the United States would sponsor an international consortium to assist in Lebanon's reconstruction once domestic tranquillity was restored. Nevertheless, ongoing hostilities made the offer seem remote, and Brown terminated his five-week mission without tangible accomplishments.

American inability to take constructive initiatives in the Lebanese crisis was acknowledged at a meeting sponsored by Secretary of State Kissinger on 22 June. Discussions with the American ambassadors to Syria, Egypt, Saudi Arabia, and Jordan, as well as Ambassador Talcott W. Seelye, temporarily named to the embassy in Beirut, yielded a consensus that there were no promising opportunities for American mediation. Instead, the United States lent its support during the final months of the war to efforts at Arab mediation. Close American ties with Saudi Arabia and the growing rapport with Egypt since the October War of 1973 enhanced the flow of information to the United States about inter-Arab developments during the Lebanese crisis. The United States reportedly urged Saudi Arabia, which had assisted both pro- and anti-establishment groups early in the war, to be more selective in its support. The United States encouraged Saudi mediatory attempts and applauded the achievement of an enduring cease-fire at the Riyadh summit conference in October 1976.[9]

Most important in explaining American influence over Lebanese developments, despite the lack of an overt military or diplomatic

[9]Stookey, "The United States," pp. 225–248, passim.

role, was the improved relationship between the United States and Syria since the October War. Direct access to Syrian officials assured that the United States would, at minimum, be able to monitor the Syrian intervention in a more informed way. However, American influence was not translated into leverage that constrained the Asad regime's options.

The U.S.-Syrian dialogue over Lebanon contrasted to the circumstances of the 1970 Jordanian Civil War, when no diplomatic relations existed between the two countries. Syria had severed ties with the United States after the June 1967 Arab-Israeli War. Indeed, American ability to react to the Jordanian crisis was impaired by the lack of reliable information, especially with respect to the Syrian involvement. Although photographic and signal surveillance was used to follow the fighting, Henry Kissinger relied on briefings twice a day by the Israeli Ambassador as a prime source of intelligence. Political analysis was even less accurate, and the United States consistently underrated the importance of domestic politics in the Syrian intervention. The split between Salah Jadid and Hafiz al-Asad in the Syrian leadership was not understood, nor could the United States gauge the degree to which Syria's decisions were influenced by the Soviet Union. Moreover, the United States apparently never considered a diplomatic overture to Syria as an alternative to a military response.[10]

Eventually, Syria moved gingerly toward opening a dialogue with the United States in response to American peacemaking initiatives after the October War of 1973. Although Syrian leaders were suspicious of American overtures to Egypt, they were also wary of allowing Egypt to remain the sole beneficiary of American diplomacy. If Henry Kissinger could bring about territorial withdrawals by Israel, Syria was willing to consider participation in the "step-by-step" diplomatic process. In December 1973, Kissinger visited Damascus and reached agreement on the opening of interest sections between the United States and Syria, as a prelude to renewed diplomatic relations.

The delicate diplomacy leading to a disengagement accord between Israel and Syria in May 1974 was followed by President

[10]Dowty, "The U.S. and the Syria-Jordan Confrontation," pp. 175–176, 182, 187.

Richard Nixon's visit to Syria in June and official resumption of diplomatic ties. A new posture was formally adopted by the Twelfth National Congress of the Ba'th Party in July. The "transitional policy" of the Congress legitimized Syria's participation in negotiations for agreements of a partial or comprehensive nature with Israel under American auspices. The fact that further progress was not reached may be attributable to a shift in American strategies and priorities, rather than to a Syrian change of heart. When the United States decided to seek a second Egyptian-Israeli accord as well as a Jordanian-Israeli agreement before pursuing further initiatives with Syria, the Asad regime reverted to its earlier suspicion of the United states.[11]

Nevertheless, even in its disillusionment with U.S. strategy, Syria saw value in the American connection. During the Lebanese Civil War, in fact, Syrian-U.S. cooperation reached unprecedented levels. Although the United States was initially wary of Syrian objectives in Lebanon, by early 1976 the American attitude changed. In the absence of alternative candidates to mediate in the Lebanese crisis, an enhanced role for Syria appeared inevitable and, increasingly, even desirable. The tone of the February reform plan advocated by Syria, with its provisions for moderate change in the Lebanese system, was consistent with U.S. policy. After Syria's relations became strained with its traditional anti-establishment allies in Lebanon (whereas Maronite leaders had accepted the reform plan), the United States lent its support openly to the Syrian initiative. A State Department spokesman endorsed Syria's proposals explicitly, saying on 29 March:

> [T]he political compromise worked out with constructive Syrian assistance in connection with the 22 January ceasefire appears to us to provide a fair basis for such a solution [which gives security to all communities in Lebanon].

In his mediatory efforts in April and May, L. Dean Brown encouraged Lebanese parties to adopt the Syrian plan. Before leaving Lebanon on 12 May, Brown praised President-elect Iliyas

---

[11]Galia Golan and Itamar Rabinovich, "The Soviet Union and Syria: The Limits of Cooperation," in *The Limits to Power,* ed. Yaacov Ro'i (New York: St. Martin's, 1979), pp. 216–225, 228.

Sarkis, expressing his conviction that Lebanon would not be transformed into a "Syrian satellite."[12] Ambassador Brown later stirred controversy by commenting in an interview that American opposition to Syrian military intervention in Lebanon had been unwise. By objecting to military involvement, he said, the United States aroused Syria's suspicions of American intentions in the Middle East. Moreover, by influencing Syria to decelerate its military advance, additional and unnecessary bloodshed had been caused. Brown believed that Syria had succeeded in providing security for the beleaguered Maronites and creating conditions conducive to the restoration of constitutional government. Brown's remarks departed from the official American position, and he quickly received a telegram of reproof from the State Department.[13]

Despite formal criticism of Brown's remarks, speculation persisted that he may have been articulating a new, more receptive American attitude toward direct Syrian intervention in Lebanon. Early in April, Henry Kissinger described Syria's role in Lebanon as "highly responsible," and President Ford said that the United States did not expect Syria to take control in Lebanon. Even after Syria had introduced some regular military units into Lebanon on 9 April, the United States was sanguine about their objectives. Kissinger contended on 23 April that "the danger of outside intervention has been reduced," and that "it is our impression that they [the Syrian forces] are there as part of the immediate situation and not a permanent feature of the Lebanese scene."[14] Tacit American approval of Syria's military escalation persisted after the large-scale intervention of regular Syrian forces in June.

The American attitude reflected gradual recognition of a convergence of interests between the United States and Syria. The United States believed that Syria was in a position to impose order in Lebanon, thereby averting two outcomes that both Syria and the United States opposed. First, the partition of Lebanon would be forestalled, with its potentially destabilizing implications for the region. Second, the emergence of a regime dominated by the Leb-

---

[12]Naseer Aruri, "The Syrian Strategy and the Lebanese Conflict," in *Lebanon: Crisis and Challenge,* Special Report, no. 1, ed. Fouad Moughrabi and Naseer Aruri (Detroit: Arab American University Graduates, 1977), p. 24.

[13]Stookey, "The United States," pp. 237–238.

[14]Aruri, "The Syrian Strategy and the Lebanon Crisis," p. 24.

anese National Movement and Palestinians, and perhaps responsive to Iraqi and Libyan interests, would be prevented. The United
States and Syria were both concerned that such a regime might
provoke hostilities with Israel, into which Syria might be drawn.
By contrast, a satisfactory outcome to the Lebanese crisis might
enable President Asad to resume participation in the American-
sponsored peacemaking process with Israel.[15]

Superpower Proxy?

The preceding analysis suggests that Syria, while remaining a client
of the Soviet Union, developed a convergence of interests with
the United States during the Lebanese Civil War. Other observers
have explained Syria's behavior through a variety of conspiracy
theories, all of which share the assumption that great powers are
capable of manipulating the behavior of regional actors. In analytical terms, conspiracy theories offer a hierarchical image of the
international system in which small states regularly serve as proxies
for the great powers.

The curious feature of conspiracy theories about the Lebanese
Civil War is that Syria is alternatively portrayed as a proxy of the
United States or the Soviet Union. For Western commentators
accustomed to thinking of Syria as a Soviet proxy, the notion of
a Syrian-American conspiracy is preposterous. Yet the evidence
for Syrian-American coordination of policy during the war, while
not sufficing to substantiate a conspiracy theory, is actually more
convincing than evidence of Syrian-Soviet complicity.

Those who believe there was collusion between Syria and the
United States in Lebanon argue that President Asad was part of
Henry Kissinger's "game plan" for a Middle East peace solution.
Once Egypt, Syria, and Jordan agreed to participate in Kissinger's
diplomacy, only the PLO was an obstacle to achieving a "Pax
Americana." From the U.S. perspective, no better candidate for
a "police mission to bring the PLO in line" could be found than
"progressive" Syria. Syria initially assumed that it could co-opt
the PLO and suppress the Lebanese left. When the PLO main-

[15]Stookey, "The United States," pp. 238, 245.

tained its alliance with the Lebanese National Movement, Asad considered direct intervention against both. He could not proceed, however, without American assurance that Israel would be restrained from counterintervention. The "task of securing a clearance was assigned" to King Husayn, who lobbied on Syria's behalf during a visit to the United States in March. Husayn conveyed assurances to President Ford that Syria would withdraw quickly from Lebanon once it reversed the trend toward leftist ascendancy. The United States was requested to keep Israel from intervening once Syrian forces advanced across the border.

The results of the Syrian intervention represented "a diplomatic coup for the United States." The elements of Kissinger's peace proposals had already been assembled, and once Lebanon was "pacified," the United States and Syria could perpetrate a "final solution" to the Palestinian problem in the name of a Middle East settlement. Henry Kissinger declared in Congressional testimony on 17 June:

> It is quite possible that as the situation in Lebanon is being resolved
> . . . we can go back to the peace process. I believe that the events
> in Lebanon may have crystallized forces that may make a return to
> the Middle East peace negotiations more hopeful.

The reason that Kissinger could afford to be so optimistic is that he felt assured of the cooperation of America's Syrian "proxy," in pursuing "a special brand of Vietnamization in the Middle East."[16]

This conspiracy theory suggests that Syria's quest for regional influence was merely one facet of a grand design derived from Syrian-American collusion. In this line of argument, Syria attempted to consolidate its position in the inter-Arab arena— through influence over Jordan, Lebanon, and the Palestinians— to enhance its capacity to achieve a settlement in the Arab-Israel arena. The crucial obstacle to be overcome was opposition by the Palestinian Resistance. Once the Resistance was "tamed," Syria could negotiate with Israel for the return of the Golan Heights (captured in the June 1967 War) and perhaps for a solution in the West Bank that would further advance Syrian influence. While this

[16]Aruri, "The Syrian Strategy and the Lebanese Conflict," passim.

process would further Syria's own regional ambitions, the con-spiracy theorists perceived a guiding American hand in the back-ground, using the Syrian proxy to advance the United States' own objectives in the Middle East.

The premises of this argument are invalidated by the foregoing analysis, which indicates the primacy of Syria's regional objectives and the limited utility to Syria of the American connection. The superpower that did possess substantial leverage over Syria was the Soviet Union. Syria's deep military and economic dependence on the Soviet Union meant that Soviet preferences could only be flouted at substantial cost. In the Lebanese Civil War, however, the absence of Soviet vital interests in the outcome of the con-frontation permitted Syria substantial autonomy in pursuing its regionally based priorities. Nevertheless, a divergence of views in the latter phase of the war gave rise to a serious crisis in Soviet-Syrian relations. No one could convincingly argue that Syria was serving as a Soviet proxy in Lebanon in June-October 1976, al-though some Western observers insisted on sustaining this image.

By contrast, during the 1970 crisis in Jordan, American poli-cymakers took it for granted that Syria was intervening as a proxy for the Soviet Union. The Jordanian crisis engendered substantial tension between the superpowers because of this American as-sumption. When hostilities first broke out between Palestinian guerrillas and King Husayn on 17 September 1970, the United States hoped to deter Syrian or Iraqi intervention that would fur-ther challenge the King. On 18 September, Henry Kissinger so-licited and reportedly received assurances from the Soviet Union that Syria would not intervene.

When Syrian tanks began to cross the border into Jordan under a PLA banner the next day, President Nixon and Henry Kissinger felt that they had been deceived. Anger at Soviet duplicity was linked to American annoyance over Egyptian violations of a cease-fire accord that had taken effect along the Suez Canal in August 1970. Contrary to the provisions of the American-negotiated cease-fire, Soviet-made surface-to-air missiles (SAMs) were advanced toward the banks of the canal. Nixon and Kissinger regarded the Syrian intervention in Jordan as a second test of American will by the Russians, and determined to respond forcefully.

The American military response to the Jordanian crisis thus

served the twin purposes of supporting King Husayn and responding to a perceived Soviet challenge. A decision to move the Sixth Fleet and alert the 82nd Airborne Division was taken even before Syrian tanks crossed the Jordanian border. A further selective alert of American forces in the United States and Europe occurred on 19 September. As plans were formulated for an American-supported Israeli military response, a U.S. aircraft carrier moved to within sixty nautical miles of the Israeli coastline and established direct communications with the Israeli government by 21 September. This American show of force was accompanied, on the diplomatic level, by daily meetings between Assistant Secretary of State Joseph Sisco and Soviet Chargé d'Affaires Yuli Vorontsov. In one of these exchanges, on 20 September, Sisco reportedly declared:

> Remember, you are to report very carefully to the Kremlin that we cannot give you any assurance whatsoever on the question of Israeli intervention or American intervention, directly in this situation.[17]

Was the American perception of the Syrian role in the Jordanian crisis as a proxy intervention accurate? According to one interpretation, "[w]hile the available evidence does not indicate that the Soviet Union precipitated the Syrian invasion of Jordan, it is clear that it acquiesced in and gave support for the Syrian move." A Soviet official subsequently acknowledged that Soviet advisers accompanied Syrian tanks to the Jordanian border. Three possible considerations may have motivated Soviet behavior. Most important was the close Soviet relationship with the Jadid regime in Syria. The Soviet leadership did not want to jeopardize these ties by opposing the Syrian initiative, just as it hesitated to criticize the Egyptian missile buildup near the Suez Canal for fear of antagonizing the Egyptian elite.

Second, the Soviet Union stood to gain if the Syrian intervention achieved its apparent objectives. If King Husayn was overthrown, one of the strongest supporters of Western influence in the region

[17]Robert Freedman, "Detente and .U.S-Soviet Relations in the Middle East During the Nixon Years," in *Dimensions of Détente,* ed. Della Seldon (New York: Praeger, 1978), pp. 93–94; Dowty, "The U.S. and the Syria-Jordan Confrontation," pp. 174, 177, 182, 189.

would be eliminated, and perhaps the Soviet Union could cultivate ties to a successor regime. Third, even if Husayn prevailed, he might be obliged to make further concessions to the Palestinian guerrillas in Jordan. The Palestinians, in recognition of Soviet support for their cause, would then be further available as a "potential lever of Soviet influence in the Middle East."

In this view, the Soviet leadership was surprised by the American show of force on behalf of Husayn, and was obliged, reluctantly, to tone down its support for the Syrian intervention. Moscow Radio supported a suggestion, on 22 September, for an Arab summit conference to resolve the crisis, apparently seeking a face-saving device to help the Syrians out of a difficult situation. It is impossible to judge, however, whether the Syrian decision to withdraw their armored forces from Jordan on 23–24 September was primarily due to Soviet advice, to the American-Israeli military buildup, or to Defense Minister Asad's refusal to provide air support for the invasion.[18]

A more convincing interpretation suggests that the United States overestimated Soviet leverage over Syria at the time as well as the degree of Soviet involvement in the Jordanian events. The United States was preoccupied with the global dimension of the crisis, which was perceived as a Cold War confrontation testing American resolve. In its concern over checking Soviet expansion, the United States was unable to distinguish the global from the regional aspects of the crisis. In fact, however, Syria was acting in furtherance of its regional goals, with scant concern for Soviet objectives. Internal rivalries within the Syrian leadership were more important than superpower reactions in affecting the pace and the scope of the Syrian intervention, although Soviet warnings may have contributed to Syrian restraint and its ultimate decision to withdraw.[19]

Strains in Soviet-Syrian Relations

The fact that a superpower and its client may have different objectives and priorities during a crisis comes as no surprise. During

[18]Freedman, "Detente and U.S.-Soviet Relations," passim.
[19]Dowty, "The U.S. and the Syria-Jordan Confrontation," pp. 177, 187; Quandt, "Lebanon, 1958, and Jordan, 1970," pp. 222–223.

the crisis in Jordan, the Soviet Union's hesitation to back a con-
tinuation of Syria's high level of commitment connotes an asymmetry of motivation,[20] but does not necessarily reflect tensions in
patron-client relations.

In a longer-term perspective, however, one may note cyclical
shifts in Soviet-Syrian relations since 1963, when the Ba'th came
to power in Syria and initiated close ties with the Soviet Union.
Hafiz al-Asad continued cooperative relations with the Soviet
Union, despite the fact that the Russians had lent their support to
Salah Jadid in Syria's intra-elite rivalries of 1969–1970. The ad-
vantages of friendship were obvious, since the Soviet Union was
Syria's major supplier of arms and its main external supporter in
the conflict with Israel. Nevertheless, Asad insisted on preserving
Syria's autonomy in decisionmaking, repeatedly spurning Mos-
cow's offer of a treaty of friendship similar to those concluded with
Egypt in 1971 and Iraq in 1972.

Syrian sensitivities were persistently jarred by the perception
that the Soviet Union assigned secondary priority to Syrian interests, attaching greater political and strategic significance to Egypt
and Iraq. The strains in Soviet-Egyptian relations since 1971, culminating in the expulsion of Soviet military advisers in July 1972,
led to a Soviet reassessment of the relative value of its relationship
with Syria. Enhanced interest in Syria was reflected in a major
arms deal in 1972; a project to enlarge Syrian ports to accommodate Soviet ships; and the construction of air bases in northeastern Syria. However, Syrian leaders were again convinced
during the October War of 1973 that despite military resupply of
both countries, Soviet strategic calculations gave priority to Egypt's
interests.[21]

Unprecedented friction in Soviet-Syrian relations was aroused
by Syria's decision to participate in American diplomatic initiatives. Whereas the needs of Arab States for arms in the conflict
with Israel accentuated dependence on the Soviet patron, the decision by Egypt and then Syria to pursue peacemaking efforts with
Israel put the Soviet Union at a disadvantage. Having severed
diplomatic relations with Israel, the Soviet Union could not match

[20]See above, pp. 21–22.
[21]Golan and Rabinovich, "Soviet Union and Syria," pp. 213–215.

American diplomatic assets in facilitating the territorial concessions that Israel's neighbors sought. Moreover, rifts in inter-Arab
relations over negotiations with Israel often set Moscow's protégés
against each other, sapping the regional basis of Soviet prestige.

Although Syria shared Soviet suspicion of American peacemaking initiatives, even conditional Syrian willingness to participate in
American-sponsored diplomacy represented a net Soviet loss. The
Soviet Union repeatedly emphasized the advantages of a comprehensive approach to peacemaking, by reconvening the Geneva
Peace Conference at which the Soviet Union had presided as co-
chairman with the United States in December 1973. By contrast,
Henry Kissinger's "step-by-step" diplomacy, promoting negotiations between Israel and individual Arab States, precluded a meaningful Soviet role.

While negotiations were under way from February to May 1974
for an Israeli-Syrian disengagement accord, the Soviet Union publicly reminded Syria that the Geneva Conference was the "authoritative forum" for negotiations and that grave dangers could
emerge from Kissinger's "partial settlements." Nevertheless, Soviet overtures toward Syria emphasized the carrot rather than the
stick. In April, a large shipment of weapons and equipment included the prized MiG-23 fighter aircraft. Moreover, the Soviet
Union granted Syria a twelve-year moratorium on repayment of
its military debt. Soviet references to military assistance during
President Asad's visit to Moscow on 11–16 April may have underscored for both the United States and Israel the fact that Syria
had options other than Kissinger's diplomatic efforts. From this
point of view, Soviet support probably strengthened Syria's bargaining position in the negotiations and may have yielded more
advantageous terms for Syria. Nevertheless, the Soviet role went
unacknowledged, and Henry Kissinger won recognition as the orchestrator of the disengagement accord of May 1974.[22]

The Lebanese Civil War brought to the fore many latent sources
of strain in Soviet-Syrian relations. Syria's efforts to consolidate
its regional influence could work to the Soviet advantage as long
as Syrian alignments were compatible with those of the Soviet
Union. As a result, convergence of interest between Syria and the

[22]Ibid., pp. 216–219.

Soviet Union emerged early in the war, while Syria supported its traditional Lebanese allies. The subsequent Syrian shift of alignments, however, was threatening to the Soviet Union. Soviet concern over the crisis did not reflect any intrinsic interest in Lebanon. For the Soviet Union, even more than the United States, the local conflict was subordinated to preoccupation with its broader regional repercussions.

When the Lebanese conflict erupted in April 1975, Soviet reaction was extremely cautious and noncommittal. During the first few months of the war, the Soviet media refrained from even categorizing the Lebanese factions according to their positions on the ideological spectrum. After the second Egyptian-Israeli disengagement accord in September 1975, however, the Soviet media began to identify with anti-establishment demands in Lebanon. Soviet sources mirrored the Syrian charge that the United States, Israel, and Arab reaction were fomenting civil strife in Lebanon to divert attention from the unpopular Sinai accord. The Soviet Union espoused a Syrian-led northeastern Arab alliance, to counteract the alleged Cairo-Riyadh axis pursuing American initiatives.[23]

Despite ongoing Soviet-Syrian consultations during the Lebanese Civil War, it is difficult to determine how much coordination of policy occurred. Syrian Foreign Minister Khaddam visited Moscow in April 1975, and President Asad led a high-ranking Syrian delegation to Moscow in October. The joint communiqué at the end of the latter visit was vague and unrevealing. In November, the Soviet Ambassador in Beirut met with Lebanese Prime Minister Rashid Karami, and Yasir 'Arafat led a Palestinian delegation to Moscow which included Zuhayr Muhsin, the leader of the Syrian-backed Sa'iqah guerrilla organization.[24]

When Syria intervened indirectly in Lebanon in January 1976, the Soviet media complimented Syria's "constructive role" in stopping the bloodshed. Soviet anxieties were aroused, however, by L. Dean Brown's mission to Lebanon and his vocal support for the Syrian-sponsored reform plan. As Syria and the United States

[23]Ilana Kass, "Moscow and the Lebanese Triangle," *The Middle East Journal* 33 (Spring 1979): 166–168.

[24]Golan and Rabinovich, "Soviet Union and Syria," pp. 222–224; Kass, "Moscow," p. 169.

began to promote common measures with the apparent aim of restraining the Palestinian Resistance and the Lebanese National Movement, Soviet authorities worried that Syrian-American cooperation might go too far. Palestinian condemnation of the Brown mission and of the Syrian plan were reported in the Soviet press, and on 5 May *Pravda* featured an interview with Yasir 'Arafat in which he praised the Soviet Union and advocated closer ties.[25]

Particularly troubling to the Soviet Union was the attempt by Saudi Arabia and Kuwait to arrange a Syrian-Egyptian meeting in Riyadh in May 1976. Egypt had officially abrogated its Treaty of Friendship and Cooperation with the Soviet Union in March. Radio Moscow charged that the purpose of the meeting was so that "Egypt and Saudi Arabia, which are coordinating their policies with those of the U.S., will be able to exert pressure on Syria to refrain from criticizing the American step-by-step policy."

The Soviet Union realized that Syria was being courted at the time by both Saudi Arabia and Libya, advocating Syrian participation in opposing regional coalitions. Obviously, the Soviet Union wished to encourage Syrian identification with the Rejectionist camp. Coordination between Syria, Libya, Iraq, and Algeria would be beneficial to Soviet objectives; just as Syrian cooperation with Saudi Arabia, Kuwait, and Egypt would be detrimental. These considerations may explain why Soviet Prime Minister Aleksei Kosygin embarked on a personal mission to Iraq and Syria late in May. Perhaps Soviet leaders hoped to facilitate a rapprochement between their Iraqi and Syrian protégés, helping to resolve the Lebanese crisis and promoting Soviet regional objectives.[26]

Soviet Verbal Assault

During the night of 31 May–1 June, thousands of Syrian forces crossed the border into Lebanon. By the time Prime Minister Kosygin arrived in Damascus on 1 June, he was greeted with an "insulting *fait accompli.*" Even if the date of the intervention was

[25]Robert O. Freedman, "The Soviet Union and the Civil War in Lebanon, 1975–76," *Jerusalem Journal of International Relations* 3 (1978): 71; Kass, "Moscow," p. 170.
[26]Freedman, "Soviet Union and Civil War," pp. 71–74.

not intentionally chosen to embarrass the Soviet leadership, the timing was highly disconcerting. Perhaps President Asad sought to emphasize Syria's autonomous decisionmaking in the face of anticipated Soviet efforts to influence his policy choices.[27]

Initial Soviet accounts claimed that the Syrian intervention was requested by Lebanese "official authorities," and that Syrian forces were "guided by national duty toward a sister nation and by compassion for the victims of bloodshed between Arab brothers." By 10 June, however, the official news agency, TASS, charged that despite Syrian assertions that its troops were sent to stop the bloodshed, "the bloodshed continues in Lebanon today and blood flows in even greater streams."[28]

Once the objectives of Syria's June offensive became clear, the Soviet Union evinced discomfiture over the direction of Syrian policy. Syria's decision to confront the Palestinian Resistance pitted long-standing Soviet clients against each other. The Soviet Union vented its anger over Syrian conduct through expressions of sympathy for the Palestinian predicament. Meanwhile, Soviet leaders were surely troubled by the emerging coincidence between Syrian and American objectives and alignments.

Early in June, Soviet authorities permitted a protest demonstration against the Syrian intervention by three hundred Lebanese and Palestinian students outside the Syrian Embassy in Moscow. The Russians pledged shipments of food and medicine to Palestinians who had come under attack by Syria. On 22 June, long-sought permission was granted to the PLO to open a permanent mission in Moscow.[29] By July, a barrage of criticism was leveled against Syria in the Soviet press. The Soviet Afro-Asian Solidarity Committee, a semi-official foreign policy organ, blamed Syria for "complicating the situation in Lebanon," and appealed for worldwide support of the Palestinian Resistance and the "National Patriotic Forces" (i.e., the Lebanese National Movement). Syria was accused in the media of "stabbing the PLO in the back," and *Pravda* complained that "PLO units found themselves under attack

[27]Golan and Rabinovich, "Soviet Union and Syria," p. 226.

[28]Kass, "Moscow," pp. 171–174.

[29]Freedman, "Soviet Union and Civil War," pp. 76–78; Kass, "Moscow," pp. 174–175.

from the rear and the front—from the Syrians and the Rightist Lebanese formations."[30]

A personal letter reportedly sent by Leonid Brezhnev to Hafiz al-Asad on 11 July was published by *Le Monde* on 20 July, although its authenticity was never confirmed. In the letter, the Soviet leader called for the withdrawal of Syrian forces from Lebanon; blamed the Syrians for failure to achieve an effective cease-fire; and warned that the prospects for "further strengthening" of Soviet-Syrian relations would be impaired if Asad did not change his course in Lebanon. Another unconfirmed report carried by the Iraqi News Agency cited "reliable diplomatic sources" as saying that the Soviet Union had suspended delivery of all arms, armor, and spare parts to Syria "until the Syrian forces are withdrawn from Lebanon and until an end is put to Syria's clashes with the Palestine Resistance Movement and the National Movement."[31]

Although both of the above-cited sources may be questioned, the tone of rebuke in Soviet commentary about Syrian conduct was unmistakable during this period. The Soviet Union was wary, however, about alienating Syria through excessive criticism, and also attempted to use its own leverage with the Palestinian leadership to achieve reconciliation between its protégés. On several occasions, Abu Iyad, second-in-command of Fath, complained of Soviet pressure to come to terms with Syria. In August 1976, he declared:

> What have you given us? We do not want you to tell us to reach an understanding with the Syrians. You have lost many of your positions in the Arab world because you did not understand the conspiracy. We are not asking the impossible; we want a ship carrying flour and hoisting the Russian flag to come to Sa'ida [Sidon] and defy Israel.

During August and September the Russians continued their diplomatic exchanges with Palestinian leaders while withholding tangible support, prompting Abu Iyad to accuse the Soviet Union on 27 September of "giving the order to Syria to intervene militarily

---

[30]Freedman, "Soviet Union and Civil War," pp. 79–81; Kass, "Moscow," p. 175.
[31]Kass, "Moscow," p. 176; Freedman, "Soviet Union and Civil War," p. 81.

against the Palestinian Resistance in Lebanon, [with the aim of] shattering the Palestinian Resistance."[32]

Soviet frustration with its inability to modify Syrian policies or promote Syrian-Palestinian accommodation was fully evident during the final weeks of the Lebanese crisis. Restraint in criticizing Syria was dropped as *Pravda,* on 27 August, advised that "the withdrawal of Syrian troops from Lebanon would be of great importance in resolving the Lebanese crisis." Nor did the Soviet press hesitate to identify Syria, on 30 September, as part of "an extensive conspiracy by imperialism and Arab reaction against the Palestinian Resistance Movement."[33]

Basis for Reconciliation

Focusing literally on Soviet comments from June through October 1976, one might conclude that irreparable harm had been done to Soviet-Syrian relations. In reality, however, both the superpower and its wayward protégé respected outer limits to their disagreement. Although Soviet military supplies to Syria may have been temporarily curtailed, a complete cutoff did not occur. Although Syria considered canceling port privileges to the Soviet Mediterranean squadron, it did not act on this inclination. Criticism of Syria in the Soviet press was often attributed to semi-official or low-ranking sources, and the Syrian press refrained from responding to the Soviet attacks.

Both patron and client recognized a long-term convergence of interests despite obvious incompatibility during the Lebanese crisis. The Soviet Union did not wish to lose its influence with the Syrian confrontation state and to be identified exclusively with the Rejectionist Arab States of Iraq, Libya, and Algeria as well as the Palestinians. Syria, for its part, recognized that the freedom of maneuver achieved by contacts with the United States could best be sustained through relations with both superpowers.[34] Moreover, the United States showed no signs of willingness to replace

[32]Freedman, "Soviet Union and Civil War," pp. 83–84; Kass, "Moscow," pp. 176–182.

[33]Freedman, "Soviet Union and Civil War," pp. 84–89.

[34]Golan and Rabinovich, "Soviet Union and Syria," pp. 226–229.

level of economic and military support that the Soviet Union regularly provided. What the Lebanese Civil War did demonstrate, however, was that on an issue of prime importance to Syria as a regional actor, and of only tangential concern to the superpowers, Syria was endowed with impressive freedom of maneuver in pursuing its own objectives.

V

IMPLICATIONS

12

The Balance Sheet

The distinctive features of Syria's intervention in Lebanon may best be highlighted by citing the experience of other interveners. Conceptual tools for studying intervention, set forth in Chapter 1, have thus far only been applied to the Lebanese case. It would be presumptuous to draw definitive theoretical conclusions based on one case study. Yet a complete inventory of comparative cases is obviously impossible. Instead, selective reference will be made to particular cases that raise analogous theoretical issues.

Variations in the intervention process reflect several different levels of analysis. First, structural characteristics of the international system determine the degree of autonomy available to a great or small power intervener. Second, regional norms may be particularly important in evaluating the behavior of a small state intervener seeking leadership in its regional environment. Third, domestic factors shape the intervener's decisionmaking process as well as the balance of forces between incumbents and insurgents in the target state, sometimes even giving rise to parallel cleavages in the two societies. Finally, if transnational linkages exist between the intervener and the target — especially if a transnational actor plays a significant role in each — the dynamics of the intervention process may be dramatically affected.

By noting the constraints facing other interveners in pursuing their objectives, one gains more insight into why Syria fell short of its goals in Lebanon. A comparative perspective also assists in evaluating the longer-term outcome of the Syrian intervention. The conclusions of this study may best be scrutinized from the perspective of several years later. Was Syria's behavior in Lebanon after the official termination of the Lebanese Civil War in 1976 guided by similar objectives and calculations? How did the impact of the intervention affect Syria's options in subsequent years?

Superpower Leverage

A small state intervener faces different dilemmas than a great power in pursuing its goals. Nevertheless, in the international system of the 1970s, ambitious small states could exercise considerable autonomy. Syrian objectives in Lebanon were not tailored to suit superpower preferences, but rather to advance foreign policy goals embraced by Syria's leaders.

A desire to minimize constraints posed by superpower patrons is common to aspiring regional powers. Third World leaders evaluate their regional environment in terms of deep-seated attitudes and objectives. A patron's level of support may determine how vigorously objectives are pursued, but calculations of costs and risks of intervention reflect indigenous criteria.

Use of the proxy concept is inherently problematic when referring to the foreign policy behavior of states. Substantiating the conceptual argument advanced in Chapter 1, the evidence clearly negates an image of Syrian intervention in Lebanon as a Soviet— or American—proxy. Yet this was not a particularly difficult case to argue, since neither superpower had vital interests at stake in Lebanon and therefore neither used the maximum influence at its disposal to exert leverage over Syrian behavior. The evidence for discounting the image of a state-proxy is less clear-cut with respect to Cuba's intervention in Angola in 1975 and Israel's readiness to intervene in Jordan's civil strife in 1970.

Several characteristics of Cuba's intervention in Angola arouse skepticism about the intervener's autonomy of decision. First, it is highly unusual for a small state to be involved in a civil conflict so far from its borders. The overwhelming majority of interventions by small states are directed at next-door neighbors or at least within the same region. Second, expenditures for the Angolan intervention far exceeded the resources of the Cuban economy. Cuban leaders could not afford to act on so large a scale without reasonable assurance of backing by Cuba's sole economic and military benefactor, the Soviet Union.

Do these conditions indicate that Cuba was serving as a Soviet proxy in sending combat troops to Angola in November 1975? Closer examination reveals that Cuba had long-standing ties to the Popular Movement for the Liberation of Angola (MPLA), having supported the guerrilla movement since 1964. Moreover, these ties were a natural outgrowth of the Cuban regime's ideological commitment to "national liberation movements." During the 1960s, when Cuba was frustrated from exercising influence in Latin America, it sought outlets further afield to carry out its ideological commitments.

Cuba initiated small-scale assistance to the MPLA during a period when its relations with the Soviet Union were strained. Even after Soviet-Cuban relations improved in the early 1970s, sub-Sahara Africa remained an area of low priority for Soviet foreign policy. There is no evidence for Soviet encouragement of Cuba's initial decision to send troops to Angola; and even when close Cuban-Soviet coordination occurred in the latter stages of the war, there are indications that Cuba may have taken the initiative in prodding a deeper level of Soviet commitment.[1] Analytically, one may conclude that dependence on a patron's material support does not suffice in its own right to establish a proxy relationship. Far more persuasive is the image of a symbiotic Soviet-Cuban partnership in Angola.[2]

Israel was another superficially convincing candidate for the proxy label in its willingness to intervene in Jordan to avert the downfall of King Husayn in September 1970. The unusual candor of Israeli Prime Minister Yitshaq Rabin, American President Richard Nixon, and Secretary of State Henry Kissinger in their respective memoirs, revealing intimate joint planning for Israel's intervention, increases the persuasiveness of this hypothesis. Once U.S. decisionmakers realized that they lacked viable military options to assist the beleaguered monarch, they concluded that Israel might accomplish this objective more effectively and at lower political risks. Joint planning included a division of labor between

[1]William M. LeoGrande, "Soviet-Cuban Relations and Cuban Policy in Africa," in *Cuba in Africa,* ed. Carmelo Mesa-Lago and June S. Belkin (Pittsburgh: Center for Latin American Studies, University of Pittsburgh, 1982), pp. 15–26.

[2]Bertil Duner, "Proxy Intervention in Civil Wars," *Journal of Peace Research* 18,4 (1981): 358.

the two states, with Israel pledging active deterrence (and, if it failed, air and ground attacks) against Syrian forces, while the United States would deter Egyptian or Soviet countermeasures.[3]

Yet the perception by a superpower that a client state is serving as its proxy does not suffice to define the relationship. American officials did indeed believe that they were "using" Israel as a proxy in safeguarding the U.S. commitment to King Husayn's regime. The analyst must try to determine, however, whether Israel's decision to intervene was conditional on the initiative of an American "activator." The answer is clearly negative, insofar as Israel considered its vital interests at stake in preventing a Syrian-backed triumph of Palestinian guerrillas over King Husayn. Israel would surely have intervened to prevent that eventuality; in fact, one concern of American policymakers was to restrict the scope of Israeli unilateral intervention through coordinated planning.[4] No doubt, the specifics of Israel's strategy were modified in response to this coordination, but the essence of Israel's decision to intervene did not reflect the status of a proxy.

These episodes confirm that the proxy concept beclouds more than it elucidates about superpower-client state relations. However, even if a client exercises sovereign will in decisions to intervene, the high costs of intervention may deepen its dependence on a superpower patron. On the eve of its massive invasion of Kampuchea in December 1978, the Socialist Republic of Vietnam concluded a Treaty of Friendship and Cooperation with the Soviet Union. The Russians had been urging such an agreement since 1975, but Vietnam avoided entering an explicit strategic alliance so as not unduly to antagonize the People's Republic of China. Once Vietnam launched its invasion, China increased its support for the Pol Pot regime in Kampuchea, labeling the Vietnamese as "the Cubans of the Orient" in advancing Soviet aims in Indochina.

Vietnam was really soliciting Soviet backing for its own long-standing regional ambitions. While denying Kampuchean allegations that they sought a Vietnamese-dominated Indochina federation, Vietnam's leaders emphasized their "special relationship" with the Kampuchean Communist Party as members of a regional

---

[3]Yaacov Bar-Siman-Tov, "Crisis Management by Military Cooperation with a Small Ally: American-Israel Cooperation in the Syrian-Jordanian Crisis, September 1970," *Cooperation and Conflict* 17 (1982): 152–158.

[4]Ibid., pp. 154–155.

socialist bloc. The Vietnamese charged that Pol Pot's regime in Kampuchea had deviated from socialist norms. In response, Vietnam first encouraged domestic dissent and then imposed a ruler of its own choosing in the wake of its intervention.

Although Vietnam was pursuing regional imperatives in its Kampuchean intervention, the venture ultimately reduced its flexibility in global alignments. The massive entry of Vietnamese troops into Kampuchea precipitated a limited Chinese counterintervention, after which the Soviet Union rallied to Vietnam's support with an airlift of military supplies and increased economic assistance. In the longer term, Vietnam remained substantially more dependent on the Soviet Union, and its efforts to normalize relations with the People's Republic of China were frustrated so long as its military occupation of Kampuchea continued.[5]

In a similar vein, the high costs of Syria's intervention in Lebanon, far exceeding initial expectations, contributed to deepened dependence on the Soviet Union. Especially once the intervention was transformed into extended occupation, Syria was increasingly reliant on Soviet military assistance. Developments in Lebanon weighed heavily, although Syria's alienation from the United States was another major factor restricting the country's global options. Syria, like Vietnam, succumbed to Soviet urging to conclude a Treaty of Friendship and Cooperation with the Soviet Union after nearly a decade of refusing to do so. President Asad's signature on the agreement in October 1980 was an implicit acknowledgment of increased vulnerability to Soviet leverage.[6]

Regional Norms

The degree of Syrian room for maneuver vis-à-vis its superpower patron reflected current characteristics of the international system,

[5]Gareth Porter, "Vietnamese Policy and the Indochina Crisis," in *The Third Indochina Conflict,* ed. David W. P. Elliot (Boulder, Col.: Westview, 1981), pp. 105–115; Stephen P. Heder, "The Kampuchean-Vietnamese Conflict," in Ibid., pp. 35–42; Banning Garett, "The Strategic Triangle and the Indochina Crisis," in Ibid., p. 208.

[6]Yoseph Olmert, "Syria," in *Middle East Contemporary Survey,* Vol. VI: *1981–82,* ed. Colin Legum et al. (New York: Holmes and Meier, 1984), pp. 866–868. See also Karen Dawisha, "The USSR in the Middle East: Superpower in Eclipse?" *Foreign Affairs* 61,2 (Winter 1982–83): 438–452.

as a realist perspective would predict. In exercising influence in its regional environment, by contrast, Syria was obliged to couple normative with power-political considerations. While the limitations posed by power politics are more readily generalizable, normative constraints are distinctive to a particular region, reflecting its historical, cultural, and ideological predispositions.

Syria was particularly sensitive to regional norms because it was seeking recognition of its leadership claims from fellow Arab states. Leadership relies heavily on the manipulation of symbols and can only be measured in nonquantifiable, attitudinal terms of followers' responses. Syria therefore emphasized its credentials as champion of the Palestinian Resistance, a consensual value in the Arab system, in its quest for leadership.

Arab reaction to Syria's intervention in Lebanon revealed both the viability and the limitations of the Arab consensus. One might argue that the efficacy of the Arab League in curtailing Syria's attack against the Resistance demonstrated fidelity to its consensual norm. Conversely, the length of time that passed until the Arab League intervened, as well as the limited concessions it extracted from Syria, might merely signify lip service to the League's ideals. Because of the motivational variables involved, the analyst cannot definitively prove whether ideological norms are being cynically manipulated by political leaders or serve as genuine guidelines for behavior.

The Lebanese Civil War did show that, insofar as commitment to the Resistance was at play, Syria's behavior was restrained only after extreme deviation, when it threatened the liquidation of the Resistance in Lebanon. Years later, in 1983, Syria went even further, backing dissidents within the Resistance opposed to Yasir 'Arafat's leadership, and ultimately obliging Yasir 'Arafat to flee Lebanon after heavy fighting against his forces in Tripoli. Although Saudi intercession may have prevented 'Arafat's removal from his leadership position, the Arab consensus functioned even less reliably in 1983 than it had in 1976.[7]

Another inter-Arab example and an extraregional case illustrate the differential effectiveness of consensual norms, as embodied in state behavior or in regional organizations. The Egyptian inter-

---

[7]See "The PLO Split," *MERIP Reports* 13, 9 (November-December 1983).

vention in Yemen of 1962–67 reflected Egypt's claim to Arab leadership under President Gamal 'Abd al-Nasir. Egypt's promotion of Arab unity was most concretely expressed in the formation of the United Arab Republic with Syria in February 1958. Syria's secession from the union in September 1961 was therefore a major blow to Nasir's leadership credentials. Nasir attributed the UAR's failure to the "forces of reaction" in the region, declaring that a progressive, socialist ideology must henceforth be the basis for Arab unity. Accordingly, Nasir assisted the planners of a September 1962 coup d'état which overthrew the monarchy (or imamate) in Yemen, declaring a revolutionary Yemen Arab Republic. Nasir responded promptly to the Republicans' appeal for support to combat the Royalist forces of the Imam. Egyptian troops were transported 3,000 miles to Yemen, eventually reaching a maximum strength of 70,000 men.

The ideological values embraced by Nasir in his intervention did not enjoy consensus in the region; all traditional regimes, and especially the Arab monarchies, felt threatened by Nasirist incitement. Saudi Arabia, which borders Yemen and considered the Arabian Peninsula part of its own sphere of influence, was most incensed by Nasir's actions. Moreover, the Saudi monarchy believed that the Egyptian military presence next door was intended to spark domestic Saudi unrest. Saudi rulers responded with lavish economic and military assistance for the Royalists, although they refrained from direct counterintervention.

This unusual example of contested intervention in Arab civil strife reflected a high point of ideological polarization in the Arab world. The Arab League refrained from even meeting to discuss the crisis in its early stages, and never made any concrete contribution to mediating a political settlement. The inter-Arab crisis in Yemen ended only when Nasir found himself in need of Saudi largesse after Egypt's defeat by Israel in June 1967. As a condition for aid from the oil-rich states to enable Egypt to recover from the war, Nasir pledged at the Arab League summit in Khartum in August 1967 to withdraw Egyptian troops from Yemen.[8]

In Africa, as well, a regional organization embodies commitment

[8]Ali Abdel Rahman Rahmy, "The Egyptian Policy in the Arab World: Intervention in Yemen, 1962–1967" (Ph.D. Dissertation, University of Geneva, 1981), pp. 112–148, 173–174, 205–218, 248–267, 321–326.

to consensual norms, while often falling short of their implementation. The goal of liberation from colonial rule and from domination by white racist regimes is universally endorsed by members of the Organization of African Unity (OAU). Beyond rhetorical cohesion, the OAU has achieved concrete results in pursuing this objective. In recent years, the five "front line states" designated by the OAU played a critical role in the transition to independence in Zimbabwe and in negotiations toward self-rule in Namibia. Nevertheless, adherence even to consensual norms is not universal, and economic pressures coupled with weaker ideological commitment prompt some OAU members to continue dealing with South Africa.[9]

The OAU has no effective sanctions to wield against those who deviate from its norms. By contrast, effective sanctions have occasionally been wielded against Arab interveners in the name of the Arab League, but in reality on the part of individual members. In the Yemeni Civil War, Saudi Arabia was protecting its own state interests in opposing the Egyptian intervention. Ultimately, however, Arab League auspices finessed the demand for Egyptian withdrawal from Yemen as a condition for aid from a consortium of Arab states. Just as Egyptian economic dependence was critical in 1967, Syrian vulnerability to Saudi economic pressure was decisive in bringing President Asad to the bargaining table in 1976. In this case, Saudi Arabia was not championing narrow state interests, but rather a broader regional consensus for commitment to the Palestinian Resistance.

The ideology of Arab nationalism and the goal of Arab unity encourage permissive norms toward Arab intervention in civil strife, on behalf of either incumbents or insurgents. A more conservative attitude in the OAU condones an appeal for outside assistance by a central government faced with civil strife, but discourages support for insurgents. The most acceptable intervener from the OAU perspective is another African state, rather than an extraregional power. Because of the relative equality of power among African states, intervention has been viewed as a relatively innocuous activity. No intervening African state has achieved en-

[9]William J. Foltz, "The Organization of African Unity in Trouble: How and Why It Works and Does Not Work," Department of State, Bureau of Intelligence and Research (INR), Report 698–AR, 29 September 1983, pp. 7–11.

during influence in a target state. Since the mid-1970s, however, several African states (including Nigeria, Algeria, and Libya) made incipient claims to regional power status based on enhanced military capabilities or oil wealth. In several cases, the capacity to engage in intervention on behalf of another beleaguered government enhanced these states' leadership credentials.[10]

By contrast, Arab responses to intervention have often been negative, when a regional power was perceived as trying to dominate its neighbors. Saudi Arabia perceived Nasir's actions in Yemen as the first step toward dominating the Arabian Peninsula. Other Arab regimes were relieved that the opportunity costs of a lengthy military stalemate in Yemen prevented Nasir from promoting his goals of revolutionary socialism within their borders.[11]

Syria's leadership ambitions at the time of the Lebanese intervention were confined to the Fertile Crescent, and consequently Iraq was the only Arab state directly challenged by Syria's aspirations. Since no other Arab state had interests in Lebanon remotely paralleling those of Syria, there was little incentive to challenge the primacy of Syria's influence over its troubled neighbor. Yet insofar as Syria's leaders hoped that success in Lebanon might enhance their country's leadership credentials, perhaps even permitting influence beyond the Fertile Crescent, subsequent years revealed precisely the opposite outcome. The opportunity costs of lengthy involvement in Lebanon were reflected, by 1978, in Iraq's assertion of a leadership claim at Syria's expense. One indication of the shift was Jordan's volte-face in allegiance toward the rising Iraqi Fertile Crescent power.

Another useful point of comparison between the Arab League and OAU experiences is the inability of either organization to field a credible regional peacekeeping operation. In theory, a regionally sponsored effort to restore stability might offer many advantages over unilateral intervention. Yet the OAU has lacked the economic, technical, and military resources to establish an effective force, as its 1982 effort in Chad revealed.[12]

The Arab League's deficiency was not in resources but rather in political will. The Arab Deterrent Force in Lebanon, created

[10]Ibid., pp. 17–19.
[11]Rahmy, "Egyptian Policy in the Arab World, pp. 173–174, 205–206.
[12]Foltz, "The Organization of African Unity," pp. 19, 28–33.

at the League's summit in October 1976, was multilateral in name only. It consisted of token units from several Arab states alongside a Syrian force approximating 30,000 men; and even these small units were removed by 1980. When the Lebanese National Movement and the Palestinian Resistance called for Arabization of the Lebanese crisis in June 1976, they specifically advocated an Arab peacekeeping force as a substitute for the Syrian military presence. Instead, the ADF was a mechanism for legitimizing Syria's unilateral intervention after the fact. In subsequent years, Syria cited Arab League sponsorship as proof that its forces in the ADF were pursuing a peacekeeping mission rather than the military occupation of Lebanon.

The Transnational Dimension

In response to its external environment, Syria's relationship with the Palestinian Resistance was conditioned by regional norms. But the fascinating aspect of the relationship is that it also governed Syria's role as intervener in the Lebanese target state. The ambivalence and struggle in Syrian-Palestinian relations precipitated Syria's switch of alignments, the most distinctive feature of its behavior as an intervener. Indeed, the transnational dimension of Lebanese strife is rich in theoretical implications, requiring incorporation of an additional, intermediary level of analysis between the intervener and the target state.

Any external actor must assess the balance of forces between parties to civil strife when contemplating a decision to intervene. Miscalculations are common, as the theoretical literature and abundant case studies reveal. For Syria, the challenge of assessment was even more difficult than usual, because of the ambiguous status of Palestinian guerrillas in Lebanon. To what extent would the Resistance become actively involved in civil strife? In view of the diversity of guerrilla groups, would some be involved and others detached? How would participation by the guerrillas affect the political and military balance?

Even more important and more difficult to predict from the Syrian perspective was the degree to which Resistance leaders would be answerable to Syrian influence. The deepest disappointment to Syria in its intervention stemmed from Yasir 'Arafat's refusal to break ranks with the Lebanese National Movement despite Syrian urging. Even when Syria applied the full weight of its forces through direct military intervention, 'Arafat stood his ground.

Why was the Palestinian leader able to do so? Precisely because Syria was not the sole patron of the Resistance, whose basic premise of operation was not to become exclusively dependent on the backing and goodwill of any single Arab regime. 'Arafat was therefore able to resist demands that he serve as a Syrian proxy. In doing so, he was also fortified by the broad domestic base of support for the Lebanese National Movement, which, despite the departure of several component groups during the Civil War, retained indigenous strength as a subnational actor not heavily dependent on any single external backer.

The Lebanese case is therefore suggestive of circumstances in which transnational or subnational actors might or might not engage in proxy relationships. Forces of the Palestine Liberation Army did participate in Syria's indirect intervention of January 1976, when a convergence of interests existed between the PLO leadership and Syria. Once a conflict of interests emerged, however, Palestinian leaders essentially declared that, even while remaining Syrian clients, they were not proxies and could say no to unacceptable Syrian demands. By the time Syria intervened in direct combat with the Resistance, even the minimal prerequisites for the patron-client relationship were suspended.

In seeking to influence transnational and subnational actors, Israel faced some analogous dilemmas in its 1982 intervention in Lebanon. Israel's principal objective was to deliver a crushing blow to the Palestinian Resistance. A secondary objective was to bring to power a subnational actor, the Kata'ib (Phalangist) Party, which shared Israel's goal of liquidating the Palestinian guerrilla presence in Lebanon. However, Israel miscalculated both its own leverage over the Kata'ib and the balance of forces between this subnational actor and groups in Lebanon antagonistic to Kata'ib domination. Unlike the forces of Maj. Sa'ad Haddad in Southern Lebanon, the Kata'ib were not prepared to serve as Israeli proxies, and when a divergence of interests occurred after Israel's military invasion, Kata'ib leaders refused to accede to Israeli demands. Moreover,

De Facto Partition of Lebanon on the Eve of Israel's 1982 Invasion

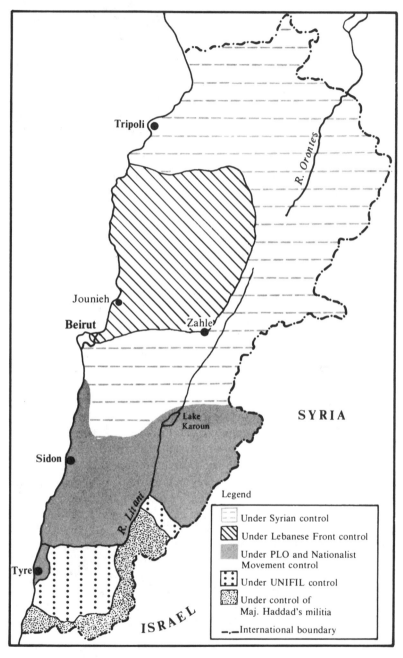

Legend

- Under Syrian control
- Under Lebanese Front control
- Under PLO and Nationalist Movement control
- Under UNIFIL control
- Under control of Maj. Haddad's militia
- International boundary

Source: Itamar Rabinovich, *The War for Lebanon, 1970–1985*, p. 46. Copyright © 1984, 1985 by Cornell University Press. Used by permission of the publisher.

the Kata'ib faced constant challenges by other Lebanese leaders who viewed them as a minority clique rather than legitimate rulers. Most critically, the Kata'ib could not command the loyalty of a rebuilt Lebanese Army. When Israel could no longer sustain the costs of direct occupation in Beirut and the Shuf and found itself without reliable Lebanese clients, its ability either to affect the domestic Lebanese equation or to prevent the reintroduction of a Palestinian guerrilla presence were significantly undermined.[13]

Linkage Politics

However salient the role of the Palestinian Resistance, one must recall that Syrian interests in Lebanon long predated the PLO presence on Lebanese soil. Deep historical bonds necessarily affected perceptions by Syria's leaders of their neighbor's domestic affairs. In effect, Syria's intervention in Lebanon exemplified the interplay between domestic politics and foreign policy in an unusually intense way. When theorists of intervention discuss linkage politics, they generally emphasize constraints posed by domestic constituencies on decisionmaking by interveners. Distinctive to this case was the presence of parallel cleavages in the intervener and the target state, whose salience was intensified by geographic proximity and historical bonds.

Syrian leaders therefore believed that the outcome of civil strife in Lebanon would affect not only the viability of their claim to regional leadership, but even the stability of their regime. The fear of contagion was very real, especially insofar as partition of Lebanon along sectarian lines could set a precedent inimical to the stability of the minoritarian Syrian regime. Defensive motivations at play in the initial decision to intervene intensified during the intervention process.

An emphasis on the significance of parallel social cleavages should not, however, discount the dramatic contrasts between the Syrian and Lebanese political systems. Perhaps the single most

[13]Itamar Rabinovich, *The War for Lebanon, 1970–1983* (Ithaca: Cornell University Press, 1984), pp. 121–173. See also Ze'ev Schiff and Ehud Ya'ari, *Israel's Lebanon War,* ed. and trans. by Ina Friedman (New York: Simon and Schuster, 1984).

glaring difference was the role of the Army in each state. In Syria, the monopolization by the Army of the instruments of coercion and the close identification between the Army and the political elite form the basis for authoritarian politics. In Lebanon, the lack of trust between communities led them to keep the Army deliberately weak. As a result, when the elite came under challenge, it was deprived of the coercive capacity to enforce its authority.

The weakness and ultimate disintegration of the Army is a vital factor in contrasting the outcome of Lebanon's civil strife and that of Jordan in 1970. The loyalty of the Army to King Husayn was ultimately more important than the conduct of external actors in enabling the King to assert his authority. In Lebanon, the collapse of the Army was a critical event in intensifying civil strife, and also in precipitating an escalated Syrian commitment.

The centralization of authority in Syria's military elite was significant not only in accentuating political differences between the intervener and the target state. The structure of Syria's narrowly based elite also conditioned its commitment in Lebanon. In its decisionmaking process, the veneer of official consensus projected by the Syrian regime glosses over any dissent within the elite. One is tempted to conclude that foreign policy, including decisions on intervention, are made more expeditiously and with fewer societal costs in authoritarian than in democratic regimes.

Nevertheless, the far more open and complete record of the U.S. intervention in Vietnam reveals parallels in the dynamics of the intervention process. A secular trend in any costly and lengthy intervention process gives rise to an escalatory dynamic and fluctuations in commitment. Regardless of the political composition of the elite, miscalculations may lead to initial underestimation of the costs of intervention. Higher costs then prompt rising stakes for the intervener. What varies most between different types of regimes is not the process of escalation, but rather the dynamic of decommitment.

This generalization is not intended to discount constraints posed by democratic systems even in early stages of commitment. Calculation of costs by leaders who are accountable to their electorates at frequent intervals places a high premium on short-term results. Therefore, one analysis concludes that "[d]emocratic governments are inherently maladapted to . . . decisive long-range planning."

However, the record reveals that throughout most of the lengthy American commitment in Vietnam, Presidential options were not severely limited by domestic politics, because the basic objectives of the American commitment were widely shared. In effect, the United States displayed a "remarkable continuity of basic objectives," centering around the goal of preventing a Communist victory in South Vietnam. Comparably to Syrian decisionmakers in Lebanon, American leaders made some fundamental miscalculations of the costs required to pursue consistent objectives, substantiating the conclusion that "no system can compensate for errors of judgment . . . pervasive among authorities." The common outcome was "progressive escalation in the face of progressive failure of policy."[14]

Once the domestic American consensus over Vietnam War objectives eroded, however, the democratic system provided specific mechanisms for undermining the will of the executive branch and triggering a decommitment process. The filtering of dissent from the bottom up was channeled through democratic institutions, especially the Congress. By 1974–75, Congress used its legislative powers to cut drastically administration requests for military and economic aid to Saigon, and to ban American reinvolvement in Vietnamese combat. These assertive measures left the President no choice but to curtail the American commitment.[15]

In an authoritarian state, discontent over foreign policy must be deferred or expressed indirectly. For example, there were many indications of the unpopularity of the war in Yemen with Egyptian citizens during years of military stalemate. The intervention inflicted a heavy burden on Egypt's struggling economy, whose inability to reach the ambitious goals of the 1960–65 development plan were widely attributed to the war. Egyptians did not understand why they were being asked to make sacrifices to subsidize a war in a remote country in which Egypt had no vital interests. Although some elements in the Egyptian military viewed the war as a means of enhancing their political influence, many officers expressed discontent over the handling of the war effort. Moreover, the opportunity costs of the Yemen War were evident in

[14]Leslie H. Gelb with Richard K. Betts, *The Irony of Vietnam: The System Worked* (Washington, D.C.: Brookings Institution, 1979), pp. 2–4.

[15]Ibid., pp. 347–369.

deficiencies of manpower and military capabilities for the June 1967 War with Israel. No wonder President Nasir subsequently referred to Yemen as "my Vietnam."[16]

In Syria, there was no legitimate channel for expressing discontent with the Asad regime's strategy in Lebanon or with the costs of the Lebanese war. Nevertheless, the toll of popular discontent was merely deferred. In a wave of political assassinations by religious fundamentalists in Syria beginning in 1977, dissidents repeatedly expressed grievances over the regime's Lebanese policies. One alleged perpetrator asserted that "these acts [of assassination] were bound to splinter the domestic front and to sow sectarianism similar to that in Lebanon." Responsibility for the assassinations was assumed by a group known as the *Mujahidun* (Strugglers), whose members have been identified with Syria's Muslim Brethren. The group's publications referred to their battle against "atheism ruling in Syria," characterizing the country's 'Alawi rulers as "infidel Nusayris [a pejorative appelation for 'Alawis] who are outside Islam."[17] The spreading impact of sectarian-tinged violence was evident in country-wide civil disturbances in the spring of 1980, and came to a head in the popular uprising in Hamah of February 1982 that was suppressed by the regime with enormous civilian casualties.

Although grievances against Syria's narrowly based regime had many causes and were latent for years, the controversial Lebanese intervention was clearly responsible for triggering social unrest. In the aftermath of the intervention, one analyst maintains, "sectarianism . . . affected not only the Ba'th Party apparatus, the armed forces and other security institutions, but the larger part of Syrian society."[18]

Appraising the Outcome

For six years after the Lebanese Civil War officially ended, Syria's large-scale military presence persisted without significant chal-

[16]Rahmy, "Egyptian Policy," 157–166, 298, 307–321, 371–384.
[17]Nikolaos Van Dam, *The Struggle for Power in Syria*, 2d. ed. (New York: St. Martin's, 1981), pp. 92–93, 104–106.
[18]Ibid., p. 14.

lenge. Although Syrian forces served under the auspices of the Arab Deterrent Force, a great many Lebanese felt that their country was subject to Syrian military occupation.

The transformation of an intervention into a military occupation represents failure by an intervener to reach its initial objectives. Occupation is an unsatisfactory outcome for the intervener, first, because it requires ongoing military engagement at high costs. Direct costs of occupation entail both financial outlays and attritional casualties if indigenous resistance arises. Indirectly, severe opportunity costs may constrain the occupier's broader foreign policy options.

A second reason that occupation is an unsatisfactory culmination of intervention is that, in these circumstances, the external actor has obviously not reached its goals in the target state. Insofar as interveners claim to be stabilizing the target state, inability to depart without reigniting civil strife symbolizes a failed venture. In many cases, the occupier installs a new government in the target state whose leaders are politically beholden and subordinate to the occupying power. In this predicament, the "penetrated" state suffers from a dilution of its sovereign status.[19] The domestic legitimacy of the new incumbents is severely tarnished by their subordinate status, underscoring their inability to assert authority without the outside prop of foreign forces.

For the student of intervention, cases in which decommitment does not occur present peculiar analytic dilemmas. Should one refer to the "routinization" of intervention, or to a distinct postintervention phase? The answer depends on whether civil strife continues in the target state and whether the occupying forces are committed militarily on the side of either incumbents or insurgents. If both conditions obtain, intervention persists. A clear-cut case of occupation as an ongoing intervention strategy was the Soviet military presence in Afghanistan after December 1979. For several reasons, the Syrian presence in Lebanon after October 1976 was more ambiguous.

The Soviet Union pursued an active commitment in Afghanistan since a Communist regime, led by the People's Democratic Party of Afghanistan (PDPA) came to power in 1978. When popular

[19]Handel, *Weak States in the International System,* p. 137.

resistance against the PDPA government of Hafizullah Amin threatened its overthrow in December 1979, Soviet leaders decided to intervene directly. Their motives were primarily defensive— aimed at preventing the replacement of a Communist regime with one that might be neutral or hostile to the Soviet Union, as well as forestalling instability on the Soviet Union's southern border, with possible contagion effects due to the ethnic affinity of the Afghan population with that of Soviet Central Asia.

The Soviet leaders' portrayal of their intervention as invitational strains credulity. On 24 December 1979, Soviet military transport planes began landing troops at the Kabul airport, achieving control of the capital by 27 December. Only after Hafizullah Amin was killed by the Soviets on 27 December was his Soviet-chosen suc- cessor, Babrak Karmal, flown into Kabul on a Soviet plane. Karmal then announced that he had invited the Soviet intervention with full support of the PDPA underground leadership opposed to Amin's rule. Karmal's lack of domestic legitimacy was an obvious outgrowth of his association with the Soviet occupiers, whose pres- ence "intensified the conflict from essentially a civil war among Afghans into primarily a national war of resistance to foreign in- vaders and their local puppets."

The Soviet Army in Afghanistan engaged in bloody combat with Afghan resistance fighters, or *mujahideen,* and Soviet casualties were estimated at up to 15,000 by Western analysts during the first three years of occupation. Yet there were no indications that the Soviet superpower deemed these attritional costs unacceptably high or considered terminating its Afghan commitment. Although the occupation of Afghanistan required active intervention to de- fend weak incumbents against persistent insurgents, maintaining Afghanistan as "an obedient member of 'the socialist community of nations' " was likely to figure as a necessary commitment by Soviet leaders for the foreseeable future.[20]

In Lebanon, the government of President Iliyas Sarkis was elected with at least the tacit support of Syria in May 1976, while Syria's commitment in Lebanon was already intense but interven- tion had not yet occurred. Despite the invitational dimension of

[20]Henry S. Bradsher, *Afghanistan and the Soviet Union* (Durham, N.C.: Duke Press Policy Studies, 1983), esp. pp. 3–8, 126–188, 205–255.

Syria's initial indirect intervention in Lebanon, the massive entry of Syrian forces in June 1976 was penetrational. The enduring presence of 30,000 Syrian forces (on average) then received an aura of legitimation from the Arab League and, unlike the Soviet forces in Afghanistan, there was no organized resistance to their presence. Yet the widespread perception of President Sarkis as a weak leader was attributable at least in part to his heavy reliance on Syria. The ineffectuality of the Sarkis government was symbolized in its inability to implement plans for rebuilding the Lebanese Army, a vital prerequisite for regaining stability in the absence of Syrian troops.[21]

Syrian officials insisted that, as participants in the Arab Deterrent Force, they were pursuing the identical objectives that led them to intervene in Lebanon in the first place—i.e., restoring stability to Lebanon, preventing Lebanon's partition, and safeguarding the Palestinian Resistance. Yet these objectives came no closer to realization in the phase of occupation than in the phase of intervention. No doubt, the tactical flexibility that characterized Syrian behavior in 1975–76 persisted in subsequent years. Shifts in the direction of Syrian alignments with domestic parties in Lebanon included annulment of the marriage of convenience between Syria and certain Maronite groups, especially the Kata'ib. There was also a temporary rapprochement between Syria and the PLO under Yasir 'Arafat's leadership. One consequence of this rapprochement was a resumption of Syrian support for Palestinian guerrilla activities in Southern Lebanon.

Renewed Syrian support for the PLO was a factor in Israel's decision to intervene in Lebanon in 1982. Israeli forces did not succeed in dislodging the ADF from its stronghold in the Biqa' Valley and the Lebanese north. However, Israel's support for the election of Bashir al-Jumayyil to the presidency and subsequent conclusion of a security agreement with the government of President Amin al-Jumayyil undermined the primacy of Syrian influence in Lebanon. President Jumayyil went so far as to request officially the termination of the mandate of the Arab Deterrent Force in Lebanon at an Arab League meeting in September 1982.

---

[21]Joseph A. Kechichian, "The Lebanese Army: Capabilities and Challenges in the 1980's," *Conflict Quarterly* 5, 1 (Winter 1985): 20–25.

Through its support for Jumayyil's domestic opponents, Syria prompted abrogation of the agreement with Israel and orchestrated the formation of a National Unity Government headed by its long-standing ally, Rashid Karami, as Prime Minister. Despite this impressive accomplishment, one must distinguish between the negative and positive components of Syrian influence over Lebanese domestic politics. Syria repeatedly demonstrated its "veto power" in Lebanon, averting political outcomes antithetical to its interests. However, Syria consistently fell short of positively building "a constructive consensus around a formula for national reconciliation."[22] This was Syria's problem in February 1976, when its reform proposal was rejected by the Lebanese National Movement; and it remained Syria's problem in 1984, when the National Unity Government could not reach agreement on the most fundamental principles for restoring national harmony.

Unlike the Soviet Union in Afghanistan, Syrian leaders probably did not contemplate occupying Lebanon indefinitely or consider the costs of doing so acceptable. For a small state, the direct costs of occupation are harder to bear and the opportunity costs in terms of regional objectives more clear-cut. Moreover, Syrian leaders at various junctures apparently considered at least a partial withdrawal from Lebanon. Early in 1980, the Syrian government announced plans to withdraw the ADF, in a decision explained by Minister of Information Ahmad Iskandar Ahmad:

> We took a decision to withdraw from all of Lebanese soil, because our entry into Lebanon and our remaining in Lebanon was to carry out the humanitarian [Arab] nationalist mission toward our brothers in Lebanon, which cost us many burdens and sacrifices.... Our forces were obliged to take on the role of the police in Lebanon, and this could weaken their preparedness for fighting. This also could make them receptive to the influence of Lebanese vices.... Everyone knows that Syria's decision was a serious decision, and we began to implement it. Therefore, all of them—even those who had abused us and abused our forces, and who said that those forces were not acceptable to them — came to us running, begging us and pleading with us that we should not withdraw those forces.[23]

[22]Itamar Rabinovich, "Syrian Weakness," *The New York Times*, 23 March 1984.
[23]Ahmad Iskandar Ahmad, Syrian Minister of Information, interview with author, November 17, 1982.

The outcome of this episode was that Syria merely redeployed its forces, concentrating them in the Biqa' Valley and in northern Lebanon.

An irony of Syria's enduring presence in Lebanon was that it furthered the one consequence that the Asad regime was ostensibly most intent on avoiding. The partition of Lebanon was closer to realization after the introduction of Syrian forces than before. From the outset, some Lebanese had suspected that Syria really desired Lebanon's partition, ultimately hoping to annex the Biqa' and the north. They were convinced by Syria's subsequent behavior that in this sector of Lebanon at least, indefinite occupation was an acceptable strategy for the Syrian elite. Once Syria's intervention was followed by that of Israel, competing Israeli and Syrian spheres of influence emerged in a Lebanese state whose integrity may be fatally compromised.

Even more ironic was the ultimate balance sheet of Syria's multiple miscalculations in Lebanon. At the outset of the Lebanese intervention, the Syrian regime was at the height of its domestic prestige, regional standing, and fluidity in global alignments. After years of intervention and subsequent occupation, Syria suffered reduced stature in each domain. Syria's Lebanese adventure should provide cautionary lessons for other small or great powers contemplating intervention.

SOURCES CONSULTED

Ahmad, Ahmad Iskandar. Minister of Information, Damascus, Syria. Interview, 17 November 1982.

Ahmed, Naveed. "The Lebanese Crisis: The Role of the PLO." *Pakistan Horizon* 29,1 (1976): 31–46.

Ajami, Fouad. "The End of Pan-Arabism." *Foreign Affairs* 57 (Winter 1978–79): 355–373.

———. "The Struggle for Egypt's Soul." *Foreign Policy* 35 (Summer 1979): 3–30.

———. "Third World Intervention: Orphans in Search of a Patron." *The Nation* 228,22 (9 June 1979): 662–667.

Al-Ayubi, [Major] Haythum. "Tabi'ah al-Harb al-Lubnaniyyah" [The Nature of the Lebanese War]. *Shu'un Filastiniyyah* 62 (January 1977): 70–78.

Al-Azmeh, Aziz. "The Progressive Forces." In *Essays on the Crisis in Lebanon,* pp. 59–72. Edited by Roger Owen. London: Ithaca Press, 1976.

Al-Nahar (Beirut).

Altman, Israel. "The Palestine Liberation Organization." In *Middle East Contemporary Survey,* Vol. 1: *1976–1977,* pp. 181–208. Edited by Colin Legum. New York: Holmes and Meier, 1978.

An-Nahar Arab Report and Memo (Beirut).

Antonius, George. *The Arab Awakening.* New York: Capricorn Books, 1965.

Aruri, Naseer. "The Syrian Strategy and the Lebanese Conflict." In *Lebanon: Crisis and Challenge,* Special Report, no. 1, pp. 21–25. Edited by Fouad Moughrabi and Naseer Aruri. Detroit: Arab American University Graduates, 1977.

Asad, Hafiz al-. Text of Speech Delivered on 20 July 1976 (in Arabic). *Al-Bath.* Periodic Publication, no. 10 (4 August 1976).

Bannerman, M. Graeme. "Saudi Arabia." In *Lebanon in Crisis*, pp. 113–132. Edited by F. Edward Haley and Lewis W. Snider. Syracuse, N.Y.: Syracuse University Press, 1979.

Bar-Siman-Tov, Yaacov. "Crisis Management by Military Cooperation With a Small Ally." *Cooperation and Conflict* 17 (1982): 152–158.

———. *Linkage Politics in the Middle East: Syria Between Domestic and External Conflict, 1961–1970*. Boulder, Colo.: Westview Press, 1983.

———. "The Strategy of War by Proxy." *Cooperation and Conflict* 19 (1984): 263–273.

Batatu, Hanna. "Some Observations on the Social Roots of Syria's Ruling, Military Group and the Causes for Its Dominance." *The Middle East Journal* 35, 3 (Summer 1981): 331–344.

———. "Syria's Muslim Brethren." *MERIP Reports* 110 (Nov.-Dec. 1982): 12–20.

Be'eri, Eliezer. *Army Officers in Arab Politics and Society*. Translated by Dov Ben-Abba. Jerusalem: Israel Universities Press, 1969.

Binder, Leonard, ed. *Politics in Lebanon*. New York: John Wiley and Sons, 1966.

Black, Cyril. "The Relevance of Theories of Modernization for Normative and Institutional Efforts at the Control of Intervention." In *Law and Civil War in the Modern World*, pp. 53–69. Edited by John N. Moore. Baltimore: Johns Hopkins University Press, 1974.

Blechman, Barry M. "The Impact of Israel's Reprisals on Behavior of the Bordering Arab Nations Directed at Israel." *Journal of Conflict Resolution* 16 (June 1972): 155–181.

Blechman, Barry, and Kaplan, Stephen. *Force Without War*. Washington, D.C.: Brookings Institution, 1978.

Bradsher, Henry S. *Afghanistan and the Soviet Union*. Durham, N.C.: Duke University Press, 1983.

Brandon, Henry. "Jordan, the Forgotten Crisis: Were We Masterful. . . . " *Foreign Policy* 10 (Spring 1973): 164–169.

Claude, Inis. *Swords Into Plowshares: The Problems and Progress of International Organizations*. 4th ed. New York: Random House, 1971.

Cobban, Helena. *The Palestine Liberation Organization: People, Power and Politics*. Cambridge: Cambridge University Press, 1984.

Convoy, Elizabeth. "Syria and Lebanon: The Background." In *The Syrian Arab Republic: A Handbook*, pp. 80–83. Edited by Anne Sinai and Allen Pollack. New York: American Academic Association for Peace in the Middle East, 1976.

Dawisha, Adeed I. *Syria and the Lebanese Crisis.* New York: St. Martin's, 1980.

———. "Syria in Lebanon: Asad's Vietnam?" *Foreign Policy* 33 (Winter 1978–79): 135–150.

———. "The Transnational Party in Regional Politics: The Arab Ba'th Party." *Asian Affairs* 61,1 (February 1974): 23–31.

Dawisha, Karen. "The USSR in the Middle East: Superpower in Eclipse?" *Foreign Affairs* 61,2 (Winter 1982–83): 438–452.

Deeb, Marius. *The Lebanese Civil War.* New York: Praeger, 1980.

———. "Lebanon: Prospects for National Reconciliation in the Mid-1980's." *The Middle East Journal* 38,2 (Spring 1984): 267–283.

———. "Sa'udi Policy Toward Lebanon Since 1975." Paper presented at the 9th Annual Symposium of the Center for Contemporary Arab Studies, Georgetown University, Washington, D.C., 12–13 April 1984.

Dishon, Daniel. "Greater Syria: Reviving an Old Concept." In *The Syrian Arab Republic: A Handbook,* pp. 83–85. Edited by Anne Sinai and Allen Pollack. New York: American Academic Association for Peace in the Middle East, 1976.

———. "The Lebanese War—An All-Arab Crisis." *Midstream* (January 1977): 25–32.

Dowty, Alan. "The U.S. and the Syria-Jordan Confrontation, 1970." *Jerusalem Journal of International Relations* 3 (1978): 172–196.

Drysdale, Alasdair. "The Asad Regime and Its Troubles." *MERIP Reports* 110 (Nov.-Dec. 1982): 3–11.

Duner, Bertil. "Proxy Intervention in Civil Wars." *Journal of Peace Research* 18,4 (1981): 353–361.

Eley, John. "Toward a Theory of Intervention: The Limitations and Advantages of a Transnational Perspective." *International Studies Quarterly* 16 (June 1972): 245–256.

Elliott, David W. P., ed. *Third Indochina Conflict.* Boulder: Westview, 1981.

Enloe, Cynthia H. *Ethnic Conflict and Political Development.* Boston: Little, Brown and Co., 1973.

Entelis, John P. "Palestinian Revolutionism in Lebanese Politics: The Christian Response." *Muslim World* 62,4 (October 1972): 335–351.

Evron, Yair, and Bar Simantov, Yaacov. "Coalitions in the Arab World." *Jerusalem Journal of International Relations* 1 (1975): 71–108.

Falk, Richard. "The Prospects of Intervention: Exporting Counterrevolution." *The Nation* 228 (9 June 1979): 659–662.

Foltz, William J. "The Organization of African Unity in Trouble: How and Why It Works and Does Not Work." Department of State. Bureau of Intelligence and Research (INR). Report 698–AR, 29 September 1983.

Freedman, Robert O. "Detente and US-Soviet Relations in the Middle East During the Nixon Years." In *Dimensions of Detente,* pp. 84–121. Edited by Della Seldon. New York: Praeger, 1978.

———. "The Soviet Union and the Civil War in Lebanon, 1975–76." *Jerusalem Journal of International Relations* 3 (1978): 60–92.

———, ed. *World Politics and the Arab-Israel Conflict.* New York: Pergamon Press, 1979.

Garrett, Banning. "The Strategic Triangle and the Indochina Crisis." In *Third Indochina Conflict,* pp. 193–242. Edited by David W. P. Elliot. Boulder, Colo.: Westview, 1981.

Gelb, Leslie, with Betts, Richard. *Irony of Vietnam: The System Worked.* Washington, D. C.: Brookings Institution, 1979.

George, Alexander L.; Hall, David K.; and Simons, William E. *The Limits of Coercive Diplomacy: Laos, Cuba, Vietnam.* Boston: Little, Brown and Co., 1971.

Golan, Galia, and Rabinovich, Itamar. "The Soviet Union and Syria: The Limits of Cooperation." In *The Limits of Power,* pp. 213–231. Edited by Yaacov Ro'i. New York: St. Martin's, 1979.

Gurr, Ted Robert. "The Relevance of Theories of Internal Violence for the Control of Intervention." In *Law and Civil War in the Modern World,* pp. 70–91. Edited by John N. Moore. Baltimore: Johns Hopkins University Press, 1974.

———. *Why Men Rebel.* Princeton, N.J.: Princeton University Press, 1970.

Ha-Arets (Jerusalem).

Haddad, George. *Revolutions and Military Rule in the Middle East.* Vol. 2: *The Arab States.* New York: Robert Speller, 1971.

Hagopian, Elaine, and Farsoun, Samih. *South Lebanon.* Special Report, no. 2. Detroit: Arab American University Graduates, 1978.

Haley, P. Edward, and Snider, Lewis W., eds. *Lebanon in Crisis: Participants and Issues.* Syracuse, N. Y.: Syracuse University Press, 1979.

Handel, Michael. *Weak States in the International System.* London: Frank Cass, 1981.

Harik, Iliya F. "The Ethic Revolution and Political Integration in the Middle East." *International Journal of Middle East Studies* 3 (July 1972): 303–323.

Heder, Stephen P. "The Kampuchean-Vietnamese Conflict." In *Third Indochina Conflict,* pp. 21–67. Edited by David W. P. Elliot. Boulder, Colo.: Westview, 1981.

Heikal, Mohamed H. "Egyptian Foreign Policy." *Foreign Affairs* 56 (July 1978): 714–727.

Hitti, Philip. *History of Syria, Including Lebanon and Palestine.* London: Macmillan, 1951.

Hourani, Albert H. "Ideologies of the Mountain and the City." In *Essays on the Crisis in Lebanon,* pp. 33–40. Edited by Roger Owen. London: Ithaca Press, 1976.

———. "Race, Religion, and Nation-State in the Near East." In *Readings in Arab Middle Eastern Societies and Cultures,* pp. 1–19. Edited by Abdallah Lutfiyya and Charles Churchill. The Hague: Mouton, 1970.

———. *Syria and Lebanon.* London: Oxford University Press, 1946.

Hudson, Michael. *Arab Politics: The Search for Legitimacy.* New Haven: Yale University Press, 1977.

———. "Democracy and Social Mobilization in Lebanese Politics." *Comparative Politics* 1 (January 1969): 245–263.

———. "The Lebanese Crisis and the Limits of Consociational Democracy." *Journal of Palestine Studies* 5 (1976): 109–122.

———. "The Palestinian Factor in the Lebanese Civil War." *The Middle East Journal* 32 (Summer 1978): 261–278.

Hurewitz, J. C. "Lebanese Democracy in its International Setting." In *Politics in Lebanon,* pp. 213–238. Edited by Leonard Binder. New York: John Wiley and Sons, 1966.

———. *The Middle East and North Africa in World Politics: A Documentary Record.* 2nd ed. Vol. 1: *European Expansion, 1535–1914.* New Haven: Yale University Press, 1975.

———. *Middle East Politics: The Military Dimension.* New York: Praeger, 1969.

Hussain, Mehmood. "The Palestine Liberation Movement and Arab Regimes: The Great Betrayal." *Economic and Political Weekly* 8 (10 November 1973): 2023–2028.

"Intervention." *The Nation* 228 (9 June 1979).

Jureidini, Paul, and McLaurin, Ronald. "The Hashemite Kingdom of Jordan." In *Lebanon in Crisis,* pp. 147–160. Edited by P. Edward Haley and Lewis W. Snider. Syracuse, N.Y.: Syracuse University Press, 1979.

Kass, Ilana. "Moscow and the Lebanese Triangle." *The Middle East Journal* 33 (Spring 1979): 164–188.

Kaylani, N. "The Rise of the Syrian Ba'th: Political Success, Party Failure." *International Journal of Middle East Studies* 3 (1972): 3–23.

Kechichian, Joseph A. "The Lebanese Army: Capabilities and Challenges in the 1980's." *Conflict Quarterly* 5, 1 (Winter 1985): 15–39.

Kelidar, Abbas, and Burrel, Michael. *Lebanon, The Collapse of a State: Regional Dimensions of the Struggle.* Conflict Studies, no. 74. London: Institute for the Study of Conflict, 1976.

Keohane, Robert O. "Theory of World Politics: Structural Realism and Beyond." In *Political Science: State of the Discipline,* pp. 503–540. Edited by Ada Finifter. Washington, D.C.: American Political Science Association, 1983.

Keohane, Robert O., and Nye, Joseph S. *Power and Interdependence: World Politics in Transition.* Boston: Little, Brown and Co., 1977.

Kerr, Malcolm. *The Arab Cold War: Gamal 'Abd al-Nasir and His Rivals, 1958–1970.* 3rd ed. London: Oxford University Press, 1971.

———. "Hafiz al-Asad and the Changing Patterns of Syrian Politics." *International Journal* 28 (1973): 689–706.

———. "Political Decision-Making in a Confessional Democracy." In *Politics in Lebanon,* pp. 187–212. Edited by Leonard Binder. New York: John Wiley and Sons, 1966.

———. "Regional Arab Politics and the Conflict With Israel." In *Political Dynamics in the Middle East,* pp. 31–58. Edited by Paul Hammond and Sidney Alexander. New York: American Elsevier, 1972.

———. "The Syrian Intervention in Lebanon: An Interpretation." Paper presented at the conference of the Middle East Studies Association, New York, November 1977.

Khalaf, Tewfik. " 'The Phalange and the Maronite Community': From Lebanonism to Maronitism." In *Essays on the Crisis in Lebanon,* pp. 43–56. Edited by Roger Owen. London: Ithaca Press, 1976.

Khalidi, Rashid. "The Palestinians in Lebanon: Social Repercussions of Israel's Invasion. *The Middle East Journal* 38,2 (Spring 1984): 255–266.

Khalidi, Walid. *Conflict and Violence in Lebanon: Confrontation in the Middle East.* Harvard Studies in International Affairs, no. 38. Cambridge: Center for International Affairs, Harvard University, 1979.

———. "Thinking the Unthinkable: A Sovereign Palestine State." *Foreign Affairs* 56 (July 1978): 695–713.

Khouri, Fred. "The Arab-Israel Conflict." In *Lebanon in Crisis,* pp. 161–178. Edited by P. Edward Haley and Lewis W. Snider. Syracuse, N.Y.: Syracuse University Press, 1979.

Khuwayri, Antwan. *Al-Harb fi Lubnan* [The War in Lebanon]. 3 vols. Junyih: Al-Matba'ah la-Bulsiyyah, 1977.

———. *Hawadith Lubnan: 1975.* [The Events in Lebanon: 1975]. Junyih: Al-Matba'ah al-Bulsiyyah, 1976.

Koury, Enver M. *The Operational Capability of the Lebanese Political System.* Beirut: Catholic Press, 1972.

Kurtzer, Daniel. "Palestine Guerrilla and Israeli Counterinsurgency Warfare: The Radicalization of the Palestine Arab Community to Violence, 1949–1970." Ph.D. Dissertation, Columbia University, 1976.

Lawson, Fred H. "Syria's Intervention in the Lebanese Civil War, 1976: A Domestic Conflict Explanation." *International Organization* 38, 3 (Summer 1984): 451–480.

LeoGrande, William M. "Soviet-Cuban Relations and Cuban Policy in Africa." In *Cuba in Africa,* pp. 13–50. Edited by Carmelo Mesa-Lago and June S. Belkin. Pittsburgh: Center for Latin American Studies, University of Pittsburgh, 1982.

Lijphart, Arend. "Consociational Democracy." *World Politics* 21 (1969): 207–225.

Little, Richard. *Intervention: External Involvement in Civil Wars.* Totowa, N.J.: Rowman and Littlefield, 1975.

Longrigg, Stephen Hemsley. *Syria and Lebanon Under French Mandate.* New York: Octagon Books, 1972.

Lutfiyya, Abdallah, and Churchill, Charles. *Readings in Arab Middle Eastern Societies and Cultures.* The Hague: Mouton, 1970.

McLaurin, R. D.; Mughisuddin, Mohammed; and Wagner, Abraham R. *Foreign Policy Making in the Middle East.* New York: Praeger, 1977.

Ma'oz, Moshe. "Alawi Military Officers in Syrian Politics." In *The Military and State in Modern Asia,* pp. 277–297. Edited by H. Z. Schiffrin. Jersualem: Academic Press, 1976.

——. *Ottoman Reform in Syria and Palestine, 1840–1861: The Impact of the Tanzimat on Politics and Society.* Oxford: Clarendon Press, 1968.

——. *Syria Under Hafiz al-Asad: New Domestic and Foreign Policies.* Jerusalem Papers on Peace Problems, no. 15. Jerusalem: Hebrew University Press, 1975.

Mitchell, C. R. "Civil Strife and the Involvement of External Parties." *International Studies Quarterly* 14 (June 1970): 166–194.

Moore, John N., ed. *Law and Civil War in the Modern World.* Baltimore: John Hopkins University Press, 1974.

Moughrabi, Fouad, and Aruri, Naseer, eds. *Lebanon: Crisis and Challenge.* Special Report, no. 1. Detroit: Arab American University Graduates, 1977.

Mughisuddin, Mohammed. "Egypt." In *Lebanon in Crisis,* pp. 133–146. Edited by P. Edward Haley and Lewis W. Snider. Syracuse, N.Y.: Syracuse University Press, 1979.

Norton, Augustus Richard. "Harakat Amal (The Movement of Hope)." *Political Anthropology* 3 (1984): 105–131.

――――. "Making Enemies in South Lebanon: Harakat Amal, the IDF, and South Lebanon." *Middle East Insight* 3,3 (Jan.-Feb. 1984): 13–20.

Olmert, Yoseph. "Syria." In *Middle East Contemporary Survey*. Vol. VI: 1981–1982, pp. 845–877. Edited by Colin Legum et al. New York: Holmes and Meier, 1984.

Owen, Roger, ed. *Essays on the Crisis in Lebanon*. London: Ithaca Press, 1976.

Pearson, Frederic. "Foreign Military Interventions and Domestic Disputes." *International Studies Quarterly* 18 (September 1974): 259–290.

Perlmutter, Amos. "From Obscurity to Rule: The Syrian Army and the Ba'th Party." *Western Political Quarterly* 22,4 (1969): 827–845.

"The PLO Split." *MERIP Reports* 13,9 (Nov.-Dec. 1983).

Porter, Gareth. "Vietnamese Policy and the Indochina Crisis." In *Third Indochina Conflict*, pp. 69–137. Edited by David W. P. Elliot. Boulder, Colo.: Westview, 1981.

Quandt, William. "Lebanon, 1958, and Jordan, 1970." In *Force Without War*, pp. 222–288. Edited by Barry Blechman and Stephen Kaplan. Washington, D.C.: Brookings Institution, 1978.

Quandt, William; Jabber, Fuad; and Lesch, Ann Mosely. *The Politics of Palestinian Nationalism*. Berkeley: University of California Press, 1973.

Quarterly Economic Review of Syria, Lebanon, Cyprus. Spencer House, London: The Economist Intelligence Unit, 1975–1976.

Rabinovich, Itamar. "The Limits of Military Power: Syria's Role." In *Lebanon in Crisis*, pp. 55–74. Edited by P. Edward Haley and Lewis W. Snider. Syracuse, N. Y.: Syracuse University Press, 1979.

――――. "Syrian Weakness." *The New York Times*, 23 March 1984.

――――. *The War for Lebanon: 1970–1983*. Ithaca; Cornell University Press, 1984.

Rabinovich, Itamar, and Zamir, Hanna. "Lebanon." In *Middle East Contemporary Survey*. Vol. I: *1976–1977*, pp. 492–525. Edited by Colin Legum. New York: Holmes and Meier, 1978.

――――. "Syria." In *Middle East Contemporary Survey*. Vol. I: *1976–1977*, pp. 604–621. Edited by Colin Legum. New York: Holmes and Meier, 1978.

Rahmy, Ali Abdel Rahman. "The Egyptian Policy in the Arab World: Intervention in Yemen, 1962–1967." Ph.D. Dissertation, Institut Universitaire de Hautes Etudes Internationales, Geneva, 1981.

Ro'i, Ya'acov, ed. *The Limits to Power: Soviet Policy in the Middle East.* New York: St. Martin's, 1979.

Rosenau, James N. "The Concept of Intervention." *Journal of International Affairs* 22 (Summer 1968): 165–176.

————. "Intervention as a Scientific Concept." *Journal of Conflict Resolution* 13 (June 1969): 149–171.

————. "Theorizing Across Systems: Linkage Politics Revisited." In *Conflict Behavior and Linkage Politics*, pp. 25–55. Edited by Jonathan Wilkenfeld. New York: David McKay, 1973.

————, ed. *Linkage Politics.* New York: Free Press, 1969.

Salibi, Kamal. *Crossroads to Civil War: Lebanon, 1958–1976.* Delmar, N.Y.: Caravan, 1976.

————. *The Modern History of Lebanon.* London: Weidenfeld and Nicolson, 1965.

Sampson, Anthony, *The Arms Bazaar.* New York: Viking, 1977.

Schiff, Ze'ev, and Ya'ari, Ehud. *Israel's Lebanon War.* Edited and translated by Ina Friedman. New York: Simon and Schuster, 1984.

Seale, Patrick. *The Struggle for Syria: A Study of Post-War Arab Politics, 1945–1958.* London: Oxford University Press, 1965.

Seldon, Della, ed. *Dimensions of Detente.* New York: Praeger, 1978.

Sharif, Hasan. "South Lebanon: Its History and Geopolitics." In *South Lebanon.* Special Report, no. 2, pp. 9–34. Edited by Elaine Hagopian and Samih Farsoun. Detroit: Arab American University Graduates, 1978.

Sinai, Anne, and Pollack, Allen, eds. *The Syrian Arab Republic: A Handbook.* New York: American Academic Association for Peace in the Middle East, 1976.

Sirriyyeh, Hussein. "The Palestinian Armed Presence in Lebanon Since 1967." In *Essays on the Crisis in Lebanon*, pp. 73–89. Edited by Roger Owen. London: Ithaca Press, 1976.

Skaf, Wadi', ed. *Mawkifuna Min al-'Azmah al Lubnaniyyah* [Our Position Vis-à-Vis the Lebanese Crisis]. Damascus: Institute of the Union of Studies and Consultations, 1979.

Smock, David, and Smock, Audrey. *The Politics of Pluralism: A Comparative Study of Lebanon and Ghana.* New York: Elsevier, 1975.

Smoke, Richard. "Analytical Dimensions of Intervention Decisions." In *The Limits of Military Intervention*, pp. 25–44. Edited by Ellen P. Stern. Beverly Hills: Sage, 1977.

Snider, Lewis W. "Inter-Arab Relations." In *Lebanon in Crisis*, pp. 179–206. Edited by P. Edward Haley and Lewis W. Snider. Syracuse, N.Y.: Syracuse University Press, 1979.

Snider, Lewis, et. al. "Israel." In *Lebanon in Crisis*, pp. 91–112. Edited by P. Edward Haley and Lewis W. Snider. Syracuse, N.Y.: Syracuse University Press, 1979.

Stoaks, Frank. "The Civil War in Lebanon." *World Today* 32 (January 1976): 8–17.

Stookey, Robert. "The United States." In *Lebanon in Crisis,* pp. 225–248. Edited by P. Edward Haley and Lewis W. Snider. Syracuse, N.Y.: Syracuse University Press, 1979.

Suleiman, Michael. "Lebanon." In *Governments and Politics of the Contemporary Middle East,* pp. 231–250. Edited by Tareq Ismael. Homewood, Ill.: Dorsey Press, 1970.

"Syria's Troubles." *MERIP Reports* 12, 9 (Nov.-Dec. 1982).

Tibawi, Abdul Latif. *A Modern History of Syria, Including Lebanon and Palestine.* London: Macmillan; New York: St. Martin's, 1969.

Van Dam, Nikolaos. "Sectarian and Regional Factionalism in the Syrian Political Elite." *Middle East Journal* 32 (Spring 1978): 201–210.

———. *The Struggle for Power in Syria.* 2d ed. London: Croom Helm, 1981.

Van Dusen, Michael. "Political Integration and Regionalism in Syria." *Middle East Journal* 26 (Spring 1972): 123–136.

———. "Syrian Politics and the Future of Arab-Israel Relations." In *World Politics and the Arab-Israeli Conflict,* pp. 250–266. Edited by Robert O. Freedman. New York: Pergamon, 1979.

Vatikiotis, P. J. "The Politics of the Fertile Crescent." In *Political Dynamics in the Middle East,* pp. 225–263. Edited by Paul Hammond and Sidney Alexander. New York: Elsevier, 1972.

Weinberger, Naomi Joy. "Peacekeeping Options in Lebanon." *The Middle East Journal* 37,3 (Summer 1983) : 341–369.

Young, Oran R. "Systematic Bases of Intervention." In *Law and Civil War in the Modern World,* pp. 112–126. Edited by John N. Moore. Baltimore: Johns Hopkins University Press, 1974.

Younger, Sam. "After the Cairo Summit." *World Today* 32 (December 1976): 437–440.

———. "The Syrian Stake in Lebanon." *World Today* 32 (November 1976): 399–406.

Zartman, I. William. "Intervention Among Developing States." *Journal of International Affairs* 22 (1968): 188–197.

Index